Praise for *MASTER OF LEVERAGE*

"The well-organized insights shared in this book could be worth thousands of dollars to those who follow its guidance. Ryan lays the groundwork for a clear and simple path for investing in real estate."
—Lori Lyons, Real Estate Broker, Bridgestream Realty

"*Master of Leverage* understands the financial process involved to acquire real estate and gives you detailed calculations to maximize your wealth. Where most books lack mortgage literacy, this one has all the knowledge needed to start your real estate journey."
—Greg Allen, Mortgage Senior Sales Manager, First Financial Bank

"We often come across real estate investor material that misses foundational building blocks. Ryan Henderson is the mason who fills the void."
—Evan Kaufman, Founder and Owner, WeVett Realty

"Ryan delivers ground zero insight into the myriad of opportunities for leverage. In particular, his synopsis in real estate can save new investors a lot of grief (and a lot of money!)"
—Jeremiah Shockley, PhD, Co-Owner Prima Management & Aim High Construction

"*Master of Leverage* is hands down the most complete collection of information for anyone wanting to get into or understand real estate transactions from personal responsibilities one must make to finding the right team to implement your dreams and finally leveraging yourself and real estate to be able to buy your properties and secure your future."
—Dr. Fredric Marc Francis, DBA, EA

MASTER OF LEVERAGE

THE ART OF
LEVERAGING REAL ESTATE
TO UNLOCK THE
MOMENTUM OF WEALTH

FOUNDATIONS OF REAL ESTATE

LENDING

BUILDING YOUR TEAM

LOCATING PROPERTIES

ACQUIRING PROPERTIES

RENOVATING PROPERTIES

SELLING AND REFINANCING

RENTING

NETWORKING

BUSINESS STRUCTURES

TAXES

RYAN HENDERSON

Ballast Books, LLC
www.ballastbooks.com

ISBN: 978-1-955026-66-6

Edited by Good Comma Editing

Printed in Hong Kong

Published by Ballast Books
www.ballastbooks.com

For more information, bulk orders, appearances, or speaking requests, please email: info@ballastbooks.com

I dedicate this book to my parents, who have
taught me more than they will ever know, and
to my brother, the most courageous person I know,
who reminds me every day that life is a gift
that should be lived to its fullest.

To the family, friends, teachers, and coaches
that have encouraged and mentored me
throughout my life, thank you, for the slightest act
may change the trajectory of a journey.

To those who have challenged and burdened me,
thank you, for without your adversity, I would
not have the fortitude to overcome many
of life's challenges and obstacles.

To my brothers and sisters in arms, thank you for
keeping our nation safe against the many known and
unknown perils threatening our way of life.

And to the reader, thank you for taking the next
of many steps toward improving not only your
own life but also the lives of those around you
and the lives of those yet to come.

The Man in the Arena

It is not the critic who counts; not the man who points out how the strong man stumbles, or where the doer of deeds could have done them better. The credit belongs to the man who is actually in the arena, whose face is marred by dust and sweat and blood; who strives valiantly; who errs, who comes short again and again, because there is no effort without error and shortcoming; but who does actually strive to do the deeds; who knows great enthusiasms, the great devotions; who spends himself in a worthy cause; who at the best knows in the end the triumph of high achievement, and who at the worst, if he fails, at least fails while daring greatly, so that his place shall never be with those cold and timid souls who neither know victory nor defeat.

Theodore Roosevelt,
26th president of the United States

TABLE OF CONTENTS – High Level

Introduction 1

SECTION I: FOUNDATION 9

Chapter 1: Leveraging the Basics 10

Chapter 2: Leveraging Key Real Estate Concepts 33

Chapter 3: Leveraging Other People's Money (Funding) 55

SECTION II: EXECUTION 91

Chapter 4: Leveraging ... When You Have None (Creative Financing) 92

Chapter 5: Leveraging Your Team 112

Chapter 6: Leveraging Location ... Location, Location!. 134

Chapter 7: Leveraging the Acquisition 164

Chapter 8: Leveraging the Rehab 194

Chapter 9: Leveraging Your Equity ("To Sell or Not to Sell" and Renting). . . 234

SECTION III: ENHANCEMENTS 257

Chapter 10: Utilizing Liability Protection 258

Chapter 11: Retaining Your Leverage 284

Chapter 12: Maximizing Your Leverage with Networking 311

SECTION IV: MASTERY 327

Chapter 13: Strategizing Your Leverage. 328

Chapter 14: Mastering Your Leverage 345

Final Thoughts 407

TABLE OF CONTENTS – Detailed

Introduction . . . 1
What This Book Is and What It Isn't . . . 3
Assumptions . . . 4
Icon Lexicon . . . 5
Are You 'Fit' or 'Misfit' for Investing in Real Estate? . . . 6

SECTION I: FOUNDATION . . . 9
Chapter 1: Leveraging the Basics . . . 10
Economics 101 . . . 11
Price . . . 12
Quantity . . . 12
Demand . . . 13
Supply . . . 13
Equilibrium . . . 13
Consumer Surplus . . . 14
Producer Surplus . . . 14
Increased Supply . . . 15
Increased Demand . . . 15
Shortage . . . 16
Surplus . . . 16
Supply Barrier . . . 17
Demand Barrier . . . 18
Trend Analysis . . . 18
Point . . . 19
Vector . . . 20
Trend . . . 20

Types of Wealth 21
Realized Wealth 21
Realized Wealth: Active Income 21
Realized Wealth: Passive Income 22
Unrealized Wealth 22
Types of Properties 22
Residential Property 23
Apartments 23
Attached Housing 24
Condominiums (Condos) 24
Co-Operative (Co-op) 24
Townhomes 24
Single-Family Home 24
Commercial Property 25
Mixed-Use Property 25
Undeveloped Land 25
Types of Cost 25
Cost of Business 26
Transaction Cost 26
Price of Lending 26
Opportunity Cost 27
Sunk Cost 28
Key Values and Ratios 29
After Restoral Value (ARV) 29
As-Is Value (AIV) 29
Debt-to-Income (DTI) Ratio 30
Fair Market Value (FMV) 30
Loan-to-Value (LTV) 31
Objective: Leveraging the Basics 31

Chapter 2: Leveraging Key Real Estate Concepts 33
Inertia of Real Estate 34
Appreciation. 35
Inflation 36
Equity Generated 37
Amortization 38
Equity Available 39
Velocity of Money. 41
Rental Income. 41
Expenses 42
Passive Income 43
Profitability Ratios 45
Return on Investment (ROI) 46
Return on Equity (ROE) 46
Momentum of Wealth. 47
Objective: Leveraging Key Real Estate Concepts 53

Chapter 3: Leveraging Other People's Money (Funding). 55
Lending Process 56
Application 57
Pre-Approval 57
Appraisal 58
Underwriting 58
Lending Risk Factors. 59
Debt-to-Income (DTI) 59
LTV 60
Credit Score. 60
Payment History 61
Outstanding Debt. 62
Length of Credit History 62
Recent Inquiries 62

Type of Credit 63
Number of Properties Owned 63
Bankruptcy Status 65
Closing 65
Closing Costs and Other Fees 66
Funding 66
Types of Lending Entities and Institutions 67
Qualified Mortgage Loans vs. Nonqualified Mortgage Loans 69
Qualified Mortgage Loans 69
Nonqualified Mortgage Loans 70
Fixed-Rate vs. Adjustable-Rate Mortgage Loans (Amortization) 71
Conventional vs. Portfolio Loans 72
Mortgage Insurance Premiums (MIPs) 74
Federal Housing Administration (FHA Loans 74
Veterans Affairs (VA) Loans 75
U.S. Department of Agriculture (USDA) Rural Development Loans 76
Collateral Loans 77
Construction and Renovation Loans 78
FHA 203(k) Improvement Loans 79
FHA Energy Efficient Mortgages 79
Jumbo Loans 79
Commercial Real Estate (CRE) Loans 80
Individual vs. Business Entity Characteristics 80
Loan Repayment Schedule and Prepayment Penalties 81
LTV 81
Debt-Service Coverage Ratio (DSCR) 81
Down Payment Assistance Programs 82
Alternative Lending Options 83
Friends and Family 83
Peer-to-Peer (P2P) Lending 84
Hard Money Lenders 84

Expedience 85
Flexible Approval 85
Flexible Terms 85
Refinancing 86
Objective: Leveraging Other People's Money 87

SECTION II: EXECUTION 91
Chapter 4: Leveraging ... When You Have None (Creative Financing) 92
House Hacking 94
Low- to No-Money-Down Financing 94
Perils of Overleveraging – Part I .99
Down Payment Assistance (DPA) Programs 99
Live and Upgrade 100
FHA 203(k) 101
Seller Financing 102
Partial Seller Financing 104
Syndication – 506(b) 105
Objective: Leveraging Creative Financing 109

Chapter 5: Leveraging Your Team 112
Understanding Your Team's Dynamic 113
Core and Ancillary Team Members 115
Centers of Gravity 116
CORE 116
Real Estate Attorney 116
Certified Public Accountant (CPA) 116
The Deal Finder 117
The Deal Finder: Attorney 118
The Deal Finder: Fellow Real Estate Investor 119
The Deal Finder: Real Estate Agent 120
The Deal Finder: Wholesale Agent 121

Insurance Agent 121
Property Manager 122
Real Estate Lender 123
Title Company 124
ANCILLARY 125
Appraiser 125
Contractors 126
Dumpster Companies 127
Electrician 127
Handyperson 128
Heating, Ventilation, and Air Conditioning (HVAC) Technician 128
Home Inspector 129
Landscape Workers 129
Plumbing Technicians 130
Roofing Technician. 130
Other Specialists: Cabinets and Countertops 130
Other Specialists: Concrete Companies 130
Other Specialists: Hardwood Refinisher 131
Other Specialists: Tile Setter 131
Team Depth 131
Objective: Leveraging Your Team 131

Chapter 6: Leveraging Location ... Location, Location! 134
Narrowing Your Search. 135
Outer Circle: The Region 136
Climate 137
Economy of Force 137
Landlord Laws and Regulations. 138
Natural Hazards 139
Medial Circle: The City 139
Employment Opportunities 140

Income and Wages . . . 141
Industry . . . 141
Types and Diversification of Jobs . . . 142
High-Growth Jobs . . . 142
Stabilizing Jobs . . . 142
Education . . . 143
Government . . . 143
Health Care . . . 144
Unemployment . . . 144
Other Enticements . . . 145
Up-and-Coming Areas . . . 145
Hip and Niche . . . 146
Direction of Growth . . . 147
Economic and Geographic Barriers . . . 147
Inner Circle: The Neighborhood/Suburb . . . 148
Buyer's Market vs. Seller's Market . . . 149
Sales Volume . . . 150
Determining Desirability and Demand . . . 150
Crime Statistics . . . 151
School Rankings and Statistics . . . 152
Transit Score . . . 152
Walkability Score . . . 153
Days on Market (DOM) . . . 154
Increasing Rents . . . 155
Vacancy Periods . . . 155
Determining Availability and Supply . . . 156
New Construction and Absorption . . . 156
Target: The Property . . . 157
Quick Determination Assessments . . . 158
Property Value Trend . . . 158
Price-to-Rent Ratio . . . 160

The 1 Percent Rule . . . 160
The 2 Percent Rule . . . 161
Objective: Leveraging Location . . . 161

Chapter 7: Leveraging the Acquisition . . . 164
Turnkey vs. Distressed Properties . . . 165
Market Distress . . . 166
Personal Distress . . . 166
Property Distress . . . 167
Auctions and Sheriff Sales . . . 168
Real Estate Owned (REO), Short Sales, and Notices of Default (NODs)/Tax Liens . . . 168
Properties in Disrepair . . . 169
Things You Should Know about a Property . . . 169
Amount Owed . . . 170
Homeowner's (or Business Entity's) Name . . . 170
Homeowner's Situation . . . 170
Lien-Holder Information . . . 170
Property Condition . . . 171
Property FMV . . . 171
Property Assessment . . . 171
Income . . . 173
Expenses . . . 173
Principal and Interest (P&I) . . . 173
Taxes . . . 174
Property Insurance . . . 174
Damage . . . 174
Liability . . . 175
Additional Living Expenses . . . 175
Actual Value . . . 175
Replacement Cost . . . 175

Extended Replacement Cost 175
Utilities 176
Property Management 176
Capital Expenditures (CAPEX) 176
Condo/Homeowners Association (COA/HOA) 177
Vacancies 177
Out-of-Pocket Expenditures 177
Down Payment 178
Closing Costs 178
Holding Costs 178
Appreciation 178
Cash Flow 179
Return on Investment (ROI) and Return on Equity (ROE) 179
Target Price Range (How Much House Can You Afford?) 180
Determining FMV 181
Market Data (Sales Comparison) Approach 182
Cost Approach 182
Income Capitalization 182
Submitting an Offer 183
Real Estate Agent vs. For Sale by Owner (FSBO) 183
Turnkey vs. Distressed Properties 183
Offer Composition 184
Possible Outcomes 185
Earnest Money 186
Contingencies 186
Inspection Contingency 186
Appraisal Contingency 187
Loan Contingency 187
Offer Strategies 187
Early Bird 188
Cash Offer 188
Best Offer Up Front 190

Pre-Approval Letter 190
Escalation Clause 190
More Earnest Money 190
Objective: Leveraging the Acquisition 191

Chapter 8: Leveraging the Rehab 194
Rehabbing Points of Note 196
Location. 196
Season 196
Skill and Demand for Contractors. 196
Specifics to the Property 197
Quality of Material 197
Necessities and Niceties 197
Conducting a Walk-Through 200
Annotations. 200
Developing Objectives and Tasks 201
Contractor Bids 203
Disclosure of Work 203
Bid Negotiations 204
Accepting the Bid 206
Exterior Rehab Components 207
Roofing 207
Gutters 208
Siding 209
Exterior Paint 210
Decks/Porches 211
Garage 212
Landscaping/Curb Appeal 213
Septic System 214
Concrete/Foundation 215

Interior Rehab Components . . . 216
Plumbing . . . 217
Electrical . . . 218
HVAC . . . 219
Framing and Insulation . . . 220
Drywall . . . 221
Carpentry . . . 221
Interior Painting . . . 222
Cabinets and Countertops . . . 223
Flooring . . . 224
Miscellaneous Components . . . 225
Demolition . . . 226
Permits . . . 227
Inspections . . . 228
Forced Appreciation . . . 229
Additions . . . 229
Bedrooms . . . 230
Bathrooms . . . 230
Kitchen . . . 231
Objective: Leveraging the Rehab . . . 231

Chapter 9: Leveraging Your Equity ("To Sell or Not to Sell" and Renting) . . . 234
Profitability and Financial Determination Measures . . . 235
Low ROI . . . 236
Negative ROE Rate . . . 236
High DTI Ratio . . . 237
Leasing and Selling . . . 238
Screening and Leasing Tenants . . . 238
Advertising and Finding Tenants . . . 239
Signage . . . 239
Online Sources . . . 240

Networking . . . 240
Preliminary Screening Process . . . 241
Application Process . . . 242
Application Fee and Release of Information . . . 242
In-Depth Screening and Verification of Application . . . 243
Accepting or Rejecting Tenants . . . 243
Lease Agreement . . . 244
Turning Over the Keys . . . 246
Short-Term Rentals . . . 246
Selling Your Property . . . 248
List Price . . . 249
Preparation Expenses . . . 249
Holding Costs . . . 249
Transaction Costs . . . 249
Taxes . . . 250
Steps to Sell a Property . . . 250
Step 1: Determine the FMV of the Property . . . 250
Step 2: Prepare the Property for Sale (Repairing, Cleaning, and Staging) . 250
Step 3: Market the Property for Sale . . . 252
Step 4: Negotiate the Sale . . . 252
Step 5: Handle the Closing . . . 253
Contract for Deed . . . 253
Objective: Leveraging Your Equity . . . 253

SECTION III: ENHANCEMENTS . . . 257
Chapter 10: Utilizing Liability Protection . . . 258
Asset vs. Personal Liability Protection . . . 259
Asset Liability Protection . . . 260
Anonymity (through a Business Entity) . . . 261
Primary Residence Homestead Exemption . . . 263
Personal Liability Protection . . . 265
Insurance . . . 265

Security through Obscurity (Business Structuring) 266
Grantor "Land" Trust 268
Equity Stripping. 270
Second Mortgage 270
Cash-Out Refinance 270
HELOC. 271
Establishing a Business Entity. 272
Step 1: Select Your Business Structure. 273
Sole Proprietorship 273
Joint Venture. 273
General Partnership 274
Limited Partnership (LP) 274
Cooperative (Co-op) 275
Corporation 275
Limited Liability Company (LLC) 276
Umbrella Company 277
Step 2: Select Your Business Name. 277
Step 3: Register Your Business 278
Articles of Incorporation and Articles of Organization 278
Bylaws and Operating Agreements. 279
Step 4: Receive Your Federal and State Tax ID. 280
Objective: Utilizing Liability Protection. 281

Chapter 11: Retaining Your Leverage 284
Key Terms and Concepts 286
Tax Preparer vs. Tax Advisor 286
Active vs. Passive Business 287
Capital vs. Passive Gains and Losses. 287
Real Estate Professional (Status). 288
Property Use (Personal, Rental, Mixed-Use, and Arbitrage). 289
Personal Property 289

Rental Property 290
Mixed-Use 290
Arbitrage 291
Business Entity Tax Considerations and Flow-Through Taxation 292
Decreasing Taxes through Business Deductions and Expenses 293
Deduction Categories 293
Deferring Taxes through 1031 Exchange 298
Reclassifying Taxable Income by Funding Retirement Accounts. . . . 300
Transforming Income by Funding Investments
through Retirement Accounts 301
Exit Strategies 303
Cash-Out Refinancing – Part II 303
Seller Financing – Part II 305
Inheritance 306
Objective: Retaining Your Leverage 308

Chapter 12: Maximizing Your Leverage with Networking 311
Types of Networking 312
Relationships Are about Give and Take, Authenticity, and Consistency 313
Professional Networking 314
Chamber of Commerce 314
Local Community Boards and Committees 314
Online Forums and Social Media 315
Seminars 315
Personal Networking 317
Classes 317
Fitness/Sports Teams 317
Social Events 317
Religious/Spiritual Gatherings 318
Volunteering 318

Pre-Established Relationships . . . 320
High-Producing Agents and Team Members . . . 320
Family, Friends, and Word of Mouth . . . 321
Fellow Real Estate Investors . . . 322
Objective: Maximizing Your Leverage with Networking . . . 323

SECTION IV: MASTERY . . . 327
Chapter 13: Strategizing Your Leverage . . . 328
Strategy Components . . . 329
Operational Art and Operational Design . . . 330
Determine End State and Conditions . . . 331
Objectives and Effects (Operational Design) . . . 331
Determine the Centers of Gravity . . . 333
Basing . . . 334
Operational Reach . . . 334
Lines of Operations (LOO) . . . 334
Lines of Effort (LOE) . . . 335
Phasing . . . 335
Timing and Tempo . . . 336
Culmination . . . 336
Strategy-to-Task Framework . . . 336
Decisive Points . . . 340
Development of Branches and Sequels . . . 340
Risk (Task Assessment) . . . 341
Objective: Strategizing Your Leverage . . . 342

Chapter 14: Mastering Your Leverage . . . 345
Niceties, Necessities, and the Desired End State . . . 346
Unlocking the *Momentum of Wealth* . . . 349
Objective: Strategizing Your Leverage . . . 349
Determine End State and Associated Conditions . . . 350

Determine Various Strategic Objectives (or Effects) Required for the End State . . . 351
Determine Subordinate (Operational and Tactical) Objectives and Tasks . 353
Operational Tasks/Tactical Objectives and Tactical Tasks . . . 354
Assess Adequacy of Centers of Gravity and Basing . . . 361
Presence of Basing . . . 362
Limitations of Operational Reach . . . 362
Establish Lines of Operation (LOO) and Lines of Effort (LOE) . . . 362
Establish Sequencing of Tasks and Objectives . . . 363
Phasing . . . 369
Timing and Tempo . . . 371
Culmination . . . 371
Decisive Points . . . 371
Develop Contingencies (Branches and Sequels) . . . 373
Perils of Overleveraging – Part II . . . 373
Overleveraging . . . 374
Overextending . . . 374
Overborrowing . . . 376
Overassessing . . . 376
Excessive Ambition . . . 377
Economic Downturn . . . 379

Final Thoughts . . . 407
Appendix A: Key Topics . . . 408
Good Idea . . . 408
Remember . . . 411
Note . . . 414
Caution . . . 419
Appendix B: Index . . . 424

Introduction

Wealth opens doors and provides opportunities unavailable to most. The harshness of disparity doesn't make it any less of a reality. Regardless, there are steps you may take to change your position and live a more successful life. Discovering and accessing those doors of opportunity is what I refer to as the *Momentum of Wealth*. One of those doors is real estate, a time-tested means by which wealth is generated.

The military provided me the opportunity to travel the world, interact with the liberated and the oppressed, the rich and the poor, the jubilant and the somber, those who do what they can and those who suffer what they must. In all of these interactions, I have found that success is attained by a combination of two factors: effort, which is within your control, and opportunity, which is not but may be cultured and developed. Opportunity comprises both knowledge and availability (or accessibility, given context). Knowledge may be attained, but availability exists (initially) more by happenstance.

The difference between one person's and another's initial knowledge or happenstance (starting opportunity) is the crux of disparity and a major determinant of their attainable level of success. For example, a flower planted in a garden with ample sunlight and plentiful water possesses all of the opportunity needed to bloom into a beautiful creation. Another like flower planted in the desert, deprived of water and subject to harsh conditions is far less likely to blossom in the same manner. The disparity of opportunity will prevent it from reaching the same potential, even if it tries its utmost to "bloom where it is planted." Metaphorically, the desert flower can learn (knowledge) and adapt (availability) to its environment to overcome its current conditions and thrive. I have written this book to equip you with the knowledge of effective practices and strategies to help you blossom. Applying these practices and strategies will help negate the disparity of investors in real estate. I cannot impact your current happenstance (current wealth, debt, credit score, life situation, etc.); however, I can provide you the tools to allow effort to be the primary delineator for your future success.

While other educational books on real estate exist, I have found few of them provide a comprehensive strategy to acquiring and building wealth. Many offer insightful information on aspects or topics of generating wealth but do not tie the topics together into a cohesive approach. Conducting a simple search will turn up books covering investing in residential real estate, investing in commercial properties, how to buy a home, flipping houses, foreclosures, taxes, and the list goes on. These are all important topics of which a seasoned real estate investor should be knowledgeable. However, most available resources do not inform a novice investor on how to get started. They assume the reader possesses prior knowledge of a broad range of topics or is interested only in the subject matter of that book. These are two very dangerous assumptions. Some of these books, while insightful, are useful only to experienced investors who are established and looking to modify their strategy or become more effective. Other books provide little to no utility. They are simply documentaries on how this or that person created their wealth. The worst examples are pitches to use their services. I use those books for tinder when I'm camping.

I decided to write this book as a pleasant alternative to those. This book is intended to provide detailed information on the various topics required for success, incorporate those topics into a cohesive and proven real estate strategy, warn the reader about common or dangerous pitfalls, and highlight beneficial tips. I have included examples to help with understanding and a little humor to entertain the reader along the way.

This book is constructed to educate novice investors and to be a quality reference for the more experienced. It includes strategies ranging in benefit to those who do not yet own their first home to those who have amassed a large portfolio and are looking to expand.

What This Book Is and What It Isn't

This book provides knowledge and insight into effective strategies for investing in real estate. In the military we have an old adage:

"Intelligence informs planning; planning drives operations."

Most people want to do operations (ops) because ops are fun and sexy. It's true. But ops are unsuccessful without precursors. This book is your high- to mid-level intel as well as your foundation of planning. It's not intel from a spy satellite in orbit or a spy plane flying in the stratosphere. Think of this intel as from a drone, providing timely support, surveying the path ahead, and relaying pertinent information. Diligently educating yourself and adhering to the techniques in this book will ensure the effort you put forth in ops is far more effective. YOU must still put forth the effort!

This book is not:

A get-rich-quick scheme. Wealth accrual in real estate is exponential. It takes time and effort; shortcuts often result in devastation. Whether your journey takes a moderate or a long amount of time is up to you. If you are looking to get rich quick, investing in real estate may not be the vehicle you're looking for.

A motivational book. This book is intended to educate, inform, guide, and level the opportunity field to the greatest extent possible, allowing your effort to carry you to wealth and success. But it is not a motivational book.

All-inclusive. This book isn't all-inclusive or comprehensive. There are investment techniques outside of this strategy. Some are for more advanced real estate investors. This book is a half mile wide and a half mile deep. Furthermore, this book does not include prices (or costs) for material and labor. Prices vary geographically and seasonally.

Assumptions

Most real estate investment books have several assumptions for their readers. I've often chuckled when authors name this section of the book "Foolish Assumptions," because they foolishly assume things about the reader. I've written this book for investors of all experience levels; therefore, it has been written absent of most assumptions. Rather than assume, I provide recommendations that should be heeded by novice investors but may be disregarded by more veteran investors. **I maintain four primary assumptions:**

You seek knowledge. You may be familiar with the expression "knowledge is power." You grasp this concept and embrace educating yourself on endeavors that you view as important. You've already proven this assumption by taking the time to read this book. You may or may not have already invested in real estate, but you are searching for proven strategies as well as one that is a fit for you.

You seek wealth. You could say that everyone seeks wealth. However, many people do not take the appropriate steps to attain it. You seek wealth and are willing to educate yourself on strategies to garner it effectively.

You have interest in real estate. Investing in the real estate market is a time-consuming process. It can be fun and exhilarating for those who enjoy real estate but taxing for those who do not. If you are reading this only to attain wealth and have no interest in real estate itself, I recommend you partner with another investor who is a real estate enthusiast.

You are not faint of heart. This business is not for the meek or fainthearted. You should never be cruel or seek to unfairly take advantage of others' situations; however, you should be willing to pursue opportunities when they arise. This journey pursues exponential growth over time; profits may be negligible when you are first getting started. You will make mistakes, and you will experience highs and lows along the way; you must have perseverance to reap the benefits real estate provides. You should also be aware that you become the target of envy (and greed) as you accrue wealth. You need to be willing and able to stand for, protect, and defend what you have earned.

Icon Lexicon

I've inserted several icons throughout this book intended to call your attention to key points and topics. The key points vary in significance and are denoted accordingly. For your convenience, all key points are aggregated and provided in Appendix A.

Good Idea: This key point provides insight that is advantageous to eager investors looking to expand their portfolio. While beneficial, these insights may also require additional effort.

Remember: This key topic is one you should note and adhere to.

Note: Denotes a key point with salient or useful information that is helpful but may not be crucial to your success.

Caution: Denotes key topics and advises caution. Seek professional guidance if attempting to pursue.

Anecdotes and Factoids
Throughout this book, I have included several anecdotes and factoids intended to provide additional context to specific topics. Each anecdote is detailed within a gray text box with a double lined border (as is this description). The anecdote is intended either to communicate an abstract idea or to provide information about a topic referenced within the main text.

Are You 'Fit' or 'Misfit' for Investing in Real Estate?

Investing in real estate is a phenomenal method to generate wealth, and generating wealth through equity is more feasible than most people believe. Over 10 percent of the world's wealthiest individuals became so through investing in real estate. While this process of generating wealth is attainable for many individuals, it isn't for everyone. Investors interested in entering the real estate market need to honestly assess their traits and personalities to determine if this method of generating wealth is "fit" for them. A few traits you may want to home in on are discipline and focus, risk tolerance, and perseverance.

Discipline and Focus. Do you get distracted easily, go off on tangents, or persistently seek immediate gratification? Do you budget, or do you splurge? If discipline and focus aren't your strong suit, that's okay; just be sure to have a partner or system to keep you on track.

Risk Tolerance. Do you hate debt (even the good kind), avoid using credit cards, and save up money to buy things in full or with cash? There isn't anything wrong with this; however, acquiring wealth through real estate investments will be a very slow process for you.

Perseverance. You will make mistakes; if you seldom go for opportunities because you fear failure, get over it, and get after it!

The "Stanford marshmallow experiment" is a helpful experiment you can think about to assess your personality and preparedness for real estate investing. A group of scientists conducted the "Stanford marshmallow experiment" in the 1970s to test children's ability to delay gratification. A simplified version of this experiment includes giving a child a marshmallow and giving them a choice: they may have the one marshmallow now or, if they wait an hour, they may have a second marshmallow. Ask yourself, which person are you? Are you the person who is content with one marshmallow? Or are you the person with the discipline to wait for a second one? Do you arbitrate for a third marshmallow on your terms, or are you the person who forgot they had a marshmallow to begin with?

Stanford Marshmallow Experiment

The Stanford marshmallow experiment is a study conducted by Mischel, Ebbesen, and Zeiss in 1972. Relying upon prior research pertaining to self-control, Mischel et al. asserted that distracting activities increased delay of gratification for an anticipated reward. The team hypothesized a combination of mental avoidance, fantasizing, and overt activity would assist with delaying gratification by means of self-distraction. Mischel et al. also asserted that subjects would likely adapt to an otherwise frustrating situation by creating a more productive one or creating a less adverse situation. The researchers established three separate tests to evaluate participants' reactions: one with an overt activity, one with a covert activity, and one with no activity at all. The three different tests were conducted with various numbers of children. The average age of the child was around 4.5 years old.

The prevailing prediction was that delayed gratification would decrease with no activity but would increase under the other two environments. These separate experiments demonstrated impressive findings. The key determinant in an effective delay of gratification was contingent upon the suppression of thought of the reward. When active thought of the reward was present, delayed gratification was as difficult to obtain as when the reward was physically present. The Stanford marshmallow experiment demonstrates that delay of gratification is most effectively achieved by cognitive suppression and avoidance techniques intended to reduce anger and irritation.

Testimonials: Aloof Aaron, Cautious Carl, Sensible Sarah, and Risky Rick

At the end of most chapters, I have included case studies and stories of endeavors experienced by real estate investors. Rather than simply appending relevant yet disparate examples, I have intwined them in a logical, progressive manner that further assists the reader in understanding the compounding effects of decisions made when investing in real estate. The progressive examples are demonstrated through the narrative of four individuals advancing through their real estate journey. These four fictitious individuals are Aaron, Carl, Sarah, and Rick.

Each of the four are somewhat knowledgeable on investing in real estate. They've read a few books, heard a few stories, and binge-watched DIY shows on HGTV. Carl, Sarah, and Rick recognize the importance of knowledge and continuously seek to educate themselves on their endeavors. Aaron, on the other hand, is the dangerous combination of cavalier and a little dull. Sarah and Rick are the ambitious members of the group; however, Rick has been known to be overzealous from time to time. Carl, having witnessed many of Rick's prior endeavors, is the more cautious and conservative member of the group.

Carl is your one-marshmallow child, Sarah is willing to wait an hour for the second, Rick will attempt to argue for a third, and Aaron has already forgotten that he had a marshmallow.

SECTION I:

FOUNDATION

Section I includes key terms, topics, and concepts, an understanding of which is essential for building wealth through real estate. These principles will become the cornerstone on which the remainder of the real estate strategy and the book will be established.

Chapter 1: Leveraging the Basics

Every person who invests in well-selected real estate in a growing section of a prosperous community adopts the surest and safest method of becoming independent, for real estate is the basis of wealth.
—Theodore Roosevelt, *26th president of the United States*

In this chapter, we are going to cover the following:

Economics 101
Price, Quantity, Supply and Demand, Equilibrium, Consumer and Producer Surplus, Increased Supply, Increased Demand, Surplus and Shortage, Supply and Demand Barriers

Trend Analysis
Point, Vector, Trend

Types of Wealth
Realized Wealth
Active Income
Passive Income
Unrealized Wealth

Types of Properties
Apartments, Attached Housing (Condominiums, Co-op, Townhomes), Single-Family, Commercial, Mixed-Use, Undeveloped Land

Types of Cost
Cost of Business, Transaction Cost, Price of Lending, Opportunity Cost, Sunk Cost

Key Values and Ratios
After Restoral Value (ARV), As-Is Value (AIV), Debt-to-Income (DTI), Fair Market Value (FMV), Loan-to-Value (LTV)

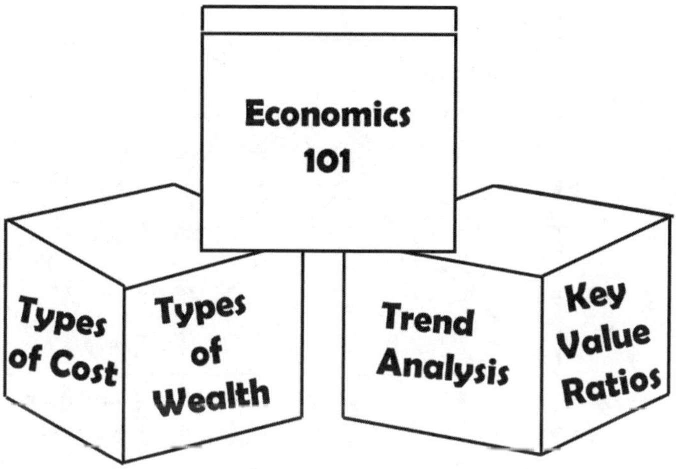

Figure 1-1: The Basics

This first chapter delves into the fundamentals of economics and real estate investing to ensure you invest in real estate correctly. The chapter covers a multitude of terms and definitions. Stick with it; it gets better. While some of the topics covered in this chapter may appear to be simplistic or possibly impertinent, when combined, they become immensely relevant, and your success in real estate is largely contingent upon your understanding of these foundational concepts and how they interrelate.

Economics 101

When covering the basics, we must include the fundamentals of economics; it is the foundation on which real estate is built. Understanding these principles is paramount to your success as a real estate investor. The core of economics is the relationship between *supply* and *demand* and how it corresponds to changes in *price* and *quantity*. Please refer to Figure 1-2 to see the relationship between these core components.

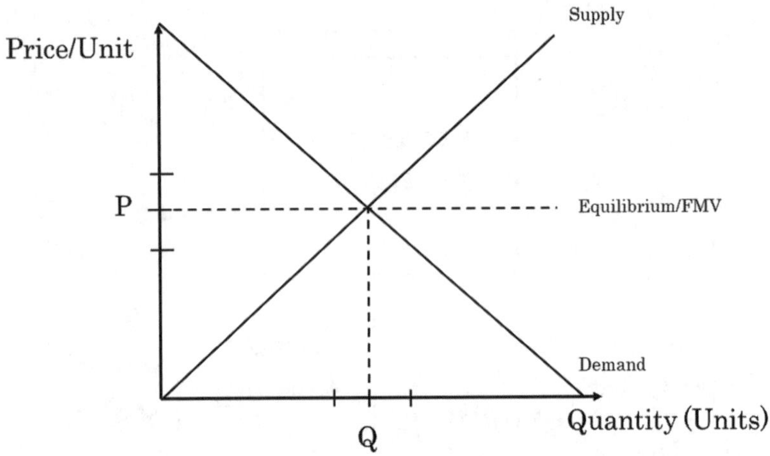

Figure 1-2: Supply and Demand Curve

Price

Price is something all but the overprivileged understand intimately well; it is the cost of use or ownership. As far as real estate is concerned, price primarily pertains to the value at which a property may be purchased and sold or the value at which rent may be charged and paid. Price is the focus area for many novice investors, but while this is an important factor, it is far from the only factor worthy of attention. Price represents the Y-axis on the *Supply and Demand Curve.*

Quantity

Quantity is adjacent to price. Whereas price pertains to value, quantity pertains to amount or volume. The quantity of real estate is equally important, as it is one of the many determinants of future value or price. Quantity represents the X-axis on the Supply and Demand Curve.

Demand

Demand is the inverse corollary of price, although it is also impacted by quantity. Generally, the more something costs, the lower the demand; conversely, lower costs correspond to higher demand largely due to the relationship with the *Supply Curve*. The *Demand Curve* is diagonal, spanning from the upper left to the lower right corner.

Supply

Supply is the converse of demand and is the direct corollary of quantity. Small quantity, minimal supply. Large quantity, higher supply. The Supply Curve is diagonal, spanning from the lower left to the upper right corner.

Equilibrium

The point at which supply and demand intersect is referred to as the *equilibrium price* on the Supply and Demand Curve. This point is of the utmost importance to investors; it is synonymous with the term *Fair Market Value (FMV)*, which will be discussed later in this chapter. This is the value that people are willing to pay and capable of paying, as well as the quantity in which no excess exists (*consumer surplus* or *producer surplus*).

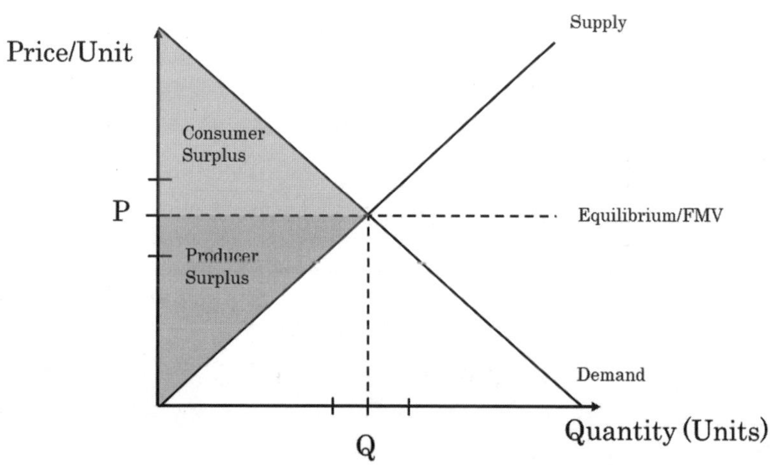

Figure 1-3: Consumer and Producer Surplus

Consumer Surplus

Consumer surplus is the area (under the Demand Curve but above the equilibrium price) in which a consumer is able to pay less than they are willing to pay. For example, they are willing to rent a residence for $1,000 but are able to rent one for $800 due to lower demand in the market.

Producer Surplus

Alternatively, producer surplus is the area (over the Supply Curve but under the equilibrium price) in which a producer may charge more than a consumer is willing to pay. For example, a consumer is willing to pay $1,000 for rent but must pay $1,100 due to higher demand in the market.

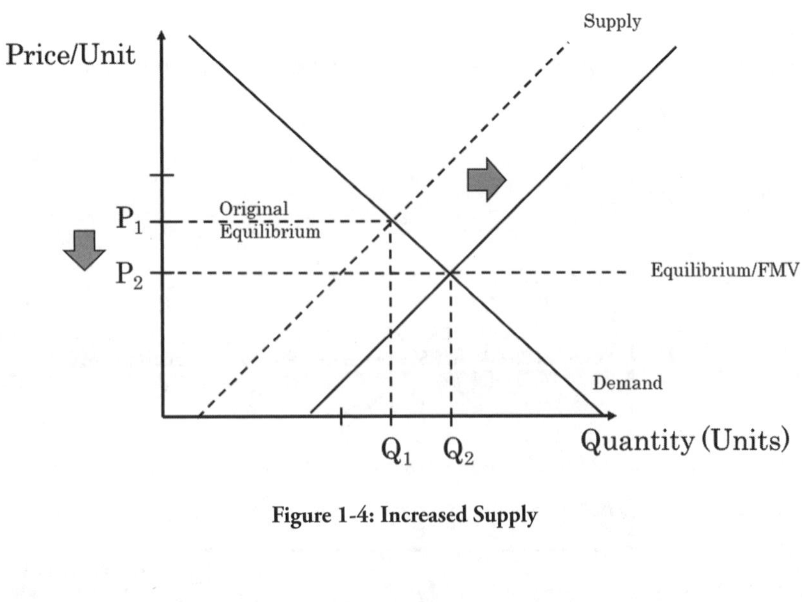

Figure 1-4: Increased Supply

Increased Supply

The relationship between price and quantity and supply and demand is a critical factor. We've previously covered that supply is increased by an increase in quantity.

Now, please refer to Figure 1-4. As you move from Quantity 1 (Q_1) to Quantity 2 (Q_2), the Supply Curve will shift to the right. Note: this action also causes the equilibrium price to drop from Price 1 (P_1) to Price 2 (P_2). The inverse is also true: a shift to the left (a decrease in quantity or available real estate) will result in an increased price.

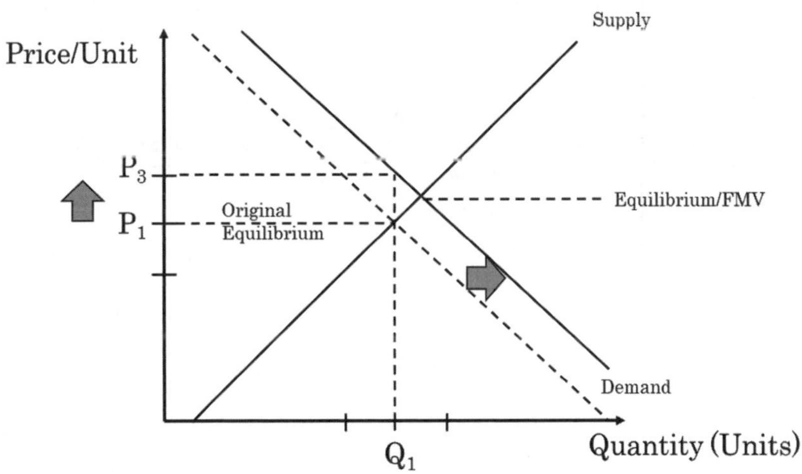

Figure 1-5: Increased Demand

Increased Demand

We've also indicated the relationship of price to the Demand Curve. When demand increases, one of three results will occur. If the quantity remains constant, the price will increase. However, if the price remains constant, the quantity will need to increase. Normally, both the quantity and the price will increase (as indicated in Figure 1-5).

Shortage

A *shortage* is when an excess of demand exists. In layman's terms, more consumers desire a property than there are properties to be occupied. This results in a shift along the Demand Curve to a new *above-equilibrium price*. A shortage of properties is always good for the real estate investor who owns within a market; however, acquiring *assets* within this market will be more difficult or at least more costly. (Refer to Figure 1-6.)

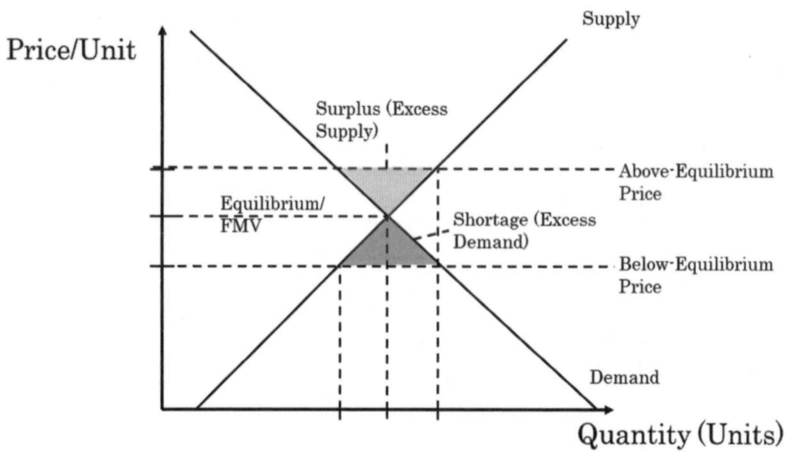

Figure 1-6: Shortage and Surplus

Surplus

A *surplus* is the converse of a shortage, and it occurs when more properties are available than demanded, resulting in a shift along the Demand Curve toward a *below-equilibrium price*. Obviously, this is not ideal for investors. (Refer to Figure 1-6.)

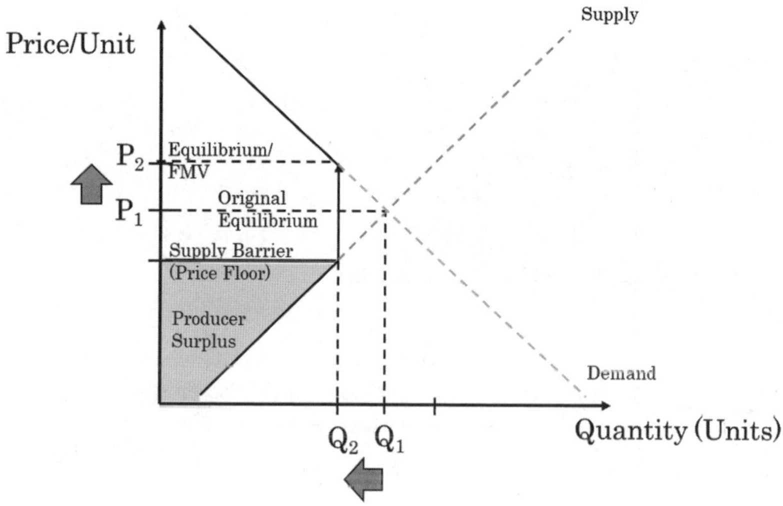

Figure 1-7: Supply Barrier

Supply Barrier

A *supply barrier* is an impediment to reaching the *equilibrium quantity*, which thereby creates a supply shortage. When this occurs, the price increases from the Original Price (P_1) to the New Price (P_2) or the FMV. Supply barriers are also referred to as *price floors*. Identifying supply barriers is key to determining the *path of growth* and confirming future demand for real estate. While this isn't the only basis for future demand, the impact of supply barriers on the path of growth is a major factor in determining property value trends in a given area over time.

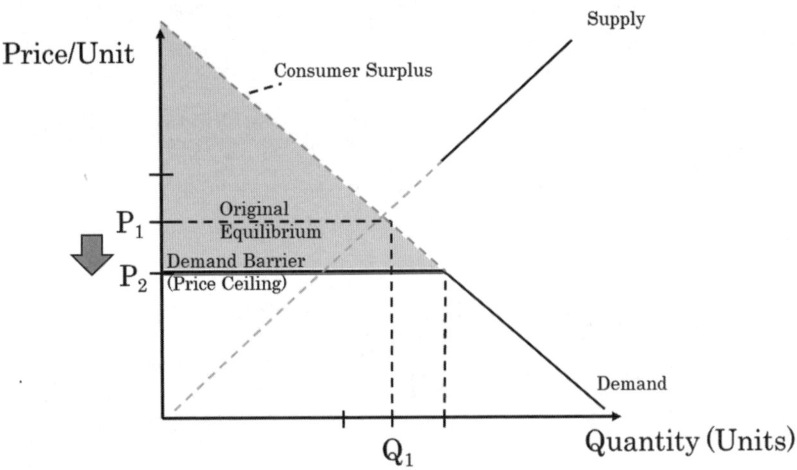

Figure 1-8: Demand Barrier

Demand Barrier

A *demand barrier* is an impediment to attaining equilibrium price—commonly referred to as a *price ceiling*. Regardless of the actual *supply* or demand for real estate in the given area, the price is capped at the demand barrier. A prime example of a demand barrier/price ceiling is *rent control.*[1] It is important for real estate investors to understand and steer clear of demand barriers unless they have an ingenious manner of legally overcoming the obstacle.

Trend Analysis

So, do you remember when I said that some things would look simplistic or possibly impertinent? I was referring mainly to this section, but I must cover it. Why? The ability to perform trend analysis will enable you to determine a more accurate *profit potential* in properties you are looking to acquire. This section covers the differences between a *point*, a *vector*, and a *trend.*

1 Municipal laws enacted to keep the rents affordable for low-income families.

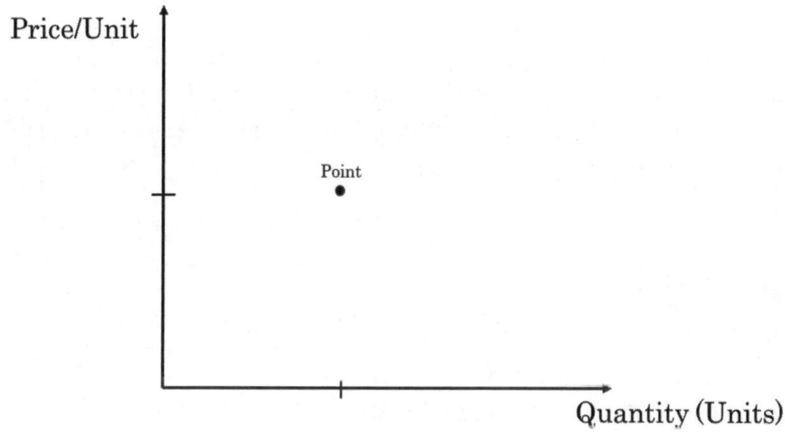

Figure 1-9: Point

Point

A point is merely an observance—or more importantly, a snapshot in time. For example, when shopping for an investment property, you identify its price. That price is a point.

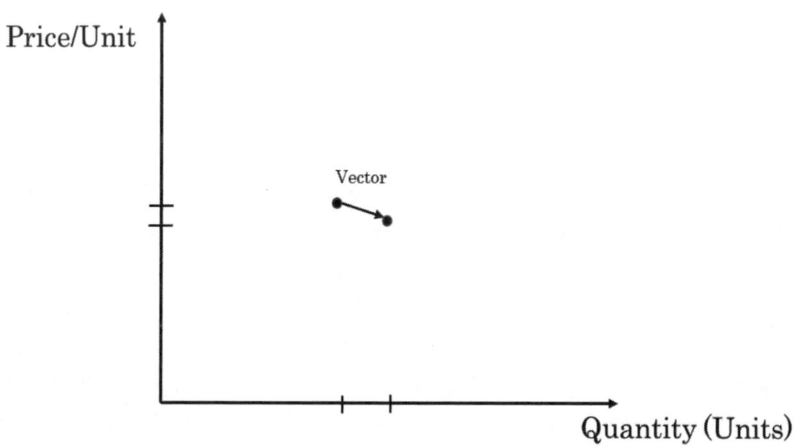

Figure 1-10: Vector

Vector

A vector is the combination of two points in sequence. It shows the direction in which an observable is moving. For example, you compare the property's price to a comparable property from a year ago to establish the vector of the property's value.

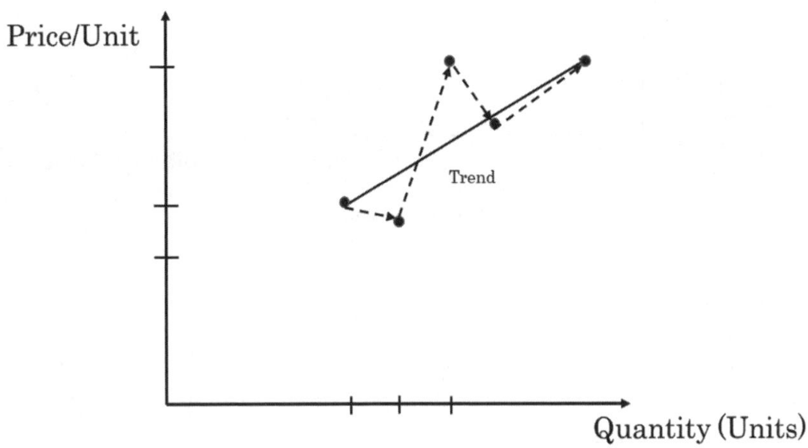

Figure 1-11: Trend

Trend

A trend is the combination of at least three points in sequence that provides a more reliable sense of direction. It is observable because it shows movement over time. Trends compensate for anomalies[2] and outliers,[3] whereas a vector is more susceptible to being swayed by them. When investing in real estate, it behooves you to establish trends before making your ultimate decision as opposed to relying solely upon a point or a vector.

2 A deviation from the norm or standard.

3 A legitimate data point that is outside the range considered normal.

Failing to analyze trends is a mistake of a novice investor that could have ruinous repercussions.

Types of Wealth

Wealth is measured in numerous ways. When referring to money or fiscal value, there are two types of wealth: *realized and unrealized.*

Realized Wealth		Unrealized Wealth
Active	Passive	
• Capital Gains	• Rental Income	• Asset Appreciation
• Wages	• Stock Dividends	• Stocks

Table 1-1: Realized and Unrealized Wealth

Realized Wealth

Realized wealth is wealth that a member has attained or currently possesses (also referred to as *capital*). Realized wealth can further be compartmentalized into active and passive wealth (also referred to as *active income* and *passive income*). (Refer to Table 1-1.)

There is only so much work (active income) any one person can accomplish due to physical limitations or time. When work stops, income stops.

Active income is intuitively termed to indicate any type of income in which a member must be "active" to earn their income (or capital). Examples of realized wealth/*active income* include *capital gains,*[4] *wages,* [5] and *salary.*[6] (Refer to Table 1-1.)

4 Income generated from selling an investment, item, or service for a profit.

5 Income generated as compensation for work performed at an agreed upon price per given period (usually hourly).

6 Income generated as compensation for work performed at an agreed upon price per year.

Realized Wealth: Passive Income

Passive income is a type of income that is garnered without persistent effort from the recipient. Often, all that is required is ownership. Prime examples of realized wealth/passive income include *rental income*[7] or *dividends*.[8] (Refer to Table 1-1.)

> Unrealized wealth/equity value is speculated on demand, meaning that it can increase or decrease in value while possessed.

Unrealized Wealth

Unrealized wealth (also referred to as *equity*) is the projected *appreciation* of the value that is owed to a recipient in exchange for their ownership of an asset/investment. Unrealized wealth (equity) is usually transferred to realized wealth (capital) via an exchange. Examples of unrealized wealth include assets[9] (real estate, rare paintings, vintage wines, classic cars, etc.) and *stocks*.[10] Another undervalued form of unrealized wealth is knowledge. An understanding or in-depth knowledge of how to accomplish various tasks is inherently valuable; its value may be realized by means of savings in capital and equity in pursuit of accomplishing the aforementioned tasks.

Types of Properties

There are several variants in property types you should be aware of as an investor. Demand, *expenses*, *governance*, *lending*, profit potential, supply, *taxation*, and *valuation* may all differ among the property variations. Each property type may be considered a subsegment of the larger real estate market. The demand for one type of property may be decreasing

7 Income generated by an owner from charging rent to tenants dwelling inside of a property possessed by the owner.

8 Sum of money paid regularly (typically quarterly) by an entity (usually a company) to its stock owners (shareholders) from profits garnered during the specified period.

9 Material item owned by an individual that maintains an amount of monetary value.

10 A fraction of ownership over a given company or business.

in an area while the demand for another is increasing. The most common forms of property include the following:

- Residential Property
  - Apartments
  - Attached Housing (Condominiums, Co-op, Townhomes)
  - Single-Family
- Commercial Property
- Mixed-Use Property
- Undeveloped Land

> You may also own industrial real estate; however, that is not covered in this book.

Residential Property

Residential properties (residences) are dwellings that people use for habitation. They reside on land zoned for residential use. In the city-building video game *SimCity*, these are green. The inhabitants may be owners themselves or may rent the dwelling from other owners. As previously mentioned, residential properties include *apartments*, *attached housing*, and *single-family* homes. Residences within a city are considered *urban*; residences outside a city are considered *rural*.

Apartments

An apartment is a room or combination of connected rooms fitted for inhabitance. This is also referred to as a unit. The building in which the collection of apartments (or units) is located is referred to as an *apartment building*. Each unit within an apartment building is normally leased[11] individually, while the entire building is owned.

11 I generally refer to the act of having someone else reside in your unit in exchange for money as leasing and the act of a person exchanging money to reside in a unit as renting.

Attached Housing

Attached housing refers to dwellings that are adjacent (horizontally or vertically) to each other and are individually owned rather than individually leased. For example, a high-rise residential building that is individually leased is an apartment building, whereas a high-rise residential building where each unit is individually owned (owner occupied or leased) is considered a *condominium*. Each unit is billed individually per the *lease agreement*.

Condominiums (Condos)

Condominiums (condos) are buildings that contain many individually owned units, generally under the same roof. Each unit is billed individually since they are separately owned. Condos may be found in both urban and rural areas.

Co-Operative (Co-op)

A *Co-Operative* (building) is a modified concept in which ownership of the building (as well as all associated expenses) is shared by the members of the business entity (*Co-op*). Members who have bought into the Co-op reserve the right to live within the dwelling. Units within the Co-op may be leased to external members; however, the member of the Co-op is still responsible for paying the associated expenses.

Townhomes

Townhomes are dwellings that contain many individually owned units but, in contrast to condominiums, are typically under different roofs (or at least different segments of a roof). Townhomes may be found in both urban and rural areas.

Single-Family Home

A single-family home is a dwelling intended for inhabitance that is not attached to another dwelling. Most dwellings located in rural areas are single-family homes. They can also be found in urban areas, typically for a higher price.

Commercial Property

Alternatively, *commercial properties* are buildings or complexes that are intended for *retail* ventures as opposed to *residential* inhabitance. (In *SimCity*, these properties would be constructed in the blue zones.)

Mixed-Use Property

These are properties that may be used for *retail* and/or *residential* purposes.

Undeveloped Land

Buy land, they're not making it anymore.
—Mark Twain, *writer*

Undeveloped land is exactly what the term defines: land that is undeveloped. Property may be constructed on purchased, undeveloped land so long as it is zoned correctly and not protected.

Types of Cost

We live in a largely transactional society; if you want something, you generally have to pay for it (in one way or another). The amount you must pay is the *cost.* Alternative definitions for cost are to suffer or to lose something. This section covers the various associated costs in real estate:

- Cost of Business
    - Transaction Cost
- Price of Lending
- Opportunity Cost
- Sunk Cost

These terms will frequently be referenced throughout the book.

Cost of Business

This term does not require a definition; however, it may require an explanation. In the context of real estate, *cost of business* refers to expenses incurred in the process of acquisition, maintenance, or disposition of real estate. For example, advertising costs, insurance fees, lending costs, maintenance fees, property management fees, tax fees, and travel (related to your real estate) are all costs of business.

> Most costs of business are tax deductible.

Transaction Cost

The *transaction cost* is the associated charge for a service or exchange. For example, *closing costs* are transaction costs for lending. *Capital gains taxes* are the transaction costs for selling a property (and making a profit). Real estate agent fees (or commissions) are the transaction costs for using a real estate agent to buy or sell a home. Investors must be aware of the transaction costs associated with their endeavors; these costs can quickly eat away at the bottom line and often make a profit on paper become a loss in reality.

Price of Lending

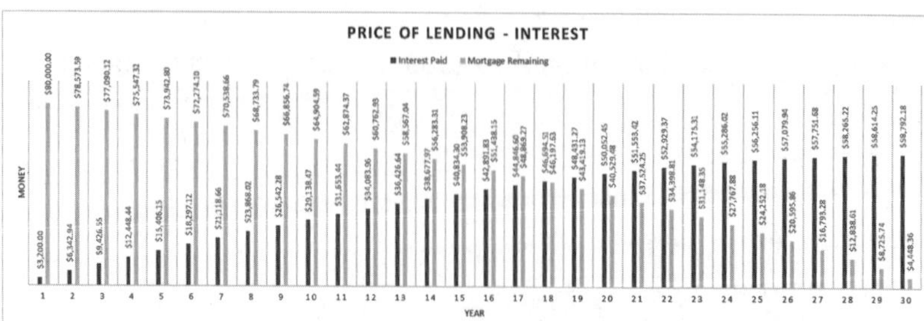

Figure 1-12: Price of Lending – Bar Graph

The price of lending is one that many people are aware of, and many people resent and commonly misunderstand it. I use the term *price* to indicate a persistent suffering, as opposed to cost, which is a singular loss. When you take out a *loan* with a financial institution, your loan is amortized; you will pay interest on that loan. If an investor borrows $80,000 at 4 percent interest, they will pay $58,791.18 in interest in the life of a 30-year loan (see Figure 1-12 for an example). Many homeowners and novice investors anticipate the day when they have paid off their mortgage balance. For homeowners who are not investors, this is a great day; for investors, this is the wrong approach for a multitude of reasons. One reason is *opportunity cost*, and the other is the *Inertia of Real Estate*.

Opportunity Cost

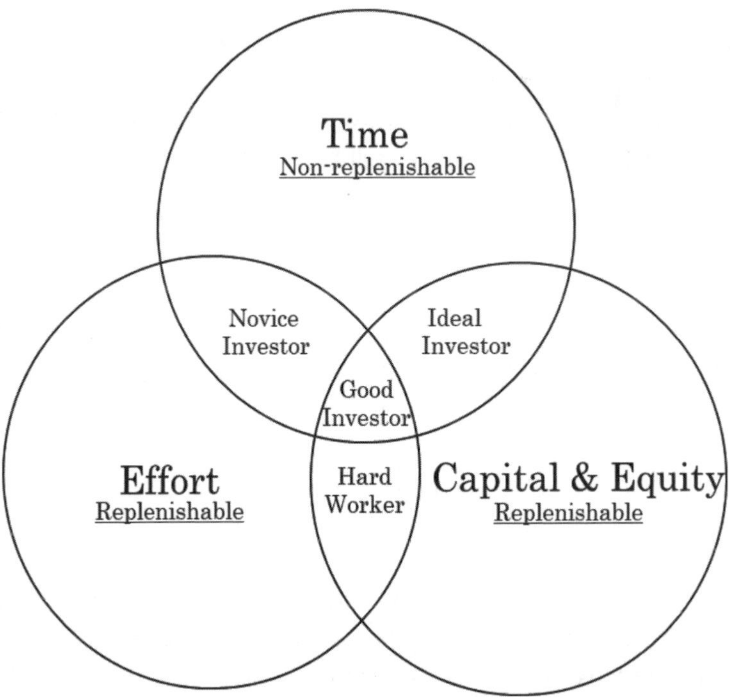

Figure 1-13: Convergence of Effort, Money, and Time

Opportunity cost is something many people are familiar with when it pertains to money: "If I spend money on this, I cannot spend money on that." In this context, whatever "that" is has become the opportunity cost. If you're a millennial referring to experiences, this term is known as "fear of missing out" (FOMO). Opportunity cost is critical to an investor. Opportunity costs should be considered for three main commodities: effort, money, and time. All commodities are finite; however, some can be regenerated, whereas others cannot. Effort can be exhausted but may be replenished. It may also be substituted (for a price). Money is also finite but can be generated both actively and passively. Time, conversely, is finite and cannot be regenerated; it is, therefore, your most precious commodity as an investor (and a living being). Many people exert time and effort to save money, and this may be required initially. But ultimately, we should be asking, "How much money and effort is my time worth?" Other questions you should be asking that pertain to the cost of lending are "What is the opportunity cost of using your own money as opposed to borrowing?" and "What is the associated opportunity cost of paying off a mortgage with rental income profits?" The opportunity cost is the cost of delaying the acquisition of more properties that could be generating you more wealth.

Sunk Cost

Sunk cost is the manner in which most people tend to gravitate and think. This cost refers to the amount (time, money, effort) of a commodity that has already been invested into something. Most people have a tendency to believe a larger sunk cost means that they must commit to and retain the endeavor. This is dangerous when it comes to real estate. Economics teaches you to always ignore the sunk cost and look at the endeavor for its potential merits. When it comes to real estate, look at the numbers and ignore the sunk cost. If the numbers work, proceed; if they do not, cut your loss like it's a tumor threatening to infect the rest of your body (or your investment portfolio).

Key Values and Ratios

Have you seen the movie *Inception*? It is arguably one of my favorite movies because it is so thought-provoking and open to interpretation. The main premise of the movie **(*SPOILER*)** is that a group of individuals can send subliminal messages by means of a "mind heist." The gang of thieves has the ability to enter a shared dream space of other people. Time is relative while in the dream state, and anyone in it can lose track of whether they are dreaming. So, seasoned dreamers carry a small tangible token called a "totem" with them, which helps them distinguish reality from their "dream state" so they never get lost within the dream.

The following key values and ratios are your "totems" for distinguishing a good deal in your reality from a good deal in your "dream state" of investing. Your totems include *After Restoral Value* (ARV), *As-Is Value* (AIV), *Debt-to-Income* (DTI), Fair Market Value (FMV), and *Loan-to-Value* (LTV).

After Restoral Value (ARV)

The After Restoral Value (ARV) is the monetary value of a property that was distressed/in need of repair after repairs have been conducted. In most circumstances, the ARV is the same as the equilibrium price. The ARV is frequently an *appraised*[12] or *assessed*[13] price rather than an *actual* price.[14] The actual price may be more or less than the ARV.

As-Is Value (AIV)[15]

The As-Is Value (AIV) is the monetary value of a property in its current condition without any adjustment for repairs or necessary work.

12 The monetary value an appraiser determines a property to be worth.

13 The monetary value an investor or (non-appraiser) surmises the property to be worth.

14 The price a property sells for during negotiations between buyer and seller.

15 As-Is Value is a term in real estate; however, the abbreviation (AIV) is not official.

Debt-to-Income (DTI) Ratio

Debt-to-Income is an important ratio for junior investors. This is one of the major ratios *lending institutions* use to determine a borrower's ability to repay a loan. The calculation for DTI is simple:

$$DTI = \frac{Total\ Hard\ Debt}{Total\ Income}$$

Total hard debt refers to debts the borrower must pay and cannot easily resolve. This may include alimony, car payments, homeowner dues, mortgages, personal and student loans, etc. This does not include other payments for items that may more easily be curtailed or abstained. Examples of these payments include bills associated with cell phones, Disney+ accounts, gym memberships, wine clubs, etc. The magic number for lending institutions is normally 43 percent. A DTI above this percentage makes you a risky borrower for the bank and limits your options as an investor. Junior investors should avoid actions that increase this ratio.

> Although lesser routine expenses are not included in hard debt, lending institutions do review credit card balances. Make sure to keep your balance beneath 43 percent.

Fair Market Value (FMV)

Fair Market Value (FMV) is the equilibrium price for which a buyer and seller are willing to exchange property (or the *rental price* a landlord and tenant mutually agree upon). When purchasing real estate, the goal is to purchase at or below the FMV if at all possible. If purchasing above the FMV, make sure the acquisition fits your investment strategy.

Loan-to-Value (LTV)

Loan-to-Value is the ratio of the amount that a lending institution is willing to lend to a borrower and the value (actual or *appraised*) of a property. The equation is simple:

$$LTV = \frac{Loan\,Amount}{Value\;of\,Property}$$

Most (not all) LTVs are 75–80 percent. If you are purchasing a home for $100,000, the bank will be willing to lend you $80,000. You must front $20,000 as the *down payment*[16] for the loan. Chapter 3 will address unique loan types that offer different LTV ratios and will cover steps to lending in more granular detail.

Objective: Leveraging the Basics

Ensure you understand the concepts covered in this chapter; they are foundational concepts upon which the remainder of this book and real estate strategy is established. Give serious thought to opportunity costs and whether your current lifestyle is conducive to investing in real estate. There is no shame in admitting you aren't ready, although chances are that you are ready and don't realize it. The biggest shame would be attempting to take on more than you can handle because you didn't take the time to properly assess and prepare for the endeavor.

You should also calculate your DTI if you have not already done so (or have not done so in a while). If your DTI is high, one of your first steps will be to decrease it. The most efficient way to decrease your DTI is to honestly assess your current expenses and determine which are your *necessities* (needs) and which are your desires (wants). Pursuing a desire/want is fine and, in fact, is encouraged to a degree. We have to live life a little. Otherwise, why go through all this effort? But make sure the pursuit of your wants does not impede your goals. A desire/want that unduly prevents the attainment of a goal is, at best, a distraction but could become an impediment or hindrance if left unchecked. If

16 The initial or partial payment provided up front when purchasing an object using credit.

attempting to lower your DTI, determine how much you really "want" these desires in comparison to how much you want to invest in your goals and future via acquiring wealth through real estate.

Finally, assess your current realized and unrealized wealth; if either type is not performing effectively or efficiently, consider leveraging them for real estate acquisitions.

Tasks:

- Calculate your DTI.
- Assess your current realized and unrealized wealth efficiency.

Chapter 2: Leveraging Key Real Estate Concepts

> **Give me a lever long enough and a fulcrum on which to place it, and I shall move the world.**
> —Archimedes, *Greek mathematician*

In this chapter, we are going to cover the following:

Inertia of Real Estate

Appreciation, Inflation, Equity Generated, Amortization, Equity Available

Velocity of Money

Rental Income, Expenses, Passive Income

Profitability Ratios

Return on Investment (ROI), Return on Equity (ROE)

Momentum of Wealth

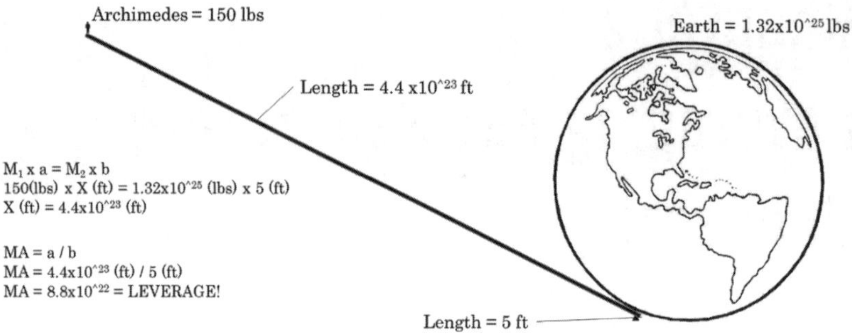

Figure 2-1: Archimedes' Leverage

Archimedes understood how leverage works. That is why he could confidently imagine moving the globe by doing nothing more than applying his body weight to a right-sized lever and fulcrum. Now, that lever would need to be 4.4 septillion feet long, placing him nearly 1.5 million light-years away, which is more than halfway to our neighbor galaxy Andromeda. But his calculations still prove a point: leverage is powerful!

Imagine if you applied this leverage to your current capital (money). Over time, every dollar you invested could yield a return of $880 sextillion! Obviously, real estate doesn't yield that high of a return; no investment does. However, leveraging real estate does yield consistent returns over time that far surpass the majority of other investments—if done correctly. This is the result of the compounded factor of the *Velocity of Money* and the *Inertia of Real Estate* that I refer to as the *Momentum of Wealth.*

Inertia of Real Estate

Real estate is one of the few investments that offers returns that consistently surpass the yields of others. This is due to its inherent ability to generate additional equity passively. Wise investors leverage such equity to acquire additional revenue-generating properties, which can then begin generating equity of their own. To best understand this concept in its entirety, one must first understand the concepts of *appreciation, inflation, generated equity, amortization (mortgage payoff)*, and *available equity*. The aggregate of these factors results in the *Inertia of Real Estate.*

$$Inertia\ of\ Real\ Estate = I_{Real\ Estate}$$

Appreciation

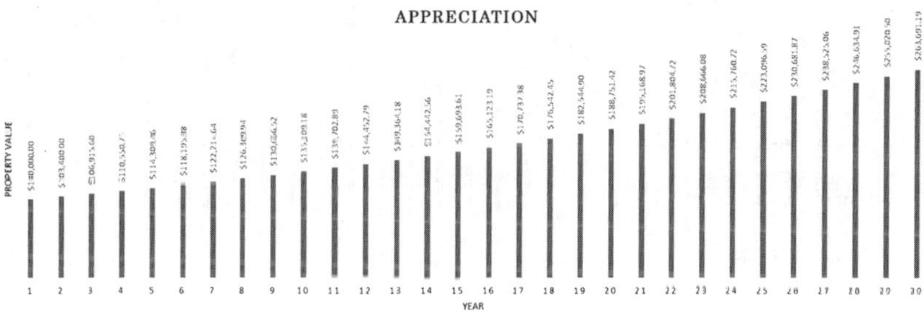

Figure 2-2: Appreciation – Bar Graph

Appreciation is the increase in value of an asset over a period of time. Appreciation may be calculated with the following equation:

$$P_1 = P_0 \times (1 + r)^n$$

$$P_{rice\ Appreciated} = P_{rice\ Original} \times \left(1 + r_{ate\ of\ appreciation}\right)^{n_{umber\ of\ payment\ periods}}$$

In the U.S., property, if in the appropriate location, appreciates at 3.4 percent per year on average (at least it did between 1991 and 2021). If an investor purchases a property that is worth $100,000, what will its appreciated value become at the end of a 30-year period?

$$P_{Appreciated} = \$100{,}000 \times (1 + 0.034)^{30}$$

$$P_{Appreciated} = \$263{,}691.19$$

That's $163,691.19 in appreciation (a 164 percent return on value!) simply from owning the property for 30 years (the standard mortgage period). Refer to Figure 2-2 to see the incremental appreciation of a $100,000 property throughout the entirety of the period. Now, you do need to account for inflation in order to have a more accurate depiction of your unrealized wealth or equity in this property.

Inflation

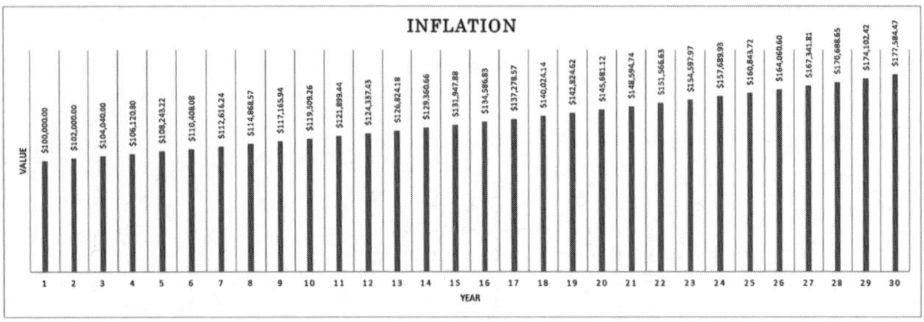

Figure 2-3: Inflation – Bar Graph

The dollar today will be worth more than the dollar a year from now. For example, let's review the price of staple goods in the year I was born: 1990.

1 gal. of gasoline:	$1.16	1 dozen eggs:	$1.00
1 gal. of milk:	$2.68	First-class stamp:	$0.25

The rate at which the dollar depreciates in value (compared to today) is referred to as inflation. Any good investor accounts for inflation when looking at the longevity of their portfolio. Inflation may be calculated with the following equation:

$$I = P_0 \times (1 + i_r)^n$$

$$I_{nflation} = P_{rice\ Original} \times (1 + i_{nterest\ rate})^{n_{umber\ of\ periods}}$$

$$I_{nflation} = \$100{,}000 \times (1 + 0.02)^{30}$$

$$I_{nflation} = \$177{,}584.47$$

In 30 years, $177,584.47 will be worth the same amount as $100,000 is today, assuming an average yearly inflation rate of 2 percent. Refer to Figure 2-3 to see inflation over the 30-year period.

Equity Generated

The difference between appreciation and inflation is the equity generated, and this is the true value we care about as investors. It is the unrealized wealth you have attained by owning the property.

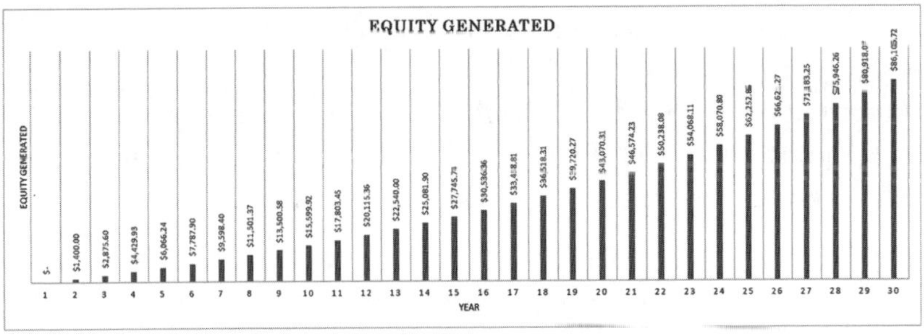

Figure 2-4: Equity Generated – Bar Graph

Generated equity may be calculated by subtracting the inflation value from the appreciation value. The depiction of generated equity over the 30-year period is illustrated in Figure 2-4. Over this period, the amount of equity generated is $86,106.72 ($263,691.19 – $177,584.47) in today's dollars, which is an 86 percent return on the initial $100,000 investment. It's not the 164 percent unadjusted return on value we noted before, but it is still far better than most other investments, and its full benefit has yet to be discussed.

Amortization

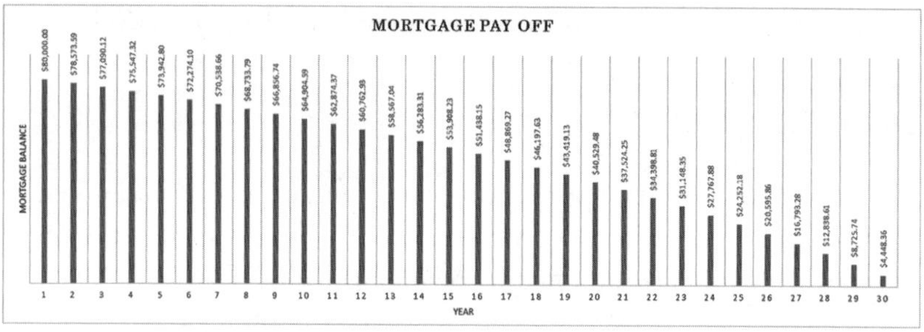

Figure 2-5: Amortization – Bar Graph

Amortization is found by dividing mortgage payments over multiple periods (years). Essentially, this is the payoff schedule for a loan. Amortization may be calculated with the following equation:

$$A = P \times \frac{i \times (1+i)^n}{(1+i)^n - 1}$$

$$A_{mortized\ Payent} = P_{rinciple\ remaining}$$

$$\times$$

$$\frac{i_{nterest\ rate} \times (1 + i_{nterest\ rate})^{n_{umber\ of\ payment\ periods\ (total)}}}{\left(1 + i_{nterest\ rate}\right)^{n_{umber\ of\ payment\ periods\ (total)}} - 1}$$

Interest rates will play a large factor in this calculation. For this example, we will assume an interest rate of 4 percent. If an investor were to purchase a property for $100,000, they would pay $20,000 for the down payment and assume a loan of $80,000. The amortized payment would normally be the installment amount from one payment period to the next. For simplicity, the period will be 30 years rather than 360 months. The total amount paid for the first year would be the following:

$$A = \$80{,}000 \times \frac{0.04\ \times\ (1 + 0.04)^{30}}{(1 + 0.04)^{30} - 1}$$

$$A = \$80{,}000 \times \frac{0.1297}{2.2433}$$

$$A = \$4{,}626\,.4$$

Note: of this product, $3,200 is interest paid ($80,000 x 0.04), and $1,426.14 is the actual amount of the mortgage that's been paid. The ratio of interest paid and the mortgage invert as the mortgage period progresses. Refer to Figure 2-5 to see the mortgage payoff schedule for an $80,000 loan over a 30-year period.

Equity Available

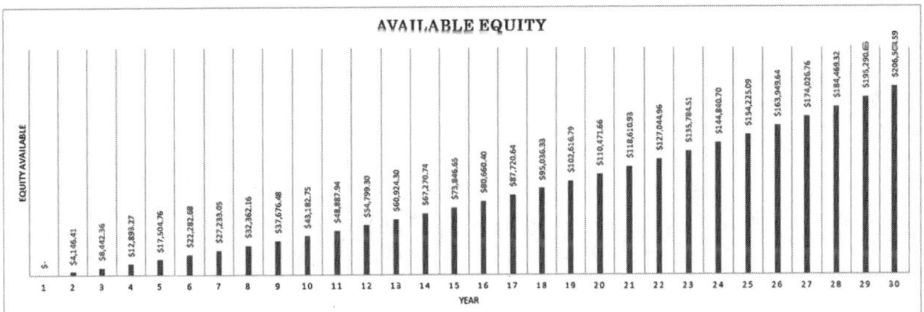

Figure 2-6: Available Equity – Bar Graph

Leveraging the equity available in attained assets is how an investor compounds their wealth. Purchasing real estate is the first step toward unlocking the *Momentum of Wealth*; leveraging the available equity is the second. This is the path to success, or as my idol Mando would say:

This is the way!
—Din Djarin, *The Mandalorian*

Available equity is determined by adding the equity generated (appreciation – inflation) to the original mortgage balance minus the amortized balance.

> Be careful not to refinance too often. There are transaction costs associated, which will eat away at the profitability of this strategy or cause you to invest additional capital of your own if you're not careful.

Ten years into the period of a property initially worth $100,000, the available equity would be $43,182.75. The action of extracting equity (*equity stripping*) from an asset and transferring it to capital is referred to as a *cash-out refinance.*[17] Determining when to execute your cash-out refinance depends upon several factors, including available capital, current interest rates, DTI, leads on new acquisitions, and lending options, among other personal factors.

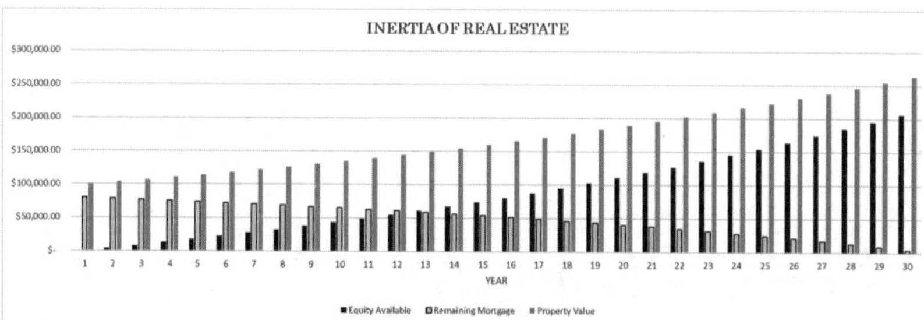

Figure 2-7: Inertia of Real Estate – Bar Graph

The equity available increases as you pay off your mortgage and your property's value increases (refer to Figure 1-16 for a graphical depiction). Do you remember the section pertaining to opportunity cost? The opportunity cost for the accumulated equity for this property at 10 years is the ability to afford two other properties, which may begin to generate additional equity (which means more passive income for you).

17 A loan taken out on a property in which the loan amount is more than any existing debt on the property and any associated transaction fees.

The *Inertia of Real Estate* is real estate's ability to self-generate equity while also providing the leverage to procure additional equity-generating assets without the need for investment of any additional capital.

Do you grasp the magnitude of this impact? An investor's initial investment of $20,000 (plus closing costs) would, after 10 years, grant the investor an opportunity to own two more income-generating properties. Imagine another 10 years down the road. Your three properties may become nine—all with little or no additional investment of capital. Now you grasp the concept!

Velocity of Money

If you don't find a way to make money while you sleep,
you will work until you die.
—Warren Buffet, *business tycoon and philanthropist*

The *Velocity of Money* is a term you may have heard before. Normally this refers to the number of times money is exchanged in a given period as a measure of commerce. When used in the context of real estate, it refers to the ability money possesses to make you more money. To best understand this principle, you will need a firm understanding of the following subjects: rental income (rent), property expenses, mortgage payments, and passive income.

Rental Income

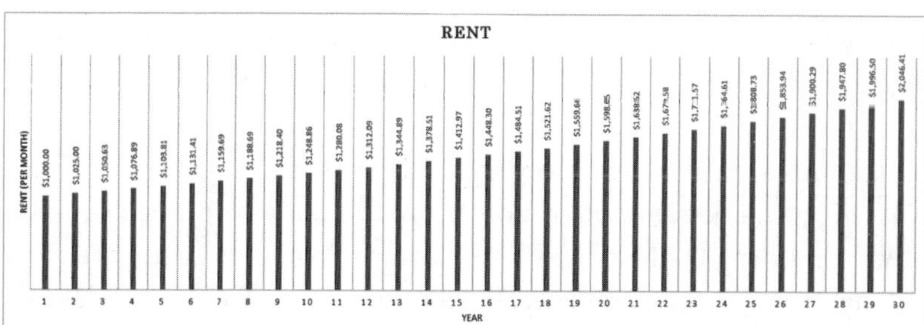

Figure 2-8: Rental Income – Bar Graph

Rental income is the first factor involved in the *Velocity of Money* in the context of real estate. As you may surmise, this is the income generated from leasing your property to someone else. Continuing with the example of the property acquired for $100,000, we will assume the investor is strictly adhering to the 1 percent rule (see Chapter 6) and charges the tenant 1 percent of the value of the property. This would equate to $1,000 per month.

Rent has at least two compelling aspects: someone else is paying you more than your mortgage to live in your property, and rent regularly increases by a small percentage every year. Rent in an area with moderate demand will increase between 2.5 to 5 percent per year. In 10 years, the investor would collect $1,280.08 per month for a property that yielded $1,000 when the contract was established. Not bad, right (especially since inflation is roughly 2 percent per year)? Refer to Figure 2-8 to see the full depiction of rental income growth over the duration of a 30-year period.

The equation to calculate future rental income would be the following:

$$I_1 = I_0 \times (1 + r)^n$$

$$I_{ncome\ (new)} = I_{ncome\ (original)} \times \left(1 + r_{ate\ of\ appreciation}\right)^{n_{umber\ of\ payment\ periods}}$$

$$I_1 = \$1000 \times \left(1 + .025\right)^{10}$$

$$I_{ncome\ (new)} = \$1{,}280.08$$

Expenses

Owning a property doesn't mean you can just charge rent and call it a day. You must also pay for the associated expenses for owning and leasing a rental property. These expenses tend to include insurance premiums, mortgage payments, property management fees, and taxes. These will take a chunk out of your monthly profit, and—with the exception of your mortgage—they do not expire, meaning you will pay them for as long as you own the property. Furthermore, the cost of your expenses tends to follow the same rate as that of inflation (2 percent per year). Refer to Figure 2-9 to see the trend of expenses over time.

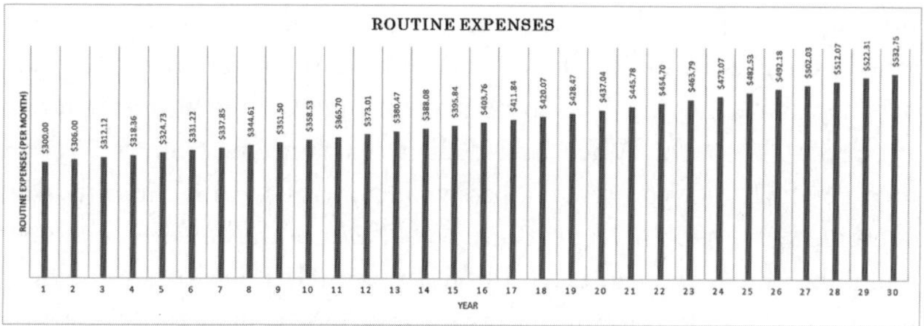

Figure 2-9: Expenses – Bar Graph

The calculation to determine the future cost of expenses is the following:

$$P_1 = P_0 \times (1 + r)^n$$

$$P_{rice\ Appreciated} = P_{rice\ Original} \times \left(1 + r_{ate\ of\ appreciation}\right)^{n_{umber\ of\ payment\ periods}}$$

$$P_1 = \$300 \times (1 + .02)^{10}$$

$$P_{rice\ Appreciated} = \$365.59$$

If an investor paid a combined $300/month for insurance, property management fees, and taxes today, they could expect to pay $365.59/month in 10 years. Fortunately, as we've covered previously, the mortgage does not increase over time (assuming it's a fixed-rate loan). If the mortgage was initially $365.59/month, it would still be $365.59/month 10 years later.

Passive Income

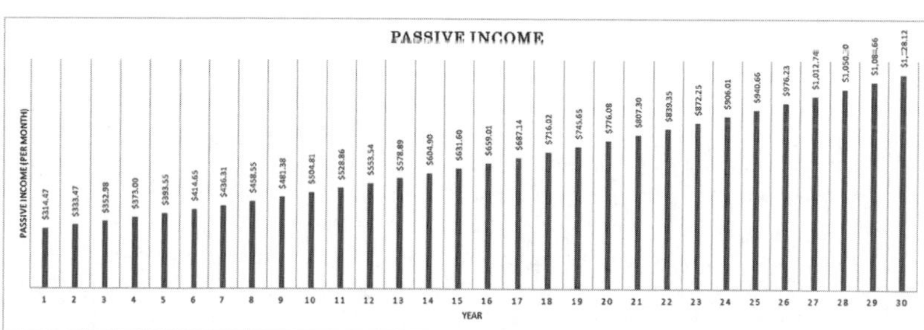

Figure 2-10: Monthly Passive Income – Bar Graph

I'm sure you've already figured out the next step: you deduct the combined expenses (including the mortgage) from the rental income to garner the passive income. The combined expenses for this property today are $685.53/month. When you deduct that amount from the rental income of $1,000, you reveal a passive income of $314.47/month. The combined expenses in 10 years are $744.06/month; however, the new rental income in 10 years is $1,248.86/month. The new passive income in 10 years is $504.80/month. Yes, your money is increasing its velocity! Refer to Figure 2-10 for the incremental increase of monthly rental income depiction. For easy comparison, the annual passive income would be $3,773.64 today and $6,057.66 in 10 years. Refer to Figure 2-11 for a graphical depiction of the annual income.

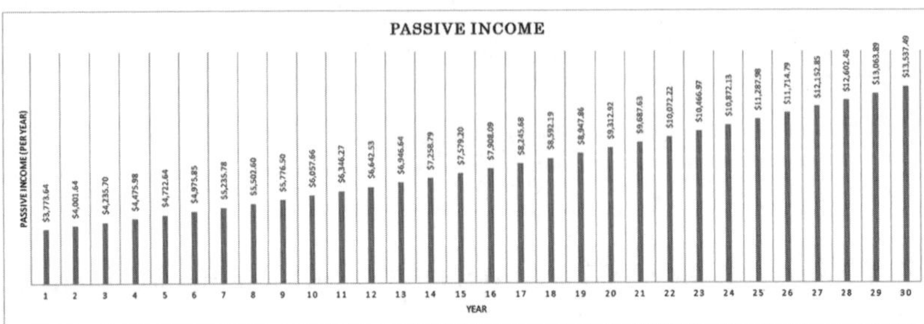

Figure 2-11: Annual Passive Income – Bar Graph

Figure 2-12 combines passive income, mortgage expenses, rent, and routine expenses together to show the true power the *Velocity of Money* provides. This chart also provides an additional five years beyond mortgage payoff to show the notable increase in passive income after the mortgage has been paid.

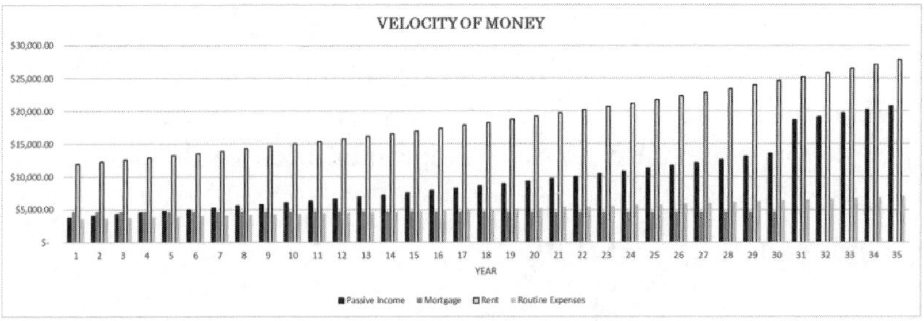

Figure 2-12: Velocity of Money – Bar Graph

Profitability Ratios

I've used phrases such as "make sure it fits your strategy" or "make sure the numbers work" in this chapter. Your *profitability ratios* are the means by which you determine whether the real estate fits into your strategy and whether the numbers work. Profitability ratios are necessary measurements at many steps of acquiring properties and at many stages of this investment strategy. The two profitability ratios are: *Return on Investment (ROI)* and *Return on Equity (ROE).* As far as ratios are concerned, these two combined are the holy grail.

> Bridge Keeper: "What … is your name?"
> King Arthur: "It is Arthur—King of the Britons."
> Bridge Keeper: "What … is your quest?"
> King Arthur: "To seek the Holy Grail."
> Bridge Keeper: "What … is the airspeed velocity of an unladen swallow?"
> King Arthur: "What do you mean? An African or a European swallow?"
> Bridge Keeper: "I don't know that. Aaaaaaaaagh!"
>
> —*Monty Python and the Holy Grail*

When people ask, "What is your *profit return*?"[18] they are usually referring to ROI. They should specify, because ROI is not the only

18 The positive rate of return for a given venture.

important profitability ratio. ROE is a less commonly leveraged yet an equally (if not more) useful ratio for determining the *profit return*. An investment's ROI and ROE can be very different, much like the air-speed velocity of an African or a European unladen swallow.

Return on Investment (ROI)

Return on Investment (ROI) is the annual percentage of return (passive income) on your initial investment (down payment + closing costs). This is an important calculation because it allows the investor to determine how long the *Velocity of Money* (unadjusted) will take to recuperate the initial investment. If given an option between two properties, it is often beneficial to acquire the property with the higher ROI. The calculation for ROI is the following:

$$ROI = \frac{(Positive\ Cash\ Flow*12)}{Initial\ Investment}$$

The sample property would yield the following ROI at the end of the first year, assuming closing costs were $4,000:

$$ROI = \frac{(\$314.47*12)}{(\$20{,}000 + \sim\$4{,}000)}$$

$$ROI = \frac{\$3{,}773.64}{\$24{,}000}$$

$$ROI = 0.0157\ or\ 15.7\%$$

Remember, ROI is a measure used to gauge and assess profitability. It should be used to differentiate the profitability of various investments.

Return on Equity (ROE)

Return on Equity (ROE) is the annual percentage of return (passive income) on the available equity in the investment, which in this case is the property. In my opinion, this should be an investor's preferred ratio because it is not only a profitability ratio but also an efficiency ratio. This calculation allows the investor to determine how efficiently their equity is being leveraged. The calculation for ROE is the following:

$$ROE = \frac{(Positive\ Cash\ Flow * 12)}{E_{quity\ Available}}$$

Once again, if using the sample property, the ROE at end of the first year would be the following (refer to Figure 2-6 for available equity after year 1):

$$ROE = \frac{(\$314.47 * 12)}{\$4{,}146.41}$$

$$ROE = \frac{\$3{,}773.64}{\$4{,}146.41}$$

$$ROE = .965\ or\ 96.5\%$$

I think that just about every teacher would say that a 96.5 percent score is an A, and it might even be an A+ if they're grading on a curve. With this percent in hand, you can feel comfortable investing in this sample property. As you can see, ROE is an important ratio to be cognizant of. Remember, the goal is to garner as much money as possible while retaining as much time as possible in exchange for the least exertion possible.

Momentum of Wealth

The *Momentum of Wealth* is the effective and efficient leveraging of both the *Velocity of Money* and the *Inertia of Real Estate*. Extracting the equity that has accrued and is now available while also utilizing the accumulated capital from rental income will enable you to acquire both real estate and generational wealth.

When should you cash out of a property? **The point in time in which to capitalize on the *Momentum of Wealth* is when the cumulative accrued capital (sum of all rental income) equates to the available equity and is also equal to the price of another mortgage for a**

similar or like property. This occurs when the cumulative ROI intersects with the current year's ROE.

Jump forward 10 years in our ongoing example and assess the ROI and the ROE at that point in time.

$$ROI = \frac{\$6{,}057.66}{\$24{,}000} = .2524\ (25.2\%)$$

$$ROE = \frac{\$6{,}057.66}{\$43{,}182.75} = .1402\ (14\%)$$

In 10 years, the ROI increased from 15.7 to 25.2 percent; however, the ROE plummeted from 96.5 percent to 14 percent. The investor may continue to increase their return but will do so in a very inefficient manner (refer to Figure 2-13 for the projection of ROI and ROE over time if uninterrupted).

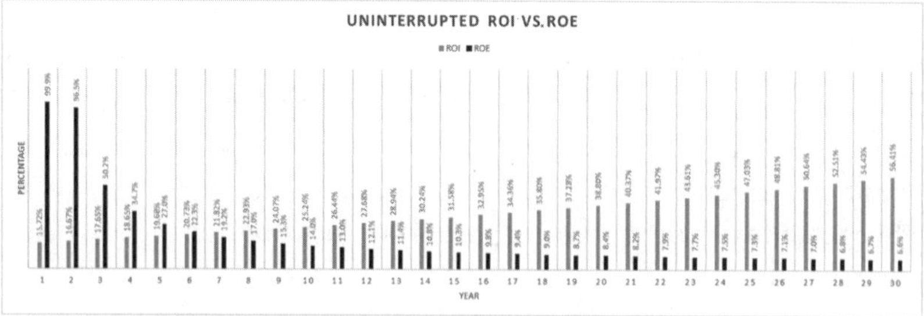

Figure 2-13: Uninterrupted ROI vs. ROE – Bar Graph

How do you avoid this? How do you continue to procure additional wealth more efficiently? You do what was discussed previously and cash-out refinance the loan. This resets the ROE to 99 percent, and if reinvested as previously discussed, the ROE can cover two more properties with an individual ROI of 15.7 percent or a combined ROI of 31.4 percent. Remember, the investor still only invested the initial $20,000. Had the investor decided to forgo the cash-out refinance, the ROI at six years would have been 20.7 percent. It doesn't take a grand chess master to know the strategic approach is to cash-out refinance and acquire another asset.

Coincidentally, six years is also the duration of time in which this property would have recouped its own cost to the investor. Yes, you have correctly concluded that simultaneously accruing passive income combined with cash-out refinancing at six years provides the opportunity to purchase an additional two properties at the end of the sixth year, as indicated by Figure 2-14.

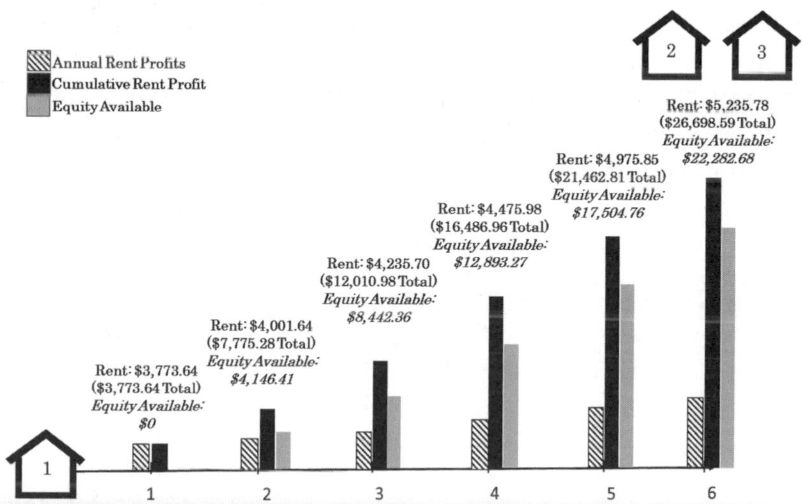

Figure 2-14: ***Momentum of Wealth*** **Strategy (Over Six Years)**

The combined passive income of the first three properties (or units) from years seven and eight is enough for yet another down payment on a like property. Continue the cycle, refinancing each individual property every six years (and at six-year intervals thereafter), and witness the exponential growth of the real estate portfolio.

As you can see, the rate of growth is exponential with an impressive spike occurring again at year 12. Units 1–3 are cash-out refinanced (again), doubling the portfolio, while the passive income allows for an additional purchase in conjunction. This strategy executed over a 30-year period would lead to results like those in Figure 2-15.

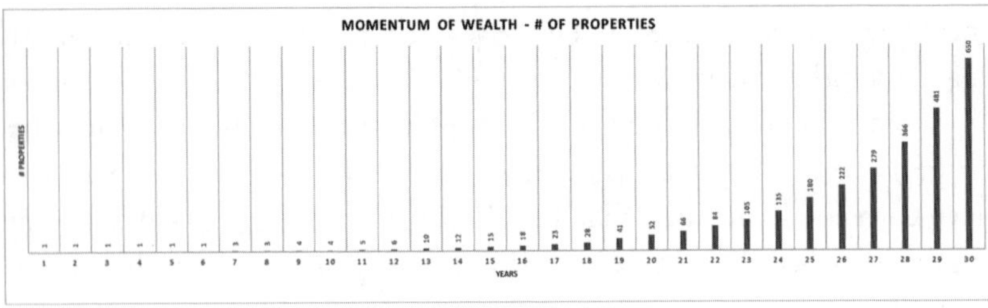

Figure 2-15: ***Momentum of Wealth*** **Strategy: Number of Properties – Bar Chart**

Yes, that is correct; if this strategy is applied for 30 years, the portfolio would increase to 650 units! And all of that wealth came from the $20,000 (and ~$4,000 in closing costs) investment in the form of a down payment for the first property. All subsequent passive income and cash-out refinances are reinvested into expanding the portfolio. The following graphs (Figures 2-16, 2-17, and 2-18) demonstrate the ROI trend, ROE trend, and (what you've been waiting for) the annually generated passive income.

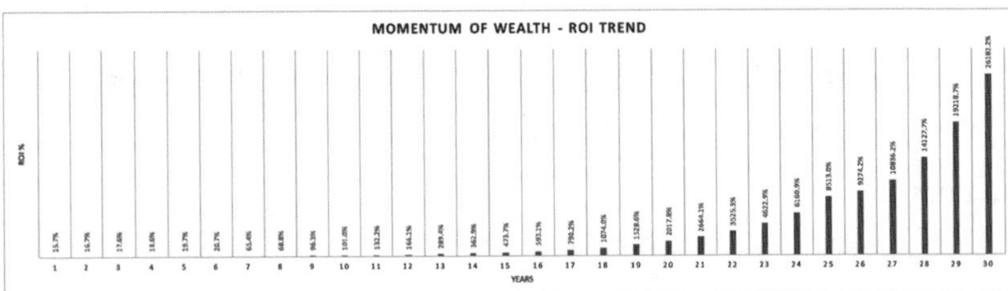

Figure 2-16: ***Momentum of Wealth*** **Strategy: ROI Trend – Bar Chart**

ROI increases exponentially, even with persistent cash-out refinances. In actuality, the cash-out refinances and subsequent purchases boost the ROI.

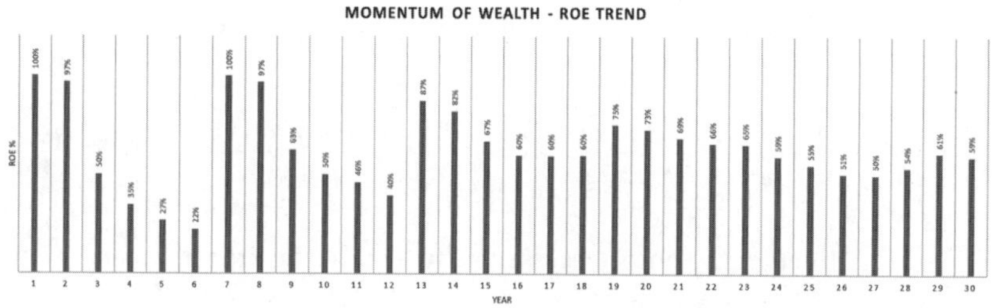

Figure 2-17: ***Momentum of Wealth*** **Strategy: ROE Trend – Bar Chart**

The ROE oscillates as properties are refinanced. ROE can be made even more efficient by reducing the number of years between *cash-out refinancing* in the later years of the strategy.

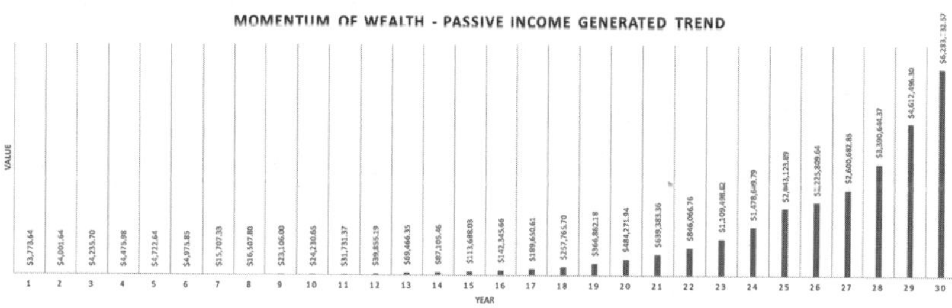

Figure 2-18: ***Momentum of Wealth*****: Passive Income – Bar Chart**

When this journey concludes, the 650 units would yield an impressive $8.8 million in annually generated passive income! That's a 36,700 percent ROI. Granted, it's not Archimedes' $913 sextillion, but you don't need to travel halfway to Andromeda to get it either. In reality, $8.8 million 30 years from today is approximately $3.1 million (generated annually) in today's money. You should be able to live off of those residuals. This is with one property to start. Imagine beginning with 2, 3, or 10!

Keep in mind, this model was extrapolated from the specific ROI and ROE associated with the sample property. This property's convergence point (the intersection of ROI and ROE) was around six years. (Refer to Figure 2-19 for line graph.)

Your property may have another convergence point and different periods in which it would be optimal for you to cash-out refinance.

Remember the following equation for the convergence point:

$$ROI = \frac{(Positive\ Cash\ Flow{*}12)}{Initial\ Investment} = \frac{(Positive\ Cash\ Flow{*}12)}{E_{quity\ Available}} = ROE$$

The convergence point is essentially when the initial investment equals the available equity.

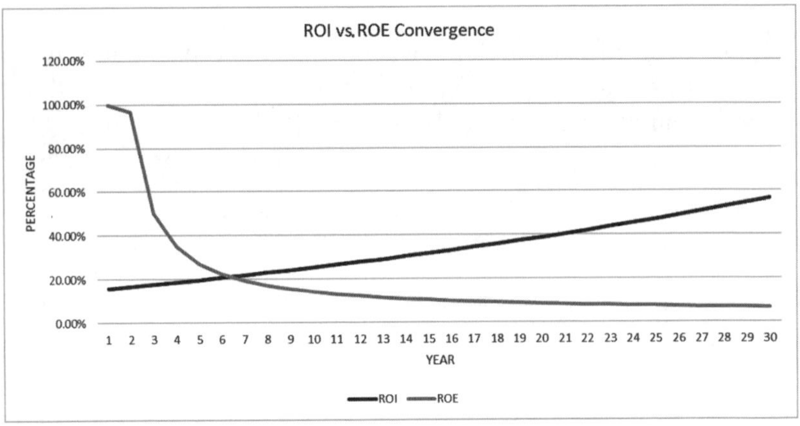

Figure 2-19: ROI and ROE Convergence

Visit our website (masterofleverage.info) by using this QR code to calculate your specific ratios. This resource also contains other key figures and ratios you may find useful as you read this book and continue your journey of generating wealth through real estate.

Visit our website (masterofleverage.info) by using this QR code to access key figures and references you may find useful as you read this book and continue your journey of generating wealth through real estate.

Objective: Leveraging Key Real Estate Concepts

This chapter was dedicated to the principles in real estate that an investor **MUST** be familiar with to succeed. They are the foundation upon which the *Momentum of Wealth* strategy is built, the strategy that every chapter after this one refines. Think of it as a prism constructed in the following manner:

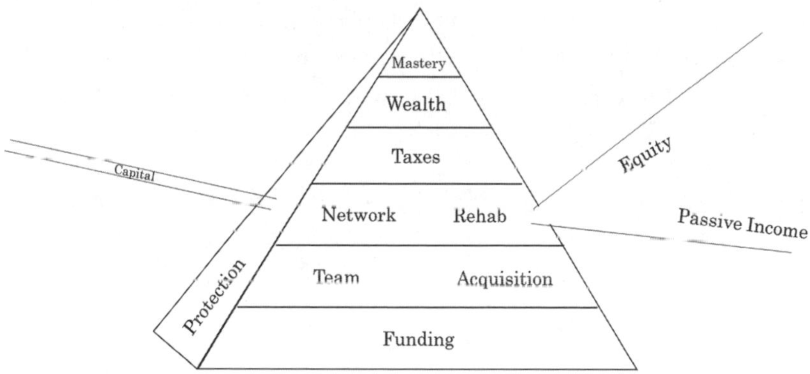

Figure 2-20: *Momentum of Wealth* – Prism

Chapters 1 and 2 addressed the "what" and skimmed the surface on the "when and why" of the *Momentum of Wealth* strategy. The following chapters will address the "who, where, and how" as well as refine the "when and why."

Tasks:

Assess your current investments' (real estate or otherwise) ROI and ROE.

Aloof Aaron, Cautious Carl, Sensible Sarah, and Risky Rick

Cautious Carl, Sensible Sarah, and Risky Rick are each married and have two young children. In order to provide a more financially sound future for their families, they have each diligently studied the principles and concepts detailed within these first two chapters. They understand the different property types and some of the benefits associated with owning an income-generating property. Additionally, they each take special note of the impact the *Velocity of Money* has on ROI over time.

Sensible Sarah and Risky Rick also observe the impact the *Inertia of Real Estate* has upon ROE over time. Furthermore, they both realize the compounding effect (*Momentum of Wealth*) that the *Inertia of Real Estate* and *Velocity of Money* have upon one another. They each begin to save funds (capital) and plan how to initiate their investment strategies to garner and access wealth by acquiring real estate.

Meanwhile, Aloof Aaron is unaware of the aforementioned information. He is otherwise occupied living his best life as a single bachelor. He lives without a care in the world—or a single thought toward his future. He has not yet thought about how he can prepare now to access wealth later.

Chapter 3: Leveraging Other People's Money (Funding)

Commerce? It's very simple. It's other people's money.
—Alexandre Dumas, *French writer*

In this chapter, we are going to cover the following:

Lending Process

- Application
  - Pre-Approval
- Appraisal
- Underwriting
  - Lending Risk Factors
    - DTI, LTV, Credit Score, Number of Properties, Bankruptcy Status
- Closing
  - Closing Costs and Other Fees
- Funding

Types of Lending Entities and Institutions

Qualified Mortgage Loans vs. Nonqualified Mortgage Loans

Fixed-Rate vs. Adjustable-Rate Mortgage Loans (Amortization)

Conventional vs. Portfolio Loans

- Federal Housing Administration (FHA) Loans
- Veterans Affairs (VA) Loans
- U.S. Department of Agriculture (USDA) Rural Development Loans
- Collateral Loans
- Construction and Renovation Loans
- Commercial Real Estate (CRE) Loans
- Down Payment Assistance (DPA) Programs

Alternative Lending Options
Friends and Family
Peer-to-Peer (P2P) Lending
Hard Money Lenders
Refinancing

What we do in life ... echoes in eternity.
—Maximus, *from the screenplay Gladiator*

Most individuals will require lending at some point in time, and those who are fortunate enough not to require lending may still leverage it for their benefit. This chapter details the lending process, the types of lending institutions, and the types of loans, guiding you through the world of lending. To some, all *lenders* and all loans may appear to be the same, but this is not the case. While the difference may appear small to novice investors or to those just beginning their journey, poor lending choices made early on have compounding consequences and may make the difference between steady exponential growth and stagnated progress.

A clear understanding of available options is essential for any investor to be successful. There are situations where you must take one step back in order to take two steps forward, while other situations require only the willingness to leap. The lending options available to an investor are the biggest determinant of whether you may require a step back or whether you are afforded the opportunity to leap forward. Study the different options and choose your next step wisely.

Lending Process

Lending processes for various financial institutions follow the same basic phases, but the individual requirements within these phases may vary more drastically per the lending institution and the relationships you've established. The five primary phases of the lending process include *application, appraisal, underwriting, closing,* and *funding*; each phase includes its own particular requirements, steps, and processes.

Application

The application phase (also referred to as documentation) is potentially the most vital phase in the loan process; this is the phase in which all required documentation must be submitted to the institution for underwriter review. It is imperative to provide all required and requested documentation promptly (and in its entirety). Prompt submission of all documents will help ensure the loan is processed in a timely manner and without complication. Delayed (or incomplete) submission will likely result in continued delays or a barrier to successful loan processing. The standard documents a borrower may expect the lender to require are the following:

- Driver's License (copy)
- Pay Stubs (last two or three months)
- W-2s and 1099s
- Tax Returns (previous two years)
- Bank Statements (last two or three months)
- Mortgage Statements (last two or three months)
- Insurance Declarations (for any owned property)
- Property Tax Statements
- Investment Statements (if applicable)
- Other Required Documentation (as required)

Pre-Approval

If the loan process is proceeding smoothly, the lender may *pre-approve* you for a loan. This may occur as early as the application phase. Pre-approval will make your offer on a property more competitive and, in "hot" markets, may be a requirement for your offer to be considered. A *loan estimate*[19] is typically provided at this time as well.

19 Provides important details about a mortgage loan, typically including the interest rate, P&I payment, escrow, etc.

> Always ask your lender if they are willing to offer a letter of pre-approval.

Appraisal

Most, if not all, lenders will require an appraisal of the property when it is being financed. The appraisal is performed by an appraiser to determine the FMV of the property as well as its general condition. The degree of your success as an investor is directly correlated to the appraiser's evaluation and assessment of your property's worth; this can be either a blessing or a hindrance. It's typically the latter. If you are purchasing a property, conforming loans can be offered without additional constraint if the purchase price is within a "reasonable" margin of the appraised value. If the listed price is higher than the appraised, the buyer can customarily negotiate the purchase price down. Non-conforming loans and cash offers do not have this stipulation, so they offer more flexibility and, therefore, more buying power. Seldom do moments occur when I actively root for natural selection (okay, maybe that isn't true), but my engagements with appraisers comprise the majority of these instances.

Application > Appraisal > Underwriting > Closing Disclosure > Funding

Underwriting

Underwriters are responsible for reviewing the documents (the loan file) submitted during the application phase and ensuring that you, as a borrower, meet the required qualification guidelines. They are determining your worthiness as a borrower and your ability to repay a debt incurred to purchase a property. This determination is made by assessing various lending risk factors. During this phase of the loan process, you may expect a myriad of "invasive" questions pertaining to these risk factors as well as a request for additional documentation (bank statements, proof of employment, Starbucks card, Marriott rewards number, etc.). Also, should the process progress slower than anticipated, it's not uncommon for them to require you to resubmit newer versions of documents you have already submitted. They may also set the terms for the loan depending upon the borrower's risk factors; these terms could include higher interest rates or other modifications to offset the risk the lending institution assumes. Typically, the more dire the market, the more persnickety the underwriter. The underwriting process for many, especially investors with multiple properties, is inefficient and cumbersome.

Application > Appraisal > Underwriting > Closing Disclosure > Funding

> While applying for your loan, try to avoid co-signing on another loan and making any large deposits. **DO NOT UNDER ANY CIRCUMSTANCE** 1) quit your job or 2) spend money set aside for closing.

Lending Risk Factors

Lenders need to assess the borrower's ability to repay a debt. Furthermore, for many loan types, borrowers need to meet strict criteria set forth by the lending institution or other governing authorities. The primary lending risk factors assessed by underwriters include DTI, LTV, credit score, the number of properties owned by the borrower, and bankruptcy status.

Debt-to-Income (DTI)

DTI was covered in Chapter 1 and is an assessment of your debt management level. If your debt is not managed effectively (you have too high of a DTI), then you are viewed as a riskier option for lenders. If you have a lower DTI, the lender views you more favorably. The key ratios the borrower must be aware of are 36 percent and 43 percent. Lenders view a DTI below 36 percent as favorable and will demand less scrutiny from underwriters. Lenders view a DTI between 36 and 43 percent as risky. Lending institutions may still lend to higher-risk borrowers; however, the underwriters may run amok and levy additional requirements upon you. Lenders view a DTI above 43 percent as unfavorable, and certain lending options may no longer be available to you. In addition to overall DTI, institutions take particular interest in hard debt that is unlikely to expire (the "hardest" of these debts they inquire about are *alimony*[20] and *child support*[21]).

LTV

The LTV is another critical factor that underwriters assess. It has less to do with the borrower than it does with the type of loan in which the borrower is intending to leverage. Primary residences generally require a down payment of 15 to 20 percent (investment properties are 25 percent, commercial loans are over 30 percent); anything less will require a *mortgage insurance premium (MIP)*.[22] A lender may permit a borrower who has a riskier profile to front less than the 15 to 20 percent down payment on a loan, regardless of the MIP.

Credit Score

The borrower's credit score is possibly the biggest criterion of creditworthiness and determinant of a lending institution's willingness to lend to a borrower or debtor. Higher scores indicate better creditworthiness. Credit scores are offered and maintained by three credit reporting agencies (otherwise referred to as bureaus). They are Equifax, Experian, and TransUnion. You can view your credit score by going to their websites. (You can typically receive one free credit report per year.)

Equifax:	(800) 685-1111, www.equifax.com
Experian:	(888) 397-3742, www.experian.com
TransUnion:	(800) 916-8800, www.transunion.com

20 Funds an individual is obligated to provide their former spouse after a divorce.

21 Funds an individual is obligated to pay their former "partner" after conceiving a child.

22 Monthly payment paid by borrower which is used to protect the lender and mitigate losses should the borrower default on the loan.

Each bureau categorizes an individual's credit with one of five labels: poor, fair, good, very good, and excellent. Additionally, credit score ranges vary per bureaus in the following manner:

Bureau Ranking	Equifax	Experian	TransUnion
Poor	280 - 559	300 - 550	300 - 499
Fair	560 - 659	550 - 649	500 - 600
Good	660 - 724	650 - 699	601 - 660
Very Good	725 - 759	700 - 749	661 - 780
Excellent	760 - 850	750 - 850	781 - 850

Table 3-1: Credit Bureau Score Comparison

The credit score is composed of various factors, each of which is weighted according to its significance to the credit bureaus. A credit score is determined by the following criteria:

Credit Score Factor/Weight	Equifax	Experian	TransUnion
Payment History	35%	35%	40%
Outsanding Debt	30%	30%	20%
Length of Credit History	15%	15%	21%
Recent Inquiries	10%	10%	11%
Types of Credit	10%	10%	5%

Table 3-2: Credit Bureau Score Factors

Payment History

Payment history reflects your payment behavior on your various credit accounts, including activity related to credit cards and loans. This is the most influential factor related to your credit score. Payment history is a collection of bill payment punctuality, and poor payment history results in lenders viewing you as a riskier debtor. The best way to maintain a good credit history is to pay at least the minimum payment on time.

Avoid falling behind on your other accounts and mortgages.

Outstanding Debt

Outstanding debt or credit use is the second most influential factor related to your credit score; it assesses the ratio of debt to available credit. Maintaining a high credit balance (debt) is detrimental to your credit score. If possible, use less than 30 percent of your available credit on any given account to maintain or improve your overall credit score.

Length of Credit History

The length of time an individual has used credit (length of credit history) is another factor that contributes to the overall credit score. The credit bureaus seem to believe that the longer an individual has had credit, the more reliable or creditworthy they must be. This doesn't mean an individual is not creditworthy right out of the gate; it just means they haven't proven their creditworthiness to the credit bureaus yet. This is an outdated way of thinking; however, it's the manner in which the credit bureaus persist in operating. This factor looks at three primary components: 1) how long accounts have been open; 2) how long specific types of accounts (*revolving*[23] and *installment*[24]) have been open; or 3) how long it's been since an account has last been used.

This should be intuitive, but it is worth stating clearly: the best way to improve your credit score by means of credit history length is to not open new accounts that you do not intend to use. Having more credit cards is not a good thing.

Recent Inquiries

Another antiquated way in which credit bureaus operate is that credit scores are impacted during a credit inquiry. A credit inquiry occurs when a member applies for credit and a lender acquires a copy of the debtor's credit report. Simply applying for a loan triggers a credit inquiry, and every inquiry triggers an automatic and unfair reduction in your credit

---

23 Credit accounts such as credit, retail, or gas cards as well as Home Equity Lines of Credit (HELOC).

24 Credit accounts such as mortgage, car, or student loans; they have steady monthly payments.

score. Note: there are two types of credit inquiries: *hard inquiries*[25] and *soft inquiries*.[26] Soft inquiries do not impact your credit score.

> When rate shopping, try to target a 30-day window in which to narrow and select a loan; the bureau will group the inquiries and treat them as one.

Opening multiple credit accounts within a short period of time is viewed as risky and will have a larger impact. *Rate shopping*[27] is viewed less harshly but still impacts your credit, nonetheless.

> Inquiries may have a more detrimental impact if you are early on in your credit journey (few accounts or short credit history). Avoid making large purchases (vehicles, etc.).

Type of Credit

The type of credit or credit mix is an assessment of revolving or installment credit accounts. A combination of both is preferred; an abundance of revolving accounts will bring down your credit score. Minimize, but do not eliminate, revolving accounts.

Number of Properties Owned

Lending institutions get particular about the number of properties a borrower owns. Investment properties to lending institutions are not deemed to be "safe" investments (although real estate is far safer than most other investments). Some lending institutions limit the number of mortgages a borrower is able to have. Note: this limit is on the total number of properties owned, not on the number of properties the lending

25 Inquiries that pull your credit report from the credit bureau and impact your credit score.

26 Inquiries that do not impact your credit score.

27 Researching rates at multiple lending institutions in search of the best interest rate for a mortgage loan.

institution has loaned to them. This is more common with banks than *credit unions* or *mortgage lenders*. This is also an important criterion for the type of loan the borrower is pursuing and is a critical point of note for investors lacking capital in the early phases of this investment strategy. (This importance will be elaborated on in the next chapter.) As of 2021, a borrower can have a maximum of 10 government-backed loans, which essentially limits the borrower to 10 *conventional loans* within their portfolio (20 if jointly owned with a spouse).

Always ask if the institution allows mortgage loans on investment properties and infer their limit.

DID YOU KNOW?

In 2020, as part of their ongoing review of consumer credit and debt data, Experian assessed the latest trends and tendencies. They've released the following information:

- Average FICO score in the U.S. for 2020: 711

- Standard increase in FICO score is usually 2 points per year

- Recent spike in score is likely due to:
    - Decreased credit utilization
        - Average credit card utilization decreased by 12 percent
    - Drop in delinquencies
        - The average number of consumer accounts ever delinquent dropped by 10 percent
    - Shrinking debt

Bankruptcy Status

If lending institutions are going to penalize a missed payment, no one should be surprised that they deem borrowers who have filed for bankruptcy to be risky. There may be limitations on a borrower's ability to apply for a loan depending on the type of bankruptcy the borrower underwent. The two primary types of bankruptcy are Chapter 7[28] and Chapter 13 bankruptcies.[29] A Chapter 13 bankruptcy is often deemed as the less serious of the two because it has less impact on the borrower's credit, and the borrower may keep their assets. Nonetheless, both types of bankruptcy typically bring with them a waiting period before borrowers may apply for additional loans.

The wait time associated with conventional loans after a Chapter 13 bankruptcy is contingent on whether or not a court dismisses or discharges the borrower's bankruptcy. If dismissed (without discharge), the borrower must wait four years from the dismissal date; if discharged, the borrower must wait four years from filing and two years from dismissal. After a Chapter 7 bankruptcy, the borrower must wait four years from dismissal.

Government-backed loans (such as USDA, FHA, and VA) are more relaxed in their standards; lenders may offer these sooner after dismissal (generally within one year). If you've had a bankruptcy within the last few years and/or have a low credit score, an FHA loan may be the best option for you; it will be discussed at length later in this chapter.

A Chapter 7 bankruptcy will remain and impact your credit report for 10 years. A Chapter 13 bankruptcy will do the same to a lesser extent for 7 years.

Closing

The closing is the final review of all mortgage documents. If you've made it this far, breathe a sigh of relief because you have survived underwriting.

28 Bankruptcy where trustee gathers and sells the debtor's assets and uses proceeds to pay claimholders to debts.

29 Bankruptcy that involves a reorganization of a borrower's debts and scheduled payments.

This phase entails two tasks: *disclosure* and *signing*. Disclosure is when the documents outlining the terms of the mortgage have been provided. This is done to ensure the borrower is aware of what they may expect when it comes time to sign the documents. When reviewing the closing disclosure, be thorough. Pay careful attention to the interest rate, LTV, closing costs, and other fees.

Closing Costs and Other Fees

The interest rate and LTV have been covered extensively up to this point in this book. Closing costs require a more thorough explanation. These costs are those associated with the processing and execution of the loan as well as the transfer of the deed. The rule of thumb for closing costs is between 2 to 5 percent of the overall purchase price of the property. The itemized cost and fees cover the following services:

- Processing Fees
- Underwriting Fees
- Loan Administration
- Discount Points (if applicable)
- Appraisal
- Flood Certificate
- Attorney Fees
- Inspection Fees
- Title Courier Fees
- Settlement Fees
- Owner Title Insurance
- Lender Title Insurance
- Title Guarantee and Recording Fees
- Other Recording Fees
- Survey Fees

Note: this list is not all-inclusive.

Funding

Funding is the final phase of the lending process. This merely entails the distribution of funds to the appropriate entities. This phase is transparent to the buyer and is a celebratory event for a seller or investor refinancing the property. If you are fortunate, you will have a windfall of capital, and if you are wise, you will use that capital to purchase additional properties that will then generate more capital and equity.

Application > Appraisal > Underwriting > Closing Disclosure > Funding

Types of Lending Entities and Institutions

> Banks typically only offer HELOCs on primary residences. Always inquire.

What is the difference between banks, credit unions, and mortgage lenders? All three will lend an investor money for real estate and offer refinances and Home Equity Lines of Credit (HELOCs). But all three are different. Knowledge of these differences is what separates novice investors from experienced ones. Simply put, a bank is a financial institution licensed and insured to take receipt of deposits and process loans. They offer several other features, such as checks, bill payments, certificates of deposit, etc. An important note is that the funds deposited (up to $250,000 per individual and $500,000 per married couple) are insured via the Federal Deposit Insurance Corporation (FDIC).[30] More often than not, when you think of banks, you think of JP Morgan Chase, Wells Fargo, PNC, Huntington, or, if you're military, possibly USAA. The biggest perk pertaining to banks is that they have reciprocity across the United States, meaning a good lender from a bank can often work with you to fund real estate endeavors wherever you may come across them. If you are a fan of accessing a brick-and-mortar financial institution, banks are your best bet. Banks, however, generally do not offer *portfolio loans* and typically only offer loans they may sell off in an exchange with other banks.

> Not all banks offer the most competitive loans on investment properties.

30 Independent federal agency insuring deposits to U.S. banks in the event of failure.

Credit unions are another and—depending upon your circumstances—better option. They offer many of the same services as a traditional bank; however, they may offer better interest rates on mortgages than your traditional banks or mortgage lenders. This is usually the case when they offer portfolio loans that they intend to keep in house. Credit unions are frequently smaller than most banks, which is advantageous to investors who are seeking to acquire REO properties or negotiate short sales. Credit unions offer an attractive option for investors looking to imbed into a specific location.

> Lenders from credit unions may not be able to assist or offer the same rates for properties outside of their lending jurisdiction.

Mortgage lenders offer what it sounds like they offer: loans on mortgages. They typically offer mortgage refinances as well. These lenders can be either angelic or demonic, depending on which you should look at. They generally have higher closing costs and sometimes have higher interest rates; however, sometimes, they are less restrictive in lending to investors, and they are available in every state. While some banks or credit unions may offer better rates or terms, a mortgage lender may be your best option if you have yet to find a better deal or you are not eligible for a better deal. The following chart offers a quick reference to the benefits and drawbacks of the three types of lending options.

	Federal Banks	Credit Unions	Mortgage Lenders
Nationwide Availability	Yes	No	Yes
Mortgage Refinance	Yes	Yes	Yes
Home Equity Line of Credit (HELOC)*	Yes	Yes	No
Other Loans (Business, Personal, etc.)	Yes	Yes	No
Interest Rates & Closing Costs	Median	Lowest	Highest

Table 3-3: Lending Entity Comparison

Regardless of the lending entity or institution you select, they will likely require documentation of your assets, credit, employment, expenses, and income to assess the risk exposure associated with lending to you.

Qualified Mortgage Loans vs. Nonqualified Mortgage Loans

Not all loans are created equal. Some loans are constructed in such a manner that offer more favorable terms to the borrower should the lender determine them to be low risk. Lenders call these *qualified loans*, and they use the aforementioned lending risk factors to determine them. Lending institutions have various strict criteria for members seeking a qualified loan. If borrowers don't meet the institution's criteria, they may not be approved; instead, they may be offered a *nonqualified loan*. Nonqualified loans are not necessarily bad; a nonqualified loan is better than no loan at all. While these loans often have higher interest rates or conditions, they may be the better choice for the real estate investor in certain situations.

Qualified Mortgage Loans

A qualified loan is a loan that conforms to the requirements of the Dodd-Frank Act, meeting the following criteria:

- Must not be constructed as a subprime mortgage[31]
- Must not have borrower DTI of over 43 percent
- Must not have excessive upfront costs and fees
- Must not have loan terms over 30 years

Members seeking a qualified loan may also expect to undergo a more extensive and strenuous underwriting process. Nonetheless, qualified loans are generally preferred by both the lender and borrower. The financial institution has greater assurance that the borrower is more likely to repay their loan, and the *Federal National Mortgage Association (Fannie Mae)* and *Federal Home Loan Mortgage Association (Freddie*

31 Loans that are interest-only, can balloon, or have negative amortization schedules.

Mac) back the loans. For the borrower, he is able to acquire a mortgage with more favorable terms.

> **DID YOU KNOW?**
>
> Fannie Mae was initially established as a federal government agency in 1938 by an amendment to the National Housing Act. Its primary purpose was to act as a secondary mortgage market (purchase, hold, and sell) for FHA-insured loans. Fannie Mae transitioned into a public agency by the Federal National Mortgage Association Charter Act of 1954. Furthermore, the Housing and Urban Development Act of 1968 transformed Fannie Mae to a for-profit organization, thereby removing it from the federal budget. Finally, in 1970, the secondary mortgage market was expanded, and Freddie Mac was established by Congress with the passing of the Emergency Home Finance Act to better manage the risks of variable interest rates.

Nonqualified Mortgage Loans

A nonqualified mortgage loan is one that does not comply to the provisions established by the Dodd-Frank Act. These loans are beneficial for members who do not meet the strict requirements for a qualified loan. The main reasons members seek and apply for nonqualified loans are if …

- Their income varies monthly
- They do not meet income verification requirements (limited documentation)
- Their DTI is more than 43 percent

Interest rates for both qualified and nonqualified loans will vary by lending institution. When seeking a nonqualified loan, you should expect higher interest rates compared to qualified loans, regardless of the lending institution.

Fixed-Rate vs. Adjustable-Rate Mortgage Loans (Amortization)

The previous section detailed how not all loans are created equal, and this remains true for the amortization schedule of loans. Loan amortization schedules may be applied to qualified or nonqualified loans and may be categorized as either fixed-rate or adjustable-rate. The simplified definition of each schedule is the following:

- ***Fixed-Rate Mortgage*:** The interest rate and mortgage payment remain consistent throughout the duration of the loan.
- ***Adjustable-Rate Mortgage (ARM)*:** The interest rate and mortgage payment remain consistent for an initial, pre-defined fixed period (such as five or ten years). But after the fixed period subsides, the interest rate and, therefore, the monthly payment may adjust up or down on a pre-negotiated basis (usually annually). The terms are customarily denoted in the following format:

Fixed Period / Adjustable Basis

For example, in a 10/1 ARM, 10 years is the fixed period. After the first 10 years, the rate may adjust once every year thereafter. (The most common ARM is 5/1.)

Fixed-rate mortgages may be applied to all varieties of loans, including *Conventional, Federal Housing Administration (FHA), Jumbo, Renovation, United States Department of Agriculture (USDA),* and *Veterans Affairs (VA) loans.* Fixed-rate loans are often the preferred choice for individuals planning to reside or own a property for more than 10 years. The duration of fixed-rate loans is typically between 10 to 30 years, offered in five-year increments; the biggest advantage is consistency and predictability of the interest rate and mortgage payment for the duration of the loan.

ARMs may be applied to the same variety of loans with the exception of USDA and renovation loans. ARMs are typically preferred for individuals who will not reside in, own, or intend to refinance a property before the end of the fixed period. It is important to note that ARMs have payment caps that limit the amount the interest rate may change within the adjustable periods. Individuals may refinance an

ARM before, during, or after the fixed period (which is highly recommended to leverage the generated equity).

DID YOU KNOW?

In 2020, the National Association of Realtors conducted a study and filed a report pertaining to down payment expectations and hurdles to home ownership. The study highlighted insightful statistics as to the readiness and challenges of the average American in pursuit of purchasing a home. Some of the many findings are provided below:

- 32 percent of first-time buyers (and 8 percent of repeat buyers) received a gift (or loan) from a relative/friend toward the down payment of their home purchase (in 2019).

- 26 percent of first-time buyers (and 7 percent of repeat buyers) indicated that saving for a down payment was the most difficult challenge in the home buying process (in 2019).

- Percentage of first-time home buyers' factors that prohibited or delayed savings for a down payment (in 2015):
    - Student Loans – 51 percent
    - Credit Card Debt and Car Loans – 45 percent
    - Limited Income – 32 percent
    - Health Costs – 22 percent
    - Medical Costs – 16 percent

Conventional vs. Portfolio Loans

We've discussed the differences between qualified and nonqualified loans as well as fixed-rate and adjustable-rate loans. Now we will discuss the difference between *conventional* and *portfolio loans.*

Have I mentioned the fact that all loans are not created equal? Conventional and portfolio loans are defined as follows:

- Conventional Mortgages: Also commonly referred to as conforming loans, these loans are issued by private lending institutions that are not yet backed by government agencies. Regardless of the government securities backing them, lending institutions typically sell mortgages on the secondary market after origination to generate additional capital for the lending institution.

- Portfolio Mortgages: These are loans issued by private lending institutions that the institution does not intend to sell.

> Conventional loans have loan limits for standard areas and higher limits for high-cost areas. Be sure to check the loan limits when buying a home.

Conventional mortgages are often the available and preferred option for novice investors or those who potentially want a low down payment on their primary residence. (Down payments may be as low as 3 percent.) This is also the novice investor's preferred option until they have gained access to *portfolio loans*. Conventional loans are available for those with at least a "Good" credit score (above 620).

Portfolio loan standards may help borrowers in certain circumstances. With this type of mortgage, lending institutions may offer loans to borrowers who may otherwise have difficulty. Since the loan will not be sold, the lending institution may modify the terms of the loan to be more favorable to the borrower. Some modifications and benefits may include:

- Non-conforming loan limits
- Minimal down payment requirements
- Exclusion of private mortgage insurance (PMI) or mortgage insurance premiums (MIP)[32]
- More flexible underwriting (This is a big one!)

32 Form of insurance collected by the lender to offset the risk of default by the borrower when the LTV of a loan is less than 80 percent.

Portfolio loans are attractive to individuals and investors alike. Keep in mind, however, that these loan offerings are rare. They are generally offered to the lending institutions' best clients, those who show the most promise of continued future business. Although lending institutions may be more flexible in their lending practices with portfolio loans than with conforming loans, the borrower must still meet and satisfy the lending institution's internal requirements.

Mortgage Insurance Premiums (MIPs)

MIPs actually have two components, and this often misleads many investors. There is the *upfront MIP* (equal to a specified percentage of the base amount) and the *annual MIP* (collected on a monthly basis).

> [+] You may be able to deduct your premium from your taxes; it is likely you will need to itemize your deductions.

The upfront MIP may either be paid at the time of closing or may be rolled into the loan. These payments are escrowed and used as collateral in the event that the borrower defaults on the loan. The annual MIP rate may range depending upon several factors, including the loan amount, loan duration, and the LTV.

For example, if you have a $200,000 loan (assuming an MIP rate of 0.9 percent), you will make annual MIP payments of 0.009 x $200,000 = $1,800 ($150/month). This payment or premium will be paid in addition to the upfront MIP.

Federal Housing Administration (FHA) Loans

The U.S. government created FHA loans to stimulate the housing market during the Great Depression and to enable borrowers to qualify for loans more easily while also reducing risks to the lender. A Federal Housing Administration (FHA) loan is an insured mortgage issued by an FHA-approved lender. They are designed for lower- or moderate-income borrowers. Typically, lenders require a lower minimum down payment and lower credit score for FHA loans than for conventional loans. The preferred minimum credit score for FHA qualification is 580. (Scores lower than 580 but above 500 may still qualify; however, a lender may require a higher down payment.) Additionally, your lender must be an FHA-approved lender. Furthermore, borrowers must have consistent employment history (meaning they have worked for the same employer for the past two years). If you have been self-employed within the last two years, there are mitigating actions you may take; however, the lender may require additional documentation, including demonstrated consistent revenue for the elapsed duration.

Finally, the property you seek to finance must be the borrower's primary residence, meaning it must be owner-occupied. Simply put, investment or rental properties are out of bounds for this program; however, the limitation of owner occupancy is typically one year. Beyond this duration, the owner-occupied limitations cease to apply. Multifamily homes (one to four units) are eligible for FHA financing.

> Financial gifts from family members or grants for down payment assistance are acceptable for down payment and closing costs of FHA loans.

The FHA loan may be ideal for novice investors lacking capital or other requirements yet still seeking to expand their real estate portfolio. It may also be leveraged even if a borrower qualifies for conventional loans. Remember to assess the ROI and the ROE. Although lenders may require an MIP when leveraging an FHA loan, the ROI and ROE may very well be more favorable.

Veterans Affairs (VA) Loans

Veterans Affairs (VA) loans are similar to that of FHA loans; however, they are backed by the U.S. Department of Veterans Affairs rather than the Federal Housing Administration. VA loans operate in a similar manner with a few variations from the FHA loan. The primary differences include:

- The member must be an eligible veteran.
- The loan requires a servicing/funding fee.
- The loan does not require or include any MIP.
- The loan may be acquired with no down payment.

The minimum credit score for VA loans is customarily 580, although some exceptions apply. This loan is available to eligible military service members, veterans, and surviving spouses. The funding fee varies but usually does not exceed 3.3 percent of the value of the home. This fee may be rolled into the loan or possibly paid by the seller. It is important to note that, like the FHA loan, the VA loan is intended for the primary residence of the borrower, not for investment properties.

> Gifts from family members, grants, and contributions from sellers are also permitted to be used toward closing costs of VA loans.

However, like the FHA loan, this requirement expires after one year of residing within the property. VA loans may also be leveraged to purchase multifamily properties (one to four units), but they cannot be used for properties containing five or more units. If you are eligible for a VA loan, compare the loan with FHA and conventional loans to ensure the terms of the loan best fit your investment strategy.

U.S. Department of Agriculture (USDA) Rural Development Loans

USDA loans are those where mortgages are backed by the U.S. Department of Agriculture (instead of other government agencies) as part of the USDA Guaranteed Housing Loan program. Like FHA loans, USDA loans are available to borrowers and home buyers with lower incomes for their area. It offers specific advantages not afforded by other loan types. The first and foremost advantage is 100-percent financing (akin to the VA loan) with a reduced MIP. The minimum credit score for USDA loans is typically 640.

The USDA loan does, however, have specific mandates associated with its terms of use:

- The loan may only be used on single-family residences (or eligible property types).
- The loan must be used for primary residences only.
- The loan must be located in eligible rural areas.
- The borrower must follow strict post-bankruptcy and post-foreclosure regulations.

The USDA loan may only be used for eligible types of properties, which generally include single-family homes, new construction of single-family homes, modular homes, planned unit developments, and eligible condominiums. The home must also be located in an eligible rural area, which are generally the suburbs located close to or far from city centers. Be sure to check the USDA limits, as they vary by location.

Gifts from family members, grants, and contributions from sellers are also permitted to be used toward closing costs of VA loans.

Collateral Loans

Collateral loans are those where the loan is secured by an asset. If the loan defaults, the lending institution may claim or collect the collateral asset to offset the losses of the loan. Collateral loans are synonymous with secured loans. In other words, loans without collateral are deemed to be unsecured loans. Secured loans are generally easier to come by than unsecured loans, and they provide short-term liquidity and generally allow the borrower to qualify or be eligible for larger loans. In order to leverage a collateral loan, you must have valuable assets that may be used as collateral. The most common type of collateral loan is a Home Equity Loan, where a second mortgage may be taken on the property up to 80 percent of the value of the property. For example, assume an individual owns a property worth $200,000, and they paid $100,000 over the life of the loan. They may then take a second mortgage ($60,000) up to 80 percent ($160,000) of the FMV ($200,000). The terms of the loan may be structured as either fixed or adjustable.

Another popular option is the Home Equity Line of Credit (HELOC). This operates in a similar manner as the Home Equity Loan; however, it operates as a line of credit that may be drawn when needed rather than upon closing (and regardless of the current need). This option is a viable alternative for lending if capital is only needed for short durations of time (such as quickly buying and selling a home for a profit, otherwise referred to as "flipping"). HELOCs are not recommended for long-term investment purchases; the interest rates on lines of credit are variable. If pursuing this option, be sure to weigh the opportunity cost. A refinance (if interest rates are favorable) or a second mortgage may be the better option.

The biggest risk associated with collateral loans (and lines of credit) is the possibility of losing the asset should the debtor fail to repay in accordance with the terms. Take caution when leveraging this option on your primary residence.

Construction and Renovation Loans

Simply put, *construction loans* are loans taken to purchase a property that is contracted to be built. It may be structured in such a manner where payments (other than a down payment) are not required to be paid until after construction has been completed.

Renovation loans are a great option should the property in question require upgrades or renovations and you need extra capital to complete these renovations. These loans are constructed for individuals who find a less-than-move-in-ready home located in a phenomenal location. Many leverage this loan type when procuring properties that are distressed (*foreclosure*, *short sale*, *REO*, etc.).[33] The loan combines the cost of purchase and renovations into a singular first mortgage, with no extra capital or line of credit required. There are many variants of construction and

33 These property types will be covered more in Chapter 7.

renovation loans; two main variants are the FHA 203(k) Improvement loan and the FHA Energy Efficient Mortgage loan.

FHA 203(k) Improvement Loans

This loan includes the cost of certain repairs and renovations into the loan. These repairs and renovations include upgrades to the kitchen and bathrooms, flooring, paint, electrical, plumbing, roofing, and siding, as well as exterior modifications, such as landscaping and additions (detached garages, swimming pools, etc.).

FHA Energy Efficient Mortgages

This program is similar to the FHA 203(k) Improvement loan; however, it focuses on upgrades that make the property more energy efficient. It promotes the notion that an energy-efficient home will have lower operating costs and will, therefore, be more affordable.

Jumbo Loans

Jumbo loans are mortgages for amounts exceeding the conforming limits established by Fannie Mae and Freddie Mac. The maximum size of and qualifications for a jumbo loan may vary by lender and location. High-cost living areas will commensurately allow for larger jumbo loans. Furthermore, jumbo loan rates may be higher or lower than the conforming mortgage rates. The biggest discriminants for being approved for jumbo loans are the following:

- Larger income requirements
- Minimum credit score of 700 (although 740 is average)
- Higher level of reserves
- Down payment minimum of 10 percent

Lenders may approve borrowers if they do not meet these criteria; however, lenders may impose additional requirements such as higher interest rates or larger reserves to offset the risk.

DID YOU KNOW?

According to the aforementioned study by the National Association of Realtors in 2020:

- 82 percent of members surveyed said their typical buyers were informed on down payments.
- 70 percent of members surveyed said their typical buyers were informed on closing costs.

Commercial Real Estate (CRE) Loans

Commercial loans are generally used for *commercial real estate (CRE).*[34] Examples of CRE include larger, more extensive properties, such as retail venues, shopping centers, office buildings, and hotels. Commercial loans are structured as collateral loans and are secured by liens[35] against the commercial property. Contrary to most residential loans, independent lenders, private investors, and other sources provide capital for commercial real estate loans. Additionally, commercial loans have several other differences from those previously identified in this chapter:

- Individual vs. Business Entity Characteristics
- Repayment Schedules and Prepayment Penalties
- LTV
- Debt-Service Coverage Ratio (DSCR)

Individual vs. Business Entity Characteristics

CRE mortgages are typically made to business entities (corporations, developers, partnerships, etc.) specifically formed with the intended

34 Income-generating property usually used for business purposes.

35 A charge against an asset as collateral until a debt is paid.

purpose of owning real estate. (I will discuss business entities in greater detail in Chapter 10.) If the business entity does not have an established credit rating, the lender may ask the owner (or group of owners) to provide a personal credit rating(s) to reassure the lender and provide recourse. If the property is the only collateral for the loan, the lender may consider a non-recourse loan.

Loan Repayment Schedule and Prepayment Penalties

Loan repayment schedules for commercial loans operate differently than residential loans; the duration of a commercial loan can vary up to 20 years. Furthermore, the amortization period may be longer than the duration of the loan, resulting in a balloon payment of the remainder of the loan balance at the end of the loan period.

Conversely, CRE loans may also have restrictions or penalties for prepayment. The lender will want to make sure they get their share or yield of the expected profit. There are many structures involved in prepayment penalties, all of which revolve around an established maturity date.[36] Be sure to check with your lender and review any terms associated with prepayment penalties.

LTV

Commercial real estate loan LTV ratios range from 65 to 80 percent as opposed to the 75 to 100 percent ranges previously mentioned. This often depends upon the property type the loan is requested for. It's important to note that borrowers may not utilize VA and FHA loan programs for commercial lending use.

Debt-Service Coverage Ratio (DSCR)

Commercial lenders assess a property's Debt-Service Coverage Ratio (DSCR).[37] This is essentially the inverse of an individual's DTI; in fact, it is the property income-to-debt ratio. Lenders determine the maximum

36 The due date in which a borrower must pay back a loan in full.

37 To learn to calculate a Debt-Service Coverage Ratio, visit https://www.investopedia.com/terms/d/dscr.asp.

loan quantity by looking at the generated cash flow of the property. Most lenders will want a DSCR of at least 1.25.

Down Payment Assistance Programs

Down Payment Assistance (DPA) programs assist home buyers with grants or low-interest loans by reducing the amount they will need to save for a down payment. These programs are governed by states and counties, so they vary by location. DPA programs come in four main types:

- Grants[38]
- Secondary mortgage paid down over the life of the loan along with the first mortgage
- Secondary mortgage deferred until the owner moves, refinances, or sells
- Secondary mortgage forgiven over a specified number of years

Always, always, always ask if you are eligible for DPA programs.

Many DPA programs allow for utilization toward closing costs in addition to the down payment. Always check to see if they are included.

All DPA programs require the borrower to use a lender who provides approved mortgage programs. Approved mortgage programs often include many previously discussed loans, such as:

- Conventional
- USDA
- FHA
- VA

DPAs secure funding from various sources: federal, state, city, county, and other funds. They each will establish their own eligibility criteria and designate their own target areas.[39] Most individuals

38 Money given that doesn't require repayment.

39 Areas undergoing modernization or revitalization in which individuals are incentivized to buy.

who have a low income, are a minority, or work in specific professions (teachers, servicemembers, civil service, etc.) may qualify.

DPA programs are offered to first-time and repeat home buyers alike.

Alternative Lending Options

Many investors will at some point need to leverage alternative lending options to satisfy their immediate funding needs. These bridge loans are lending options intended for short-term use, meant to carry the borrower over the bridge from now until when they can secure more favorable financing. This may occur earlier or later in an investor's real estate journey. Alternative lending options are ordinarily used when the borrower has poor credit, has exceeded their threshold for conventional financing, hasn't secured access to portfolio loans, or is attempting to purchase a property that cannot be otherwise financed (such as a foreclosure or a fixer-upper in need of repair). Some of the most common alternative lending options include:

- Friends and Family
- Peer-to-Peer Lending
- Hard Money Lenders

Friends and Family

The "friends and family" category is self-explanatory. But be careful with this one; lending money from friends and family can either be a phenomenal option or a terrible mistake. If you have people around you who are both willing and able to support your endeavors without imposing undue demands, this can be great. If not, steer clear of this option. Even if you do have friends and family willing to support you, do not abuse or comingle the relationship of business and family.

Peer-to-Peer (P2P) Lending

Peer-to-peer (P2P) lending is an alternative form of lending that enables borrowers to obtain loans directly from other individuals who are lenders/investors. This method of lending removes financial institutions from the equation. P2P is commonly known as "crowd lending" or "social lending."

Several lending websites (Prosper, Lending Tree, Upstart, etc.) have become popular. Each website is able to establish rates and define terms in exchange for enabling a transaction between a borrower and lender. Similar to lending institutions, lending sites offer a range of interest rates based upon the creditworthiness of the borrower. The investor receives profit by means of the interest, and the platform collects on the transaction cost.

Although processes may vary, the basic process for P2P lending flows as follows:

1. Investors establish an account and deposit capital to be distributed in loans.
2. The applicant/borrower completes a financial risk assessment; this determines their risk category, which determines the interest rate they will pay.
3. The applicant/borrower reviews various offers and selects one (or many).
4. The platform transfers initial funds and manages monthly payments.

Hard Money Lenders

You may ask yourself, what is *hard money*? Is it fiat money,[40] commodity (gold, silver, etc.), or credit? It's none of these things. Hard money denotes funds provided in exchange for collateral. Hard money lenders are worried less about your creditworthiness and more about your collateral. You may think of them as a legal form of a loan shark but to a lesser extent. If you fail to pay, they may take your collateral. Hard money loans also have higher interest rates than any of the

40 Government issued paper money, not backed by a commodity (such as gold or silver) yet still considered legal tender.

aforementioned loans. Most investors tend to use hard money lenders for three primary reasons:

- Expedience
- Flexible Approval
- Flexible Terms

Expedience

Since the lender is less concerned with the borrower's creditworthiness, they spend considerably less time verifying the borrower's financial position, which drastically cuts down the time required to provide funds. If a relationship has already been established with the lending institution or entity, the time may be reduced, even to a matter of days. This is extremely important when negotiating for properties in a hot market and allows the borrower to provide cash offers that would otherwise be unavailable.

Flexible Approval

Hard money lenders typically value the collateral more than the borrower's financial position. If the property in question holds value or will have value, the borrower is more likely to find approval, even if their personal finances are not ideal. Hard money lenders also keep a lower LTV in an attempt to keep the borrower vested and better ensure they will garner a return. (Standard hard money LTVs range from 50 to 75 percent of ARV.) Investors will likely need to front some of their own capital to pay for expenses unless they have stumbled across and acquired an asset well beneath ARV.

Flexible Terms

Finally, lenders may offer agreements that are more flexible than traditional loan agreements. The underwriting process is often not standardized, which allows for modifications such as the interest rate or repayment schedule.

Refinancing

Refinancing is the process of replacing an existing mortgage or loan with a new one. The most common reason to refinance a loan is to change the terms of the loan. The terms modified could include any of the following:

- Lowering the monthly payment
- Eliminating private mortgage insurance (PMI)
- Reducing the length of the loan
- Changing from adjustable-rate to fixed-rate
- Consolidating mortgages
- Cash-out refinancing

The process remains the same regardless of intention and resembles the standard loan process. Each of these reasons are rather self-explanatory, with the exception of the cash-out refinance; this process entails constructing a new loan for the new appraised value of the property. Rather than changing the terms of the loan by any of the aforementioned reasons, the borrower is able to transfer a portion of the available equity accumulated in the property into capital—capital that they can then use to purchase additional wealth-generating properties.

The cash-out refinance LTV is typically 75 to 80 percent (80 if primary residence) of the appraised value of the home (or ARV if renovating a home). When undergoing this process, the amount of equity that may be transferred into capital is the sum of the remaining mortgage balance deducted from the LTV percentage of ARV. For example, if a property is worth $160,000 and the remaining balance (or the price you paid) for the property is $60,000, the following equation expresses the amount of equity that could be exchanged into capital:

$$C_{ash\ Out} = \left(ARV * LTV_{rate}\right) - R_{emaining\ Balance}$$

$$C_{ash\ Out} = \left(\$160{,}000 * 0.75\right) - \$60{,}000$$

$$C_{ash\ Out} = \textbf{\$60,000 (\$120,000 if no remaining balance)}$$

> If intending to refinance a property owned for less than a year, always ask if the lending institution has a seasoning period and if the lender uses LTV or LTC for their cash-out refinance ratio.

This calculation is contingent upon an LTV calculation. Some lending institutions will leverage a loan-to-cost (LTC) calculation. (This is especially common if the property has not yet been owned for the full duration of its seasoning period.) Most lending institutions' seasoning period is six months to a year. After the seasoning period concludes, the lender should use the LTV metric for calculating the cash-out value.

This is a tremendous difference in value and can make or break an investor's profit margin. Use the same example, but instead use the LTC:

$$C_{ash\ Out} = \left(P_{urchase\ Price} * LTC_{rate}\right)$$

$$C_{ash\ Out} = \left(\$60{,}000 * 0.75\right)$$

$$C_{ash\ Out} = \$45{,}000$$

In this endeavor, the investor would have spent $60,000 and received back $45,000. Now, a $15,000 down payment (excluding any repairs or transaction costs associated with the endeavor) on an investment property worth $160,000 is not bad; that's 9.4 percent compared to the standard 20 or 25 percent typically required for an investment property that the investor has not used as his/her primary residence. The ideal timeframe to seek a cash-out refinance is when the available equity is sufficient to leverage as a down payment on a like property and the interest rates are favorable.

Objective: Leveraging Other People's Money

Hopefully, you've realized exactly how crucial the ability to leverage lending options is to your real estate portfolio's rate of growth. Become familiar with the lending options available to you but don't shop around for rates just yet unless you are ready to begin purchasing a property. You can and should talk with lending institutions to determine what they offer but be wary of their need to perform a credit inquiry, remembering that an inquiry to the credit bureau negatively affects your rating. Always review available DPA programs in your area and their respective qualification criteria. Finally, work on and maintain your creditworthiness. This is the most important preparation you can do other than educating yourself on the process and the intricacies of lending.

Tasks:

- Improve and maintain creditworthiness.

- Research and assess available lending options.
  - Lending institutions
  - Loan types
  - DPA programs

Not all lending institutions allow cash-out refinancing on investment properties. Always verify when first engaging with a lender.

If while reading this chapter, there were concepts you wished to see that were either not covered or where you desired additional detail, please annotate and provide feedback via this QR code.

Visit our website (masterofleverage.info) by using this QR code to access key figures and references from this chapter.

Aloof Aaron, Cautious Carl, Sensible Sarah, and Risky Rick

Cautious Carl, Sensible Sarah, and Risky Rick spend numerous hours researching and comprehending the intricacies associated with leveraging other people's money (getting a loan). Not only do they understand the process required, people involved, and various types of lending options available, but they also comprehend the importance of maximizing their available conforming loans first due to the combination of lower interest rates and longer terms that result in a potentially higher ROI than various portfolio loans.

Furthermore, Sensible Sarah and Risky Rick pay close attention to the process of cash-out refinancing their real estate assets, specifically this process's importance to leveraging the *Inertia of Real Estate* by accessing the equity accrued over time. They take special notice to cash-out refinance their assets when the ROE of a unit converges with its ROI.

Aloof Aaron is still partying every weekend and, on occasion, thinking about taking out a loan to purchase a vehicle that he could use to stock up on beer for his friends' house parties. The primary form of lending Aaron is familiar with is from his friends and family.

SECTION II:

EXECUTION

Section II walks through the various actions and activities a real estate investor or home buyer is likely to encounter throughout their journey and details the methods to use to accomplish these activities.

Chapter 4: Leveraging ... When You Have None (Creative Financing)

The secret of getting ahead is getting started.
—Mark Twain

In this chapter, we are going to cover the following:

House Hacking
- Low- to No-Money-Down Financing
- Perils of Overleveraging – Part I

Down Payment Assistance (DPA) Programs
- Live and Upgrade

Seller Financing
- Full Seller Financing
- Partial Seller Financing

Syndication – 506(b)

This chapter of the book is the section that covers *creative financing*. While this term is simultaneously praised and disdained, it is important to note that I will cover only the legal means of using creative financing. I could have included this information in Chapter 14, "Mastering Your Leverage," but these techniques are so critical that leaving them near the end of the book would do an injustice to even the more experienced investors. These creative financing techniques offer phenomenal opportunities for individuals to jumpstart their real estate investment portfolio; more experienced investors can use these techniques to accelerate their portfolio growth far more efficiently than they would have otherwise.

The primary methods disclosed in this chapter include *house hacking*, *seller financing*, and *syndication*. It is also important to note that just because you can leverage some of these techniques doesn't always mean you should. As I say to some of my closest friends, "time and place (T&P) tend to dictate most things." It is always important to assess the numbers and account for various scenarios. This could not be truer than when leveraging creative financing. When conducting military planning, we often assess the most likely and the most dangerous course of action or outcome. Each has an associated probability.

The most likely outcome is, intuitively, the outcome that is most probable to occur. When related to real estate, this scenario would tend to involve acquiring a property at FMV and garnering average rental income and a moderate rate of appreciation. It assumes the home requires low repairs, low tenant turnover, and minimal capital expenditures. The most dangerous outcome represents the direst scenario. You can use your imagination, but this could involve purchasing a property with little-to-negative equity, receiving rents that don't cover the mortgage, and dealing with depreciating property values, multiple repairs, high tenant turnover, and large capital expenditures. If a moderate-to-high possibility of the most dangerous outcome exists in a property you're considering, be cautious with some of these creative financing approaches. These techniques can cut through tough financial obstacles; however, like all sharp objects, they can just as easily cut you if you're not experienced using them.

House Hacking

The term *house hacking* is often used synonymously with creative financing. In reality, it simply refers to leveraging many of the aforementioned government-sponsored programs to the investor's advantage within the confines of the imposed regulations and requirements. The two primary methods covered within this chapter are *low- to no-money-down financing* and "*live and upgrade.*" These options are likely the preferable options for individuals reading this book and thinking, "This is great, but I don't have 20-plus percent for a down payment," or "I spent all of my capital on my primary residence, and there isn't enough available equity for me to leverage."

Low- to No-Money-Down Financing

Low- to no-money-down financing is a great way to get started in real estate investing if done correctly. In reality, this technique is nothing more than using a combination of several options already explained in Chapter 3. Specifically, it's leveraging government-backed loan programs that guarantee or subsidize the loan on behalf of the borrower. Let's recap a few of these options using two examples: a single-family home and a duplex. For each example, we assume the individual/investor is leveraging the minimum down payment. The financial figures for these two properties are listed below.

Single-Family

Price: $100,000 **Taxes:** $175/month
Size: 3 Bed, 2 Bath **Insurance:** $25/month
Avg Rental Demand: $1,100/month

Duplex

Price: $150,000 **Taxes:** $200/month
Size: 2 Bed, 2 Bath (Each) **Insurance:** $40/month
Avg Rental Demand: $850 (Each)/month

> You may refinance any of these deals to a conventional/portfolio loan to enable their re-use!

If you recall, the government-sponsored programs are the Federal Housing Administration (FHA), U.S. Department of Agriculture (USDA), U.S. Department of Veterans Affairs (VA) loans, as well as Down Payment Assistance (DPA) programs.

Loan: Federal Housing Administration (FHA)
Terms: 15- or 30-year fixed
Down Payment Percentage: (As low as) 3.5%
Constraints: Monthly Insurance Premiums (MIP) Required, Primary Residence Only (1 year)

We will use an exemplar who will now be referred to as Investor Bob and run through the numbers for both the single-family property and the duplex, using the figures from the provided examples. Let's start with the single-family property.

Down Payment: $3,500
Closing Costs: ~$4,000 (Funding fee ~3%, MIP fee ~1%)
P&I: $380/month
MIP: $60/month

Using these figures, Investor Bob would need to front approximately $7,500 to pay for the out-of-pocket expenditures (assuming no repairs). The total monthly expense (PITI[41] + MIP) is $640.

P&I:	$380 +
Taxes:	$175 +
Insurance:	$ 25 +
MIP:	$ 60
Total:	$640

41 P&I combined with Taxes and Property Insurance is typically referred to as PITI.

The profit would be $460/month or $5,520/year. The ROI on this property would be 73.6 percent. Once Investor Bob vacates the property, it will take just under 1.5 years to recoup the initial investment. All around, this is not a bad deal, but there are two exceptions: 1) Investor Bob doesn't receive the 73.6 percent while it is still his primary residence, meanwhile the $640/month is a non-tax-deductible expense. 2) Investor Bob can do better if he is willing. Let's assess the duplex.

Down Payment: $5,250
Closing Costs: ~$6,000 (Funding fee ~3%, MIP fee ~1%)
P&I: $570/month
MIP: $90/month

The out-of-pocket expenditure increases to $11,250, and the monthly expenses increase to $1,000.

P&I:	$570 +
Taxes:	$200 +
Insurance:	$ 40 +
MIP:	$ 90
Total:	$1,000

With these figures, Investor Bob will still need to leverage his own funds for the mortgage but only part of it. If the other half of the duplex is leased, he will have immediate rental income of $850/month or $10,200/year (not including deductions for property management, vacancies, or capital expenditures), which offsets the majority of the mortgage cost. Instead of paying $640/month for the mortgage out-of-pocket, he must only pay $150/month (savings of $490/month). The $5,880 saved during that first year is significantly more than the extra $3,750 required for out-of-pocket expenditures. If you skew the numbers and consider the monthly savings to be the profit, the ROI would be 52.3 percent. That's an immediate ROI of 52.3 percent for the duplex as opposed to a delayed ROI of 73.6 percent for the single-family home; the initial investment is recouped in fewer than two years.

Let's assume that after some time (at least one year), Investor Bob decides to move again and leases both sides of the apartment. The new rental income is now $1,700/month or $20,400/year. That's an ROI of 181.3 percent. This is house hacking!

Now, if we perform the same analysis on the USDA loan, which, if you recall, can only be applied to single-family homes, we receive the following:

Loan: U.S. Department of Agriculture (USDA)
Terms: 15- or 30-year fixed
Down Payment Percentage: (As low as) 0% (a.k.a. no money down)
Constraints: Must be Located in Rural Area, Primary Residence (1 year), Single-Family Homes Only
Down Payment: $0
Closing Costs: ~$3,000 (~3%)
P&I: $380/month
MIP: N/A

These numbers look a little different. Note that no MIP is required for USDA loans. The out-of-pocket expenditures required for the single-family home would be the closing costs and miscellaneous fees, roughly $3,000 for easy math. Furthermore, the monthly payment would only be $580.

P&I:	$380 +
Taxes:	$175 +
Insurance:	$ 25
Total:	$580

After Investor Bob vacates the property (after at least one year), the rental income would be $520 ($6,240/year). Because the out-of-pocket expenditure was cut by more than half, the ROI on this figure is 208 percent, which isn't half bad!

But wait, it still gets better. Let's assess the VA loan. (Remember, this loan option is only available to eligible service members and veterans).

While similar to the USDA loan with no required down payment and no MIP, a VA loan can be used on multifamily homes (up to four units). The VA loan example for a single-family home is the same as the USDA example. But the following demonstrates its application toward the duplex.

Loan: Veterans Affairs (VA)
Terms: 15- or 30-year fixed
Down Payment Percentage: (As low as) 0% (a.k.a. no money down)
Constraints: Primary Residence (1 year), Eligible Veterans Only
Closing Costs: ~$6,000 (~3%)
P&I: $600/month

The out-of-pocket expenditure would be roughly $6,000, and the monthly expenses would be $840.

P&I:	$600 +
Taxes:	$200 +
Insurance:	$ 40 +
Total:	$840

In this scenario, if Investor Bob leases one side, that tenant is essentially covering all PITI expenses and allowing the owner to live in the other half for free. Yes, **FOR FREE**, with an extra 10 bucks a month. Investor Bob could bank the $10 for miscellaneous expenses or treat himself to a McDonald's Happy Meal for a job well done. Once again, we'll skew the math and use a savings of $640/month (the mortgage cost for a single-family home). The savings would be $7,680 in the first year, with an immediate ROI of 128 percent. Investor Bob would recoup his investment within the first year. If he applies the savings toward the P&I, he could refinance in three years and repeat the same process on another property.

Alternatively, Investor Bob could also move (after a year) and lease out both sides of the duplex. The rental income and ROI would then be $1,700/month ($20,400/year), a 340 percent ROI. Yes, 340 percent!

That's not even the best part; he is also eligible to use the FHA loan and the USDA loan.

> Bob could actually use the VA, then FHA, then USDA consecutively in back-to-back (to-back) years!

Perils of Overleveraging – Part I

Up to this point, house hacking looks great. But be wary. If used incorrectly, leveraging these options could diminish an investor's ability to continue leveraging other mainstream funding sources and could curtail the rate at which they grow their portfolio. The worst-case scenario (a.k.a. the most dangerous outcome) is that the individual must contend with an upside-down mortgage (a mortgage balance more than the property value). Adhering to the cautions listed in the forward section of the chapter will help you avoid being in this situation.

Down Payment Assistance (DPA) Programs

This is where it gets interesting. Recall the DPA programs overview in the last chapter. Most individuals are unaware that DPA programs are available to assist in subsidizing the down payment and closing costs required for purchasing a property. (I was completely unaware when I purchased my first primary residence.)

Leveraging a DPA program can be a game changer in jump-starting an investor's real estate portfolio. Many DPA programs offer up to 5 percent of the purchase price of the property to be used toward the down payment and/or closing costs. That may be enough to cover the closing costs for a USDA or VA loan and even enough to cover either the down payment or closing costs for the FHA loan (including the 1 percent upfront MIP fee). Leveraging DPA programs is potentially the easiest way to turn a low-money-down loan into a no-money-down loan. There are, however, income limitations to DPA programs (identified in Chapter 3).

Live and Upgrade

Low- to no-money-down loan options are not the only house hacking technique. The other popular technique to rapidly generate equity and potentially accelerate the appreciation of a property is to live in and upgrade a distressed or less desirable property located in a nice or upcoming neighborhood. This is a great opportunity to acquire a property for less than market value and repair it to market standards. Let's use the previous single-family property as an example, but this time, the property is distressed and is being acquired for $50,000. Repairs are required to restore the property to FMV. Let's estimate repair costs to be $20,000. The equity generated would be $30,000.

Value:	$100,000 –	80% LTV:	$ 80,000 –
Purchase Price:	$ 50,000 –	Purchase Price:	$ 50,000 –
Repairs:	$ 20,000	Repairs:	$ 20,000
Equity:	$ 30,000	**Equity Available:**	$ 10,000

* LTV is 80 percent due to it being a primary residence.

If Investor Bob were to refinance, he would likely conclude the process with a zero-sum expenditure (same amount of capital in reserves at the start and end of the endeavor), but he would have a primary residence (or income-generating investment property). He could also maintain the possibility of force appreciating the property's value. The techniques for forced appreciation are covered in Chapter 8. Let's assume Investor Bob wants to transform the home into a four-bedroom, three-bathroom property. We'll assume it will cost an additional $10,000 to do so; after all, it's already in need of repair. This process would increase the value from $100,000 to $120,000. The new figure would resemble the following:

New Value:	$120,000 –	80% LTV:	$ 96,000 –
Purchase Price:	$ 50,000 –	Purchase Price:	$ 50,000 –
Repairs:	$ 35,000	Repairs:	$ 35,000
Equity:	$ 35,000	**Equity Available:**	$ 11,000

The difference between $5,000 in equity and $1,000 of available equity may appear minuscule, but this is an example for a $100,000 property. Higher values yield better results for less proportionate repair costs. Even so, we have not factored in the higher rental value. Let's assert the new rental demand is $1,400/month ($16,800). Once Investor Bob has vacated and leased this property, the ROI, previously 73.6 percent, will increase exponentially (the initial investment has already been recouped, if refinanced). The benefit of low- to no-money-down loan options is that they do not require the individual/investor to have much capital to begin; the drawback is little to potentially negative equity at first. The "live and upgrade" approach requires the individual/investor to have capital up front but offers the opportunity to recoup their capital in addition to generating immediate equity.

An option exists that allows an individual to recoup their investment and generate equity immediately while not requiring much capital up front. This is Section 203(k) of the FHA loan.

FHA 203(k)

Section 203(k) of the FHA loan program enables individuals to finance repair or improvement/upgrade costs into their mortgage with no additional costs imposed upon the borrower. This is a great tool to leverage for individuals who do not have residual capital yet seek to pay for any deficiencies identified by inspectors or ensure the property is move-in ready by handling all remodeling and renovations before they move in.

> The FHA 203(k) loan program is capped at 110 percent of the value of the home. Additionally, licensed contractors must perform the work.

Seller Financing

Using financial institutions to acquire funds for major acquisitions is a relatively new advent in comparison to other forms of lending. A more dated version of lending (and leveraging) is seller financing. Seller financing is exactly what it indicates: the seller is financing the deal to the buyer. Essentially, the seller assumes the role of the lending institution and may engage directly with the buyer/borrower. The ownership of the property transfers from the seller to the buyer, and the buyer pays the seller in pre-defined, negotiated installments.

Seller financing is ideal for individuals who may not acquire traditional financing and for investors who are looking to expand their portfolio with little of their own capital. Using the same single-family example, let's assume the seller negotiates for a 10 percent down payment and a 10 percent (fixed) interest rate over 30 years. The negotiated deal would then resemble the following:

Loan: Seller Financed
Term: 30-year fixed (any term is possible)
Down Payment Percentage: 10%
Constraints: N/A
Closing Costs: N/A
P&I: $790/month

Since the seller is the one financing, this would mean no constraints, no closing costs, and no real estate agent fees, in addition to no MIP. However, the tradeoff is a substantially higher interest rate. The monthly expense would then become:

P&I:	$790 +
Taxes:	$175 +
Insurance:	$ 25 +
Total:	$990

Should Investor Bob lease the property for $1,100 a month, he would earn a monthly rental income of $110/month ($1,320/year). This is an ROI of 13.2 percent. It's better than the average stock yield but is not anything incredible. If he was able to negotiate for a 5 percent down payment, this would be another story. Here's the perk: Investor Bob maintains ownership of the property and may refinance it to pay off the seller/lender if it appreciates. If we assume the rate of appreciation is 3.4 percent, the property will have appreciated to a significant enough point in four years to refinance and pay off the seller/original lender. When refinancing, a better lending deal could be constructed to drastically improve the ROI. The original example of a financed deal using FHA had an ROI of 73.6 percent. This ROI would be notably higher due to the lack of MIP required.

Seller financing is unlikely to show up on a member's credit report (unless the seller registers and reports the debt).

When pursuing seller financing, it is imperative to be up front with your intentions to the seller. Do you plan to reside in the property as your primary residence, or do you plan to lease it to a tenant? Do you plan to make payments for the full loan term, or do you intend to refinance and pay them off early? If the seller still has a mortgage on the property, are you paying the mortgage directly and paying them the remainder, or are they handling the original mortgage? These are all things that must be discussed, agreed upon, annotated, and recorded.

If the seller still has a mortgage when attempting to seller finance a deal, the lending institution may elect to invoke the "due-on-sale" clause. This allows the bank to demand that the remainder of the loan be paid in full, effective immediately. If the owner is not able to pay, the lender may repossess/foreclose upon the home.

A lender executing the due-on-sale clause would be highly unfortunate for both the buyer and the seller. It would make the most sense to avoid this pitfall by engaging in seller financing in situations where the seller has no mortgage on the property. This enables them to fully finance the property without fear of the "due-on-sale" caveat. This type of seller financing is referred to as *full seller financing*. Fortunately, there is such a thing as *partial seller financing*, which is useful in such situations where the seller still retains a mortgage on the property.

Partial Seller Financing

This is, in essence, the process of having two mortgages on a property, the first mortgage being the original mortgage maintained by the owner/seller and the second mortgage being the seller financed mortgage to the new buyer of the property. Using the single-family property as an example, let's assume the owner owns 50 percent of the equity in the property but wishes to sell. The buyer could seek to have the owner execute a partial seller finance of the property. For example, the borrower negotiates with the owner's bank for the deal and gets them to agree to a $60,000 first mortgage. This mortgage is now assumed by the buyer, and that $60,000 pays off the original owner's $50,000 mortgage (and provides $10,000 in cash as profit). The remaining $40,000 of the purchase price is seller financed to the buyer, allowing the seller to continue to generate passive income for a defined period of time. The buyer is essentially now paying on two (smaller) mortgages for the same property, one of which required a (smaller) down payment, the other of which (the seller financed loan) did not require a down payment directly from the borrower but instead received a payout and profit from the first mortgage.

Complex, right? It's also very creative. There are several manners in which this might be accomplished. I encourage you to research this technique if it is something you are considering. Also note that not all lending institutions permit partial seller financing. You won't know until you inquire, so always inquire!

Syndication – 506(b)

If you are reading this book and thinking: "My capital is tied up in other successful ventures, so I'm forced to pass up on fruitful opportunities due to a lack of accessible capital," syndication may be useful to you. Simply put, syndication is an effective team that works together as real estate investors. A syndication is a group of individuals/investors aggregating their money together to acquire a real estate asset and split the subsequent responsibility and profits commensurately. There are both managers and members of a syndication. Leveraging a business entity to syndicate—a highly recommended arrangement—requires specific roles, responsibilities, and liabilities. These will be covered later in the book.

Since a real estate syndication is a business, the regulations and policies establishing governance are dictated by the Securities & Exchange Commission (SEC).

Multiple forms of real estate syndication exist, all of which have rules that govern the business. The most common real estate syndications are 506(b) and 506(c). The figure below displays some differences between the two:

	506(b)	506©
Solicitation:	No	Yes
Accredited Members:	No Limit	No Limit
Non-Accredited Members:	Up to 35	Not Permitted

Figure 4-1: Real Estate Syndication Comparison

Two notable differences include solicitation and legal membership. With 506(b) syndications, the group may not solicit investors/members; however, provisions allow for investing with up to 35 non-accredited investors. With 506(c) syndications, soliciting is accepted but only accredited investors[42] are permitted. Violating rules of syndication may have serious ramifications for the members of the syndicate, including

42 Investors with a net worth of over $1 million and whose annual income exceeded $200,000 ($300,000 if married) over the last two years.

heavy fines and/or jail time. However, when done correctly, it can be a useful tool to increase your real estate portfolio.

Syndication 506(b) is ideal for house hacking because it allows family and friends to join together for business ventures. You might ask how syndication is useful since all who join share the profit. I would argue that sharing a profit is better than owning no share of the profit. Also, keep in mind that sharing does not necessarily mean splitting. As an example, let's assume Investor Bob wanted to acquire a multi-unit property with the following specifications:

Multifamily (20 unit)

Price:	$500,000	**Taxes:**	$797/month
Size:	2 Bed, 1 Bath (20 unit)	**Insurance:**	$454/month
Loan:	Commercial	**P&I:**	$1,879/month
Term:	30-year fixed	**PM:**	$1,200/month
Down Payment (30%):	$150,000 (30%)	**Rent:**	$600/month (Each)
Closing Costs:	$10,000 (~2%)	**Total:**	$12,000/month
Repairs:	$100,000	**Profit:**	$7,670/month

This property would yield an annual (operating) income of $144,000 (assuming no vacancies). This is an annual profit of $92,040 and an ROI of 35.4 percent. Recouping an investment in three years is a significant achievement, one that Investor Bob aims for. If Bob does not have $260,000 plus reserves to purchase this property, he might decide to form a syndication to fund the endeavor.

Syndication may be accomplished in several methods, but let me explain three options. The first one is where all members are managing partners and share the profit as well as the liability. Note that this method does not allow for any buffer if expenditures exceed estimates or rents fall short of projections.

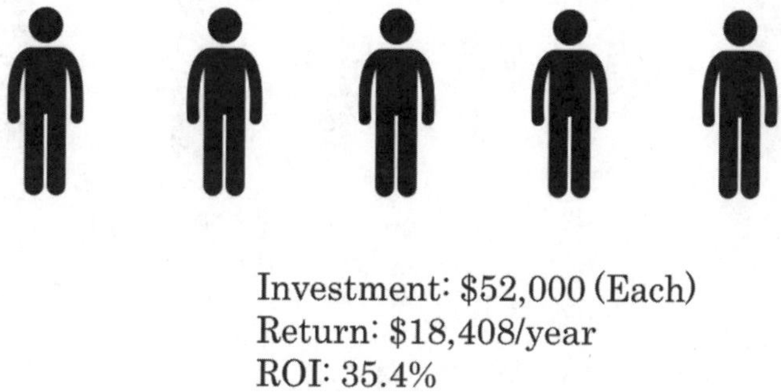

Figure 4-2: Syndication Example (All Managing Partners)

Investor Bob could bring on an additional member to help cover the expenditure as well as share the profit. This would resemble the following:

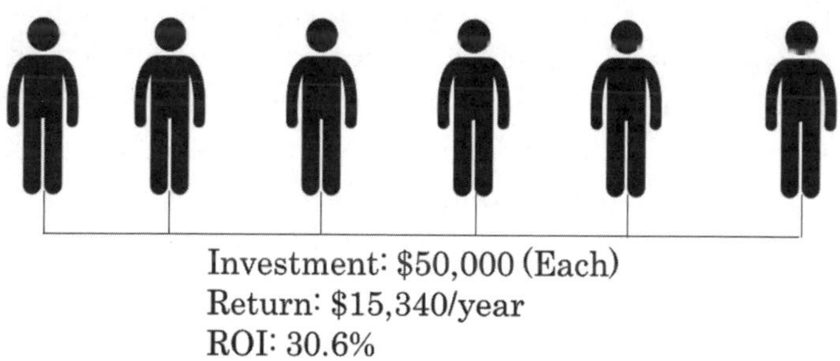

Figure 4-3: Syndication Example (All Managing Partners – 2)

Now, Investor Bob could also elect to structure the syndication so that there are managing partners and that the others are limited partners. This structure is one in which the endeavor and, therefore, the deal is "split" as opposed to "shared." Option two falls in this category, where an individual manages the venture, and others invest. This is a potential no-money-down option for an investor to generate wealth.

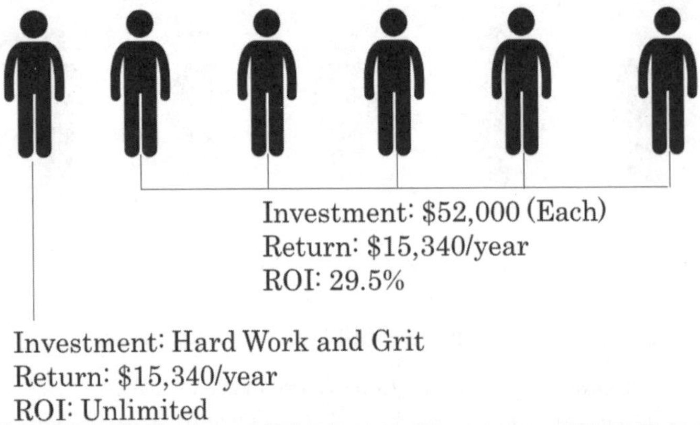

Figure 4-4: Syndication Example (Managing and Limited Partners)

Garnering an ROI of 29.5 percent starting Year 1 is also a notable investment for many investors. If you account for increases in rent over time, this number may continue to grow. Still, if the investor is ambitious, they could pursue yet another structure that will yield better returns for the managing member yet more immediate returns for the limited members. The third option offers limited members a guaranteed rate of return for a defined duration. In this example, the managing member is guaranteeing a 34 percent ROI for five years. The structure would resemble the following:

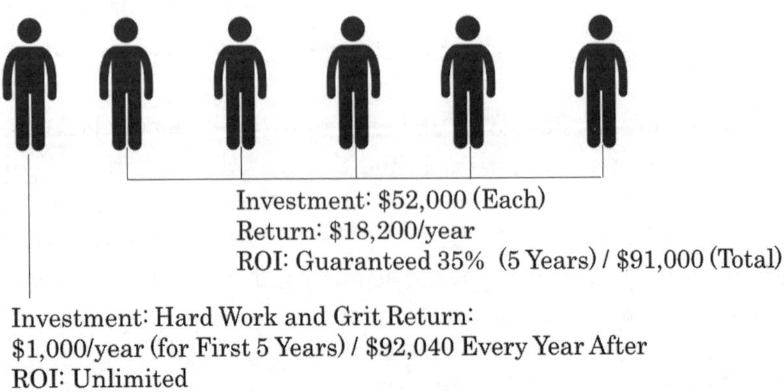

Figure 4-5: Syndication Example (Managing and Limited Partners – 2)

Syndication can be a savvy way of generating wealth for those with the ambition and commitment to follow through. In this section, I have described a 506(b); the benefits of 506(c) will be elaborated upon later in the book.

DID YOU KNOW?

According to an article written by RealWealth, in 2007, nearly 66 percent of Americans were investing in the stock market. By 2017, the number of Americans investing in the stock market decreased to just over 50 percent, the other half favoring real estate as a more stable and profitable endeavor.

Objective: Leveraging Creative Financing

All of the concepts discussed in this chapter are rather simple when viewed individually. The "creativity" arises from utilizing them in conjunction with one another in such a manner that allows for benefits that surpass what could be attained in isolation. Although these techniques offer immense potential, not all are available for everyone. There are income limitations for DPA programs and some low- to no-money-down financing options. Even so, the remaining house-hacking techniques are available. Research and assess your options. If you are properly positioned and ready to take on bigger endeavors, consider upscaling to a syndication. Whatever you decide, let this chapter inform you on how you may go about executing your real estate strategy even more effectively than you had thought before.

Tasks:

- Determine if you are eligible for low- to no-money-down financing.
- Determine if you are eligible for DPA programs.
- Determine if you have the capital for "live and upgrade" ventures.
    - After having conducted a property assessment
- Consider seller financing.
    - After having assessed the property's pertinent details
- Consider syndication to acquire larger, more profitable investments.

If while reading this chapter, there were concepts you wished to see that were either not covered or where you desired additional detail, please annotate and provide feedback via this QR code.

Visit our website (masterofleverage.info) by using this QR code to access key figures and references from this chapter.

Aloof Aaron, Cautious Carl, Sensible Sarah, and Risky Rick

Cautious Carl, Sensible Sarah, and Risky Rick continue to expand their depth of knowledge pertaining to various lending options, specifically those associated with low- to no-money-down options. They are each aware that these options are only available for primary residences. Sensible Sarah and Risky Rick both realize that a phenomenal method with which they can own a residence sooner as well as maximize their ROI is to lower the capital expenditure required for purchase.

Cautious Carl comes to the same realization; however, he is not as comfortable purchasing a home in a manner where there is minimal equity buffer against an economic/housing downturn, which may potentially result in an upside-down mortgage. Sensible Sarah and Cautious Carl both discuss these options with their spouses. Sarah and her spouse agree to proceed; Carl and his spouse decide to forgo this option despite the opportunities it provides. Risky Rick presses forward without consulting his wife.

Aloof Aaron's attention is focused on the sorority house at the end of the block, and he has no intention of owning a home at this time.

Chapter 5: Leveraging Your Team

> **Teamwork is the ability to work together toward a common vision. The ability to direct individual accomplishments toward organizational objectives. It is the fuel that allows common people to attain uncommon results.**
> —Andrew Carnegie, *American industrialist and philanthropist*

In this chapter, we are going to cover the following:

Understanding Your Team's Dynamic

Core and Ancillary Team Members

Centers of Gravity

Core Team Members:

Attorney, CPA, Deal Finder, Insurance Agent, Property Manager, Real Estate Lender, Title Company

Ancillary Team Members:

Appraiser, Contractors, Dumpster Companies, Electrician, Handymen, HVAC, Home Inspector, Landscape Workers, Plumber, Roofer, Specialists (Cabinets and Countertops, Concrete, Hardwood Refinisher, Tile Setter)

Team Depth

There are a couple of steadfast rules in life as well as in real estate. One such rule is that it is difficult to accomplish anything great on your own. Luckily, teams come in various forms and sizes, and they can accomplish various objectives. One of the most effective teams I've ever encountered is a Marine Expeditionary Unit (MEU).[43] This is a quick reaction entity, capable of responding to virtually any situation. They are light, lean, lethal, and incredibly efficient—just like I design my team to be!

If you've ever been friends with someone in an MEU, you would know they often have a distinct personality type that allows them to be effective. For your real estate endeavors, you need to assemble such a team, but before you may do so, you need to understand the team dynamics and how you fit into your team.

Men are basically smart or dumb and lazy or ambitious. The dumb and ambitious ones are dangerous, and I get rid of them. The dumb and lazy ones I give mundane duties. The smart ambitious ones I put on my staff. The smart and lazy ones I make my commanders.
—Erwin Rommel, *German Field Marshal, WWII*

Understanding Your Team's Dynamic

When you are assembling your team, you should view it as a professional business relationship, a partnership of sorts. All relationships have give-and-take. Any relationship—professional or otherwise—where one entity solely gives or solely takes will not last. The amount of give-and-take for any one deal may not always be equal, but the mutual benefits over the span of the relationship are commensurate with all parties striving toward the same goal. Build your team for mutually beneficial synergies, and it will produce a win-win for all team members.

Effective team building begins with understanding yourself. What personality type are you? What is your social style? How do other people respond or react to you? It's important that you know these things about yourself—and about the remainder of your team.

43 A Marine Expeditionary Unit (MEU) is the smallest of the air-ground tactical task forces in the United States Fleet Marines. Each unit is an expeditionary quick reaction force, ready to respond to any crisis.

Steve Rogers and Tony Stark

Early in my military career, I was a junior officer in the United States Air Force, assigned to one of the three-letter agencies within the intelligence community. We worked on some very interesting projects that had national security implications. There were many instances when we would need to be creative to ensure the success of the mission. My commander often leveraged me to solve complex or unpleasant issues, but I wasn't alone. I always had a dedicated team of enlisted airmen, a cadre of contractors, and a small cohort of peers. My commander often paired me, a captain, with a major for the less-than-pleasant issues. This was deliberate. My background and experiences were from cyber operations, and so was my way of thinking. The major's background was acquisitions. He was very effective at doing his job, but we rarely agreed upon the same approach to solving a problem initially.

Here's the thing: although we seldom initially agreed on approaches, we respected each other, and when we did work together, we developed optimal solutions that neither of us would have proposed individually. In the rare moments when we could not find an amenable solution, we also had another coworker who ensured we accomplished our mission. Our commander would routinely refer to me as Steve Rogers and to the major as Tony Stark.

You always had the Avengers. Sometimes it was Civil War; most times, it was End Game—I guess that made our coworker Captain Marvel. Our leadership realized we were strong individually but were unstoppable together.

This is ultimately what you want in a team: the right personalities with the right skills working together toward a common set of objectives.

I've come to accept and appreciate my personality and social style. My upbringing, in addition to my military background, has taught me there are times when I am ideally suited for a task and other times when I must actively fight my instincts. My MBTI[44] is ENTJ (commonly known as the Marshal/Commander). To be blunt, my personality type and social style mean I can be a little intense and somewhat Machiavellian at times. When people first meet me, I may appear to be very guarded and direct. I often talk fast, and I am very task oriented. I like to get to the point quickly. I don't like loss of control. I get aggravated by indecision. And I get irritated when people waste my time. If we were students at Hogwarts, I would be sorted into Slytherin. If we were in *Game of Thrones*, I would be House Lannister. If this were *Breaking Bad*, I would be Walter White. If we were in *Star Wars*, I would be the guy saying, "I am your father." I know these things about myself; therefore, I surround myself with trusted team members whom I charge with maintaining balance within "the force."

To build a cohesive team, you need to know your personality, your strengths, and your weaknesses. As a real estate investor, it is your responsibility to ensure you have the correct personality types in the correct roles for your team to be effective. The team may leverage your strengths, but it must also compensate for your weaknesses.

Core and Ancillary Team Members

Core and *ancillary* are not meant to designate a class system of team members. *Core* is not white collar with *ancillary* as blue. All of your team members are valuable members, and you must treat them as such. The tier designation is simply an easy way to denote groups you will frequently encounter regardless of your investment strategy. That being said, there is one team member in a tier above all others: your spouse or significant other. They are your partner in life as well as your partner in this endeavor and can be either your greatest asset or your greatest hindrance. Real estate investing is a time-consuming endeavor. You should make this choice together, as a partnership, vested in one another's future of wealth generation and financial freedom.

44 The Myers–Briggs Type Indicator (MBTI) is an introspective questionnaire designed to highlight differences in how individuals perceive the world and consequently make decisions.

Centers of Gravity

While the tier structure is not a ranked system, centers of gravity are. In astronomy, a center of gravity is a body of mass that generates a gravitational field, resulting in a pull of surrounding objects toward or around itself. From a military strategy and planning perspective, a center of gravity is where your team's power comes from. All other forces are projected from or revolve around the centers of gravity, and you will rarely attain victory without them. You should value them accordingly and protect them at all costs. In a real estate team, your centers of gravity include the *deal finder*, *property manager*, lender, and contractor(s). Each of these team members will be discussed at length below, along with other key players in each tier.

> Many investors refer to these members that I call the Centers of Gravity as the Core-4.

CORE

Real Estate Attorney

This member is on your team to help you navigate through the legal and financial complexities involved with certain types of real estate. They should be able to assist you with navigating the acquisition of distressed properties, advise you on business entity structures and required actions, help you avoid legal pitfalls, file evictions for tenants or homeowners of distressed properties you've acquired, develop strategies to maintain your wealth, and minimize taxes. You don't want just any attorney. You want one that specializes in real estate.

Certified Public Accountant (CPA)

Some individuals think accounting for real estate is as simple as calculating the profit you receive from owning the asset, subtracting the sum of all expenses, and factoring for deductions. It sounds simple but is actually far more complex. Make sure you find a CPA who understands your needs and requirements. A good accountant will ensure you avoid unnecessary expenses and various legal pitfalls. They will also find effective ways of making sure Uncle Sam gets his appropriate share, but not a penny more!

Accountant services are tax deductible.

You may consider using TurboTax or H&R Block for your taxes to save on expenses. Don't do it! Leveraging a CPA who specializes in real estate will often cost roughly the same amount but result in far more deductions and savings.

The Deal Finder

Have you ever prepared for a game of Monopoly, developed your strategy, and had a fat stack of Monopoly money ready to spend, only to have your plans crumble with the roll of the dice? You may have even wished for loaded dice to help you land on the properties you wanted to buy. Wishing works when you are playing a board game, but when the money is real, your deal finder is your loaded dice.

The deal finder is the first in your center of gravity and could be one person or a combination of individuals. They may be a real estate agent, a *wholesaler*, a *probate attorney*, a fellow real estate investor, or even a real estate–savvy neighbor. Their importance comes from being able to find deals before any of your competitors and from being in a position to provide you with a competitive advantage. They have systems in place that make them efficient—systems they have learned throughout their successful career. They are professional, resourceful, knowledgeable, and often creative. These professionals are problem solvers and typically have little patience or tolerance for people and things that impede progress. You need to prove your worthiness to them more so than they need to prove it to you. I recommend you do your research before engaging with them. Have a plan. Do not waste their time.

You should ensure they know you are looking to build a real estate portfolio, that you view them as a critical partner, and that you are looking for repeat business with them. After all, they are professionals who also expect to build wealth. You may prove your value to them in several manners. First, leave stellar reviews when you close a deal. This is an easy way to broadcast their value to the real estate investor community and earn their appreciation at the same time. Second, you may consider giving your real estate agent a small bonus if they score you a phenomenal deal. Acts of kindness go over well with most people, and granting money goes over well with all people. Third, send them referrals for other investors looking to buy, making sure you send serious buyers to your agent. Sending strong referrals results in more money in their pockets, a good realtor for your counterpart, and a better relationship between you and your realtor. This is not just a win-win; it's a win-win-win.

Your deal finder is a center of gravity that pulls in other members who will be useful to you and your goals. There is a direct benefit to you as well: good deal finders will educate you on their process because they know a more intelligent buyer makes for a more efficient system. Furthermore, some deal finders will provide you with necessary referrals such as lenders, contractors, and property managers—the other centers of gravity—as well as other crucial members of your team.

The Deal Finder: Attorney

What the caterpillar calls the end of the world,
the master calls a butterfly.
—Richard Bach, *author and aviator*

A tragic situation for one person can be a great opportunity for another. Attorneys are not just good at litigating; they can also be a valuable source of leads for properties owned by people in personal distress (covered in Chapter 7). A professional relationship with an attorney can put you in contact with individuals filing for bankruptcy. These members are looking for ways to work off their debts and may be willing to sell a distressed property for a bargain. Attorneys have also been known to tip off investors if they have a client who is going through a divorce and wants to liquidate some of their assets in a hurry. These are not rosy situations by any means; however, they do offer positive opportunities that can benefit multiple parties. If a person is facing bankruptcy, draft a contract that offers them enough of a profit to assist with their debt. Many times, the individual liquidating their assets prior to a divorce is happy to have your assistance. This is the world of win-wins. If you have already cut your teeth on real estate and are looking for methods to rapidly expand your portfolio and exponentially increase your wealth, attorneys can provide that assistance. Good attorneys are ones who are efficient, affordable, and, most importantly, accessible.

The Deal Finder: Fellow Real Estate Investor

Most people would think that other real estate investors are your competitor or even the enemy. That is not entirely correct. Real estate investing is far more collaborative than most rookies believe. If you are a gambler, think of it in terms of blackjack more than poker. In poker, you are playing against every member at the table. Players bluff and deceive each other to gain an advantage. Advantages exist to having a larger pot (equity), and some players almost bully others. Your hand (the real estate deal) is for the winner-takes-all proposition.

Blackjack, on the other hand, is a collaborative game. Every player (investor) is against the dealer (institution), not the other players. The strength of your hand (real estate deal) does not impact other players (investors). The pot (investor equity) does not impact other players (investors). Every player (investor) may walk away with a larger pot (more equity). Be cautious, though; an investor not abiding by the rules of real estate can jeopardize the equity leveraged by all investors at the table.

Other investors may help you in several ways. Remember the conversation about opportunity cost? I have had fellow investors tip me off about a phenomenal deal they discovered but were not in a position to take advantage of. Sometimes, investors will stumble across multiple deals at once and not have the capital or means to engage all deals simultaneously. Obviously, they will pursue the best deals; however, having a good deal dropped in to your lap is a blessing. Don't pass these gifts up, and be sure to keep your friends in mind when your turn comes to have multiple offers you aren't able to engage with.

Additionally, other investors may be looking to modify their portfolio, consolidate their investments, or trade up and need extra capital to do so. All of these situations would result in them potentially selling an asset. Run the numbers and see what works for you. If it's a good deal, take it.

The Deal Finder: Real Estate Agent

For most individuals and junior investors, the deal finder is a real estate agent. I recommend this for novice investors or individuals entering the market. You will gain knowledge beyond your years from real estate agents if you are willing to listen. Real estate agents offer several unique services. They can grant access to the MLS[45] or other listing services. These listing services match buyers and sellers based on specific search criteria. These criteria include location, price, style, square footage, number of bedrooms and bathrooms, etc. These listing services will typically show properties that are *turnkey*, but an agent may modify the criteria to include terms such as "REO"[46] or "FSBO,"[47] which may help locate discounted properties. Make sure you know if you are being represented by a *single agency* or a *dual agency agreement.*

> Be sure to find an agent who specializes in the property type in which you are interested.

Single agency is when an agent represents only the buyer or the seller. The only fiduciary relationship is to their respective client. Dual agency is when an agent or brokerage firm represents both the buyer and the seller. The fiduciary relationship is extended to both parties because they are both clients.

45 Real estate listing service (Multiple Listing Service) used predominantly in the U.S.

46 Term used to describe real estate owned by a bank or financial institution.

47 Term used to indicate real estate being sold by the owner as opposed to a real estate agent.

Try to avoid the conflict of interest with dual agencies. Develop rapport with an agent who is loyal to you.

The Deal Finder: Wholesale Agent

Wholesale agents or wholesalers are another group who can help find you incredible deals … or they can cost you a lot of money. They do not offer the same services nor are they likely to have as robust of a team of referrals as a real estate agent; however, they will find and bring you deals because their success depends on it. A wholesaler will acquire a property in distress for a bargain. They assess the asset's ARV and determine an appealing price to offer to you as an investor.

Many wholesalers are honest individuals, but you will need to perform due diligence to find them. Leverage other members of your team to verify the wholesaler's "comps" and reputation.

In an ideal world, partnering with a wholesaler is a win for everyone. In the real world, people are greedy, and one person's greed is usually at the expense of someone else.

When dealing with a wholesaler, the transaction is treated as if it is for sale by owner (FSBO); they have no duty to care about any of your interests. This offers a phenomenal opportunity but also has inherent risks—risks that may be perilous for novice and more junior investors.

Insurance Agent

Insurance agents are beneficial in helping you protect your asset. You will want to coordinate with them in advance of acquiring the property to ensure you are covered from day one. If a mishap occurs to your asset, to a worker while performing renovations, or to a tenant while residing in your residence, you will be held liable unless you have an effective policy. Make sure you work with an agent that is at least familiar with real estate investors and their needs. Pay specific attention to the terms of the agreement. They will be able to recommend other variances of insurance that may be beneficial and/or mandatory for you as an investor.

> **i** Look into Loss-of-Rents (business interruption) coverage for bigger assets and/or if it works for your level of risk.

Property Manager

The utilization of a property manager is a huge topic of debate. I've heard many horror stories of bad property managers or property management companies, and I've had a few less-than-pleasant experiences with them myself. However, I acknowledge that they are a necessity for long-distance real estate investing and for large portfolios. They may also be a major stress reliever and cover real estate assets you maintain within the same vicinity in which you reside.

> **i** Property managers can also be your deal finder. They often know other investors who are looking to sell their property before it goes on the market, allowing you to engage prior to other investors.

Similar to the deal finders and lending agents, the difference between a great property manager and a mediocre one is astronomical. Ideal property managers know the area in which you are investing, they know good areas to invest in, and they are willing to share that information with you. The best property managers resolve your issues without needing to get you involved, ideally in a similar manner or even better than how you would have resolved it. They are hired to interact with and manage your tenants so you don't have to. Keep this in mind: tenants are the fuel for your investments, and the property manager is your contact with your tenants. Be appreciative of this fact and don't abuse this relationship.

A few good ways to show that you appreciate a property manager's services are to be responsive, respectful, and, as you can probably guess, give good reviews and referrals. Do the collective a favor by understanding their processes as well as reading and understanding their management agreement. If you foresee an issue, address it before signing a contract instead of trying to arbitrate it afterward. It is a good idea to consult their advice when you are considering purchasing an additional property. They can provide useful information that may influence your decisions. Finally, don't call them for petty things.

The advice that I just provided you assumes that you engage a property manager. You don't have to. To borrow from Shakespeare: to use property management services or not to use property management services—that is the question. Make sure you can establish a system that works for both you and a property manager. As an investor, you must decide for yourself what works best. The following chart offers an easy depiction of the benefits and consequences associated with self-management and professional property management.

	Self-Management	Professional Management
Pros:	No one cares about your property as much as you do. You save money on property management fees.	Professionals have immense contacts and knowledge you can leverage.
Cons:	Time is your most valuable commodity. What is your time worth to you?	Good ones are few and far between.

Table 5-1: Pros and Cons of Property Management

Real Estate Lender

Great real estate lenders are diligent, and they may open up doors that enable creative possibilities. They can help you repair your credit score, find creative ways of helping you qualify for specific loans, educate you on the best ways to proceed, and even recommend you to other lenders more suited to meeting your needs. A great lender is very busy. Don't be put off if they don't answer your calls as quickly as you might like as long as they call you back within 24 hours. Real estate lenders may come in several forms, including investor-friendly banks, credit unions, or other loan institutions. (See Chapter 3.) It is your job to make sure you understand your needs and what each lender is offering.

The best way to prove your value to a lender is to give them great reviews and referrals. Similar to real estate agents, if you know serious investors who are looking for lenders in your area, send them in your lender's direction. But again, do yourself and your lender a favor; only send investors who you know are going to need a loan. If you made first contact with the lender, consider introducing them to your deal finder. Developing that professional relationship is not only good for them and their business, but it is also good for you. Finally, engage with their boss and let them know how much you appreciate their hard work and effort. This small act will pay back dividends in your continued relationship with your lender.

Title Company

This entity will be beneficial in providing certain key services. The biggest use for them will be their provision of *title insurance* or a *title commitment*. This is a document that insures the asset against claims of ownership from other individuals. They will also notify you of any liens against the asset—liens that you may inherit depending upon the manner of acquisition. While any good real estate agent will have title companies they work with, I would recommend developing a good rapport with at least one per investment area. It will alleviate frustration and may allow for more rapid expansion of your real estate portfolio.

DID YOU KNOW?

In 2018, the National Association of Residential Property Managers conducted a study of 1,857 property managers to better understand the change and current state of the property management industry. Among many statistics, this study revealed these services are offered by the majority of property management companies:

- Rent/Fee Collection – 96 percent
- Leasing Properties – 94 percent
- Maintenance/Repairs – 92 percent
- Property Inspections – 86 percent
- Marketing – 86 percent
- Evictions – 84 percent
- Cleaning – 75 percent
- Purchasing and Selling – 65 percent
- Accounting, Bookkeeping, and Taxes – 64 percent
- Outdoor Services – 61 percent

ANCILLARY

Appraiser

Good *appraisers* can be valuable allies. Bad appraisers, just like bad tenants, may make you lose faith in humanity. The appraiser is the individual who establishes the value of your property in the form of a property valuation report. Normally, they are contracted by a bank/financial institution on behalf of the buyer to establish the appraised value of the property. This is a component of the appraisal contingency (which will be discussed in Chapter 8). Appraisers may also come in handy when you are renovating a property as well as when you are refinancing a property. If the property is distressed, bringing in the appraiser at purchase will enable them to provide you with the AIV as well as the ARV. Some banks will accept your appraiser's estimate in lieu of hiring another appraiser if they have an established relationship with them. This may be contingent upon how quickly renovations are completed and the refinance is initiated.

I recommend contacting your lender to see which appraisers they frequently work with. Look to develop a relationship with one of them.

The appraiser's true value comes from their ability to provide insight into the factors that may increase your property's value. They may also provide useful leads to properties that are distressed and ready for an offer.

Make sure you have a good appraiser. Appraisers that lowball your property value will diminish your real estate inertia. Appraisers with a reputation for inflating asset values are unlikely to be accepted by financial institutions and are, therefore, equally problematic. Leverage your network!

Contractors

For any of the contractors, you want them to know three things: the work that needs to be done, how to complete that work, and how to save you money. They will most likely also know other specialty contractors who are good at their trade and won't gouge you on prices. Contractors can offer innovative solutions to accomplish your goals that are both compliant with regulations and within or under your budget.

There are several things you can do to show your contractor you appreciate their services and consider them to be a valuable member of the team. Contractors will appreciate incentives; however, they will also appreciate the removal of hindrances and obstacles to the completion of their work. This could be as simple as asking them how they like to be paid and paying them on time. It could also be asking them the type of work they enjoy compared to what they dislike. If a decision on procedure comes into play and you are indifferent, communicate value to your contractor by letting them do it their way.

> Don't micromanage. Don't ask them to work for free. Don't pester them with small stuff. This will ruin your relationship with a valuable member of the team.

Consider using a general contractor (GC) to manage large projects or the entirety of a renovation if you are either uncomfortable managing the members of the team or if you do not have the time to manage the members of the team. GCs will also pull and file the proper permits for your project. A GC will typically be willing to perform this role for 10–15 percent of the overall project cost. If you are not very handy and/or if you are working on a major renovation, I urge you to strongly consider this option. Consider it a combination of insurance and an investment in your education on how to manage a rehab team.

Dumpster Companies

For most home renovation projects, you don't want to rely upon your standard trash removal services. Many companies offer both short- and long-term, roll-off dumpster rentals. They are sized for different projects and various materials to better help the customer complete their projects efficiently and responsibly. The standard sizes for roll-off dumpsters are 10 yards, 20 yards, 30 yards, and 40 yards. Unless your property is turnkey, dumpsters will be a necessity.

Electrician

An *electrician* is a craftsman or tradesman who specializes in electrical wiring of buildings, both installation as well as maintenance and repair. When dealing with real estate, investors will often interact with either service or construction electricians. *Service electricians* normally work on repairs and upgrades in small remodels. They specialize in fixing wiring issues, installing new wiring in preexisting infrastructure, as well as making minor repairs. *Construction electricians* usually focus and specialize on the installation of new electrical systems (think larger projects or entire developments).

> When hiring an electrician, ensure you find one who is licensed, bonded, and insured. Inspect the final work.

Handyperson

A good *handyman* or *handywoman* can be a great cost saver in many instances. Not every job or task requires a master craftsman; many times, a handyperson is more than capable of performing the work and may do so at a lower cost to you. This individual is ideal for general labor, minor repairs, or small projects.

These jack-of-all-trade workers may not drive the newest pickup truck or wear a company uniform. They may or may not have flyers or business cards. They may be retired or working as a side hustle. Ultimately, these things aren't the things that matter most. You care about their performance and the reputation they have built.

> Leverage the handyperson to the greatest practical extent, then follow up with the licensed specialist where needed.

Heating, Ventilation, and Air Conditioning (HVAC) Technician

An *HVAC technician* is a person who performs installation, maintenance, or repairs on heating, ventilation, air conditioning, or refrigeration systems. These technicians will come in handy if you are having issues with any of the utilities that may be beyond the capability of a handyperson to repair.

Home Inspector

Bring both the home inspector and general contractor on site together and early. The GC can develop estimates for issues identified by the home inspector.

You will want a good *home inspector* on your team, especially when you are getting started or taking on major projects. I recommend bringing your home inspector on early in the process. They will inform you of the must-fix issues, which tend to be structural, electrical, plumbing, gas, roof, or hazard related. Any issues in these areas will result in your investment failing inspections should you choose to refinance or sell the asset. If you are the buyer, you can use these deficiencies to negotiate the cost or, at minimum, make sure they are repaired prior to taking ownership. This will enable you to better prioritize renovations associated with your project. The best home inspectors are busy ones and, ideally, ones that recommend solutions and not just simply point out issues.

Be careful not to get a home inspector who is persnickety and nitpicks unnecessarily.

Landscape Workers

A *landscape worker* is responsible for the cultivation and care of the landscape and yard surrounding a residence or building. A good or creative landscaper will artfully design attractive landscapes out of unmanaged or uncultivated areas of the property. This may include planting flowers, shrubberies, sod, or even trees. It may also include the installation of walkways and will most definitely include various groundskeeping tasks such as pulling weeds, pruning, mulching, and fertilizing.

Do not undervalue landscaping when developing your real estate portfolio. It is essential in developing curb appeal and ensuring your house is the hottest prospect on the block.

Plumbing Technicians

Plumbing technicians are commonly referred to as plumbers. They perform installation, repairs, and maintenance on piping used to transport gas, sewage, water, or other liquids. They also perform installation and repairs on sinks, toilets, and other household items, including fixtures, appliances, water heaters, and garbage disposals.

> If major plumbing work is not required, consult your handyperson first.

Roofing Technician

Roofing technicians are commonly referred to as roofers. A roofer installs roofs, repairs leaking roofs, and replaces broken roof tiles on residential dwellings or commercial buildings. Their scope of duty generally includes performing pre-inspections, smoothing and leveling roofs, installing materials, as well as completing site prep and cleanup. Most roofing companies can also install, repair, and replace siding on residential homes.

Other Specialists: Cabinets and Countertops

If you are conducting a renovation of a residence, you'll likely be replacing countertops at some point. You'll need a company that specializes in framing and installing cabinets as well as setting countertops. Big box stores such as Home Depot and Lowe's offer these services but so do other local businesses. They may not have the same variety, but they will likely be offered at better prices. Do your research and inquire with local vendors when working on your projects.

Other Specialists: Concrete Companies

Depending upon the size and complexity of your project, you may need a *concrete company* to provide their services, which include the installation of foundations and slabs for new residences and additions, concrete driveways, walkways and patios, a concrete parking lot, stairs, and terraces. They also offer repairs for cracks and chips, drainage remediation, design services, as well as demolition services.

Other Specialists: Hardwood Refinisher

Hardwood refinishers specialize in smoothening and removing imperfections in wooden surfaces, such as floors. They are knowledgeable and comfortable working with various types of wood, applying filler compounds, varnishes, and sealants.

Other Specialists: Tile Setter

Tile setters or *tile layers* are responsible for installing ceramic or natural stone tiles. They remove existing floor coverings, take measurements, cut and shape tiles to ensure they fit into the designated spaces, and spread grout to ensure clean edges and straight lines. They may also create decorative wall and floor designs by installing mosaic tiles in kitchens, bathrooms, and living rooms. Good tile setters are capable of following blueprints and plans to the letter.

Team Depth

Once you've gotten started and gained traction building a portfolio in an area in which you know you want to continue expanding, you should look to grow the depth of your team. You may not need multiple accountants or insurance agents. I hope you don't need multiple attorneys. But you should have multiple deal finders, contractors, and technicians. You will want to have a backup if your primary team member is unavailable at the time you need him/her or if you are managing more than one project simultaneously, and you cannot deconflict the work.

Objective: Leveraging Your Team

I will tell you now: you cannot build your real estate portfolio alone. You will need a team. Your team may be large or small. You could even have multiple teams to manage multiple projects. It all depends upon your means and appetite for expansion. Be cautious not to overexpand or bloat your team. A bench that's too deep equates to many players not getting the opportunity to play. Be aware that your deal finder and property manager likely have established relationships with other potential team members that you may be able to leverage on your team.

Tasks:

- Honestly assess your personality type, personal skills, and aptitude for managing and operating real estate, as well as your ability and willingness to invest your personal time and effort.

- Identify and research team members for your centers of gravity.
    - Deal finder
    - Lender
    - Property manager
    - Applicable contractors

- Determine which additional core and ancillary team members you may acquire for any property in which you are interested.

If while reading this chapter, there were concepts you wished to see that were either not covered or where you desired additional detail, please annotate and provide feedback via this QR code.

Visit our website (masterofleverage.info) by using this QR code to access key figures and references from this chapter.

Aloof Aaron, Cautious Carl, Sensible Sarah, and Risky Rick

Cautious Carl, Sensible Sarah, and Risky Rick have all been diligently developing their plans in preparation for implementing their real estate acquisition strategy. Cautious Carl, mistrusting of others, is hesitant to involve too many team members in his real estate plans. He'd rather develop and maintain only the Core-4 members (the deal finder, property manager, lending agent, and a good general contractor). Even so, Carl is deliberate in establishing and maintaining his primary center of gravity.

Risky Rick also decides to develop and maintain a leaner team but for different reasons. He believes he can increase his profits by completing portions of the work on his own. Alternatively, Sensible Sarah researches and identifies quality team members she could use for various real estate acquisitions, both those that are turnkey and those more in depth. She establishes these relationships in each major area in which she intends to establish a center of gravity. She always starts with a reputable property manager and lender. In many instances, the property manager has developed contacts or also has skills as a contractor and/or real estate agent.

Finally, Aloof Aaron's only interest in team members, at this time, is for his competitive volleyball team.

Chapter 6: Leveraging Location ... Location, Location!

> **The three most important things in retail are location, location, location. The three most important things for our consumer business are technology, technology, technology.**
> —Jeff Bezos, *founder and former CEO of Amazon*

In this chapter, we are going to cover the following:

Narrowing Your Search

Outer Circle: The Region

- Climate, Economy of Force, Landlord Laws and Regulations, Natural Hazards

Medial Circle: The City

- Employment Opportunities
    - Income and Wages
    - Industry
        - Types and Diversification of Jobs
            - High-Growth Jobs
            - Stabilizing Jobs
    - Unemployment
- Other Enticements
    - Up-and-Coming Areas
    - Hip and Niche
    - Direction of Growth
        - Economic and Geographic Barriers

Inner Circle: The Neighborhood/Suburb
- Buyer's Market vs. Seller's Market
  - Sales Volume
- Determining Desirability and Demand
  - Statistics and Scores
  - Metrics and Corollaries
- Determining Availability and Supply
  - New Construction and Absorption

Target: The Property
- Quick Determination Assessments
  - Property Value Trend
  - Price-to-Rent Ratios
    - The 1 Percent Rule, The 2 Percent Rule

Nearly every real estate investor or professional will inform you that location is key to having a successful portfolio. That's sage advice. But where do you go from there? How do you find the right locations where you might discover gem properties? With all the advertisements and listings, wouldn't it be nice to have a system to help filter and sort properties that either don't meet your needs or are distractions from the goals of your current phase? Whether you're conducting a search, building a puzzle, or painting a piece of art, you will generally go about each endeavor in the same manner: start broad and slowly home in on the details.

Note: this chapter focuses on how you can identify an ideal investment property. There are services, such as *turnkey investing*, that care for all aspects of managing investment properties (including locating, acquiring, rehabbing, leasing, and hiring property management). Do your research and see if this course of action is most effective for your investment strategy.

Narrowing Your Search

When searching for real estate, think of narrowing your target, which, in this case, is a property you wish to purchase. I imagine a scope with three concentric circles representing the layers of my search. The outer

> Technology is your friend. Use it advantageously to automate the process of searching through these criteria.

circle represents the general region I am interested in, the second circle represents the city, and the inner circle is the neighborhood or suburb in which I would like to invest. My target, or ideal property, is in the center. This chapter will guide you through the search criteria for each of these concentric circles, ideally resulting in you being able to identify the right properties for you.

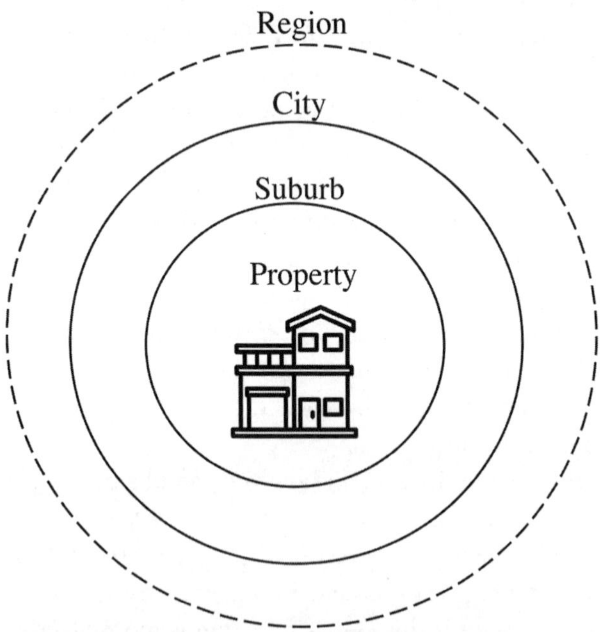

Figure 6-1: Narrowing in on a Property – Concentric Circles

Outer Circle: The Region

The exterior circle is dashed due to its inherent lack of definition. The region is whatever you define it to be. For some, this may be geographic, such as the West Coast, Midwest, East Coast, etc. Others define the region as within a certain time or distance using a specific mode of transportation. The region could also be defined by state, or even within proximity of where you currently reside. My preference is to define a region by the coverage area of my property management company and areas where my team is willing to work. This allows me to maximize the *economy of force*, which is defined below. Regardless, you must determine the boundary of the region for yourself. Your deal finder cannot be the one narrowing down your region; it's too broad of an area for him/her to be effective. I recommend considering the following criteria when establishing your region:

- Climate
- Economy of Force
- Landlord Laws and Regulations
- Natural Hazards

Climate

Why should you care about the climate? Aren't there investment opportunities in all climates? Yes, however, they don't all have the same requirements for maintenance or profit margins. Buying in areas that have frequent precipitation tends to result in more frequent repairs of roofing, siding, and other exterior features. Areas that are warm and damp or humid tend to have more mold and infestation issues than more arid or colder climates. If you choose to own in areas that have a climate that leads to persistent and predictable consequences, you will likely incur additional expenses in the form of more repairs and/or higher insurance premiums.

Economy of Force

Economy of force is one of the nine principles of war used by the military. It pertains to employing all combat power available in the most effective way possible and allocating minimum essential combat power to secondary efforts. Economy of force is the judicious employment and distribution of forces. No part of the force should ever be left without purpose. The allocation of available combat power to such tasks as limited attacks, defense, delays, deception, or even retrograde operations is calculated. This allows strategic action at the decisive point and time for the accomplishment of the objectives.

Establishing your desired region as the area in which your preexisting centers of gravity are capable of working (a.k.a., your sphere of gravity) ensures you are maximizing their efficiency. A location outside of your sphere of gravity doesn't mean the property will be unprofitable; it only means that your processes will likely be less efficient and, therefore, more costly. If multiple opportunities arise outside of the sphere of gravity, another sphere of gravity may need to be established.

Landlord Laws and Regulations

Landlord and tenant laws and regulations govern all aspects of residential rental agreements. These include the rights of the landlord, the rights of the tenant, and the rules upon which both parties must abide. The majority of these rules and regulations do not vary between the fifty states. Some statutes, however, have drastic differences between states, which you will want to know should they impact you as a landlord or an investor. While these statutes are meant to protect all parties, they can sometimes present problems. The statutes that most often come to mind are the ones pertaining to the eviction of tenants (or owners of a foreclosed property). Fair and proper notice regulations tend to differ between locations. Other major statutes to be aware of include those that pertain to discrimination.

> Property management companies and attorneys are great assets to help navigate the complexities of the landlord-tenant statutes. You, however, are ultimately responsible.

If you violate the lease agreement (or if it is drafted incorrectly), a judge may rule portions (or all) of it as unenforceable. At worst, the tenant could hold you responsible and file a lawsuit against you, the landlord. Do yourself a favor and ensure you review the pertinent laws and regulations governing the landlord-tenant relationship for any area in which you are considering investing.

I recommend conducting a quick search of the following site to ensure you are up to date with the necessary information:

American Apartment Owners Association (AAOA)
www.american-apartment-owners-association.org

Natural Hazards

Different areas of the United States have different hazards. Common natural hazards include earthquakes, flooding, high winds and tornadoes, hurricanes, sub-zero temperatures, and wildfires. Less commonly known is the impact these hazards can have on real estate. The FMV of a property accounts for these hazards—and so do the insurance agencies. You need to ensure your budget and profit margin account for the increased cost to insure the residence.

Medial Circle: The City

When people are considering places to live, they typically have two big motivators. Either they move for employment opportunities and then find other enticing aspects to narrow their search, or they move because of an enticing aspect and then look for employment. When homing in on a city or surrounding area to invest in, you should look for the same.

DID YOU KNOW?

In 2015, RealtyTrac concluded a study (initiated in 2005) on natural disaster impacts on real estate. This study determined that 43 percent of residences in the United States are located in a *high-risk* or *very high-risk* area for natural disasters. Furthermore, this study concluded the following:

- Homes located in *very low-risk* to *low-risk* areas appreciated in home sale prices by 9.5 and 6.6 percent respectively.
- Homes in *high-risk* to *very high-risk* areas experienced a decrease in home sale price by 2.5 and 6.4 percent respectively.

Conversely, the study determined that home appreciation in *high risk* and *very high-risk* areas tended to be higher than *low risk* and *very low risk* areas. This is largely due to the correlation that higher risk areas tend to be in places deemed more desirable to live (along the coastline, at the foot of the mountains, etc.)

- *High-risk* and *very high-risk* areas experienced an average appreciation of 16.6 and 20.4 percent respectively between 2012 and 2015.
- *Very low-risk* and *low-risk* areas experienced an average appreciation of 12.8 and 10.1 percent respectively over the same period.

Employment Opportunities

Your future tenants, unless they are rich or retired, are looking for employment. And if they are rich, they most likely are not looking to rent from you. You should research the following factors to evaluate an area's employment opportunity:

- Income and Wages
- Industry
    - Types and Diversification of Jobs
        - High-Growth
        - Stabilizing
- Unemployment

Income and Wages

In any given area, it is good to know that the available jobs are paying well compared to the cost of living. Increasing wages are a great sign, but an abundance of wages that are disproportionately low compared to the price of housing—regardless of availability or quantity—will prevent an increase in housing demand. It creates a work situation that is undesirable, which may result in an undesirable residential situation. Do your research. There are opportunities in this residential climate, but they may or may not be right for you.

> This is an ideal situation for owning Section 8 housing, but that is not advised for novice investors.

Industry

Industry and major businesses are the lifeblood of a city. Without them, cities age, crumble, and die. Look at the city of Detroit. What was once bustling is now old and decaying (however, it is in the process of revitalization). Making sure that you are investing in an area that is robust and healthy is a great way to ensure your wealth isn't taken out to pasture. The best way to do this is to look into the types and diversification of jobs.

Types and Diversification of Jobs

A high causation exists between industry and the types of jobs generated in the surrounding area. In most instances, the surrounding area develops and adapts to complement its major industry. If a major factory is present, the surrounding area will likely have machine shops; large technology giants will likely bring along software companies; and large areas of commerce will frequently have law firms and venture capitalists, etc. The best combination is to have a healthy mix of both high-growth and recession-resistant, or stabilizing, jobs.

High-Growth Jobs

High-growth jobs are those that have a tendency to continue expanding and can generate additional job growth in other subeconomies. They are the successful tech-startup companies, the energy companies, and the biotech companies. If you think of something that you don't need but have a strong desire for, it's that kind of company. They generate growth and create demand not only because they offer employment but also because they are an enticing type of employment for workers with the appropriate skills. If you're looking for a good example within the past decade, look no further than Amazon or Tesla.

> If the economy takes a turn, these jobs are hit the hardest.

Stabilizing Jobs

Stabilizing jobs are employment opportunities that are unlikely to be outsourced or minimized during times of recession. Many investors refer to these types of jobs as recession-resistant, but I prefer to refer to them as stabilizing because they also promote growth opportunities for subeconomies. Stabilizing jobs are generally those that are within the education, government, and health care professions.

> **i** Look for areas that have military installations; they have stable employment and move every few years, resulting in many choosing to rent instead of purchase their residence.

Education

Education in this context refers to higher-level educational institutions. These are institutions, typically colleges and universities, that require highly educated faculty and workers to maintain the facilities of the institution. They also draw students from within and without the surrounding area. Furthermore, subeconomies tend to develop around education institutions. Have you noticed the plethora of restaurants, bars, and retail venues surrounding a college? They market to young adults of various financial means. This stabilizing factor provides diversification of jobs. It also provides a diverse tenant pool for investment properties offered at targeted rates.

> **i** Typically, highly educated tenants take better care of your property and tend to generate higher wages, which enable them to afford higher rents.

Government

The second stabilizing type of employment opportunity is government. Government work is stable employment, which means stable tenants. Recognize the inherent value this provides. Additionally, subeconomic markets (retail, restaurants, and auto dealers) often develop in the surrounding area and neighborhoods.

Do you remember the three branches of government from elementary school? Did you ever imagine they would be pertinent to real estate? The three branches established by the Constitution for the separation of powers are the Legislative (lawmakers), Executive (law enforcers), and Judiciary (law interpreters) branches. Concentration centers of government workers tend to be nearby military installations and state capitals.

Government employees from each of these categories, as well as those from subeconomies, require a residence.

Refer to the table below for examples of jobs from each of the respective branches of government:

LEGISLATIVE

- Senators
- Representatives
- Other members of legislature

EXECUTIVE

- DoD
    - Military
- Civil Service
    - Law Enforcement
    - Medical Professionals
    - Firefighters
- Just about every other government worker you can think of
- Other agencies*

JUDICIAL

- Judges
- Clerks
- State Lawyers
- Other members of the judiciary

* Post office is considered "other agencies"

Figure 6-2: Branches of Government – Employees

Health Care

The third and final stabilizing job type is health care. Large municipal hospitals or specialty care hospitals have major influences on a city's economic health and are a cornerstone of a strong real estate market. Similar to educational institutions, health care facilities require a well-educated staff. They also require workers of all skill levels to ensure the facility operates efficiently.

Unemployment

Another rate you'll want to be aware of is the unemployment rate in an area, specifically in the nearest city and within the neighborhood you're looking at. Unemployment rates require deeper analysis than just "high" or "low." A declining unemployment rate (even if high) is a potential opportunity. An increasing unemployment rate (even if low) may be cause for concern.

Other Enticements

We previously discussed the two driving factors for people to relocate: employment and "other enticing factors." We've detailed considerations and search criteria for positive indicators pertaining to employment. We will now discuss what makes a location enticing.

Many people say, "It is difficult to describe. You just know it when you are present! You can feel it." Those people are correct. This is an area where there may not be a practical reason to drive demand for living there. The location's climb to desirability could be linked to pure luck, such as someone famous or rich liked it. It could have been a convergence of positive micro factors, such as minimal taxes, good weather, low cost of living, business-friendly laws, proximity to geographic features, etc. It's difficult to predict when people are going to hop on a real estate bandwagon and make a location desirable. Don't spend too much effort guessing which location will become famous or popular simply because a group of celebrities said it should be. Focus more on looking for the real estate micro factors that contribute to the demand in any given location.

Up-and-Coming Areas

Up-and-coming is really just a simple way of describing gentrification.[48] This is typically an area that was previously run down for a variety of reasons but recently had a lot of money and effort invested into it to turn it around. The Wharf and National Harbor near Washington, DC, are great examples of this. Years ago, those were unsafe or unpleasant areas to live in. Now, after lowering the crime, removing the drugs, and investing considerable amounts of money, they are becoming locations that people frequent, and properties in these areas now demand top

48 Changing the character of a neighborhood by improving housing and attracting new opportunities while displacing the current inhabitants of an area.

dollar. Purchasing properties within these areas is difficult; however, looking to purchase on "the path to progress" or in the up-and-coming areas can rapidly increase your portfolio's wealth.

> Look for nice restaurants and nice car dealerships; they are usually on the "path to progress."

> Junior investors should be cautious using this method to increase wealth. Identifying these opportunities may not be difficult but timing often is. Poor timing can easily result in you acquiring a property that takes too long to mature and undermines your overall investment strategy.

Hip and Niche

Sometimes there is just something about a place that attracts a certain kind of person. It's often unexplainable yet makes absolute sense at the same time. It's like when you notice that a quarter of the residents in Florida are retirees from Ohio who got tired of gray cloudy skies. Or when you meet a young adult who dreams of moving to New York City although they've never been before (thank you, *Friends*, *Sex in the City*, and *How I Met Your Mother*). Or when you talk to people who love the outdoors and dream about owning a place in Utah. How about the hordes of people who migrated from California to Colorado, coinciding with California raising taxes and Colorado legalizing marijuana? Also, whenever you encounter anyone who lives in Portland, Oregon, and you think, "Yeah, that makes sense."

If you know an area possesses a niche, and you have a lead on a property that fits your investment model and can leverage the character a city offers, acquire the property. Whatever drives people to those places will often also drive them to find a way to afford living in those places. Just make sure you have the reserves needed to weather any storm that may arise (such as an economic depression or a global pandemic).

Direction of Growth

Another investment technique valuable for not only assessing demand but also accelerating your asset appreciation is buying in the *direction of growth*. When cities are growing out or expanding, being among the initial buyers and investors has its advantages. Residences purchased on the leading edge of expansion historically show massive appreciation of value, whereas properties established in developed neighborhoods have already had their value realized. The ability to buy and hold in areas with high demand and signals of strong growth is key to any investor seeking to rapidly increase their equity.

> Look for new interstates, highways, and metros. Cities will not invest in infrastructure unless there are demand signals showing growth. Also, look for major retailers such as Walmart or Target.

Economic and Geographic Barriers

An *economic barrier* exists when real estate is simply too expensive for people to be able to afford, resulting in a search for other, typically nearby, places to live. Colorado Springs is such a location. Prices skyrocketed and outpaced wages between 2013 and 2020. Many within the city could not afford to purchase in the area and could only afford to rent. Landlords could charge rents at equilibrium or higher. Those wanting to buy (or not pay higher rents) sought housing further away, which increased demand in surrounding areas. The economic barrier (combined with a *geographic barrier*) generated a cascading demand for real estate throughout surrounding the area.

A geographic barrier, intuitively, is when a geographic feature makes housing unavailable. This could be a body of water, a mountain (in Colorado Spring's case), other wildlife preserves, or Native American sanctuaries. Geographic barriers impact the real estate market in the same manner as economic barriers: they act as a supply barrier (refer to Figure 1-7), which, therefore, rapidly increases demand as supply decreases.

DID YOU KNOW?

Forbes Advisor posted an online article in 2021 detailing the top "10 Most Affordable Cities" (metro areas with a population of at least 100,000). These cities are currently undervalued and have considerable potential for long-term growth due to various factors, including direction of growth, niche markets, and other enticements. In order, the top 10 include:

Detroit, Michigan
Cleveland, Ohio
Toledo, Ohio
Memphis, Tennessee
Baltimore, Maryland
Rochester, New York
Milwaukee, Wisconsin
Montgomery, Alabama
Buffalo, New York
Kansas City, Kansas

Inner Circle: The Neighborhood/Suburb

Not every neighborhood or suburb of a city will offer the same appeal. You can probably recall the good neighborhoods and the bad neighborhoods from your hometown. When you were a child, the good and bad may have been instinctual or because your family or friends told you so. As an investor, you'll also develop an instinct for identifying good investment areas in which to purchase your properties. That instinct will be built upon by clearly understanding the market and the factors that impact the desirability and availability of real estate.

This level of research is where your deal finder will come in handy.

Buyer's Market vs. Seller's Market

A *buyer's market* is when the available homes in an area exceed the demand for homes in the same area. This is also known as a consumer surplus (refer to Figure 6-3). When this occurs, homes will typically remain on the market for longer durations of time (60+ days). Additionally, the FMV of a property will likely also be less. Conversely, a *seller's market* arises when the demand for a property exceeds the available supply of housing in an area. This is referred to as a producer surplus (refer to Figure 6-4). Homes and rental listings do not stay on the market for extended periods of time (< 30 days), and the FMV is higher than comparable homes. Areas with houses selling between 30–60 days are usually considered neutral, with balanced consumer and producer surplus.

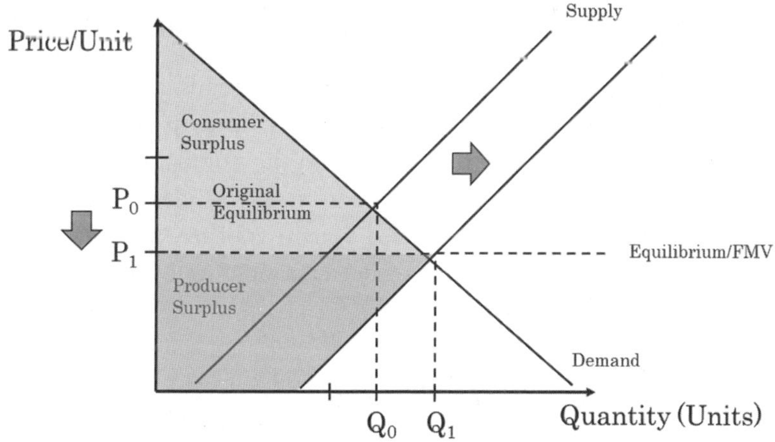

Figure 6-3: Buyer's Market – Increased Supply

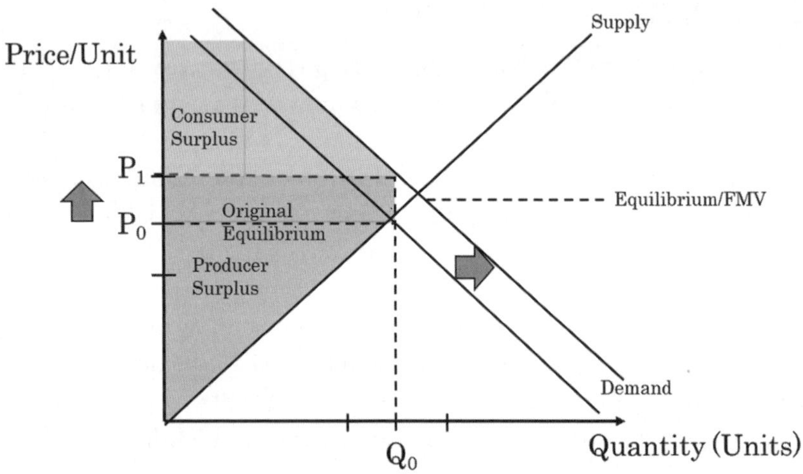

Figure 6-4: Seller's Market – Increased Demand

Sales Volume

Sales volume is a useful metric to determine trends in the market. Research the number of listings within the zip code in which you are looking to invest. Compare that number to the number of listings the previous year as well as the year prior to it. If you identify a notable increase in listed properties from one year to another, you have identified a potential buyer's market. A decrease signifies a shift toward a seller's market.

Determining Desirability and Demand

Determining the demand or desirability for a property is the key component that drives the value of your investment. Therefore, it is also a key determinant in the search for an ideal location. Incorrectly assessing the demand for a property is an error that even some veteran investors succumb to. When conducting an assessment, it is normally best to take a more conservative stance and be pleasantly surprised than to be overly ambitious and overextend. The following are several criteria that should be used in your determination:

Statistics and Scores
Crime Statistics
School Rankings and Statistics
Transit Score
Walkability Score
Metrics and Corollaries
Days on Market
Increasing Rents
Vacancy Periods

Visit our website (masterofleverage.info) to find quick references on where you can research these scores, statistics, and figures for your specific property.

Crime Statistics

Society prepares the crime; the criminal commits it.
—Henry Thomas Buckle, *English historian*

Crime is a critical metric to be aware of as it can directly impact your property's value and has the potential to immediately minimize your profit.

Crime statistics research can be conducted online with relative ease. Look at your medial circle (city level) and then refine your search to garner more specific information for various neighborhoods. The local law enforcement department can help answer questions about specific neighborhoods. In general, you will want to know the types of frequent crimes and the trend of crime occurrences.

I recommend conducting a quick search on the following sites to provide you with the requisite information:

Crime Comparison: www.bestplaces.net/crime
National Sex Offender Public Website: www.nsopw.gov

Research crime before you buy.

School Rankings and Statistics

The quality of the school is among the biggest determinants of consumer demand for a neighborhood. This is a subjective measure. You could simply use the rating provided by most online real estate search engines, or you could invest some time and effort yourself. If choosing to do the latter, look into the following statistics: graduation rates, standardized test scores, and student-to-teacher ratios. Intuitively, you're looking for higher graduation rates and standardized test scores and lower student-to-teacher ratios.

I recommend conducting a quick search of Great Schools (greatschools.org) to provide you with the requisite information."

Establish a trend to determine school rankings.

Transit Score

The development of infrastructure is a well-known yet seldomly considered aspect when determining the demand or desirability of an area. This metric is called the *transit score*, and it is the companion to the *walkability score*. You'll want an area that maintains a high score in at least one of the two, but both are ideal. This transit score generally corresponds to two components: accessibility and quality of thoroughfares for vehicles.

The accessibility component views the ease for commuters to be able to access major thoroughfares; essentially, how far away or how difficult it is to gain access to a highway or interstate. Some individuals enjoy living further away from city centers because it is more private and they can acquire more land for affordable prices. But other individuals enjoy having a short commute to their place of employment. Most will strike a balance between the two.

The quality component is measured in two ways, one of which is the quality of the roads on which residents will commute. No one likes potholes in their streets. Not only do they add wear and tear to vehicles, but they also diminish the overall aesthetics of an area. If not properly managed, a poor road quality can result in a decline in the care people provide and maintain to the neighborhood and its properties.

The other quality factor corresponds to the traffic volume or congestion. No one enjoys being in a traffic jam! If an area is poorly designed to the extent that congestion is a routine issue, residents will take note, and the demand for housing will adjust accordingly.

> The quality of roads and streets is a simple and telling assessment. Cities invest and maintain areas they value.

> Properties adjacent to roads with high traffic volume will appraise for less than comparable properties.

Walkability Score

The ability of pedestrians to commute is a major factor for many potential tenants and buyers. An area's walkability score is determined by societal and industrial factors. Societal factors are those that provide comfort, convenience, or safety. These factors include the following:

- Aesthetics
    - Variety of Buildings
    - Transparency (Aesthetic and Safety Factor)
    - Trees and Other Vegetation
- Air Quality
- Area Density
- Traffic Volume and Speed

Alternatively, industrial factors mainly pertain to the logistics of commuting from one location to another. These criteria include:

- Access to Public (or Mass) Transit
- Access to Footpaths and Walkways
- Buffers to Moving Vehicles (for Pedestrians)
- Proximity to ...
    - Employment
    - Parks
    - Retail Stores
    - Schools
    - Sport Centers
    - Town Centers
        - Bars
        - Restaurants
        - Theaters
- Pedestrian Crossings
- Street Connectivity

I recommend conducting a quick search on the following site to provide you with the requisite information:

Walkability Score: www.walkscore.com

Crime Statistics	School Statistics	Walk / Transit Score	
Low	High	High	A+
Low	High	Low	A
Low	Low	High	B
Low	Low	Low	C
High	High	High	D
High	Low	High	F
High	High	Low	F
High	Low	Low	Hard F

Table 6-1: Crime, School, and Walk/Transit – Grades

Days on Market (DOM)

Days on Market (DOM) is a metric aligned to gauge the FMV of a given property within the target neighborhood. It is a good correlating metric to determine desirability of properties in the market. Markets where similar houses go under contract in a matter of days is a great sign that the residence is either appropriately priced and/or underpriced. It is also a strong demand signal indicating a fast market. Similar residences that go under contract within 30 days is good, and even 60 days is fine. If a property hasn't gone under contract in 90 days, the market has either slowed or the property is overpriced.

Increasing Rents

Increasing rents is another direct corollary of demand for investment properties. Rent rates increasing 2.5–5 percent from year to year is typical in most locations. Rents increasing 5–10 percent or more show signs that supply is limited and demand is increasing. If you invest in this area, your wealth is likely to grow proportionately.

> Consult with your property manager or research online to determine trends in rent prices.

> Be wary about rents increasing 15 percent or more per year. These are signs of a potentially overinflated market.

Vacancy Periods

A more direct corollary to demand for investment properties is the vacancy period of similar residences. A vacancy period is the amount of time between tenants during turnover. A vacancy period of days is ideal, and a vacancy period of fewer than 30 days is good, but vacancy periods greater than 30 days provide cause for further investigation. A longer vacancy period could be caused by any number of reasons. The most common reasons include higher supply/lower demand, rents priced too high for the market, need for renovations between tenants, or possibly poor advertisement/curb appeal. Look for neighborhoods with low vacancy periods.

Determining Availability and Supply

After determining the desirability and demand of a given area, the next logical aspect to research is the supply. If an area has high demand, it will most likely have a moderated supply. Purchasing based upon demand alone will likely be at least a decent investment in the interim. Investors should be looking for what the future supply will likely be to determine whether an area will be a suitable long-term investment; after all, most mortgages are either 15 or 30 years. You'll want to ensure your future investment is stable for at least that long. The best determinant of future supply is analyzing or assessing new construction and the subsequent *absorption*.[49]

New Construction and Absorption

A unique leading indicator that often eludes more junior investors is monitoring new construction. This is different from watching a high rise being erected or new housing developments being built. These are positive indicators, but they are not the leading indicator. Before any of the aforementioned construction and development may commence, building permits must first be issued. Knowing the location and the rate at which the building permits are being issued is like having a crystal ball in which you can see the future. And by the future, I mean the future direction of growth.

Location can only grow out or grow up. Growing out entails increased building and development extending away from a city or neighborhood. In other words, the area is expanding. Growing up entails tearing down existing properties in order to put in place residences that can accommodate a larger occupancy, either high rises or more densely occupied dwellings. Both are signs of an increasing supply of real estate inventory, which is an indicator that supply is lagging behind demand. This presents an ideal investment opportunity for the properly equipped investor.

You will also want to track the absorption rate for the recently developed properties. This will inform you of whether the increased

49 Rate at which newly constructed buildings are occupied (rented or purchased).

construction is a signal for a current shortage or a future surplus. A rapid rate of growth with a negative absorption rate is a recipe for a real estate market dystopia. However, a rapid rate of growth or a stagnated rate of growth with a high positive absorption rate is a euphoric dream.

Target: The Property

Once you've identified a neighborhood that meets all of the above criteria, you're done, right? Wrong. The work you've done to narrow your search has helped you identify potential deals—but they are still only potential. You must do the work to determine whether each property is an actual deal. This determination will be largely contingent upon your overall real estate strategy and numerous other factors covered in the next chapter. Nonetheless, if you are looking to hold and maintain the asset, you will want to use a few, quick determination assessments to see if the asset is worth your time. This requires establishing the *trend of property value* and determining the *Price-to-Rent ratio.*

DID YOU KNOW?

In September of 2013, a survey was conducted by the National Association of Realtors along with Myers Research & Strategic Services to determine what kind of neighborhood people prefer. This study surveyed 1,500 and produced the following results:

When asked to specify the importance of 19 neighborhood characteristics, they indicated the following:
Sidewalks and places to walk – 80 percent
High-quality public schools – 74 percent
Proximity to community area – 69 percent

People would trade yard size if:
Shorter commute to work – 57 percent
Could walk to schools, stores, and restaurants – 55 percent
Could walk to parks and playgrounds – 53 percent

Quick Determination Assessments

Property Value Trend

Establishing the trend of property value entails two steps. The first is to determine the FMV of your home. To do this, you can use either the expedient method or the more thorough method. Which method you use depends upon your level of comfort and risk. Remember, time is your most precious commodity. I recommend using the expedient method for your initial filter, and if the numbers look promising, following up with the more thorough approach.

1. Research the estimated sale price provided on various real estate listing sites (Zillow, Realtor, Trulia, etc.).
2. Identify at least three estimated values and average them. This will provide a rough baseline for your FMV.
3. Adjust the FMV based upon "comps" from identified comparable properties that have sold in the last 60 days (sales comparison approach).

The more thorough approach involves an assessment of various property valuation approaches. These methods include the sales comparison approach, cost comparison approach, and income capitalization approach. An appraiser will provide a professional assessment and determine which approach is most suitable for the evaluated property.

In both the expedient and more thorough approaches, once you've determined the FMV, you will continue with establishing the trend of value.

4. Assess property values of comparable properties from the beginning of the year or the end of the previous year.
5. Take the average of at least three.

6. Calculate the rate of appreciation.
    a. Note: negative R_a denotes depreciation.

$$R_a = (P_{FMV} - P_{FMV\ (previous\ year)})/P_{FMV\ (previous\ year)}$$

7. Combine data with Days on Market (DOM) and Sales Volume and analyze using the paragraph below.

> **i** A shifting market does not always denote positive growth. It simply identifies ideal conditions preceding a high demand market environment.

If you have identified a property that is in either high demand or a seller's market, you've likely found a good investment. If you've identified a property in a buyer's market, a shifting market, or an underpriced market, the property may be a good investment (and some may even be your best investments). However, more in-depth research should be conducted on these opportunities. Avoid properties in low demand or in overpriced or declining markets (unless you're privy to knowledge very few people are aware of that indicates this would be a good investment or unless you're a seasoned investor who can handle more risk).

Sales Volume	Property Price	Days on Market (DOM)	
Up	Up	Low	**High Demand**
Down	Up	Low	**Seller's Market**
Up	Up	High	*Shifting Market*
Down	Down	Low	*Underpriced Market*
Up	Down	Low	*Buyer's Market*
Down	Down	High	Low Demand
Up	Down	High	Market in Decline
Down	Up	High	Overpriced Market

Table 6-2: Sales Volume, Price, and DOM – Evaluation

Price-to-Rent Ratio

The next quick assessment that should be performed is the Price-to-Rent calculation. This calculation is relatively simple:

1. Determine rental demand for a property.
    a. There are several methods you could use to determine the estimated rental price for an asset:
        i. Check out Rentometer.com
            I. Shows an average, median, and other percentiles
        ii. Review online listing companies:
            1. Craigslist
            2. Zillow, Trulia, Redfin, and Realtor.com
        iii. Consult your property manager
        iv. Consult your real estate agent
2. Divide the estimated rent for the property by the FMV of the property to ascertain the Price-to-Rent ratio.

> It's better to have lower rents to ensure a lower vacancy rate.

The 1 Percent Rule

The *1 percent rule* is simply a rule of thumb that states that a property is likely to produce positive cash flow if it would rent for 1 percent of the FMV (or the price you paid for it). This is an important factor for investors looking to hold onto the property as opposed to selling them for quick gains. Put in other terms, say you purchase a property for $100,000. The property should demand a rent of at least $1,000 per month to pass the 1 percent rule.

Note: this is a rule of thumb. Properties that meet this rule are most likely cash flow positive, but they can still produce a negative cash flow (loss). Also, properties that fail this rule may still generate income. Other factors such as insurance, homeowners associations (HOAs), property management fees, and taxes have not been factored into this quick assessment.

As a general rule of thumb, the ideal property for an investor is the worst house in the best area. This property will offer the best opportunity for appreciation while also maintaining demand.

The 2 Percent Rule

I've included the *2 percent rule* only because many readers may ask about it if I didn't. The 2 percent rule states that a property in a "less-than-optimal" market should rent for at least 2 percent of the FMV (or the price you paid for it). Less-than-optimal could mean the property is in a dangerous area (due to drugs and/or crime). Or there may be numerous hazards nearby. Or the area may be stressed, the market in decline, or a number of other potential issues. Be cautious—very cautious—when thinking about investing in this type of market. Usually, in these situations, you will typically pay more than you're expecting. It's just a question of how much. If you find a diamond in the rough within a low-demand market (one that is free from the previously mentioned hazardous conditions), you may be staring at an opportunity. Do your research! If the market is in decline, wait until it bottoms out before thinking about a risky investment opportunity.

Some properties that are low demand may be ideal for Section 8 housing. While inherently riskier, this can be a lucrative endeavor for the more experienced investor.

Objective: Leveraging Location

The approach described in this chapter is merely one of many methods you may employ to narrow your search in pursuit of an investment property. What matters most is that you find a method of locating a property that works for you. If the process described in the chapter overwhelms you, remember that I mentioned various turnkey businesses that specialize in offering comprehensive services. They can do the locating for you, but you will pay for it.

At a minimum, I recommend you define your scope based on your current residence (regardless of ownership). If you are not interested in long-distance investing, this will help you identify the boundary of the area in which you currently or may one day wish to invest. If you are interested in long-distance investing, this chapter will assist you in determining how many centers of gravity you may one day need.

Tasks:

- Determine the region of interest.
  - Assess climate, economy of force, laws, and natural hazards
- Determine the city (or cities) of interest.
  - Assess employment opportunities
  - Assess other enticements
- Determine the neighborhood(s) of interest.
  - Assess desirability and demand
  - Assess availability and supply
- Assess if you're in a buyer's or seller's market.
- Assess the property.
  - Assess the property value trends
  - Assess Price-to-Rent ratios

If while reading this chapter, there were concepts you wished to see that were either not covered or where you desired additional detail, please annotate and provide feedback via this QR code.

Visit our website (masterofleverage.info) by using this QR code to access key figures and references from this chapter.

Aloof Aaron, Cautious Carl, Sensible Sarah, and Risky Rick

Cautious Carl, Sensible Sarah, and Risky Rick adhere to the process of narrowing down and selecting cash-flowing and appreciating properties to acquire. All three investors may easily identify the conditions of a buyer's versus seller's market. Cautious Carl is the shrewdest of the group. He chooses to purchase only properties that are within a three-hour drive of his residence, even if better opportunities are available outside of his selected radius. He selects based upon employment opportunities but not upon other enticements. Sensible Sarah is selective. She defines the area in which she purchases properties by her centers of gravity. Furthermore, she also assesses an area for both employment opportunities as well as various other enticements. Finally, Risky Rick is a little more daring. He elects to purchase properties when he sees an opportunity, even if outside an established area where his centers of gravity exist.

Carl and Sarah adhere to the 1 percent rule, while Risky Rick on occasion will apply the 2 percent rule for properties in less-than-optimal locations. They have each begun to hone their ability to determine current desirability and demand and predict those for the future as well as availability and supply.

Aloof Aaron is currently unaware of these principles and is only focused on his personal desirability and demand.

Chapter 7: Leveraging the Acquisition

> **I will forever believe that buying a home is a great investment. Why? Because you can't live in a stock certificate. You can't live in a mutual fund.**
>
> —Oprah Winfrey, *media executive, TV personality, and philanthropist*

In this chapter, we are going to cover the following:

Turnkey vs. Distressed Properties

- Market Distress
- Personal Distress
- Property Distress

Things You Should Know about a Property

Property Assessment

- Income
- Expenses
- Target Price Range
- Cash Flow
- Appreciation

Determining FMV

Submitting an Offer

- Real Estate Agent vs. FSBO
- Turnkey v. Distressed Properties
- Offer Composition
- Possible Outcomes
- Earnest Money and Contingencies
- Offer Strategies

Have you ever been in a situation where seconds slowed down and took an eternity to pass? This has occurred to me twice. The first time, I was in a rollover accident during an extended tour of duty in the Arctic. I hit a patch of ice, and the truck I was driving went off the road. Its tire dug into the shoulder, and the truck proceeded to flip, two-and-a-half revolutions end over end until it came to a stop. The inside of the vehicle looked like the opening scene from *Deadpool.* My flight chief and I discovered what was roll proof and what wasn't. We both survived with minor bruises and now reminisce. "J," I sometimes remind him, "we flipped that truck!" The second instance was when I purchased a foreclosed property online for the first time. I had seen the exterior, but I had not seen the interior.

Needless to say, buying a property can be both terrifying and exhilarating, full of trepidation and uncertainty, layered with anxiety—good and bad. I'd like to think there wouldn't be much second-guessing, but that simply isn't true. Even if you score a great deal, you may second-guess the ways in which the deal could have been made better. This is a feeling that never subsides; you just learn to control it better so that it does not control you.

This chapter is dedicated to outlining the process leading into and executing the purchase of a home. Hopefully, this chapter equips you with knowledge that minimizes some of the emotions that accompany purchasing property. If you want to leverage this wealth-building strategy successfully, you're going to need to overcome your fear.

Turnkey vs. Distressed Properties

What is the difference between a turnkey property and a distressed property? There are many differences, but the two main ones are the value for which you may be able to purchase the property and the amount of work that will likely be required to restore the property to a livable or rent-worthy state. Turnkey properties require little to no work before a tenant is able to occupy them. These properties are typically sold around FMV, and in competitive markets, they typically sell for above FMV.

Distressed properties may vary in condition; some could be near-turnkey, while others may require major repairs or renovations.

The value at which you may acquire the property is typically lower than the equilibrium price. Let me say that again: the FMV may be less than market equilibrium. This may or may not be a deal. (Just because a property may be purchased under price does not mean it is being purchased under value.) Some distressed properties may require more work than the ARV. Investors should look to acquire properties under value so equity exists the moment they take possession. There are three primary types of distress related to properties: Market Distress, Personal Distress, and Property Distress.

> Make sure your spouse (or significant other) is supportive of ventures in distressed properties. It is not an easy path and requires a lot of commitment.

Market Distress

Market distress is when the market conditions have changed to the extent that a property that was once affordable no longer is due to actions outside the homeowner's control. A common example is if a home was purchased with an adjustable-rate loan and barely within an individual's buying power. If interest rates increased over time, the homeowner could go from just barely making payments to no longer being able to make payments. If they do not have the means to refinance (or cannot secure a better interest rate), they will become motivated sellers and will likely look to forgo potential profit from selling in the current market in an attempt to avoid debt.

Personal Distress

Personal distress is likely the most common reason for distressed properties. The ways in which personal distress can occur are numerous, but they tend to relate to one of the four Ds: dodge, duck, dip, and dive. Wait! Those four Ds apply to dodgeball. The four Ds of property personal distress are a little different:

- Death
- Debt
- Divorce
- Drugs and Alcohol

Unfortunately, these are far more serious than the other Ds. They present situations, however, where the seller is motivated to sell at a discount. The best way to uncover these properties and determine how best to navigate a successful deal is to find out the homeowner's situation. Remember, they are people, and these situations are unpleasant. Don't be overeager to exploit their loss for your benefit. Find the win-win. Explain how it helps them and work quickly.

> Interacting with properties involving personal distress is often a time-consuming, emotionally draining, and frustrating task. You need to be thick-skinned and resilient. Understand that people who are drowning will do anything not to drown, and that may include trying to take you with them.

Property Distress

Property distress tends to arise when a physical issue with the property exists. Some common issues that result in this form of distress include abandonment, fire damage, extensive water damage, issues with the foundation, failed remodels, or hazards on the property. These are typically the situations where an investor should anticipate more costly repairs and renovations. These are also the properties that may be purchased well under value and can be opportunities for a rapid generation of equity. These opportunities may also be the most challenging for novice investors due to the limited financing options available for full-rehab endeavors.

Distressed properties do not appear on the MLS, so your real estate agent may not be as much help in searching as they would be for turnkey properties. You will need to leverage other sources such as attorneys, fellow investors, or wholesale agents to find these deals. Usually (but not exclusively), the best way to find them on your own is by one of these main venues:

- Auctions and Sheriff Sales
- Real Estate Owned (REO), Short Sales, Notices of Default (NODs)/Tax Liens
- Property in Disrepair

Auctions and Sheriff Sales

Lenders foreclose when a homeowner is not able to maintain their monthly mortgage payments. The foreclosure is the act of the bank or lending institution that is repossessing the property. The bank, on many occasions, may attempt to sell the property via auction or sheriff's sale to recoup the debt incurred by the defaulted loan. Auctions may be held in person or online.

> Some states have statutes limiting a property from being sold for less than a certain percentage of its listed value. For example, Ohio's limit is 66 percent.

> Some auctions will inflate the valuation of a property in efforts to drive up the bids for the property. A higher valuation mandates a higher minimum accepted bid, which also diminishes profits for any investor pursuing the property.

Real Estate Owned (REO), Short Sales, and Notices of Default (NODs)/Tax Liens

REO is the term for real estate that is held in possession of the bank. This could be a property that has not yet gone to auction or that did not sell at auction. The lending institution then retains the option to sell the property for a loss as a short sale, believing that recouping some of the debt is better than recouping none. Finally, *Notices of Default (NODs)* and *tax liens* are filed when a homeowner has gone into default prior to the home being foreclosed upon (pre-foreclosure). There is still time for the homeowner to turn their situation around or make arrangements that minimize damage to their credit. This is the opportune window for angel investors to assist homeowners in distress.

Properties in Disrepair

Everyone knows the house in their neighborhood that just simply isn't as well kept as the others. The grass is longer, the paint is peeling, the shutter is crooked, and no one has fixed it in three weeks. The sun just doesn't shine as brightly on that one property. These are subtle indicators that the house may be distressed for any number of reasons. If it hasn't appeared for auction and no NODs or liens are listed, the property may be undesired or unmanaged by the owner. In this case, they may be glad to find an investor who is willing to help them part ways with the property for minimal compensation. These are the properties in which it is imperative to understand the homeowner's situation to best negotiate terms that are agreeable to all parties.

Things You Should Know about a Property

When pursuing a turnkey property and most definitely when pursuing a distressed property, there are several things of which you should be aware:

- Amount Owed
- Homeowner's (or Business Entity's) Name
- Homeowner's Situation
- Lien-Holder Information
- Property Condition
- Property FMV

While much of this information may be irrelevant when purchasing a turnkey property at FMV, it may help in price negotiations. And this information is crucial when negotiating a purchase price for properties in distress.

Amount Owed

Knowing how much is owed on the property can be useful in numerous ways. First and foremost, it is the cornerstone of your bargaining position. Unless the property is a bank-owned REO, the absolute minimum a seller is likely to accept is their remaining balance on the property. Lending institutions possessing a property may accept a short sale to relinquish the asset from their liabilities.

Homeowner's (or Business Entity's) Name

You aren't going to make it very far in the detective business if you can't get the name of a property owner. The owner's name and the property ID/lot number are the lynchpin pieces of information to which all other pieces are tied. This is often the first step to finding the pertinent information required to construct an offer as well as reach out to the member if the property is not already listed on the market.

Homeowner's Situation

Life has few absolutes, but an important one is that everyone has a story. Akin to people, properties have stories as well. The best way to find the diamond in the rough is to get to know the homeowner's situation, the circumstances surrounding the property, and the homeowner's desires. There are many instances in which the homeowner is simply looking to be rid of a problem (the property) and will accept an offer that covers (or mitigates) their expenses. This is the ideal win-win solution that may be successfully negotiated when you combine this knowledge with how much is owed on the property.

Lien-Holder Information

When pursuing distressed properties (especially from personal distress), it is common for additional entities other than the lending institution to have a lien against the property. The transfer of the property from the former owner to you also transfers the liens on the property. An individual may take possession of a property at a discount by leveraging their lien position. These methods are not covered within this book. Do not let their opportunity be to your detriment!

> Ensure you conduct a title search and check for all liens on the property.

Property Condition

The reason for wanting to know the property's condition should be clear: you want to know what you are getting yourself into. Is the property nearly turnkey and requires little work before it is rent-ready, or is the property in a state of disarray and in dire need of tender loving care? While not common, distressed properties can be in great condition, but you never know until you look. Always do your research! The next chapter covers the rehab process in extensive detail so you can better understand the state of the property.

Property FMV

The FMV of a property may be calculated in a few different manners, all of which will be covered shortly. As a buyer—and more importantly, as an investor—you want to know if you are purchasing a property that is underpriced or overpriced and under value or over value. Properties purchased under price may not be under value. Properties purchased under value will have immediately established equity. The next section covers what you should look for when assessing a property. Part of this assessment is determining the FMV of a property.

Property Assessment

Properly assessing a property for profitability is paramount. Failure to do so will result in frustration, loss of opportunity, and in the worst-case scenario, the loss of your accumulated wealth. Note that the property assessment should be conducted after narrowing your search based upon your criteria established in Chapter 6. Determining the affordability (for homeowners) or profitability (for investors) of a property can be accomplished by assessing the following factors:

- Income
- Expenses
    - Monthly Expenses
    - Out-of-Pocket Expenditures
- Appreciation

DID YOU KNOW?

According to Zillow's Home Value Index:

- The average value for a "typical" home in the United States is $354,165.
- The average home value in the United States increased 9.9 percent from February 2020 to February 2021.
- The average home value in the United States increased 19.8 percent from June 2021 to June 2022.

According to the United States Census Bureau:

- In 2019, 5.34 million existing homes were sold, compared to 682,000 newly-constructed homes.[50] [51]

According to the National Association of Realtors:

- In 2018, FSBO sales constituted 8 percent of home sales.
- Forty-six percent did not actively market the home.

50 "Existing-Home Sales," National Association of Realtors, accessed October 4, 2022, https://www.nar.realtor/research-and-statistics/housing-statistics/existing-home-sales.

51 "New Residential Sales," United States Census Bureau, accessed October 4, 2022, https://www.census.gov/construction/nrs/index.html.

Income

For the homeowner, income includes any combination of salary, income from self-employment, child support, social security, disability, and/or retirement. If he or she is married, it could also include the spouse's salary. For the investor, rent from the property is also part of the equation. Otherwise, the investment will have a negative Debt-Service Coverage Ratio (DSCR). Equity may still be generated in this situation, but the property will not provide cash flow, and therefore, no capital will be generated.

Expenses

Expenses should include any expenditures for living in or maintaining the property. This list of expenses is numerous—a fact that renters are seldom aware of and that homeowners are intimately cognizant of. Expenses should be partitioned into two categories, monthly and out of pocket. Monthly expenses include the following:

- Principal and Interest (P&I)
- Taxes
- Property Insurance
- *Utilities
- *Property Management
- *Capital Expenditures (CAPEX)
- *Condo/Homeowners Association (COA/HOA)
- *Vacancies

> For homeowners, the rule of thumb for monthly expenses is no more than 28 percent. For investors, assess ROI and ROF.

Principal and Interest (P&I)

The principal and interest (P&I) is the monthly expense owed to the lending institution for assuming the mortgage loan. The ratio of principal to interest shifts over the life of the loan; however, in a fixed mortgage loan, the amount stays the same.

Taxes

Yes, the dreaded taxes. The government requires homeowners to pay property taxes, which are a levy against land and property used as income for local and state governments.

> P&I combined with Taxes and Property Insurance is typically referred to as PITI.

Property Insurance

Think you can own a home without insurance? Think again. Property insurance is what covers the property and provides protection against many risks associated with home ownership. The standard inclusions are fire, theft, and potentially weather-related damages (flood, earthquake, etc.). There are normally three elements to a policy as well as three types of policies. The standard elements include:

- Damage
- Liability
- Additional Living Expenses

Damage

A *damage policy* provides protection from disasters and vandalism. Damages originating from unique weather-related events (such as earthquakes or floods) may require separate insurance. Unattached structures (detached garages, sheds, etc.) may also require separate riders to the policy.

Liability

Liability coverage protects you from lawsuits that could be filed by tenants (or anyone else on the property).[52] This includes coverage if something happens to them on a property you own.

Additional Living Expenses

This type of coverage reimburses the owner for incidental costs (rent, lodging, meals, etc.) incurred during the interim when the property is uninhabitable.

The three types of insurance are the following:

- Actual Value
- Replacement Cost
- Extended Replacement Cost

Actual Value

Actual value policies cover the cost of the property and the value of your possessions after deducting for depreciation.[53]

Replacement Cost

Replacement value policies cover the cost of the property and the value of your possessions without deducting for depreciation.

Extended Replacement Cost

The *extended replacement cost policy* covers the cost required to repair or rebuild the home. This policy is ideal in the event that construction

52 To learn more about liability coverage, read this article: Julia Kagan, "Liability Insurance: What It Is, How It Works, Major Types," Investopedia, last modified June 21, 2022, https://www.investopedia.com/terms/l/liability_insurance.asp.

53 To learn more about depreciation, read this article: Alicia Tuovila, "Depreciation," Investopedia, last modified June 27, 2022, https://www.investopedia.com/terms/d/depreciation.asp.

costs have increased since the time when the property was initially constructed.

Utilities

Some properties do not have individually metered utilities (water, electricity, heat, etc.). In these circumstances, it is not uncommon for the landlord/property owner to pay these expenses on behalf of the tenant. The rent may be inflated commensurately to compensate; however, the tenants are not billed for the utilities directly. In these situations, the utilities are considered an expense.

Property Management

I have already covered property management services in Chapter 5. Most property managers will charge two fees: a *leasing fee* and a *service fee*. The leasing fee is an upfront fee for finding a tenant when a vacancy occurs. This ranges in value but is typically between a half and a full month's rent. The service fee is typically a recurring monthly fee, and the standard is between 7 and 10 percent of the monthly rent. Some property managers will lower the service fee percentage if you have achieved *economies of scale*[54] using their services.

Capital Expenditures (CAPEX)

These are expenditures required for big-ticket items/repairs. Specifically, these are funds used to maintain or improve assets, such as properties or land. Ideally, these expenses will not be required in the short- or mid-term future; however, they will likely be required at some point during your ownership of the property. Smaller repairs are included within operating expenses (OPEX), so typically, capital expenditures include larger items such as a new roof, a new HVAC, repairs to the foundation or driveway, or other large expenses.

54 Cost advantages obtained by size or scale of operations.

Condo/Homeowners Association (COA/HOA)

Many properties have owner associations. These are fees charged to homeowners for maintaining common areas within a building or neighborhood. If in a shared building, these fees cover from the studs out, meaning any damage that occurs to the exterior of a property is covered by the owners association. Any damage to the interior is covered by the owner. Customarily, these fees also cover lawn and garage maintenance as well as membership to the community gym and pool if available.

Vacancies

Any experienced landlord or real estate investor will know that properties are never 100 percent occupied. Ideally, you find tenants who are looking to reside in your property for a long period of time, which would minimize any vacancy costs. I refer to the vacancy as a cost because of the associated fees in turnover (property management fees, repairs, etc.) combined with a lack of rent to offset the expenses.

> The rule of thumb for investors is to set aside 10 percent of monthly rental income for repairs and anticipated vacancies.

Out-of-Pocket Expenditures

Out-of-pocket expenditures include those the borrower (homeowner or investor) must pay up front to acquire the property. This typically includes the down payment, closing costs, and any associated *holding costs*.

- Down Payment
- Closing Costs
- Holding Costs

Down Payment

I addressed the down payment in Chapter 3. The amount of the down payment could vary from no money down to more than 30 percent depending upon the type of loan. Any borrower seeking to purchase a property using credit must have enough capital to cover this amount of money in addition to the other out-of-pocket expenditures. Otherwise (depending on the type of loan), the borrower may leverage DPA programs or receive gifts from family or friends to cover the expense.

Closing Costs

I also addressed closing in Chapter 3. Like the down payment, the borrower must have enough capital to cover the closing costs for the lending institution. Alternatively, the borrower may leverage DPA programs, receive a gift from family or friends, or negotiate with the seller to pay closing costs.

Holding Costs

Novice investors often overlook holding costs. These costs are those associated with owning the property before income may be garnered to offset the expenses. You must budget and account for these as an out-of-pocket expense. The typical holding costs may include (but are not limited to):

- Principal, Interest, Taxes, and Insurance (PITI)
- Utilities
- *COA/HOA
- *Hard Money Lender Fees
- *Other Extraneous Expenses and Fees

Appreciation

Finally, appreciation is a factor I would encourage investors and homeowners alike to assess. While not necessary to calculate current profitability, projecting appreciation gives you a glimpse of future profitability and investment outcome. Some real estate sites (Realtor, Redfin, Zillow, etc.) provide estimates on the likely appreciation of properties within a zip code. I recommend you conduct a more targeted assessment using the calculations provided earlier in this book. Consider these factors: 1) choose properties within a half mile of the subject property that have sold within the past couple of months and 2) compare these properties sold over the last four years (in annual intervals) to garner at least five plot points in your trend.

These inputs will enable you to calculate the following values, which you will ultimately use to assess affordability and/or profitability:

- Cash Flow
- ROI
- ROE
- Target Price Range

If you believe the process of purchasing a property is hellish, let these values be your Virgil—your guide through hell and purgatory.

Cash Flow

Cash flow is the simple deduction of all expenses from income. A positive number indicates a positive cash flow; a negative number indicates a negative cash flow. I recommend two calculations: 1) *projected cash flow* and 2) *actual cash flow*. Projected cash flow should include vacancy costs. Actual cash flow is retroactive and uses expenses and income actually accrued.

Return on Investment (ROI) and Return on Equity (ROE)

I addressed ROI and ROE in Chapter 2. If the cash flow is positive, assess the ROI and ROE of each property against that of other properties you are considering. Cash flow is an assessment of profitability today, while ROI is an assessment of recouping expended capital, and ROE is an assessment of profit efficiency. Be sure to select an asset with profitability ratios that fit your investment strategy.

DID YOU KNOW?

In February 2021, Redfin reported a decline of 40 percent in active property listings (compared to February 2020) across the United States. In January 2021, Realtor.com conducted a similar study that revealed a 42.6 percent decrease in listings, which is roughly 443,000 fewer homes than the previous year. This is what a shortage looks like! (See Chapter 1.)

When combined with historically low interest rates driving up potential affordability and, therefore, demand, the perfect storm becomes a dwindling supply and burgeoning demand—in other words, a highly competitive seller's market.

In these situations, it is important to:

1. Make a strong offer up front.
2. Be persistent and expand your search criteria.
3. Understand that you may be outbid by cash buyers.

Target Price Range (How Much House Can You Afford?)

Determining the target price range for property acquisition is subjective. The borrower's individual circumstances and intentions for the property dictate this figure. Some principles, such as out-of-pocket expenditures and monthly expenses, apply both to investors and to individuals seeking to own their primary residence, while others are tailored. For both groups, the out-of-pocket expenditures will be the main expense. The cash flow will determine your ability to maintain the property. The DTI will determine your ability to procure additional funding.

Primary residence homeowners should look to have a property where monthly expenses are around 28 percent of their total income. Additionally, their DTI should not breach 43 percent. Borrowers risk overextending or encountering issues procuring additional loans if they exceed these ratios. Finally, the borrower must be able to afford or acquire the funds for the out-of-pocket expenditures.

Investors should ensure the property has positive cash flow and that their DTI does not exceed 43 percent if they are anticipating leveraging conventional loans for other endeavors. They must also be able to afford the associated out-of-pocket expenditures.

Determining FMV

There are a few methods an investor might use to determine the FMV of a property; some are more expedient, while others are more effective but come at a cost. Use your time and energy wisely by starting with the expedient, and if the preliminary numbers work out, work your way toward the most effective methods. The most expedient (but also the least reliable) method is to use the cost estimates provided on various online real estate sites (Realtor, Redfin, Trulia, and Zillow). I typically research the four and take the average as my baseline. As previously stated, if the preliminary numbers check out, you may elect to hire an appraiser or consult a real estate agent. Whether you elect to hire a professional or perform the valuation yourself, there are three main methods you may use to determine value:

- Market Data (Sales Comparison) Approach
- Cost Approach
- Income Capitalization

> When performing your valuation, conduct all three and use the most conservative approach. When making an offer, you can leverage this figure, and when refinancing, you will minimize most surprises (appraisers love to take the most conservative estimate).

Market Data (Sales Comparison) Approach

This comparison approach assesses similar properties that have sold within the past few months in proximity (generally a half-mile radius) of the subject property. The valuation takes into account the various features a property may possess. With this comparison method, the property would be assessed against other properties on the basis of their amenities: the number of bedrooms and bathrooms, type of flooring, type of siding, size of yard, swimming pool, patio/deck, or any number of other amenities.

Cost Approach

The cost approach assesses the average price per square foot of properties in the nearby area (half-mile to mile radius) and multiplies that figure by the total square feet. You can easily find the cost per square foot of recently sold properties on any mortgage listing site (Realtor, Redfin, Trulia, Zillow).

Income Capitalization

This method assesses and estimates the value of real estate based on the rental demand and the anticipated resale value. Note: this valuation method is typically reserved for commercial real estate or multifamily properties (more than four units). This comparison approach is calculated by the following equation:

$$V_{alue} = \frac{N_{et\ Operating\ Income}}{C_{apitalization\ Rate}}$$

Calculate the *capitalization rate* by dividing the average net operating income (for nearby commercial real estate) by the average value of nearby commercial real estate.

Submitting an Offer

For most opportunities, there comes a time when you eventually need to either ask the question or walk away. Choose wisely but be decisive. If there is a lot of competition (or if you're pursuing something highly desirable), you may not have much time to make or submit an offer. You should consider some of the nuances involved with using a real estate agent when engaging directly with an owner listing the property as for sale by owner (FSBO) or even when attempting to purchase a property that is not on the market. However, the process is mostly the same.

Real Estate Agent vs. For Sale by Owner (FSBO)

The biggest advantage of using a real estate agent is the knowledge they provide, their access to the MLS, and the ease of having them arrange and file the abundance of paperwork. Some owners may elect to forgo using a real estate agent; such is the case with FSBO. As a buyer, if you locate a property you wish to purchase that has not been listed with an agent, you may elect to persuade the seller to engage as FSBO to better negotiate the price. Real estate agents typically collect between 3 to 4 percent (per side of the negotiation, 6 to 8 percent total). You may negotiate a lower purchase price for yourself as the buyer, along with a higher take-home profit for the seller.

Turnkey vs. Distressed Properties

Most turnkey properties are going to demand purchase prices ranging from just below to far above FMV. Always assess the numbers to determine if the purchase price and the profitability ratio work for you. There are times (in a competitive market) when the purchase price is inflated and the FMV has increased. This doesn't necessarily mean the property isn't profitable; it just may have changed from great to good.

You should always acquire distressed properties for less than market value. There is no telling what issues will arise when acquiring a distressed property. It is better to plan for the worst—and I mean the worst—but hope for the best. After all, if done correctly, acquiring distressed properties is not only your best opportunity for rapid generation of equity but also a communal benefit because it removes a potential blight from the neighborhood. Your benevolence could provide you with additional leads where neighbors will seek you out and provide you with information on other properties in the neighborhood that could use an adjustment.

> If possible, try to be all in for 75 percent ARV or less. This includes purchase price, renovations, transaction costs, and holding costs. This will ensure you have immediate equity in the property and provide you a buffer if something goes wrong. It also adds the possibility of procuring an income-generating asset after having an immediate 100 percent ROE.

Offer Composition

An offer contains a few standard components. It typically includes the following:

- Parties Involved
- Property/Asset Description
- Sale Price
- Terms of Financing
- Closing Date
- Contingencies
- Other Details and Terms

Describing the *parties involved* is as simple as detailing who is making the offer (the buyer) and who is receiving the offer (the seller). The name of the property and the lot number typically comprise the property or *asset description*. The *sale price* is the agreed-upon transaction amount. The *terms of financing* are the disclosure of how the borrower intends to finance the purchase of the property (see Chapter 3). The seller is often interested in this detail because it indicates: 1) the likeliness of a successful transaction and 2) the timeliness of the transaction because financing typically requires additional time. The *closing date* is also another indicator of how long the transaction can take. The date of closing is typically negotiable.

Contingencies are a necessary and influential part of the offer. These are the clauses that enable the buyer to lawfully back out of the deal without consequence. The contingencies will be elaborated upon shortly. Finally, you and the seller should also include any other details or terms. This may entail a clause about keeping appliances, resolving an encroachment,[55] necessary repairs, move-out dates, or any other ancillary requests.

Possible Outcomes

Once you submit an offer, three outcomes can occur: The seller will accept (hooray!), counteroffer, or reject. If the seller accepts the offer, you're in and on to the next phase of performing due diligence[56] before signing the contract. This is also the time when you need to secure lending if you haven't done so already. If the seller provides a counteroffer (typically referred to as a *counter*), they have rejected your initial offer and provided you with another. You are now in negotiations; you can either accept or continue to negotiate terms if they are willing. Finally, the seller could reject your offer. This could either be a soft rejection or a hard rejection. If listed with an agent or FSBO, they are looking to sell, just not at the price you offered. In this case, they haven't offered a counter. They are looking to see what they can get for their property, or they are sticking to their guns. If you find yourself in this situation, stick to the numbers. If the numbers work, proceed, but if they do not, walk away.

> Closing costs, home warranty, contingencies, earnest money, appliances, move-out date, rent collection, utility transfer, and necessary repairs are all excellent terms that can be used during negotiations to sweeten the deal for both parties until settling on agreed-upon terms.

55 Part of one property (within its property line) protruding into another property line.

56 Steps taken to ensure all legal requirements are met when purchasing or selling an asset.

Earnest Money

The *earnest money* is a good-faith deposit provided by the buyer to indicate that they are serious about the offer and intend to purchase the asset. It's an insurance of sorts that compensates the seller should the buyer back away from the acquisition prior to signing the contract (unless the reason for withdrawal pertains to a *contingency*). If a withdrawal is due to a failed contingency, the earnest deposit is returned to the buyer. Customarily, the amount of earnest money is 1 to 2 percent of the purchase price. The earnest money requirement is standard when working with a real estate agent; however, it may be negotiated (or even excluded) when working with owners of distressed properties or properties listed as FSBO. If the parties consummate the transaction, the earnest money is rolled into the funds required for closing.

Contingencies

A contingency is a legal provision that enables a buyer to back out or terminate a contract to purchase an asset without forfeiture of the earnest deposit or any other legal repercussion. There are typically three standard contingencies in an offer, but these may be waived. They include the following:

- Inspection Contingency
- Appraisal Contingency
- Loan Contingency

> The buyer may include additional contingencies; however, this decreases the competitiveness of the offer.

Inspection Contingency

This provision allows for an inspection to assess the property and identify any issues that may reside within it. The standard duration is 10 days for an inspection to be conducted. After this time elapses, this contingency is no longer available. You'll want to have a professional appraiser inspect during this period and annotate any and all deficiencies so that you are aware of any expenses you might incur after taking possession. If substantial work is required, you may wish to renegotiate the price. If the seller declines, you may walk away without penalty.

Appraisal Contingency

This provision allows a buyer to back out of the contract should the property appraise to a value less than the purchase price of the contract. Customarily, the parties will renegotiate the price down to the appraised value of the property (unless when using a cash offer or in a competitive market). Alternatively, some lending institutions will provide funding if the buyer/borrower funds the difference between the appraised value and the purchase price as part of the down payment.

Loan Contingency

The loan contingency is a provision established to protect the buyer in the event that the financing falls through. This is the contingency the seller has the least ability to mitigate; hopefully, the owner is aware of any deficiencies to the property and should be aware of the property's estimated value, but the buyer's ability to secure a loan is entirely out of their control. This is part of the reason cash offers are as competitive as they are; they enable the buyer to waive this provision and further secure the seller.

Offer Strategies

There are several tricks of the trade that help make an offer more competitive. If competition is high, you may want to employ some of these techniques to get the upper hand. Use any combination that fits the market and fits your style of negotiation. There is no one way to go about negotiating an offer; it's truly an art. The following six techniques are those that have worked successfully with most of the real estate investing community:

- Early Bird
- Cash Offer
- Best Offer Up Front
- Pre-Approval Letter
- Escalation Clause
- More Earnest Money

Early Bird

Most people are familiar with the phrase, "the early bird gets the worm." Sometimes deals happen quickly and the only difference between who gets the deal and who doesn't is who gets there first. I've seen deals close in a matter of hours—the fastest being just minutes after listing. It doesn't matter if other offers are more competitive if they select yours first.

Cash Offer

> If you have the capital, provide cash offers to increase your competitiveness; cash-refinance after the seasoning period to recoup your capital.

Cash offers afford the most flexibility to the buyer and are at times necessary to consummate the deal. This is especially true when pursuing properties that do not allow for standard financing, such as distressed properties or other properties requiring extensive work, or properties that are out of compliance with code and regulations. Because of these factors and others, cash is king. Let me emphasize this point one more time:

CASH IS KING!

Best Offer Up Front

The most efficient approach (necessary in competitive markets) is to submit your best offer up front. If your offer is more enticing right off the bat, the seller may be more inclined to notionally accept your offer and negotiate with only you for purchase. Additionally, submitting your best offer up front is beneficial because trying to lowball the seller always runs the risk of agitating the seller. While lowballing should be expected if the property is less desirable (for any number of reasons), it should not be abused.

Pre-Approval Letter

Offering a *pre-approval letter* is always a good practice. This helps dissuade the seller of fears that the buyer will not be able to obtain financing. This is also why it is best to have pre-approval prior to submitting an offer for a property.

Escalation Clause

The *escalation clause* is a provision the buyer elects to include that states the buyer will increase their bid (automatically) to an increment (normally $1,000) above the most competitive bidder. Ordinarily, the buyer includes a ceiling price on the escalation clause (the price that they will not exceed). For example, a buyer might place a bid for $100,000 with an escalation clause of $1,000 over competitor submissions, up to $110,000.

More Earnest Money

Finally, if the earnest deposit is meant to convey the seriousness of the buyer, fronting additional earnest money conveys that the buyer is extra serious and more invested in purchasing the property. If, as a buyer, you have no reservations pertaining to the purchase of the property (and you have secured funding), increasing the earnest deposit is an easy way to increase the competitiveness of your offer.

As a reminder, if using financing, loans have various levels of competitiveness within themselves. The following chart provides a quick reference to the competitiveness of the various funding sources.

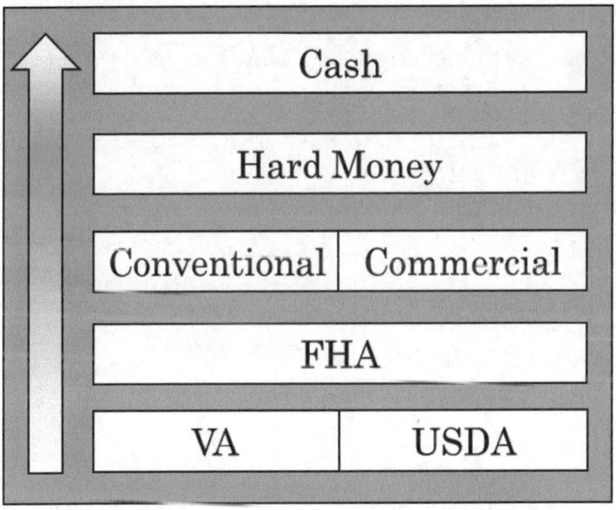

Figure 7-1: Terms of Financing Competitiveness

As a home buyer or potential real estate investor, you should know the competitiveness (or lack thereof) associated with the terms of financing you elect to leverage.

Objective: Leveraging the Acquisition

There are numerous approaches to determining what property you want to buy, and the key to all of them is preparedness. Waiting to establish your readiness until after you have found a property will likely result in your failure to acquire the desired asset. Ideally, you have already identified the area in which you would like to purchase or invest, ensured you are financially sound and creditworthy, ensured you have or can secure lending, and gathered your team. But it's hard to do more in advance of an acquisition other than to be ready.

This chapter is a guide for those next steps once you've identified your asset. Follow these tasks to conduct your quick assessments that will provide you with enough information to make an informed decision, ideally enabling you to acquire an asset at or under value.

Tasks:

- Decide if pursuing a turnkey and/or distressed property.
    - If distressed property, determine cause of distress

- Assess property pertinent details.
    - Amount owed
    - Condition
    - FMV
    - Homeowner's situation
    - Property situation

- Conduct a property assessment.
    - Income and expenses
    - Expenditures
    - Costs
    - ROI and ROE
    - Target price range

- Submit an offer.

If while reading this chapter, there were concepts you wished to see that were either not covered or where you desired additional detail, please annotate and provide feedback via this QR code.

Visit our website (masterofleverage.info) by using this QR code to access key figures and references from this chapter.

Aloof Aaron, Cautious Carl, Sensible Sarah, and Risky Rick

Cautious Carl, Sensible Sarah, and Risky Rick have all thoroughly researched the process of acquiring a turnkey (or nearly turnkey) property. Sensible Sarah has also studied the nuances of the various distressed properties as well as the methods to acquire them. Risky Rick understands these methods but struggles to locate and identify distressed properties. Cautious Carl refrains from acquiring distressed properties, as he finds them to be too risky.

Carl, Sarah, and Rick have become astute at identifying the details (amount owed, owner's name and situation, as well as the overall condition of a potential property). They are each honing their ability to assess a property to better determine FMV.

They each take differing approaches to submitting offers on properties. Carl never waives any of the contingencies. Risky Rick routinely waives contingencies in an attempt to increase his offer's competitiveness and ensure he is able to consummate the acquisition. Sarah is deliberate in her approach to deciding if and when she will waive any of the contingencies for turnkey properties. Both Sarah and Rick are fully aware that contingencies are often waived when acquiring distressed properties.

I think you understand Aloof Aaron at this point. He continues lacking a desire to look toward his future.

Chapter 8: Leveraging the Rehab

Plan and prepare for every possibility, and you will never act. It is nobler to have courage as we stumble into half the things we fear than to analyze every possible obstacle and begin nothing. Great things are achieved by embracing great dangers.
—Xerxes, *King of kings of the Persian Empire*

In this chapter, we are going to cover the following:

Rehabbing Points of Note

Necessities and Niceties

Conducting a Walk-Through

Annotations, Developing Objectives and Tasks

Contractor Bids

Disclosure of Work, Bid Negotiations, Accepting the Bid

Exterior Rehab Components

Roofing, Gutters, Siding, Paint, Decks/Porches, Garage, Landscaping, Septic, Concrete

Interior Rehab Components

Plumbing, Electrical, HVAC, Framing and Insulation, Drywall, Carpentry, Paint, Cabinets and Countertops, Flooring

Miscellaneous Components

Demolition, Permits, and Inspections

Forced Appreciation

Not every property you encounter will be turnkey. Most properties will require at least minor work prior to being ready for new tenants. Even properties you already own will eventually require some repairs, hopefully minor. This chapter will provide a cursory review of the various rehab and renovation components should you elect to undergo these on your own or take on the project manager role yourself. If you're a novice, hopefully you won't need much from this chapter. If you're ready for bigger challenges and opportunities for bigger rewards, this chapter will be immensely beneficial.

Rehabbing a property that is distressed and can be acquired for beneath FMV is a phenomenal way to rapidly appreciate the available equity in your portfolio. For example, let's assume you identify a property in distress that is worth $200,000 ARV/FMV and that you acquired the property for $100,000. You estimate closing costs to be $5,000 and estimate the rehab will cost $40,000. The available equity and immediate profit would resemble the following:

ARV/FMV:	$200,000
75% LTV:	$150,000
Purchase Price:	– $100,000
Rehab Cost:	– $40,000
Closing Costs:	– $5,000
Available Equity:	$5,000

In this example, the investors increased their equity by $5,000 and gained an income-generating property in the process. This chapter is your guide to being able to better estimate, assess, and prepare for the interior and exterior renovation costs.

Good property management will offer services ranging from minor repairs to extensive rehabs and renovations.

Rehabbing Points of Note

I feel it is important to note that not all rehabs cost the same, even if the exact same work is being performed. This is my primary impetus for not including pricing for labor and materials in this book. Prices often vary for a myriad of reasons, but in the end, it all comes down to supply and demand. Some of the determinants for pricing include the following:

- Location
- Season
- Skill and Demand for Contractors
- Specifics to the Property
- Quality of Material

Location

Location may or may not be a determinant of pricing; it depends on the work being performed and the material required. It is a determinant when an area does not naturally have easy access to a type of material and/or there are impediments that must be overcome. For example, material costs in Hawaii may be higher because the materials aren't naturally manufactured on the island and must be transported by air or freight.

Season

Varying climates also play a factor in pricing. Adverse seasons can exacerbate the locational impediment (e.g., trying to deliver materials to Alaska in the winter). But the more likely (and less drastic) example is hiring an HVAC technician in the dead of winter. Supply is stable, but demand is higher, so the price is higher. Similarly, demand for contract work in the spring and summer (when the market is most active) may increase the price. The same work may be less costly during off seasons.

Skill and Demand for Contractors

Not all contractors are created equal. The prices for contract work vary by the quality and extent of the work as well as the specialty of the trade.

General carpentry will cost less than ornate trim work. Likewise, minor plumbing for fixtures will cost less than work on the main water line. Minor electrical work for replacing a light fixture will cost less than the high-voltage work required for an electrical panel. When executing a rehab, make sure you are hiring the level of skill commensurate with the work required.

> ⊞ You don't need to hire a master craftsman when a handyperson is more than capable.

Specifics to the Property

Specifications for, or peculiarities of, the property itself may increase the price. Some properties have specific codes that must be adhered to, such as those in historic districts or neighborhoods designed for senior citizens. These typically require specialized contractors, additional work, or special materials due to the various codes and regulations and/or the age of the property.

Quality of Material

The next variance is the difference in the cost of materials. Just as not all contractors cost the same, not all materials are priced the same. For example, in the flooring industry, hardwood and tile are priced higher than vinyl and carpet. Among hardwoods, the price for the variants also differs, sometimes drastically. Assessing and selecting the proper material will be key in keeping a rehab on budget.

Necessities and Niceties

When performing rehab, it's important not to overdo it. Chapter 3 covered the concept of a profit being made at purchase as opposed to when selling or refinancing. Executing a poor rehab or overdoing the rehab kills potential profit. Investors should strive for a rehab that is under budget rather than thinking that profit may be recouped by charging a higher rent or selling at a higher price, which may lead them to execute work performed above value.

This is all contingent upon the type of neighborhood in which the property is located. In any given property, you will find amenities that require replacement or installation. Otherwise, the property will likely not attract market-value rent. These components are necessities. Table 8-1 shows a partial list of necessities segmented into interior and exterior components. The kitchen and bathroom are also specified due to their critical factor in determining FMV.

	Necessities	Niceties
Interior	• Permitting • Plumbing • Electrical • HVAC • Framing • Baseboards/doors • Flooring • Paint • Lighting	• Bookshelves • Accent walls • Framing (Crown molding)
Exterior	• Roof • Doors • Fences • Gutters • Siding • Paint • Decks/Porches • Foundation • Garage • Septic	• Fixtures • Landscaping
Kitchen	• Cabinets • Appliances • Countertops	• Backsplash
Bathroom	• Showers • Vanities • Sinks	• Specialty showerheads • Decadent mirrors

Table 8-1: Necessities and Niceties

When searching for a property, you want the worst house in the nicest neighborhood, and when rehabbing the property, you want the property to offer the best value. Some areas and properties demand the highest quality. In these instances, best value equates to higher-end amenities. These higher-end amenities are what I refer to as *niceties.* For these properties, I tend to fall back on the Air Force's third core value, "Excellence in all we do," as an adage for the quality of work and materials required. There are other instances, however, when the adage is simply neither practical nor necessary.

When I was a young lieutenant at my first assignment, I had a Senior Noncommissioned Officer (SNCO).[57] I made the following statement to her: "I know that no one will care about my career as much as I do." She cut me off at "I know that no one will care about my career." Although it came across as jarring at the time, the lesson she was

57 An officer who has not earned a commission; usually the top three tiers of the enlisted structure.

intending to convey was that no one cares about your career until you prove that you're worth investing in. She had my respect immediately, and in a short time, I had earned hers.

If I could give advice to any investor reading this book, it would be, "No one cares about your property as much as you do." You know your tenants won't care about it as much as you do. If you invest excellence in your rehab within an area that doesn't demand it, your reward will be watching excellence get slowly stripped and torn down to the level of merely satisfactory. For most properties, I default to another principle I've created from a common Air Force Academy phrase: When conducting a rehab, you want "fast, neat, average, friendly, good, [and] good."

You want the work to be completed fast, the appearance to look neat, the quality of materials to be average, the contractors to be friendly, the neighborhood to be solid, and the tenants who lease your property to be good. These properties have all the necessities and some of the niceties but not so many that your project exceeds the budget or causes unnecessary repairs down the line. You don't want to be the best house on the block; you want to be the house that provides the most value for the least cost.

Finally, you have the third rung of properties when you're acquiring a deal—ones where there may not be enough buffer in the budget to include any more than the necessities. For these properties, the focus is on the necessities and one or two niceties. My mantra for this situation is that "Excellence in all we do" is to be strived for, but sometimes "Better than the next guy" is all you can manage. I have found this has always been true, and sometimes, unfortunately, this pertains to the minimum allowed standard that still gets the job done. Investors will find themselves in this situation at times; it's a matter of when, not if. When you get into this frame of mind, don't beat yourself up over it. You are being efficient, and the tenant is getting a unit that is better than the next guy's for the same price as the inferior property, so that's still value for them and value for you.

While in the military, there were numerous occasions when my superior would task my team with something unnecessarily over the top. My standard reply would often be, "Yes, sir (or ma'am), we'll get it done." However, in my head, I'd be yelling, "Are you kidding me?!"

You will have times when a team member brings you an issue, and you think that same phrase. Relax and tell them, "We can make it work."

What matters most is that you remain cognizant of the comparable properties in the area to better assess what is acceptable. Remember, the goal is to rehab under or at budget, not create a property that is over value. Sometimes that means "Excellence in all we do"; other times, it means "fast, neat, average, friendly, good, [and] good."

Conducting a Walk-Through

Prior to executing a rehab, you (or someone on your behalf) will need to assess the work required to bring the property up to par, resulting in a proper ARV. The best way to determine the work required is to conduct a *walk-through* prior to seeking contractor bids. The walk-through consists of two components: *annotations* and development of objectives and tasks. Both should be accomplished before approaching any contractor to perform work other than your lead contractor or property manager, who will manage all other contractors.

> If possible, have your project manager and property inspector conduct the walk-through alongside you. They will start to develop efficiencies that will be to your benefit.

Annotations

I recommend annotating several specifics to ensure you capture areas requiring work. These specifics include the following:

- Overall Look and Appearance
    - Attention Areas
    - Condition
- Layout of the Property
    - Floor Plan
    - Common and Adjacent Areas

> If possible, take a video of the walk-through for you to reference and send to contractors when disclosing the work you wish for them to perform.

The first major factor you'll want to capture is the general condition of the home. This includes capturing the overall look and appearance as well as specific attention areas. The first assessment should be its condition, and this is easily assessed by a property inspector. They will enumerate any issue they find. If they identify a major deficiency, this becomes an attention area that requires fixing. The overall look and appearance is the next assessment, which will provide an estimate of how much cosmetic work will be required. If all that is required is a fresh coat of paint and changing of the locks, pat yourself on the back because you found a gem. Your frame of mind should then shift from things you must do (necessities) to things you can do (niceties) if warranted.

It is also wise to annotate the layout of the property, which includes not only capturing the floor plan but also keying in on common and adjacent areas. This will become crucial if you decide to attempt any forced appreciation rehabs (which will be covered at the end of this chapter). The floor plan is important to accurately capture amenities and square footage for comparisons. More importantly, it will be handy when specifying where work is required. Identifying the areas that are common and adjacent is also helpful for you or the contractor to establish the order of renovations so that one contractor is not unduly held up waiting on another to finish his or her work. This is also handy for planning purposes should you choose to remodel any portion of the interior. For example, you may want to remember what room is on the other side of the wall you're thinking of removing to make the dining room more open. Once you have completed annotating the walk-through, you'll advance to developing objectives and tasks for the rehab.

Developing Objectives and Tasks

This can be accomplished in many ways, and I recommend a few until you are experienced enough to develop your own system. The recommended method for approaching this is to first identify which work must be completed (necessities) and which work will add additional value to the property or increase demand (niceties). Your objective is to execute the rehab of a property; the first sub-objective is to execute the work required with remedying the necessities, and the second sub-objective is to execute any work associated with the niceties. Each sub-objective will also have associated tasks. These objectives are the groupings of work that were assessed during the walk-through. The subtasks would then be the same groupings subdivided into location of the property. For example, if assessing the installation of flooring for work, the development of objectives and tasks would resemble the following diagram represented in Figure 8-1. The military refers to this planning method as the Strategy-to-Task Technique (STT).[58]

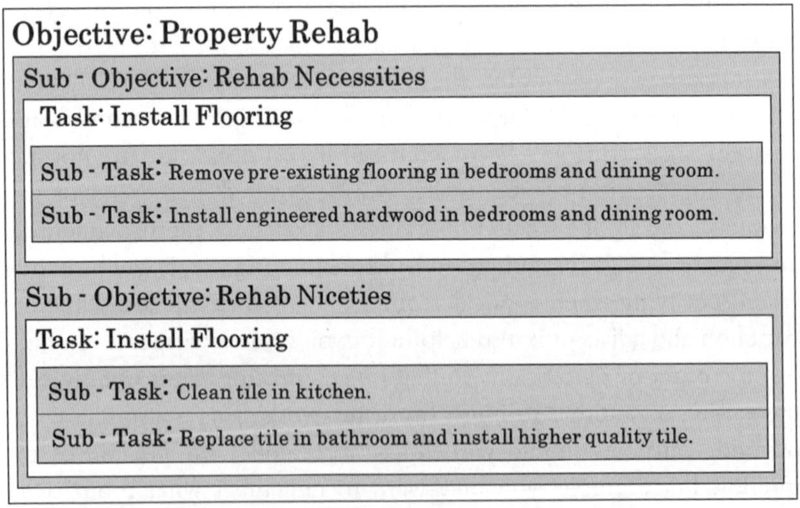

Figure 8-1: Strategy-to-Task Technique – Flooring Example

58 A decomposition methodology to identify lower-level specific tasks required for a larger objective or strategy.

DID YOU KNOW?

Sales of Do-It-Yourself (DIY) products from various retailers amounted to roughly $407.1 billion in 2019. This represents a fraction of total home improvement revenue in the United States.

Contractor Bids

Once you have developed the specific objectives and tasks you are requiring contractors to execute, you are ready to solicit bids. *Contractor bids* comprise three components: 1) the disclosure of work you wish to be performed, 2) the negotiation of the contractor bid, and 3) the acceptance of the bid. Each of these components has nuances you should familiarize yourself with should you choose to act as the project manager, as opposed to hiring someone else to perform this work for you.

Disclosure of Work

The first step in the process is to present the work you are requesting contractors bid or compete for. If you have completed the aforementioned steps for annotation, this step will more or less have already been accomplished. Work may be presented (or disclosed) according to tasks. Make sure you describe the work you would like performed, provide the video of the area (for them to give an accurate estimate), and explain the time frame for completion. You want to be respectful of your contractors' time, and you want them to be respectful of yours. They should inform you of their availability during the indicated time frame.

The contractors should provide a bid that itemizes materials and labor. Do not accept a vague offer that does not itemize the work being performed. They should also indicate the time the project will take.

You may elect to group all related tasks together for contractors to bid upon, or you may further segregate. For the flooring example (Figure 8-1), I recommend further segregation. The removal of existing flooring (both tile and other flooring in the bedroom and dining room) may be performed by a handyperson or a laborer. The same individual may or may not be laying the flooring or the tile, depending upon their specialty. Furthermore, cleaning of tile is something that can be done for much less by a cleaning service than by one of the contractors. The bottom line is that you may group these four subtasks into as few as two bids for work or as many as four. Do what makes sense.

Finally, you should specify a reasonable amount of time (known as a *suspense*) for when the contractors must submit their bids. Don't expect them to provide an estimate on site; provide at least two days for minor work and up to a week for major work.

Bid Negotiations

Once bids have been submitted or the suspense has elapsed, you may review the bid offers and make your selection. Notify the contractors of when you will make your decision. You could simply accept the bid at this point, or you could negotiate some of the terms. If I'm going to negotiate any component, it's normally negotiating payment schedules for work, applying *the carrot-and-stick method*, or negotiating the *quartermaster*'s responsibilities.

Some work requires partial payment up front, other work requires payment in installments, while the remainder requires payment upon completion. It is okay to pay for some or all materials (depending upon the size of the job) at the project onset. Labor can either be paid incrementally (for long jobs) or at completion. If payment will be paid in increments, this needs to be discussed during negotiations and agreed upon in writing when the bid is accepted. Any time after this is unfair to you and your contractor. The method of payment should also be discussed at this time.

If you are experienced in managing projects and have connections that allow you to acquire materials at competitive rates, you may elect to acquire and deliver the materials to the contractor. I generally refer to people who choose to do this as the quartermaster. This role has many perks: namely, reward and loyalty points with the vendors and lending institutions you are using. If done frequently, this value quickly accrues in your favor. Performing these responsibilities can also be time consuming and is therefore not recommended for those inexperienced or without the available time to do it properly. If you elect to perform quartermaster responsibilities (and the contractor agrees), their bid should then only reflect labor since you are paying for all the materials.

> Be wary if a contractor requests all funds (material and/or labor) up front. Many horror stories from investors start by accepting these terms.

Applying a carrot-and-stick methodology is good for both incentivizing your contractor and holding him/her accountable. The carrot is offering to pay an additional sum should they complete the work ahead of schedule. If they say the project will take three weeks to complete, offer them an extra 10 percent if they complete the work in two. Ensure you follow through and write it into the contract. Allow the contractor to estimate the amount of time; otherwise, they may feel like you are entrapping them.

However, for the stick, notify them that they will be penalized if they exceed their estimated time. If the estimation is for three weeks, a penalty of 10 percent will be enacted if they are doing work during the fourth week. An additional 5 percent deduction will be enacted for each additional week their project extends over the agreed-upon deadline.

> Ask if your contractor has an account with the vendor you intend to use; if so, purchase on their account. You ensure that you are not paying markup and they get the loyalty points and can arrange logistics. It's a win-win!

Accepting the Bid

Accepting the bid is both the easiest and the hardest component. All that must be done is to make the selection, have the contractor generate the invoice based upon the negotiated bid, and have all parties sign. Easy, right? Wrong. You have to choose the correct contractor. The highest bidder is easy to eliminate, but what about the lowest? The lowest bidder may not always be the best. Check their references and ask the real estate community prior to accepting. I'm willing to pay a little more for a reputable contractor I am confident will perform the work to the satisfaction I require for the job.

Whatever you do, make sure you make your selection above reproach; your decision criteria cannot be discriminatory in any nature.

DID YOU KNOW?

According to an online article posted by Zumper,[59] the following are the top 10 most requested amenities by renters in 2019:

1. Air Conditioning
2. In-Unit Washer/Dryer
3. Dishwasher
4. On-Site Laundry
5. Assigned Parking
6. Central Heat
7. Furnished
8. Balcony
9. Garage Parking
10. Hardwood Floors

Note: the 11th most requested amenity was a ceiling fan.

59 Julie Aiello, "What Renters Want: Top 10 Most Requested Amenities of 2019," Zumper, last updated September 16, 2020, https://www.zumper.com/manage/resources/top-10-amenities/.

Exterior Rehab Components

When executing a rehab, several components will need to be assessed on the exterior of the property. The exterior is often mishandled by novice investors. It is either overlooked or overemphasized, and both are detrimental to the bottom line. Exterior components include:

- Roofing
- Gutters
- Siding
- Exterior Paint
- Decks/Porches
- Garage
- Landscaping/Curb Appeal
- Septic System
- Concrete/Foundation

We discussed my personality type in Chapter 5; I'm all about efficiency. When executing a rehab, I generally find that it is best to work components in a methodical order; otherwise, you'll have contractors working on top of one another and hindering each other's progress. Some components may be worked concurrently while others should be worked in series. Experienced developers and contractors tend to work outside-in. At a minimum, I recommend checking and rehabbing the foundation, septic, roofing, gutters, and siding at the beginning. After this point, work on the interior and exterior components as required. You don't want to finish a rehab only to find that the foundation is cracked and needs work, or to drywall and paint the interior just in time to discover a leak in the roof. Taking care of these components first will allow you to identify and mitigate the potentially largest issues at the forefront of your project.

Roofing

The main purpose of the roof is to keep water from entering the property by way of the ceiling. Additionally, a roof also keeps water from entering the property and running down the walls along the *framing* and other interior infrastructure.

> If you see water damage or suspect a leak, check the gutters and flashing first before jumping to replace the roof.

Roofing may also be used to accent the aesthetics of a property. This is generally accomplished by the variations to roof types that may be selected. The most common types of roofing material are asphalt composite, wood, metal, clay, and slate. Asphalt (composite) shingle roofs are the most common in the U.S.; they are an all-around good choice for most home roofing needs. Replacing individual shingles is fairly easy, and a standard roof will last 15 to 30 years. Metal shingles are popular in areas with heavy snowfall or more frequent wildfires. These can be manufactured to resemble asphalt composite, and the standard lifespan of metal shingles is 30 to 75 years. Slate tile and clay shingles are the more expensive alternatives; however, they are also the longest lasting, with a lifespan of up to 200 years. Finally, wooden shingles are an option but are both expensive and not long lasting, especially in humid environments.

Associated Tasks: 1. Roof repair 2. Roof replacement (if required)	
Standard Material Measurements: 10' x 10' = 100 sq. ft. = 1 square	**Estimated Time for Completion:** Usually 1–2 days

Gutters

Gutters serve one purpose: to move rainfall and other precipitation away from the infrastructure of the property. Gutters are offered in different variants. The most common are aluminum, steel, vinyl, plastic, copper, or zinc.

> Installing gutter covers eases maintenance and extends the life of gutters. It's a good idea for wooded lots.

Aluminum and vinyl are both popular and affordable options. They offer the benefits of anti-rust, weatherproof material and are easily painted. Standard aluminum gutters have a lifespan of 30 years, whereas vinyl is closer to 20. Vinyl also tends to fade in constant sunlight and crack if persistently exposed to extreme differences in temperature. Steel gutters offer an attractive option that balances durability and cost. They are weather resistant, can be painted, and are highly durable; however, they are also heavy and prone to rust. The standard lifespan of steel gutters is approximately 15 years. Finally, copper or zinc gutters are the most expensive but longest lasting material. They are weatherproof and do not warp or fade, nor do they need to be painted. These are often only used for high-end homes or are mandated for specific instances (such as historic districts). The lifespan for a zinc gutter is roughly 50 years, whereas a copper gutter may last 100.

Associated Tasks: 1. Clean gutters 2. Replace gutters (if required)	
Standard Material Measurements: Linear feet	**Estimated Time for Completion:** Usually 1 day

Siding

The siding of a property offers a weather-resistant barrier between the interior and exterior of a property. While *siding* is the commonly used term, there are actually three components that comprise the weather-resistant barrier: siding, house wrap, and sheathing.

The siding is the exterior layer that protects the remainder of the underlying infrastructure from weather elements. The house wrap is the medial weather-resistant layer that is intended to prevent water buildup within the interior wall. The innermost layer, the sheathing, is appended to the underlying infrastructure (frequently the studs) as the last weather-resistant layer.

There are a few variants of siding, including wood, aluminum, vinyl, composite, and masonry (brick). Vinyl is the most popular choice because it is affordable and offers the most variety. While not the most durable, it's frequently the most economical. Composite siding takes the counter position by being more expensive but more durable. There are, however, fewer options with composite than with vinyl. Metal and brick offer the most expensive and durable options while also the most limited variety. Brick is used for more upscale homes as it is the most expensive and aesthetically pleasing. Finally, the wood option is easy to change the appearance as well as conduct repairs, but it is both expensive and high maintenance (not ideal for investment properties).

<table>
<tr><td colspan="2">Associated Tasks:
1. Clean and pressure wash 2. Patch and replace siding (sheathing, house wrap)</td></tr>
<tr><td>Standard Material Measurements:
10' x 10' = 100 sq. ft. = 1 square</td><td>Estimated Time for Completion:
Usually 2–3+ days</td></tr>
</table>

Exterior Paint

The primary purpose of exterior paint is for aesthetics, although some paints can also help extend the longevity of siding. The two main types of exterior paints are oil-based and latex-based paints. Oil-based are generally more durable and are more water-resistant than the standard latex-based paints. Latex is easier to apply and dries more quickly. Many advancements have been made to latex paint to narrow the margin of difference between the two types. Acrylic latex, the high-end variant of latex, possesses near comparable benefits to that of oil-based paint.

Note that if you're going from dark to light paint color schemes, you may need additional coats.

Do not put a new coat of latex over an old coat of oil-based paint; it will cause the paint to peel.

When painting the exterior of a residence, the main areas of focus are the siding, trim, doors, and shutters. Typically, a painter will select three grouped colors. Siding is the first color, trim is the second (and is selected to complement the color of the siding), and the doors and trim are the third color (normally a contrast color to add flare to the overall color scheme).

Associated Tasks: 1. Clean or power wash 2. Paint trim (if in good shape) 3. Paint exterior siding	
Standard Material Measurements: Gallons	**Estimated Time for Completion:** Less than 1 week (scope dependent)

Decks/Porches

Obviously, the only reason for a deck or porch is to string up a hammock and watch the neighbors pass by, all while drinking an Arnold Palmer. More seriously, a deck or porch is an exterior addition to the infrastructure that may be either covered or uncovered. The main components of a deck or porch are framing, decking, and railings.

The framing is the infrastructure abutting the property. Framing mostly consists of the ledger board, front and side rim joist, interior joists and posts, and footers. The *decking* is the top portion and is the most visible component. Standard types of decking are wood, synthetic, or concrete. The final component is the railing, which consists of the rails, balusters, and posts. Railings tend to be composed of wood, synthetic, composite, or metal. The decking and the railing may be (and often is) painted for aesthetics. Depending on the material, the deck is frequently painted in the same color as the trim, although properties seeking to demand attention or add pizzazz may choose a more vibrant color than the door or shutters.

> Always bring an expert (engineer or qualified contractor) to verify work.

Associated Tasks: 1. Clean or power wash 2. Paint or 3. Replace/Repair (if required)	
Standard Material Measurements: Ft. or sq. ft.	**Estimated Time for Completion:** Less than 1 week (scope dependent)

Garage

Garages are a determinant of property value and may or may not be standard for properties in a given area. Not having a garage in an area where it is standard can drastically decrease the value of a home. Conversely, the availability of a garage in an area that does not typically have them may drastically increase the value of a property. A garage has three main components: structure, door, and door opener.

Garages may be attached or detached from the property. *Attached garages* are where the structure is a portion of the main infrastructure. *Detached garages* are where the structure is not connected. The garage structure commonly has the same roofing and siding components as the main property. The second component, the garage door (not the pedestrian door), is what allows automobile access to and from the garage. Garage doors come in various materials and patterns. The most common materials include steel, aluminum, vinyl (composite), wood, and wood composite. Steel doors are economic, durable, and low maintenance, and they are offered in a wide variety. Aluminum costs less, but it is also less durable. Wood offers a traditional touch, and wood composite offers a traditional look with less maintenance. Vinyl offers a rust- and corrosion-resistant option for humid and coastal regions. Finally, the garage door opener is what mechanically opens and closes the door.

Associated Tasks: 1. Replace garage door 2. Replace door opener 3. Fix other infrastructure	
Standard Material Measurements: Standardized Door Sizing	**Estimated Time for Completion:** 1+ day(s)

Landscaping/Curb Appeal

Don't underestimate the value of landscaping and the curb appeal it provides. As a real estate investor, you want tenants to notice, desire, and gravitate toward your property.

There may be other properties that are better suited for your tenants' needs, other properties that are more affordable, and other properties that are more put together, but those properties don't matter if your tenant can't see them because they have fallen in love with your property. If exterior paint is the makeup, curb appeal is natural beauty. Simply put, you want your property to be the one everyone desires. This will make other properties more attractive by proxy and entices tenants to pay more than they normally would for the opportunity to dwell there. Additionally, offering a property that is well kept (within a neighborhood that is well kept) will often attract well-kept tenants who will keep up your property.

When conducting or contracting landscaping work, ensure items are used that will not degrade or deteriorate quickly. You want a property that keeps its appeal over time and doesn't just look good from a distance. The standard things to remove are high-maintenance or fragile items. For real estate purposes, high-maintenance and fragile are not attractive.

The four remaining aspects of curb appeal include:

- Lawn
- Shrubbery
- Trees
- Fixtures

The lawn should be maintained, and this could be as simple as lawn treatment and weed removal; as moderate as seeding or laying sod to repair areas of the lawn; or as extensive as constructing flower beds, installing drainage/irrigation, or even excavating or leveling portions of the landscape. It may sound like a large undertaking, but it may also save you a headache down the line.

Shrubbery consists of flower beds, shrubs, bushes, etc. I tend to favor bushes and shrubs over flowers. Bushes and shrubs add aesthetics to a property without demanding extensive maintenance. They are easy to maintain, and they complement the features of the property. If a tenant wants flowers, he or she can plant them.

> Do not buy expensive plants.

Trees may be a nice addition, but not always. Trees offer both aesthetics and privacy. But they can also offer insurance claims and liabilities. If a tree on a property is dead, you have it cut down. While you think a tenant would steer clear of large objects that could break and fall on them, you may be surprised. This is a potential hazard, and it's best to have it removed proactively. You or your property manager don't want to get a call when a storm knocks off a limb and it comes crashing into the property, prompting repairs. If a tree boasts large branches near the property, consider having those cut back.

Finally, properties have fixtures. Some are necessities, like a mailbox or a lamp post, and others are niceties, such as garden sculptures. Ensure the necessities are in place, and fix and repair the niceties if already on the property. This will be more than enough.

Associated Tasks: 1. Lawn maintenance 2. Trim shrubbery 3. Trim or remove trees 4. Lawn repair 5. Repair or remove fixtures	
Standard Material Measurements: (sod) sq. ft.	**Estimated Time for Completion:** 1+ day(s)

Septic System

Sometimes when doing a renovation, you'll need to get your hands dirty. Really dirty. Like *septic* dirty. It's not the prettiest work, but it is among the more critical, and it serves an essential purpose. Most properties located within a city municipal area will be connected to city sewage. But properties in rural areas may have their own septic system. There are many types of septic systems, including *chamber*, *drip distribution*, *mound systems*, etc. Most septic systems have two primary components: the *tank* and the *leaching (drain) field.* The septic tank is a buried, watertight container constructed to receive sanitary wastewater. The standard construct is for heavy solids to settle to the bottom while light solids and wastewater float to the top. The wastewater is released or discharged to the second component, the drain field, for dispersal.

> Dealing with septic tanks is not something investors do on their own. Hire a professional and save yourself a headache, time, and potentially a large mess.

Associated Tasks: 1. Clean or Empty Tank 2. Replace Tank (if unable to clean or repair)	
Standard Material Measurements: 1,000- or 1,500-gallon tank	**Estimated Time for Completion:** 1+ day(s)

Concrete/Foundation

Everything starts with and is built upon the foundation. If structural issues exist, they need to be addressed immediately before you begin any other renovations. Aside from the foundation, you will also want to check any exposed concrete walls, stairs, and patio/decking. Depending upon the scope of the project, it's likely you will need to fix minor issues, such as cracks or steps. On occasion, replacement may be required for non-foundation-related concrete work. If minor concrete work is required, a handyperson is generally up for the job. For major work, you may require a contractor who specializes or focuses more on concrete work.

> Always consult with qualified professionals/engineers on the final product.

Talk with local investors to find a good and affordable concrete layer.

If there are major structural issues to the foundation and you discover them before you've acquired the property, my advice is to let this deal pass so a better deal does not become your opportunity cost.

Associated Tasks: 1. Repair foundation 2. Repair interior walls 3. Repair deck/patio 4. Install deck/patio 5. Repair stairs 6. Install stairs 7. Repair driveway	
Standard Material Measurements: Pounds or cubic yards	**Estimated Time for Completion:** 3+ days (scope dependent)

Interior Rehab Components

When most people are thinking of executing a rehab or a home remodel, they are thinking of the interior components. For many, it is the exciting portion of the process. The interior rehab components entail the following:

- Plumbing
- Electrical
- HVAC
- Framing and Insulation
- Drywall
- Carpentry
- Interior Painting
- Cabinets and Countertops
- Flooring

This is also the area where most novice investors tend to overdo things and/or make the majority of their mistakes. The primary reason for this is the frame of mind an investor requires for a rehab. The first mistake is going over value or investing too much capital by using a quality of material that is above what the area or property demands. The second mistake is designing or renovating the property to a standard or design the investor enjoys, not what the tenant wants or needs. This is a mistake. Remember: The investment property is not for the investor to live in; it is for the tenant to live in and to generate capital for the investor. Don't fall into the trap of designing the property in a layout you like, and don't assume that most people like the things you do. Do your research and design your property for mass appeal. You may think black walls with white trim and a white ceiling is a sharp look. You may be a Michigan fan and want to paint all walls blue or maize. The masses may not agree, so stick with what appeals to them. It's better to have many people like your color palette than to appeal to the handful who have your tastes.

Plumbing

There are a few things that you never want to go awry in a property, and plumbing is one of the big ones. You may be able to work on some of the minor plumbing fixtures on your own, but you will want to have a professional work on everything else. There are four main components for which you may wish to enlist a plumber's services: the water source, the water heater, piping, and fixtures.

> If acquiring a functioning washing machine, draft a clause for the washer excluding it from the repair agreement; otherwise, do not provide a washer/dryer.

Water sources within cities are typically provided by the municipality. If a property is rural, the source may be well water. The water heater is another entity for which you may want to consult a professional or at least a reliable handyman or handywoman. Piping is bifurcated; it includes distribution piping as well as drainage. Distribution piping is the piping that transports hot and cold water. Drainage piping is designed to transport wastewater and sewage away from the property or to the septic system. Finally, fixtures are all of the smaller attachments to the distribution piping. These include sinks, faucets, toilets, tubs, showers, dishwashers, etc.

When conducting a major repair or renovation, you will want to check all fixtures (as well as the water heater) for leaks. Replace fixtures if leaking or malfunctioning, with the exception of the washing machine; remove the washing machine and dryer if malfunctioning.

Associated Tasks: 1. Replace plumbing components (if required) 2. Minor repairs (as required)	
Standard Material Measurements: Varies	**Estimated Time for Completion:** < 1 week (scope dependent)

Electrical

If plumbing is one thing you don't want to go wrong in a property, electrical is the other. Bad wiring is not only an inconvenience but also a hazard and potential lawsuit. Generally speaking, electrical includes four main components: the service meter, the circuit breaker and fuse panel, internal wiring, and outlets, switches, and fixtures.

Do not attempt to do any work on the service meter or circuit breaker yourself; hire a professional. If you elect to work on the internal wiring and other electrical fixtures, have it inspected by a professional.

Upgrading the service meter to 200 amp will ensure the property can handle the demand of modern technology.

Associated Tasks:

1. Service meter
    a. Upgrade service to 200 amp
2. Circuit breaker/fuse panel
    a. Replace circuit panel
    b. Add new circuit
3. Wiring
    a. Replace/repair faulty wiring
    b. Add new wiring
4. Outlets, switches, and fixtures
    a. Replace/install new outlets
    b. Upgrade outlet to GFCI
    c. Replace/install new switches
    d. Replace/install lighting
    e. Replace/install ceiling fans

Standard Material Measurements:	**Estimated Time for Completion:**
Varies	< 1–2 weeks (scope dependent)

HVAC

Everyone enjoys a home that is the right temperature—not too cold in the winter and not too hot in the summer. If a unit is missing or contains an outdated HVAC unit, consider replacement or installation. Without a working HVAC unit, tenants may choose to rent your unit but will soon vacate when another comparable unit that includes heating and cooling becomes available.

Standard heating comes in four different variants: *furnace*, *heat pump*, *boiler*, or *electric*. A furnace converts fuel (commonly oil or gas) into heat that is then distributed through the property. Furnaces generally consist of four components: burners (burn fuel), a heat exchanger, a blower, and an exhaust. A heat pump uses external air to both heat and cool a home. A boiler converts fuel (oil, natural gas, or electricity) into hot water or steam that is circulated using either a radiator or radiant floor system.

> **i** R22 (Freon) is used in older cooling units and is no longer available. If acquiring an older unit that has an R22 cooling system, keep in mind it will eventually need to be replaced.

Cooling is also assessed by output and efficiency. The main two types of cooling include *evaporator coil* and *compressors and condensers.* The evaporator coil absorbs the heat from the air and transfers it to the condenser coil, which generates cool air.

Finally, ventilation and ducting are the ductwork that transports hot or cold air through or away from the property.

Associated Tasks: 1. HVAC cleaning 2. Install/Repair heating 3. Install/Repair cooling 4. Install/Repair	
Standard Material Measurements: HVAC units vary	**Estimated Time for Completion:** 1–3 days (scope dependent)

Framing and Insulation

Framing is the "bones" of the property, consisting of the top plate, bottom plate, and the studs. These are constructed together to frame a wall (or a combination of walls to frame a house). The top and bottom plates represent the top and bottom horizontal components of a framed wall, respectively. The studs represent the vertical components, which are customarily spaced either 16 or 24 inches apart. Frames are usually constructed from wood; however, they can also be constructed from metal.

The second component is *insulation*. Insulation is provided in various forms, including *loose fill*, *blanket*, *board*, or *foam*. Loose fill typically consists of recycled paper and is normally blown into place between the sheathing and house wrap. Blanket insulation is mostly made of fiber and is fitted between the studs in an unfinished house. Board insulation is a rigid foam board used in the same manner. Finally, spray foam is sprayed into an unfinished wall.

Associated Tasks: 1. Install (or) replace	
Standard Material Measurements: Varies by type	**Estimated Time for Completion:** 1–3 days

Drywall

Drywall is the prepared and painted surface in view within the interior of a property. There are several types of drywall. These include greenboard, paperless, cement board, fire-resistant, and insulated.

Greenboard consists of drywall that is water- or moisture-resistant and is typically used in areas of a property that may be damp. *Paperless drywall* is composed of fiberglass instead of paper product; it is also water/moisture-resistant and is slowly supplanting greenboard in use. *Cement boards* are standard in bathrooms and other areas where puddles, spills, and higher levels of moisture are more prevalent. *Fire-resistant drywall* is made of fiberglass and other materials that act as a fire retardant. Municipalities typically require fire-resistant drywall in areas near furnaces, fireplaces, and utility rooms. Finally, *insulated drywall* is a drywall panel that also contains insulation, representing a product closer to an all-in-one package.

The complete installation of drywall requires three main steps: hanging the drywall, taping and mudding, and finishing (priming and painting). This is easy work to perform but time consuming to perfect; it's also a messy process regardless of your skill level.

Associated Tasks: 1. Hanging 2. Taping and mudding 3. Finishing 4. Patching 5. Painting Prep	
Standard Material Measurements: (Sheet) 32 or 48 sq. ft.	**Estimated Time for Completion:** 1–2 weeks

Carpentry

Carpentry is a critical element to a rehab. Keep in mind that some work may require a skilled carpenter, while other work may be accomplished by a skilled handyman or handywoman.

Carpentry generally includes the doors, windows, and trim. Both the door and framing for the door are considered carpentry. The window casing is considered carpentry, but you will need to consult a window specialist for the glass pane. Finally, trim refers to the crown molding and the baseboards. Carpenters are also leveraged for other miscellaneous components, such as railings and banisters.

Doors, window casings, and baseboards are considered necessities. Crown molding, however, is a nicety in most circumstances. Ensure you assess comparable properties in the area to determine the norm. The addition of crown molding will not add commensurate value or force appreciate a property. If done correctly, it may attract potential buyers or tenants and artificially inflate a price you could demand from them; however, it will not impact an appraiser's valuation. Strongly consider using a handyperson or general contractor for any carpentry if they are available and able.

Associated Tasks: 1. Install/Replace doors 2. Install/Repair windows 3. Install/Repair trim	
Standard Material Measurements: Varies	**Estimated Time for Completion:** 2–4 days (scope dependent)

Interior Painting

The purpose of interior paint is largely aesthetic, and it can have a large impact. Some people enjoy painting, but others loathe it. It can be meticulous work, but when done correctly can make the most notable differences in a property. The three primary steps involve preparation, the application of primer, and the actual application of paint.

Preparation includes patching, filling, and smoothening any holes. It also includes taping off nearby areas to ensure crisp lines while painting and avoiding paint drippage onto unintended locations.

New or dark walls will need a primer!

Primer covers imperfections, conceals stains, provides better cohesion and a uniform surface, as well as neutralizes the color of a surface;

this is important when painting after patchwork, painting new drywall, and going from a dark to a light color.

Most painters tend to use one paint color for the walls, another for the ceiling, and a third for the trim. Remember, this is not a house for you to reside in; it is for a tenant to live in. It should be painted for mass appeal. For walls, I suggest you use a neutral beige or gray; for ceilings, use ceiling white, and for trim, use a semi-gloss white.

Associated Tasks: 1. Preparation 2. Primer (if required) 3. Painting	
Standard Material Measurements: Gallons (covers ~ 400 sq. ft.)	**Estimated Time for Completion:** < 1 week (scope dependent)

Cabinets and Countertops

Together, cabinets and countertops make up one of three things that can make a kitchen or bathroom stand out. (The other two are the design and appliances). Both cabinets and countertops come in various quality, forms, and styles.

Cabinet quality may be stock, semi-stock, or custom. The ready-made cabinets found in big-box stores are stock or semi-stock (depending on the order). Custom cabinets are custom built to your specifications. Each cabinet may be framed or frameless and may be constructed from particle board, MDF, or plywood. The two standard veneers are laminate or wood. A framed wood veneer on semi-stock MDF should work for most instances.

> For most investment properties, a framed semi-stock MDF and wooden veneer will suffice. Refer to Figure 8-2.

Countertops may be laminate, granite, or a variety of other options. When acquiring a property, clean and reset the laminate countertop. If a replacement is required, install granite. The difference in cost is minimal, and granite is still preferred in property valuation.

	Particle Board	MDF	Plywood
Stock	Framed/Wood	Framed/Wood	Framed/Wood
	Framed/Laminate	Framed/Laminate	Framed/Laminate
Semi-stock	Framed/Wood	**Framed/Wood**	Framed/Wood
	Framed/Laminate	Framed/Laminate	Framed/Laminate
Custom	Framed/Wood	Framed/Wood	Framed/Wood
	Framed/Laminate	Framed/Laminate	Framed/Laminate

Figure 8-2: Cabinets and Countertop Variations

Associated Tasks:
1. Install (or) repair cabinets (paint if required) 2. Install (or) reset countertop

Standard Material Measurements:
Cabinet: H: 34.5" D: 24" W: varies

Estimated Time for Completion:
1–3 days

Flooring

The best component is often saved for last. Flooring is a determinant of value and is a noted feature by buyers and tenants alike. More importantly, it is the component of the property that takes the most beating. The surface is repeatedly walked on. Remember, no one will care for your property as much as you do. And pets must factor into the equation because of the wear and tear they add to flooring.

For investment properties, installing flooring that can withstand such beating will cost more initially but will likely offer a return on the investment. There are various types of flooring that you should consider, including vinyl and linoleum, carpet, wood (laminate, engineered hardwood, and solid hardwood), as well as tile flooring (ceramic or natural stone).

A good handyperson can do most flooring and small tile jobs.

Consider installing floors after painting has been completed (unless solid hardwood).

laminate and engineered hardwood, solid hardwood, and tile. The quality of vinyl flooring has improved significantly over the last several years; however, I do not recommend vinyl or linoleum. Solid hardwood is unnecessarily expensive for a rental unit (unless the market demands it). The most comparable option is to install engineered hardwood throughout the home with tile in the kitchen and bathrooms. I strongly advise against the installation of carpet, even in bedrooms. If acquiring a property with a well-kept carpet, use your best judgment. You'll likely just defer replacement until the next tenant turnover.

Associated Tasks: 1. Replace/Repair subfloor 2. Install/Repair flooring	
Standard Material Measurements: Sq. ft.	**Estimated Time for Completion:** 3 6 days

Miscellaneous Components

There are a few aspects of a rehab that apply to both the interior and exterior of the property, and I've included them in this section. Although I consider them to be miscellaneous, they are equally important, if not more important than any of the aforementioned components. These miscellaneous aspects include the following:

- Demolition
- Permits
- Inspections

Demolition and hauling trash away will be a part of nearly every remodel, every major repair, and just about every tenant turnover. Some tenants will leave some part of their belongings that they no longer want, and you will have to deal with disposal.

Permits may be required if you are changing the design or layout of the home. The requirement for a permit differs per location, so you should research whether a permit is required. Finally, you will need inspections if executing a major rehab and likely if you're performing a major repair. If selling a property or if you purchased a property turnkey and didn't modify a thing, you will still have inspections as a condition for the loan.

This section is an overview of each of these components. You should always have a professional conduct the inspections. Performing the demolition or filing the permits is something you could elect to do yourself; however, I do not recommend this for your first or second endeavor. Pay the nominal fee to let a professional do it, observe, and consider those minor costs as tuition toward your education in real estate.

Demolition

Many times, destruction comes before something else can be created. Think of it as the circle of (real estate) life. This is truly the fun part of a rehab: tearing stuff apart! Have fun with it but know what you're doing. Don't destroy something that doesn't need to be destroyed, and try to repair what makes sense to be restored. Also, don't just take out a wall without knowing what's on the other side or whether it is load bearing.

> Residents and other individuals living near your property will take advantage of your dumpster. Try to do all the demo at one time near the beginning of the project.

> It's not a bad idea to have a portable toilet on site if there is no running water.

The three aspects of demolition are simple: 1) demolish the undesired aspects of the property, 2) haul away the trash, and 3) clean up the mess you made. I won't go into much detail on how to tear something apart. That process is intuitive to most people.

The haul away is a simple process for those aware of the necessary services. If the property is within city limits, the city may provide trash hauling as part of the routine garbage pickup. You may need to stagger how much debris you leave for the garbage company. If the property is not within city limits and/or you have a large quantity of debris, you'll need at least one roll-off dumpster provided by a dumpster service. Research which dumpster services are available.

The clean-up should be intuitive; you'll want the residence to be presentable for renters or buyers, depending on your plans for the property.

Associated Tasks: 1. Demolition 2. Haul-away 3. Clean-up	
Standard Material Measurements: (Dumpster) Cubic yards	**Estimated Time for Completion:** 1–2 weeks (scope dependent)

Permits

Permits are a necessary aspect of major home renovations, repairs, updates, and additions. There are many instances where you might be surprised that a permit is required, and you don't want to find out the hard way when you are trying to refinance or sell your property.

There are two main types of permits: building and specialty. Building permits are standard for additions and structural work. This encompasses any time there is a conversion of a room (such as a sunroom to a living room, or a garage to a bedroom or office) or removal or addition of a wall. Specialty permits are standard for plumbing, electrical, and HVAC modifications; installation of windows or doors; and roofing.

> Always check your county website or local building department for codes and regulations on permits; these vary by state/area.

First you need to visit the county website (for the county your property is in) to apply for a permit. Once you have a permit, you may initiate building plans. Building plans can be drawn up by an architect or a project manager, or you could do so yourself if you have the skills and wherewithal to do so (constructing building plans is not included in this book). Once complete, schedule for approval. Execute the project once approval is granted. Finally, schedule an inspection of the work once the work has been completed.

Associated Tasks: 1. Apply for permits 2. Prepare drawings 3. File permits (schedule approval and obtain permit) 4. Inspection	
Standard Material Measurements: N/A	**Estimated Time for Completion:** Scope dependent

Inspections

Inspections are another component, and these inspections are in addition to the permit inspections covered in the previous section. Unless you purchase the property as a foreclosure, purchase as is, or waive the inspection requirement by other means, the property will undergo inspections in the process of being sold to you. If you are performing a rehab, you may also want to conduct inspections after the work is complete. If you're selling the home, the buyer is going to request them anyway, and if you're renting the property, tenants gain comfort knowing a property has been recently inspected. The three primary inspections most properties undergo are mold, termite, and radon[60] inspections.

Some states mandate disclosures to buyers.

60 A naturally occurring radioactive gas that forms when certain metals decompose in rocks, soil, and groundwater.

Associated Tasks:

1. Mold (moisture and fuel source) inspection
    a. Remediation
        i. Remove or remediate moisture/water source
            1. Check for leaks in roof, plumbing, etc.
        ii. Excise current mold
        iii. Air-quality test (AQT)
        iv. Remediation
2. Termite inspection
    a. Remediate existing termite damage
        i. Repair any damage
    b. Get a pest control company to treat and maintain
        i. Have the company write a letter of inspection
3. Radon inspection

Standard Material Measurements:	**Estimated Time for Completion:**
N/A	(Inspection) 1 day

Forced Appreciation

Forced appreciation is otherwise known as "Getting the biggest bang for your buck!" Why do investors exert effort into forced appreciation? Lower vacancies, higher rents, and higher ARV are just a few reasons (and even that is enough). Remember, real estate wealth is all about leverage, and this all plays into it. When force appreciating, you want every dollar expended to yield a dollar plus in value. There are a few key areas that are more likely to grant forced appreciation: additions, bedrooms, bathrooms, and the kitchen.

Additions

One of the primary methods to estimate a property's value is the price per square foot. One way to increase a property's value is to add square footage. If the plot has space, a complete add-on is possible but will include more effort. An easier addition would be enclosing an already covered area (a sunroom, covered patio, etc.), especially if electrical is already present.

Be wary of adding square footage when the residence is already the largest in the neighborhood. The ARV will not increase commensurately, but rental demand may still increase.

Bedrooms

If a property has only one or two bedrooms and there is space available to convert, add bedrooms. This is an immediate increase in value for a nominal cost. Three or four bedrooms with a minimum of two bathrooms is optimal. Be sure to check local regulations and statutes that determine requirements for a room to be considered a bedroom. Typically, this is a walled-off room with a doorway and a window large enough for a person to exit through in an emergency. Other specifications may apply depending upon the location.

Add a ceiling fan if there are lights already in the ceiling.

Bathrooms

Bathrooms are another easy way to increase the value of a property for little investment. Consider installing high-quality tile when the bathroom or the shower is small. Tile in small quantities is not that much more expensive, and you'll need to pay for the labor anyway. Be cautious about cabinets, countertops, and baseboards in bathrooms. Do your best to repair them when possible. If necessary, replace them, but don't overdo it. Having a fiberglass tub is more than sufficient. Another consideration is the addition of a bathroom if the residence contains only one—and has two or more bedrooms. Owners and tenants alike enjoy having their own bathroom aside from one for guests.

Stay away from installing bathtubs with jets. This is a maintenance nightmare waiting to happen. Remember, "no one cares about your property."

Kitchen

A kitchen can not only appreciate a property but also make a statement. Many people correlate a property's overall quality and condition with that of its kitchen. At a minimum, the amount of rent you demand will increase by investing in this area (if not also the actual value of the property). Look for stainless steel if you need to replace any of the major appliances (dishwasher, microwave, refrigerator, or stove). Appliances do not need to be the same brand but should match in color. Also, look at the cabinets and countertops. Refinishing the cabinets is sufficient. Maintain countertops if they're in decent-to-good condition, but if they need to be replaced, look at installing granite countertops. If you're going through the effort to replace a countertop, consider installing a backsplash, but stay within your budget.

Objective: Leveraging the Rehab

Executing a full rehab can be a lot of fun but can also be quite a bit of work. If done correctly, this process allows the investor to leverage the differential in the purchase price and ARV to maximize their equity growth. If done incorrectly, this endeavor could drain the capital invested or even devastate your investment portfolio.

The best method to ensure you stay on the correct side of the rehab is to follow two key principles: 1) Maintain an investor mindset. This is not a property for you to reside in. It's for tenants who will aid you in garnering wealth. Don't go overboard with renovations. 2) Understand the average for the area. You don't want your property to be the most expensive or require high maintenance. You want it to offer the best value.

Tasks:

- Research and understand the norm for the area.
- Understand your constraints.
- Conduct your walk-through (virtual or in-person).
- Determine necessities and niceties within your budget.
- Work exterior to interior (depending on the season).
    - Develop a practical order of work
- Don't exclude miscellaneous components.
- Target forced appreciation (if practical).
- Garner contractor bids.

If while reading this chapter, there were concepts you wished to see that were either not covered or where you desired additional detail, please annotate and provide feedback via this QR code.

Visit our website (masterofleverage.info) by using this QR code to access key figures and references from this chapter.

Aloof Aaron, Cautious Carl, Sensible Sarah, and Risky Rick

Cautious Carl (and his wife) have expressed no desire to conduct riskier and more elaborate projects such as force appreciating or rehabilitating distressed properties. They have neglected to research the principles covered within this chapter.

Sensible Sarah and Risky Rick have both embraced the benefits these actions can have on accelerating the growth of their real estate portfolios. Risky Rick plans to undergo these projects without using a large team to try and maximize his profits. Sensible Sarah plans on leveraging the skilled team members with whom she has worked hard to develop working relationships.

Aloof Aaron is not thinking about anything included in this chapter.

Chapter 9: Leveraging Your Equity ("To Sell or Not to Sell" and Renting)

Buyers decide in the first eight seconds of seeing a home if they're interested in buying it. Get out of your car, walk in their shoes, and see what they see within the first eight seconds.
—Barbara Corcoran, *TV personality and author*

In this chapter, we are going to cover the following:

Profitability and Financial Determination Measures

Leasing and Selling

Screening and Leasing Tenants

- Advertising and Finding Tenants
- Preliminary Screening Process
- Application Process
- In-Depth Screening and Verification of Application
- Accepting or Rejecting Tenants
- Lease Agreement
- Turning Over the Keys

Selling Your Property

- List Price
- Preparation Expenses
- Holding Costs
- Transaction Costs
- Taxes

Steps to Sell a Property

Step 1: Determine the FMV of the Property
Step 2: Prepare the Property for Sale
Step 3: Market the Property for Sale
Step 4: Negotiate the Sale
Step 5: Handle the Closing

Let's cut straight to the chase; this chapter is intended to equip you with the tools you need to make the crucial decision of whether to lease or to sell your property. We'll start with assessing certain profitability and financial determination measures.

Profitability and Financial Determination Measures

Ideally, no decision is required at this point in the process. If all has proceeded according to plan, you will have acquired and renovated a property with the intent to lease or to sell. Sometimes, however, things do not go according to plan, and the actual figures do not align with your projections. If you're lucky, the investment will still be cash flowing and will continue to generate wealth. If you're not so lucky (the price or renovation was more than anticipated, rents are lower than expected, etc.), you may need to cash in your investment for near-term gains in exchange for freeing up capital for better opportunities. Investors should heed a combination of profitability and financial measures.

> A positive rate of ROE denotes appreciation of value; a negative rate of ROE denotes depreciation.

You should be well versed with the two profitability ratios, ROI and ROE. An investor should assess these ratios when pursuing a property, and you should reassess them with actual values once a property has been acquired. Since you have already acquired the property, this is not an assessment of whether to attain it but rather an assessment of the opportunity cost associated with retaining it.

If you recall, ROI is a profitability measure indicating the cash-on-cash return. Essentially, it measures the duration of time required to recoup the initial capital expenditures. ROE is a measure of the income generated in comparison to the equity available. Essentially, it measures how efficiently wealth is being generated. Take note: a high ROI and/or a high ROE is good. A high ROI with a commensurately low ROE is best. A low ROI should be assessed, although a high rate of ROE may compensate depending upon your investment strategy.

ROE RATE	ROE	ROI	ACTION
Positive	High	High	Cash-Out Refinance
Positive	High	Low	Cash-Out Refinance / Sell
Positive	Low	High	Maintain
Positive	Low	Low	Maintain / Sell
Negative	High	High	Maintain / Sell
Negative	High	Low	Sell
Negative	Low	High	Maintain
Negative	Low	Low	Sell

Table 9-1: Determination Measure Quick Reference

The default action should be to maintain or cash-out refinance; however, as you can see in Table 9-1, there are several instances in which an investor may elect to sell a property. Two trends you might have identified are a low ROI or a negative ROE rate.

Low ROI

A low ROI isn't ideal but isn't necessarily bad either. If the property is located in an area that is appreciating (positive ROE rate), the ROI will increase in time. The question for the investor should be, "What is my opportunity cost?" If holding onto a property yielding a low ROI is preventing the immediate acquisition of a better investment, you may elect to sell in order to trade up.

Negative ROE Rate

Negative ROE rates are a sign of depreciating property value. The value could be depreciating due to market distress, such as a housing bubble or other economic depressions. If this is the case, and you have long-term tenants, do not sell; the market will rebound in time. If your asset is depreciating outside of these circumstances, then proceed with caution and do not allow your perception of sunk cost to overcome that of opportunity cost and practicality. If the area's values are consistently depreciating and your ROE is currently high, you should sell, especially if the ROI is low. If the ROI is high, you may be robbing Peter to pay Paul. The property will continue to depreciate in value—and eventually, the rental demand, and therefore the ROI, will also decline. If the ROI is high, look to sell when indications of decreasing rental demand are present.

Do not cash-out refinance a property that is depreciating in value; doing so may result in a situation where the amount owed is more than the value of the home.

However, if the ROI is high and the ROE is low, you may consider holding onto the property to take advantage of the rental income. Selling a depreciating property with little available equity will likely result in a loss. Hold the unit at least until you have paid off enough of the mortgage to sell the property without incurring a loss on the investment. Should the ROI and ROE both be low, sell immediately! They will continue to depreciate, and we all know bad news does not get better with time; if anything, it only gets worse.

High DTI Ratio

A third determination measure is one with which you should be intimately familiar: your DTI ratio. Remember, 43 percent is the delineation most financial institutions use to assess a borrower as acceptable or risky. The combinations of profitability ratios and your DTI should be the primary criteria in any decision to take the one marshmallow or hold out for the marshmallow factory (see the Introduction). An abundance of low ROI investments is directly correlated with high DTI. Properties with negative ROI are causation for a high DTI, and therefore a negative ROI is highly detrimental to the early and mid-level real estate investor. If the ROI calculation using actual figures is negative, strongly consider selling. If you are thinking about retaining due to a high rate of appreciation, consider the opportunity cost.

Leasing and Selling

Obviously, you should avoid selling a property for less than its FMV if at all possible. Whether you decide to leverage your team or to lease or sell a property on your own, ensure you do so in a deliberate manner. You should not haphazardly attempt to find a tenant or to sell a property; this will surely result in immediate or delayed loss of profit and worse circumstances if you are not careful. The most prominent dangers to be cognizant of are accruing holding costs, dealing with bad tenants, and not getting max value of an asset.

Delay in finding a suitable tenant or selling a property not only forgoes potential rental income to offset expenses but also increases the interim expenses the investor must carry between acquisition and disposition of the asset. If you rush and find a less-than-desirable tenant, you run the risk of evictions, potential damages and subsequent repairs to the property, court cases and fees, your tenants becoming delinquent or not paying their rent altogether, or worse.

There are several aspects you should consider whether you seek to lease or sell your newly acquired and renovated unit. A property manager will assist with finding tenants to rent your properties, and a real estate agent may assist with selling any properties. Whichever path you select, you will find the remainder of this chapter helpful. It is dedicated to the process of screening and finding tenants, as well as *staging* and selling a property.

Screening and Leasing Tenants

Finding good tenants is essential for any investor intending to generate wealth through real estate. Your tenant will either be your lifeblood or the bane of your existence. This is why the property manager should always be an integral part of your center of gravity. However, when getting started, many elect to take on the property management function themselves. I don't recommend this. Hiring a property manager is worth the opportunity cost, and it frees you up to focus on other aspects of building your portfolio. But should you choose to find and manage tenants on your own, you'll need to be familiar with the following steps:

- Advertising and Finding Tenants
- Preliminary Screening Process
- Application Process
- In-depth Screening Process
- Accepting or Rejecting Tenants
- Lease Agreement
- Turning Over the Keys

Advertising and Finding Tenants

The first action is advertising and identifying tenants for your property. There are several methods through which you may accomplish this, but the most common and efficient techniques are *signage*, online sources, and *networking*.

Signage

Signage simply entails putting a sign in the yard or window indicating that a unit is available for rent. "For Rent" signs can usually be found in hardware stores for an affordable price. You can also have signs custom designed to add a little extra flare and appeal to the advertisement. At a minimum, the sign should include the price and your contact information. Some landlords elect to include qualifiers (minimum credit score, no pets, no smoking, etc.) on the sign.

> Be wary of posting "For Rent" signs in certain areas. These signs highlight that the unit is available but also broadcast the unit's vacancy (or impending vacancy), which makes it an easy target for vandalism.

Online Sources

Most things nowadays can be accomplished online; advertising to and locating tenants is no different. This is the most common method of finding a tenant. Some services are free, while others require nominal fees. The best sites to use are Craigslist (free classifieds website), the MLS (normally for purchasing, but it also advertises rentals), and other paid sites (such as Rentals or Apartments.com). With all online sites, I recommend including as much information as possible. Specifically, include the following:

- Requirements
- Disqualifiers
- Rent Price
- Number of Bedrooms
- Number of Bathrooms
- Square Footage
- Amenities
- Neighborhood Information
- Photos

> Do not post the address of the property; make the prospective tenant call for the address.

Networking

Networking is the method that produces the highest quality tenants. This method relies upon recommendations from current tenants or your property manager. Your tenants will know friends and coworkers in need of housing. If you share knowledge of available units with them, they may help fill your vacancy. Furthermore, your property manager will be aware of tenants seeking to move for various reasons. They can also help with placement should your property meet the desired specification for their move.

Offer a small reward payment to current tenants for referrals, but be sure to pay them only after the new lease has been signed.

Preliminary Screening Process

You'll want to perform adequate screening of your tenants to see who are worthwhile leads and who are simply wasting your time. You'll save the inquirer and yourself considerable time and money by covering the essential requirements up front, even before an application. If using online sites, most of the initial screening information should be made available in advance. You'll want to request the following information for each prospective tenant:

- Gross Monthly Income (this should generally be three times the rent)
- Credit Score
- Proof of Employment / Proof of Funds
- Rental History
- Number of Occupants Planning on Occupying the Property
- Smoking Status (declare if allowed)
- Pet Status (declare if allowed)
- Any Derogatory Information

If the prospect does not meet your pre-identified requirements, politely decline their request and wish them well on finding another property. Some prospects will attempt to negotiate some of the requirements. Proceed with caution and use your discretion.

Be sure to check state laws to avoid discrimination. Protected statuses include disability, familial status, national origin, race, religion, sex, and skin color. DO NOT inquire about any of the protected statuses or traits of your prospective tenants, because it may appear to be discriminatory.

Application Process

Prospective tenants should expect to submit an application. The application should include proof of all preliminary screening questions as well as the following:

- Name
- Date of Birth
- SSN
- Phone Number
- Previous Addresses (past five years)
- Current Employer Info
- Past Employer Information
- Emergency Contact Information

If generating your own application, ensure there is adequate room for a prospective tenant to provide all the requested information. Be sure to review the application thoroughly. You must be vigilant. Some people may use deception to get what they want. Don't be cynical but be cautious when screening prospective tenants. This process is to sort the good prospective tenants from the bad. If all prospective tenants were good, we would have no need for this process. Be sure to follow up with the employer, previous employer, and previous landlords.

Application Fee and Release of Information

You should always include an application fee. An application fee helps sort the serious applicants from those who are fishing with a wide net. It also helps defray the cost of conducting the background search and investigation. Furthermore, you should also always include a "release of information" clause in the application. This will allow you to stay within the boundaries of the law and use the information prospective tenants provide to conduct your background investigation, conduct an in-depth screening, and verify their application.

In-Depth Screening and Verification of Application

Some people can be deceptive. We hope that your prospective tenants will be up front about the presence of any negative information; they should expect that a decent landlord will verify their information. In fact, if they disclose something in their past that is problematic (employment, weak credit score, eviction, etc.), I may be willing to listen to their explanation and consider leasing a unit to them. Attempts to conceal this information are an immediate disqualifier. In addition to verifying the application, a background check should be conducted to look for the following disparaging information:

- Felonies
- Evictions
- Bankruptcies
- Judgments or bad financial history

Accepting or Rejecting Tenants

Eventually, you will find a suitable prospect to be your tenant. At this point, you will need to accept the prospect and reject the others. The best way to approach this is to vet tenants on a first come, first served basis. If a prospect does not meet the requirements, move on to the next. If a prospect meets the qualifications, select that tenant unless you can prove easily and non-discriminately that another prospect is a better fit.

Regardless of accepting or rejecting a prospect, provide them a written letter (or email) indicating such. If rejecting, indicate why the candidate is being rejected, and ensure you maintain a copy for your records. When a prospect is accepted, require that they submit a non-refundable deposit to hold the unit vacant. This is to prevent them from applying, qualifying, and accepting multiple rental agreements and leaving multiple owners holding the bag and passing on other viable candidates. Furthermore, specify a length of time for the prospect to sign a lease agreement and become your tenant. I do not recommend holding the unit for longer than a one- or two-week period. If the prospect fails to sign a lease within this window, the deposit is forfeited. If the tenant does sign, the deposit should be rolled into the security deposit.

Lease Agreement

The lease agreement is the binding document between the landlord and the tenant. These agreements may be found in several locations, including online and in office supply stores. Most lease agreements include the following:

- Name(s)
- Property Address
- Lease Term
- Rent Amount
- Security Deposit Amount
- Late Fee Amount
- How and When Payments Are Executed
- Additional Provisions

Always check special provisions in your state governing landlord-tenant relationships and lease agreements.

Note: the lease agreement identifies the term of the lease. Use your best judgment; most leases are one year and revert to month-to-month after the one-year anniversary. Other leases initiate at month-to-month, while some are multiyear leases and offer discounts on rent or stipulations not to raise the rent for a duration of time. Use your discretion. In a highly competitive market, incentives are not required.

Additional provisions I recommend you include within the lease agreement are the following:

- Occupancy
- Early Termination
- Utilities

- Repairs
- Alterations
- Liabilities
- Notice to Terminate and Renewal
- Abandonment
- Insurance
- Military Clause
- Breach of Contract

Be sure to meet with the tenant at the property (or at an attorney's office) to sign the lease. Go over each section, cover important items in detail, and answer any questions. Provide a copy of the lease to the tenant and maintain one for yourself.

DID YOU KNOW?

According to the U.S. Census Bureau in their Rental Housing Finance Survey for 2018[61]:

- 44.1 million (35.9 percent) U.S. households rent their home.
- 2.48 persons is the average renter's household size.
- 6.75 million renters (5.5 percent) have lived in their home for 20 years or more.
- 42.2 million renters (34.4 percent) are under the age of 35.
- 20.3 million renters (16.5 percent) are aged 65 years or older.
- 106.1 million renters (86.4 percent) are high school graduates (or equivalent).
- 54 million rental properties (44 percent) are in suburban areas.
- 50.3 million rental properties (41 percent) are in urban areas.
- 18.4 million rental properties (15 percent) are in rural areas.
- 31.9 million renters (26 percent) live in homes categorized as "detached single family."

61 https://www.census.gov/programs-surveys/rhfs.html

Turning Over the Keys

Even after the lease agreement is signed, you are not quite finished. You will still want to complete the move-in condition report with the tenant. This is a form that annotates any preexisting damages to the property that the tenant is not responsible for. The tenant may be held liable for damages incurred after this report. It's typically best to allow the tenant to conduct a walk-through and call out any deficiencies, go over their findings with them, and take photos of any identified areas of notice. Taking photos of the entirety is not a bad practice, especially for comparison with the move-out condition report when that time arises. Do not count on remembering every detail of every property you own when it comes time to assess your property for damages.

Once the move-in condition report has been completed, the lease has been signed, and the security deposit and first month's rent has been paid, the tenant may be permitted to move in. When you hand over the keys, you can add a little housewarming gift, such as a gift basket or gift card to a nearby restaurant. This is always an appreciated—but never necessary—touch. As I previously stated, tenants are your lifeblood. Put your best foot forward and help them help you generate wealth.

DO NOT allow the tenant to move in prior to completing the move-in report, signing the lease, or paying the security deposit and first month's rent. If you allow them to move in and they decline to do any of the above items, they are technically considered a resident and must therefore be evicted. This is a slow and expensive process, especially for a tenant from whom you have not collected any rent.

Short-Term Rentals

I would be remiss if I didn't include at least a few words to discuss *short-term rentals* (also known as vacation rentals). Due to the potentially inconsistent cash flow, this is not necessarily recommended for investors who are just entering the market and planning to leverage their capital and equity for expansion. But it can be a great tool for generating capital more expediently than traditional long-term rentals.

A short-term rental is the leasing or renting of a dwelling unit for an abridged period of time (technically, less than a year) that regularly varies in duration from nightly to monthly. Airbnb, HomeAway, and VRBO are commonly recognized businesses that facilitate short-term rentals. Short-term rentals represent one of the niche markets discussed in Chapter 6. The three most common clients of this market include the following:

- Individuals traveling on vacation
- Individuals working for short periods away from home
- Individuals between homes looking for a residence to buy or rent

Short-term rentals offer a win-win solution for both the landlord and the tenant. The landlord is able to charge higher rental prices for a shorter duration than the prorated rate of a long-term rental contract. The tenant receives more amenities and space than that of a hotel and/or the amenities may come at a lower cost.

The danger or risk with short-term rentals is the possibility of inconsistent cash flow due to prolonged periods of vacancy. Long-term rentals offset this risk by offering higher probabilities of occupancy (in exchange for lower income for the landlord). Even so, short-term rentals are worth considering if you own a property in a niche market that attracts tourism or is in an area that promotes a fair amount of transient business such as expos, conferences, and trade shows.

For example, Investor Bob enjoyed living in one of the houses he purchased using low- to no-money-down. He's since put a lot of time and effort into turning the fixer-upper into a real gem. Furthermore, while living in the home, he realized that there is a considerable amount of new construction for hotels and shopping centers, signaling a demand that outweighs supply. He also noticed a notably larger population of people in the area during certain times of the year, specifically during the late spring and through the summer.

Investor Bob's total monthly expenses for the property, including the mortgage, amount to roughly $2,500. Investor Bob had previously considered renting his unit for $3,000 per month (an overall profit of $6,000 a year), but after doing a little research, he discovered that most people are looking to rent short-term rentals.

He found that the going rate for short-term rentals during the spring and early fall was around $250 per night, about $350 per night during the peak season of summer, and about $150 during the late fall and early winter. (Including cleaning fees and other charges, his income would be closer to $200 per night in the spring and fall, $300 in the summer, and $100 in the late fall and winter.)

Summer		Spring/Fall		Winter	
PITI:	$2,500	PITI:	$2,500	PITI:	$2,500
Rate (per night):	$350	Rate (per night):	$250	Rate (per night):	$150
Income (per night):	$300	Income (per night):	$200	Income (per night):	$100
Required Occupancy:	9 Days	Required Occupancy:	13 Days	Required Occupancy:	25 Days

Long-Term Rental: $3,000 income / $500 profit (per month)

Figure 9-1: Short-Term Rentals

After running these calculations, Investor Bob decided the conditions were right for him to use this specific property as a short-term rental. As luck would have it, Investor Bob experienced an average 60 percent occupancy rate during the following year, which yielded him an annual profit of $13,200 as opposed to $6,000. Not a bad job, Investor Bob!

Selling Your Property

When deciding how to sell your property, a homeowner or investor should consider a few additional items. These items include the price at which to list the property, preparation expenses, holding costs, transaction expenses, and taxes. Poor planning and consideration could result in the property selling for a less-than-optimal price or the property staying too long on the market. Poor planning can also cause inefficiencies that cost you money, which is capital that you could be reinvesting to bring you more wealth. We've all heard the phrases "It takes money to make money" and "An ounce of prevention is worth a pound of cure." Don't be afraid of investing a little capital to prepare adequately for a sale.

List Price

I covered determining FMV a number of times throughout this book. Refer to Chapter 7 if you need a refresher. FMV isn't the only price determinant for your property. The demand for properties within an area also plays an influential role in the *list price*. Some conditions, such as limited inventory and low interest rates, inflate a property's value. Be sure to assess how hot the market is when you are attempting to sell. It is not uncommon for properties to sell for tens of thousands more than the list price in the right market. Inflated markets may frustrate buyers, but they can be wealth building for the seller.

Preparation Expenses

Preparation expenses are the proverbial ounce of prevention you buy in hopes that you won't be in need of the cure (rushing to find a tenant to fill a vacancy) in the end. Generally, these expenses include services such as advertising and marketing, landscaping and lawn care, staging services, and cleaning services. While it is possible to do all of these things on your own, ask yourself how much your time and effort are worth and if you can do it as efficiently as a professional.

Holding Costs

Holding costs have already been detailed in previous chapters. These could be numerous or few, and with proper planning, they will be few. If they are numerous and the expense of the holding costs exceeds the profit garnered from selling at top price, you may consider selling for a less-than-optimal price to shorten the time it takes to close on a deal.

Transaction Costs

You must also consider numerous transaction costs, including commissions and fees for real estate agents, title companies, attorneys, etc. Many of these expenses have also been detailed in earlier chapters. Remember, you can avoid some of these fees if you elect to perform the services yourself, but some entities require unavoidable fees when transferring a property from one owner to another. The most common service homeowners may forgo is that of the real estate agent; they will attempt to list the property as FSBO. This can either allow the seller to gain a larger profit or sell at a lower price and garner the same or greater profit.

Taxes

Some investors overlook a major expense until it is staring you in the face: taxes. When you sell a property, you will pay taxes on it. If you sell within the year you acquired the asset, you will pay taxes at your income tax rate. If you sell after the first year, you'll be taxed at 21 percent or lower (as of 2021). There are strategies that may be applied to timing when you sell a property, such as aligning the sale (capital gain) to the same year when you have a major expenditure (capital loss) to defray the net amount you pay to Uncle Sam, if any.

Steps to Sell a Property

While these considerations may appear to be a little daunting at first, they can easily be simplified to only five steps:

Step 1: Determine the FMV of the Property
Step 2: Prepare the Property for Sale
Step 3: Market the Property for Sale
Step 4: Negotiate the Sale of the Property
Step 5: Handle the Closing

Step 1: Determine the FMV of the Property

I would explain this again, but the 1900s British politician, Jim Knight, is echoing in my head: "You've got to stop whipping a dead horse sometime." (See Chapter 7.)

Step 2: Prepare the Property for Sale (Repairing, Cleaning, and Staging)

This is the second most influential component of selling a property.

When you prepare properties for sale, you are preparing them to yield top dollar—or at least FMV. Preparing a property for sale frequently entails cosmetic work and conducting minor repairs. This includes patching and/or painting walls, replacing light bulbs or other fixtures, or completing any other minor repairs that may be required.

Another component of preparing a property is landscaping and lawn care. I've covered some of this in Chapter 8. When attempting to sell or rent a property, you want your property to demand attention and attract as many buyers as possible. Mass attraction creates competition. (Don't believe me? Think back to high school or college.) You want your property to be the most popular on the block, so much so that the adjacent, occupied properties appear more attractive and other available properties become nearly invisible. Competition for real estate drives up prices, which means more profit for the investor.

The easiest form of preparing a property is a thorough cleaning. When taking photos, you want surfaces to be clean and shiny, the floor to be free of smudges and footprints, and the overall appearance to look welcoming rather than dreary. Cleaning services are inexpensive, so you might as well use them.

The final step in preparing a property is staging.[62] You can do it yourself or use a staging agency. Some staging agencies will allow you to rent furniture and accessories for a limited time period, and other agencies provide more comprehensive services and will stage the property for you. The most common staging practices include:

- Clearing Clutter
- Balancing the Look of Clean and Lived-In
- Stylizing the Dining Room or Kitchen Table
- Rearranging the Furniture to the Most Open Layout
- Using Neutral Colors
- Making the Residence Gender Neutral
- Filling the Property Efficiently
- Creating the Ambiance the Neighborhood/Area Is Known For

62 A method of decorating a property with the intent to highlight the residence's most impressive features in order to help buyers imagine themselves living there.

On average, following these steps for staging a property boosts the sale price by around three percent.

Step 3: Market the Property for Sale

Advertising and marketing are what sell a home. This is one of the primary services provided by a real estate agent, along with handling and managing the paperwork and providing estimates on the value of a property. The most common form of advertising is by means of online real estate websites (Realtor, Redfin, Trulia, Zillow, etc.). Most of these services charge a fee, and you should consider that as part of the transaction cost. If you use a real estate agent, they will do this on your behalf as part of their service. Craigslist can be used as a no-cost method of advertising. Some members may also elect to use more traditional forms of advertising, including the use of flyers, brochures, and even the newspaper. Regardless of how you choose to advertise your property, you will need quality photos to capture its condition and entice a buyer. It is often best to hire a photographer. An experienced photographer knows how to adjust lighting, frame the shots, and take quality photos. They don't need to be a professional *per se*, but their photos should be better than the ones you snap on your phone. Quality photos are a good marketing tool when you're looking to lease a property as well.

Lastly, most individuals host an *open house* or have *showings* that allow for prospective buyers to tour the home. This also allows neighbors to visit and see what amenities have been included in the property. To an investor, the open house is just as much about networking as it is about attempting to sell a particular property. If staged correctly, an open house may very well be the final push for a buyer to make an offer. And if the showings provide a sense of competition, you could possibly receive an offer higher than prospective buyers would have given otherwise.

Step 4: Negotiate the Sale

The details of how to negotiate a sale are akin for buyers and sellers, just from the opposite side of the table. (See Chapter 7 for a reminder of buyer negotiation techniques.) Keep in mind the fees and other considerations discussed in Chapter 3, and use those same principles to structure the price and sale in a manner that is apropos for you.

Step 5: Handle the Closing

Finally, you will need to close the deal. The seller or the buyer can decide which title company to use in the transaction. For the seller, the purpose of the closing is to ensure the deal is finalized and the contract for the deed is signed. It's also where the proceeds distribution occurs. If there is still a mortgage on the property from the seller, it is then paid off. If there are profits, the seller must disclose where they should be sent.

Contract for Deed

The standard *contract for deed* typically includes the following sections:

- Name of Buyer and Seller
- Property
- Purchase Price
- Terms of Payment
- Encumbrances
- Maintenance and Improvements
- Condition of Premises
- Remedies on Default

Objective: Leveraging Your Equity

Deciding to sell a property can be just as stressful as deciding to purchase one. Hopefully, the decision to sell or to lease was made well in advance of the moment you initiate this phase of your strategy. If not, be sure to leverage these quick assessments to make the most informed decision possible, ideally resulting in the most ROI.

Tasks:

- Decide upon selling or leasing and assess profitability.

- If leasing (and not using a property manager) …
    - Advertise.
    - Conduct a preliminary screening.
    - Disseminate applications.
    - Conduct an in-depth screening.
    - Accept or reject tenants and solidify lease agreement.
    - Turn over the keys.

- Furnish property for short-term rentals.

- If selling (and not using a real estate agent) …
    - Determine listing price by assessing FMV.
    - Prepare property for sale (cleaning and staging).
    - Conduct marketing.
    - Negotiate potential sales.
    - Navigate closing.

If while reading this chapter, there were concepts you wished to see that were either not covered or where you desired additional detail, please annotate and provide feedback via this QR code.

Visit our website (masterofleverage.info) by using this QR code to access key figures and references from this chapter.

Aloof Aaron, Cautious Carl, Sensible Sarah, and Risky Rick

Our three informed investors (not including Aloof Aaron, who does not care to be informed at the moment) fully understand the value of passive income from positive cash flow (the *Velocity of Money*), but they take different approaches when it comes to managing their equity. Cautious Carl believes leveraging equity within a residence removes the buffer from economic downturn and is unnecessarily risky. Carl, being cautious, is also inclined to sell a property whenever he notices a decrease in the demand for properties in an area, especially if the financial determination measures are negative (low ROI, negative ROE rate, high DTI ratio). Additionally, he leaves the process of acquiring, staging, and selling assets to his real estate agent.

Sensible Sarah and Risky Rick do not have the same reservations pertaining to leveraging the equity they have accrued in real estate. Sarah assesses an asset's profitability and financial determination measures but has her real estate agent and property manager take care of most day-to-day actions and turnkey property engagements. She engages with owners when acquiring distressed properties. She refrains from purchasing high DTI/low ROI assets and is not inclined to sell her assets unless there is a negative ROE. With that being said, she's not opposed to selling an asset if it is only marginally profitable and the extra equity will enable a more profitable acquisition.

Rick doesn't mind being a little riskier in his endeavors. He elects to handle most tasks on his own, including property acquisition, staging, managing, and selling. Additionally, once he acquires an asset, he is not inclined to sell it unless it has a negative ROE rate. Even so, he'll retain the asset in his portfolio if the property meets or exceeds the 2 percent rule.

SECTION III:

ENHANCEMENTS

Section III identifies and outlines activities and strategies that are not required but will enhance the investor's ability to attain, maintain, or increase their wealth through acquiring real estate. While Section II walked through the execution of acquiring real estate in a natural progression, Section III's identified activities should be conducted continuously throughout development of your real estate portfolio and generation of wealth.

Chapter 10: Utilizing Liability Protection

Twenty years from now, you will be more disappointed by the things that you didn't do than by the ones you did do.
—Mark Twain

In this chapter, we are going to cover the following:

Asset vs. Personal Liability Protection

Asset Liability Protection

- Anonymity (through a Business Entity)
- Primary Residence Homestead Exemption

Personal Liability Protection

- Insurance
- Security through Obscurity (Business Structuring)

Grantor "Land" Trust

- Grantor, Trustee, Beneficiary

Equity Stripping

Establishing a Business Entity

- Step 1: Select Your Business Structure
    - Sole Proprietorship
    - Joint Venture
    - Corporation
    - Limited Liability Company (LLC)
    - Umbrella Company
- Step 2: Select Your Business Name
- Step 3: Register Your Business
    - Articles of Incorporation and Articles of Organization
    - Bylaws and Operating Agreements
- Step 4: Receive Your Federal and State Tax ID

We live in a society that has become highly litigious and seemingly growing more so by the day. Some people have unwittingly jumped on the cultural bandwagon of threatening legal action as the quick fix for everything. Other individuals act with more nefarious intent: they work the system for their personal gain. A third grouping are individuals who are struggling for survival. A person who is drowning will reach for anything or anyone they believe will save them.

Do not allow yourself to become the victim of any motivations that lead to litigation. Take the necessary steps to protect and defend what you've earned. This chapter will identify and explain the methods for individuals and investors to protect their real estate investments.

> I am not an attorney I am not offering legal advice. I am offering information for educational purposes. You should consult an attorney to determine which business structure is most appropriate for you.

Asset vs. Personal Liability Protection

You may be wondering what exactly is the difference between *asset liability protection* and *personal liability protection*; why isn't it all just considered "liability protection," as the title of this chapter implies? Simply put, the difference is this: asset liability protection protects your business assets when you are taken to court. Personal liability protection protects your personal assets when someone comes after your business or business assets.

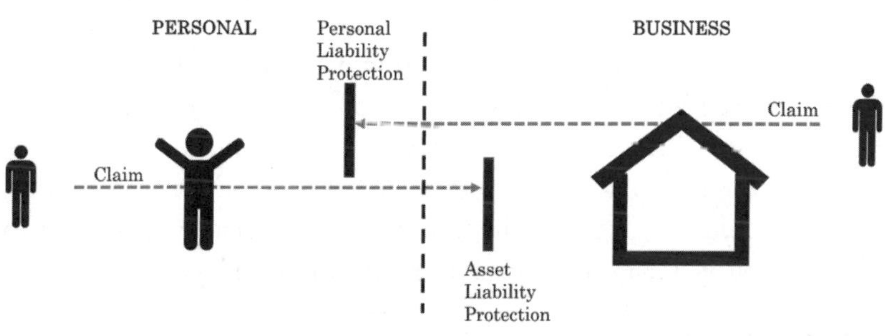

Figure 10-1: Asset vs. Personal Liability Protection

The difference may appear minuscule at first but believe me, when your assets are in jeopardy, knowing and preemptively applying these differences may be your most productive investment. In some situations, you may need to apply several strategies to both asset liability protection and personal liability protection. Some protections are exclusively for primary residences, while others may be used for investment properties. This chapter will address the following techniques for each:

- Asset Liability Protection
    - Anonymity (through a Business Entity)
    - Primary Residence Homestead Exemption
- Personal Liability Protection
    - Insurance
    - Security through Obscurity (Business Structuring)

Asset Liability Protection

Asset liability protection protects your business entity's assets in the event you personally do something ill-advised. Asset liability protection is the process of structuring your assets in the event someone attempts to litigate against you for an act you, an immediate family member, or even your family pet committed or neglected to commit. If you rear-end someone in your car, if your dog bites the neighbor, if your child is hitting golf balls off the driveway and hits a car, if your spouse gives a homeless person hot cocoa that subsequently burns the recipient's tongue, if the boy down the street trips on the ice on your driveway, etc., there is a possibility of litigation in an effort to collect garnishments[63] from a civil case. Before this happens, you want to have measures in place that prevent them from 1) thinking it's worth their time to pursue your assets and 2) accessing your income-generating assets (which are those most likely to be associated with your business). *Anonymity* is the recommended practice to protect your assets by hiding them legally from potential litigants. The homestead exemption may allow you to leverage your primary residence for protection as well.

63 A court order mandating money (or property) of a defendant be seized to satisfy a debt or grievance owed to a plaintiff.

Anonymity (through a Business Entity)

Others who seek to gain wealth quickly at your expense may see you as a target of opportunity. I'm not advising you to be paranoid, suspecting that every encounter has an ulterior motive. I'm just stating that you don't need to be a scout to be prepared. Within the military, we classify targets into two categories: hard targets[64] and soft targets.[65] You don't need to make yourself a hard target. You simply need to be a less visible target or, better yet, no target at all.

One of the ways to be less visible is to ensure your assets do not appear in your name or a name associated with you. This is the anonymity approach: make your assets appear to be unassociated with you. This is an effort to diminish your appearance as a target. Why would a person exert time and money to go after an individual who doesn't appear to have much that would benefit them? Even if an affiliation is made, which identifies you as more of a target, there are other caveats that make your assets a hard target rather than a soft one that may yield the same result.

So how does this work? There are some states (namely, Nevada and Wyoming) that allow for only the founding business manager's name to be associated. If that individual resigns, the record simply indicates the member and a status of "resigned"; they do not require an update of the managing member's name. So, if you had an attorney sign as the founding business manager and subsequently resign, you own the business and are the owner/manager; however, no public record of affiliation between the business entity and you exist. If you have established your real estate assets within the business entity, a litigator will not see your real estate assets, only your personal ones.

Always verify with an attorney to ensure your business entity is structured correctly to accomplish this imperative.

64 A person or thing that, due to their actions or mitigating protective measures, has minimized existing risks and made themselves a more difficult target to attack.

65 A person or thing that, naturally or due to their actions or lack of mitigating protective measures, is relatively vulnerable to attack.

As an example, let's assume Investor Bob has acquired five properties worth $200,000 each, in addition to his primary residence worth $250,000. Additionally, we'll assume he has $100,000 in savings. Figure 10-2 represents the gross worth visible to a litigant when no asset protection is used. Note that the total gross worth visible is $1.35M.

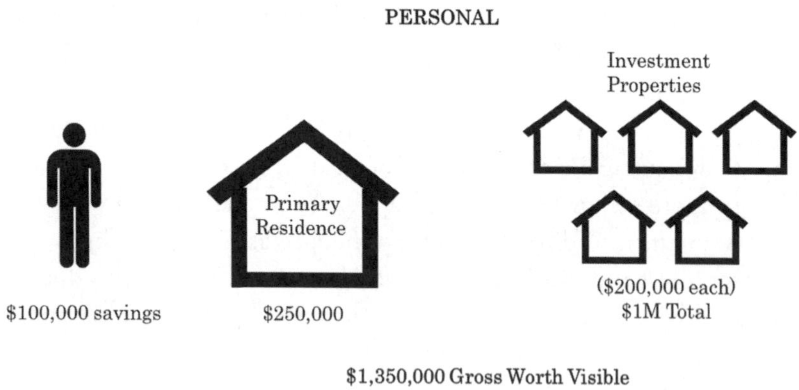

Figure 10-2: No Asset Protection

Figure 10-3 demonstrates the difference in visible gross worth when a business entity is established to encompass Investor Bob's real estate assets.

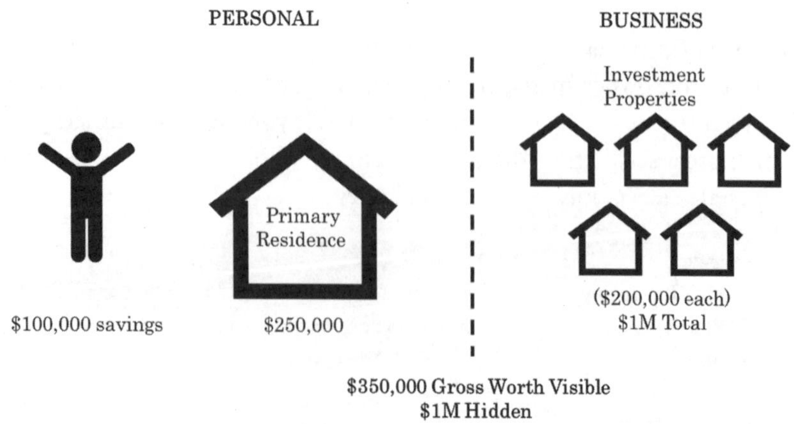

Figure 10-3: Asset Protection (Anonymity through Business Entities)

Appearing to have a gross worth of $350,000 makes Investor Bob a less attractive target than $1.35M. Even so, Bob can protect his assets even more.

Primary Residence Homestead Exemption

Simply stated, the *primary residence homestead exemption* exempts an amount or percentage of your primary residence from litigators or other potential creditors. This exemption may provide protection depending on where the investor has his or her primary residence.

Let's assume that Investor Bob resides in Ohio, where the exemption at the time is $145,425. If Investor Bob has a balance of $100,000 on his mortgage, anything over $145,425 is not protected. If a litigator filed against the owner, the court could force the owner to sell his or her residence (since it is more than the Ohio homestead exemption cap). The owner (Bob) would retain $45,425 (homestead cap minus the mortgage balance) while the litigant could profit the remainder (~$90,000 after selling expenses plus a fraction of the owner's savings) as indicated by Figure 10-4. If the litigant is your ex-spouse, and the courts entitled him/her to 50 percent, he or she is taking an extra $50,000 of your savings along with the profits from the house. Not an ideal situation for the owner.

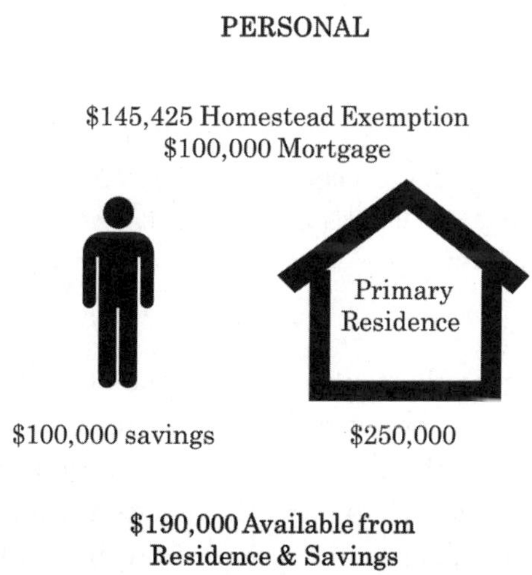

Figure 10-4: Homestead Exemption Less than Residence Value

Now, let's assume Bob's primary residence is in California or Florida, where the homestead exemption is unlimited. That's right: unlimited equal to the value of the property. In this instance, the residence is a protected asset, and no action is required to prevent a litigant from accessing the equity in the primary residence, as indicated by Figure 10-5.

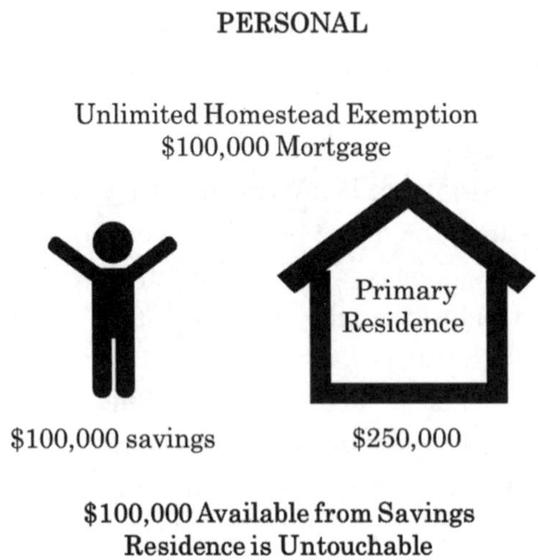

Figure 10-5: Homestead Exemption Greater than Residence Value

> If the homestead exemption in your state is greater than the value of your home, there is little risk in paying off your mortgage; if the exemption is less, take actions to strip equity from the asset.

If you live in a location with less friendly homestead-exemption policies, more actions may be taken. If the homestead is less than the value of the property (as is the case in Figure 10-4), the owner could strip equity from their residence to make themselves a harder target. Equity stripping could be taking out a second mortgage, cash-out refinancing to increase the LTV of the home, or establishing a HELOC that temporarily accomplishes the same (and only for the amount actively used). If the litigant chooses to come after your assets, he or she (or their attorney) will see that you must pay off these primary liens first, leaving them with little profit for their efforts.

> Do not trust the residence into a business entity; homestead exemption is for natural persons only.

Personal Liability Protection

Now that we've addressed how to protect your business assets, let's assess how to protect you from adverse actions taken against your business entities. Why might you need to protect your personal assets from that of your business? That answer is largely the same as for asset protection. Sometimes, you will perform actions in the operation of your business that will be incorrect, placing your business as a target of opportunity. It could be as simple as a tenant slipping and falling on your property if ice is present or a contractor getting injured working under dangerous conditions, even if they verbally agreed to do so. Furthermore, up to this point in the book, there have been 29 "Caution" key topics. Any one of these is a potential misstep that could result in a tenant or other individual attempting to litigate against you or your business entity. There are two methods discussed in this chapter that hedge against adverse actions impacting your personal assets; they are insurance and *business structuring*. Some people call this, "security through obscurity."

Insurance

Insurance is your first line of defense, and your insurance agent should structure it to take the brunt of the force. As part of your team, he or she can structure your policy effectively and appropriately for your real estate investment. If we venture back to Chapter 7, you'll find the section covering insurance as part of the acquisition, as well as the various intricacies of insurance policies. A good insurance policy will have an extended replacement rider for damage and a hefty liabilities rider to cover any accidents that occur on your property. You should explore one additional intricacy: the loss-of-rental-income rider. This policy not only protects you from potential litigants who attempt to collect your equity or from damages to the property that impact your equity value, but it also allows for continued generation of capital while a property is being restored or repaired.

Security through Obscurity (Business Structuring)

Business structuring is the next line of defense, and it's a multifaceted one at that. If done correctly, this process acts as personal liability protection for your non-business assets and offers the anonymity function for your other business assets. It is also tailorable to your acceptance of risk. Let's use the previous example in Figure 103. In this example, if an individual were to pursue litigation against Investor Bob, his personal assets would be safe. However, the business assets would be exposed—all $1 million of them! If the liability insurance does not cover the amount litigated, the remainder would come out of his business assets. Now let's say his business assets are dispersed among three business entities such as in Figure 10-6.

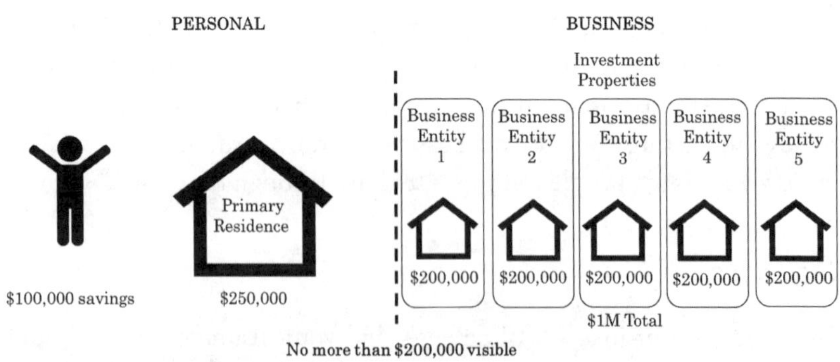

Figure 10-6: Business Structuring

As you can see, no more than $200,000 is visible or accessible, and that's only if liability insurance doesn't cover the litigation. In this example, Bob has established a separate business entity for each property in the portfolio; this is the most risk-adverse method but also the costliest. You should consider the initial expenditures required to establish each business entity as well as the fees, time, and effort required to maintain them. Apply this technique to the degree of risk you deem to be acceptable.

I advocate for establishing business entities per geographic location as well as value threshold. Let's say your value threshold is $500,000. Two properties are located in one state, and three are located in another, as indicated by Figure 10-7.

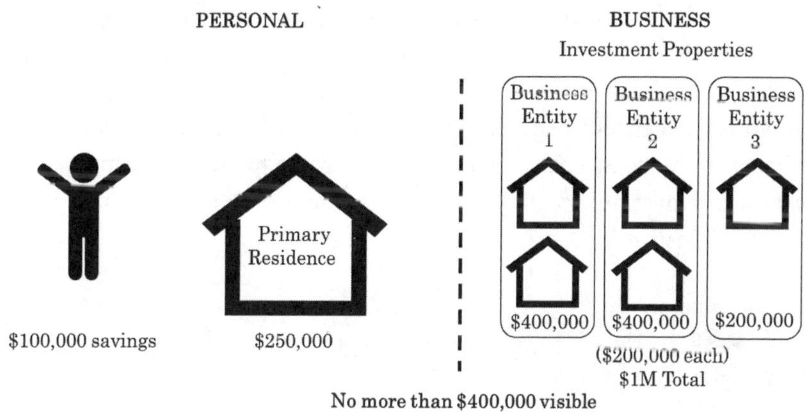

Figure 10-7: Business Structuring by Location and Threshold

The first two properties can remain in one business entity; the remaining three must be split between two business entities because their combined value exceeds $500,000, even though they are in the same location. Remember, the goal is to limit the amount of equity (and capital) available for a litigant to pursue. Business structuring is a phenomenal method to accomplish this goal; however, an intermediary, typically a lawyer, must establish the real estate within the respective business entity for this to be a possibility.

Grantor trusts are not impenetrable; a judge can order you (or your business) to disclose the owner grantor of an asset. Proper adherence to business practices may prevent a judge from making such a mandate.

Grantor "Land" Trust

Grantor trusts are the answer to the question you were probably just asking: "What if I didn't acquire my property in the name of my business entity?" A land trust is a legal system that allows for a person (or entity) to hold a property on behalf of (i.e., with the "trust" of) another. They are also able to perform specific duties on a member's behalf. This method is an easy way to shift management responsibilities of real estate to your business entity as well as ensure privacy by replacing your name with your business entity's name. This is also a phenomenal manner to transfer ownership without triggering a due-on-sale clause with their financial institution.

Not all states recognize the grantor trust; always consult your attorney or business advisor.

A grantor trust involves three pertinent members: the grantor, the trustee, and the beneficiary. They typically represent or perform the following actions:

Grantor: The individual who establishes the trust and transfers assets via the trust.

Trustee: The person (or entity) responsible for managing the trust. For this strategy, I recommend your business entity as the trustee. If your business entity requires you to list all members, use a nominee trustee who may then resign.

Beneficiary: The grantor (or investor in this instance) is the standard beneficiary. The beneficiary is the owner of the trust. If you assign someone else as the beneficiary, they then own the trust and, therefore, the property.

> Grantor trusts on their own do not offer any tax advantages.

Figure 10-8 illustrates how this would work for an investor who wishes to use a grantor or land trust to protect their assets by trusting them into a business entity.

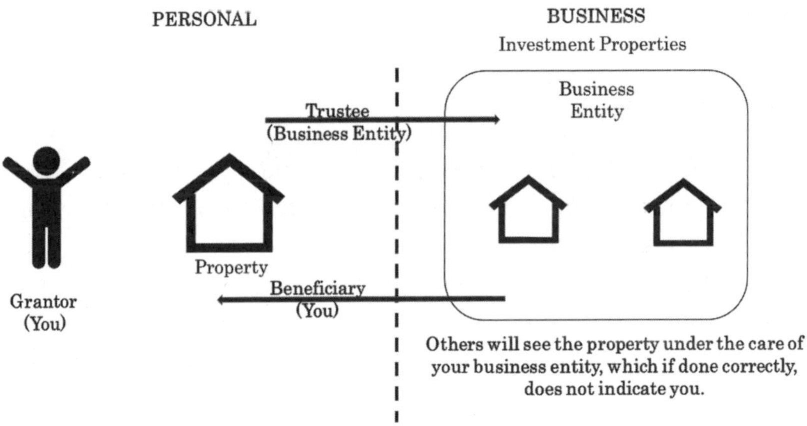

Figure 10-8: Grantor Trust Illustration

The investor could also have the beneficiary of the trust be another individual, an estate, an organization, or any combination of other entities. When legacy planning, estates are declared to be the beneficiary of the trust, and individual members (related or not) may be declared within your living will as the partial or sole beneficiary of the estate. For additional information and details on how to proceed with trusts and estate planning, consult an attorney who may assist you.

The first generation makes it, the second generation spends it, and the third generation blows it.
—Ancient Proverb

Equity Stripping

Equity stripping is the act of extracting available equity from an asset in an effort to prevent the asset's equity from being targeted by litigants and potential creditors. Leverage is the action of equity stripping applied toward the acquisition of additional capital and equity-generating properties. We have three primary techniques in which to perform equity stripping:

- Second Mortgage
- Cash-Out Refinance
- HELOC

Second Mortgage

The second mortgage is a great equity-stripping approach if interest rates have risen significantly since the first mortgage. This allows for the remaining principal balance to retain its low interest rate. The second mortgage will have the higher interest rate; however, it will strip or extract equity from the property, making it appear to be a less desirable target and will enable you to leverage the extracted equity in procuring additional assets.

Cash-Out Refinance

This equity-extracting approach consolidates the refinance of the mortgage into a new loan. (See Chapter 3.) This method of equity stripping (or leveraging) works to your advantage when interest rates are lower than when you took out your original loan. It is also far less complex to manage a large portfolio without an abundance of second mortgages.

HELOC

The HELOC is the third method of equity stripping. (See Chapter 3.) You may use this approach when the exposure to litigation is temporary or when you require funds for short periods of time. I do not recommend leveraging a HELOC for long-term investments, due to their variable interest rates. The HELOC only works effectively as an equity-stripping method if maximized to its full extent. It protects only up to the amount borrowed; a HELOC that is not actively in use offers no protection against litigants.

A HELOC cannot be used as an equity-stripping method on investment properties.

DID YOU KNOW?

In 2019, there were 28,280 complaints reported (7.5 percent drop from 2018) to the National Fair Housing Alliance (NFHA) pertaining to housing discrimination. The following is the breakout of the cases reported to the NFHA:

- Disability: 17,010 (58.9 percent)
- Race: 4,757 (16.5 percent)
- Familial Status: 2,228 (7.7 percent)
- Gender / Sex: 1,948 (6.8 percent)
- National Origin: 1,730 (6 percent)
- Color: 646 (2.2 percent)
- Religion: 328 (1.1 percent)
- Other: 3,117 (10.7 percent)

The "Other" category is comprised of the following complaints: source of income, age/student status, sexual orientation, gender identity, marital status, criminal background, victims of domestic violence, military status, retaliation, immigration status, and zoning.

Establishing a Business Entity

The early part of this chapter refers to establishing and acquiring your real estate portfolio within a business entity. First, you'll need to establish a business entity to accomplish this task. While many steps are involved in establishing a business entity, these four are primary for establishing an entity intended to retain real estate:

Step 1: Select Your Business Structure
Step 2: Select Your Business Name
Step 3: Register Your Business
Step 4: Receive Your Federal and State Tax ID

How you approach each of these steps and the manner in which you accomplish them is contingent upon the intended purpose and corresponding structure of your business entity. This section of the chapter will address the intricacies and differences involved with each of the steps in this process.

DID YOU KNOW?

In 2019, of the 28,280 reported complaints to the NFHA, 24,186 of them were rental market (potential renters against potential landlords) complaints. The rental market proportion accounts for 83.4 percent of all NFHA reportable transaction types.

Real Estate Sales accounted for 2.7 percent; Mortgage Lending, Home Insurance Transactions, and Harassment accounted for less than 1 percent each. The remaining 13 percent is comprised of "other" transaction types.

Step 1: Select Your Business Structure

The first step is deciding which type of business entity or structure is the most apropos for your real estate portfolio. The main types of business structures are provided below:

- Sole Proprietorship
- Joint Venture
    - General Partnership
    - Limited Partnership (LP)
    - Cooperative (Co-op)
- Corporation
    - C Corporation
    - S Corporation
- Limited Liability Company (LLC)
- Umbrella Company

Each business structure contains specific advantages; however, they are also paired with specific limitations. Ensure the advantages and limitations are appropriate for your venture. Once you have selected and established a business structure, you can alter it, if need be, but penalties and fees may apply. Careful business planning may prevent the need for unnecessary fees and related expenses.

Sole Proprietorship

A *sole proprietorship* is the easiest business entity to form; however, it also offers the least liability protection. In fact, no dissociation between business and personal assets and liabilities exists; therefore, the owner can be held liable for any and all debts and/or claims against the business. I don't advise a sole proprietorship for retaining real estate, due to its lack of liability protection.

Joint Venture

A *joint venture* is an arrangement between multiple individuals (or business entities) who agree to work together to achieve a common goal or objective. Several business structures function as joint ventures, and each has varying levels of integration and liability for its members. They can be constructed for temporary or more permanent arrangements. The three most common forms of joint ventures are *general partnerships*, *limited partnerships*, and *cooperatives*.

> There are specific differences between a joint venture and a syndication. Consult your attorney for advice.

General Partnership

A partnership is a business structure in which two or more individuals own a business jointly. Similar to a sole proprietorship, these do not require formal legal recognition. There is no obligation to draft or file *articles of organization* or *operating agreements* (covered later in this chapter). Also akin to sole proprietorships, no dissociation from the business and personal assets and liabilities exists either; therefore, a partnership does not provide personal liability or business asset protection for the owners.

Limited Partnership (LP)

Limited partnerships have one general (managing) partner who has unlimited (total) liability and control. All other members are limited partners who have limited liability and control. The limited partners establish the extent of liability and control in the operating agreement. This agreement should also establish the conditions that govern the distribution of profits. Taxes are passed through, meaning profits pass along to the members, and each member pays taxes on the sum of his/her earnings garnered from the partnership.

> The general manager will need to pay self-employment taxes.

This arrangement offers liability and asset protection to the limited partners; however, the general partner does not benefit from this protection. Establishing limited liability partnerships is another alternative that essentially provides limited liability to each partner and limits the liability of each partner to their own actions.

Cooperative (Co-op)

A cooperative (commonly referred to as a *co-op*) is a business or organization owned, maintained, and operated by, and for the benefit of, its own members. Members who elect to join a cooperative are referred to as *co-owners*; they split and distribute the profits as well as expenses. The managing members are referred to as the *board of directors*; these members own shares, make decisions, and run the cooperative, while the non-managing members simply receive a portion of the profit. Non-managing members may elect to join the board of directors by purchasing shares.

Corporation

A *corporation* is one of the most traditional business structures. Corporations are common because this structure offers many attractive taxation attributes and liability protections to its members. A corporation is a separate legal entity used for business; as such, it can perform any action an individual may perform, such as acquisition, renovation, developing, leasing, managing, and selling of real estate. Additionally, it can also acquire loans and pay salaries. Furthermore, if an owner or shareholder departs the company or sells their shares, the corporation may seamlessly continue operation.

This business structure is unique in that it is issued as stocks at its inception. These stocks may be privately maintained or publicly traded. Businesses that elect to maintain or privately trade their stock keep the controlling interest in the business in-house, whereas publicly traded businesses may elect to sell shares in exchange for generating capital.

The corporation business structure is also attractive because it offers the strongest personal liability protection compared to the other business structures. This generally comes at the expense of being the most expensive to maintain. It also comes with tax disadvantages. There are many taxation variants for corporations; however, the two most common are *C-type corporations (C corp)* and *S-type corporations (S corp)*. The main differences between these two entities pertain to their taxation.

Limited Liability Company (LLC)

The *Limited Liability Company (LLC)* has become one of the more popular business entities in recent years; this structure allows the owner(s) to take advantage of benefits bestowed from both the corporation and partnership business structures. Specifically, the LLC offers the business asset protection of the limited partnership and the personal liability protection of a corporation. Profits and losses—and therefore, taxation—pass through to the individual.

Take note: there is immense flexibility in establishing an LLC; state regulations regarding LLCs may differ. Check state statutes' governing formation, duration, dissolution, and termination. It's usually best to include specific clauses within the operating agreement to avoid issues with transferring ownership.

Because of the LLC's flexibility, it is imperative to be deliberate in planning for your LLC's structure. LLCs can be manager-managed or member-managed. If member-managed, all members have a say in how the business is run. This may not be an issue if the number of members is small, but it could result in paralysis if the number is large. I've spent too much time in the military, where structure tends toward hierarchical and totalitarian, to ever succumb to an egalitarian approach when my future wealth is at stake.

One of the biggest benefits the LLC provides is the ability to determine its method of taxation. You can structure the LLC as either a C corp, an S corp, or as a partnership. This impacts your taxation. Furthermore, if the business only has one member, it can be treated as a disregarded entity. I highly recommended an LLC for managing real estate due to the flexibility in the establishment and the protections provided to its owners.

Umbrella Company

An *umbrella company* is a business entityconstructed to maintain control over other business entities. This is also referred to as a *holding company*. The subsidiary companies or (sub-companies) are the business entities under the umbrella or holding company. Many advantages accompany using an umbrella company for the management of real estate, the most prominent of which are taxation and increased asset protection, which may be powerful when combined together appropriately. Some of the most prominent benefits include the following:

- Each sub-company can have a different management construct
- Each sub-company can elect how it will be taxed
- Each sub-company maintains its own assets and liabilities
- Asset protection is maintained between each sub-company
- The type of business conducted can be different among sub-companies

A series LLC operates in the same manner as the umbrella company, with the series LLC being the holding company and the sub-series LLCs being the subsidiary companies. The advantage of a series LLC is that it (as well as the sub-series LLCs) can be filed for at inception as opposed to individually.

Step 2: Select Your Business Name

Selecting your business name is the fun part of the process. You can select something that signifies your business and represents its identity. You'll want to protect your business's identity to better protect your business assets, or in this case, your real estate portfolio. The best method of protecting your business name is by registering it. The first step of selection is to ensure your desired name is available.

> Establishing a website to show "flip" remodels is a great way to advertise and potentially solicit distressed properties.

If your desired name is available and you register it with the state, it is protected at the state level. You will need to trademark your name to protect it at the federal level. Finally, if you intend to use a website with your business, you'll need to register the domain name as well.

> Using the same name for each registration is not required; doing so is good for advertising, but refraining is more discreet.

Step 3: Register Your Business

When establishing and operating a business entity, regardless of the type, you will need to file certain documents with the state Secretary of State's office. The most important among them are a company's *bylaws*, operating agreement, and articles of organization. Your attorney will be able to assist you with creating and filing these documents with a *registered agent*.[66] They will also advise on the other steps involved with establishing a business.

Articles of Incorporation and Articles of Organization

Many individuals often get confused about the difference between the articles of incorporation and the articles of organization. The simple answer is that articles of incorporation only apply to a corporation (specifically a C or S corp). Articles of organization apply to all other entities.

The most common components to the articles of incorporation include:

- Business Name and Official Location of Your Business*
- The Manner in which the Business will Operate
- Business Management (Manager- or Member-Managed)
- The Purpose of the Business
- Business Owner Names*

66 An individual (or entity) designated to process a business entity's legal actions such as formation or lawsuits. See this article for help deciding whether you should hire an agent: Drake Forester, "Should You Hire a Registered Agent or Be Your Own?," Score, May 17, 2019, https://www.score.org/resource/should-you-hire-registered-agent-or-be-your-own.

- Registered Agent's Name and Address*
- Company Stock Information
- Primary State of Operation

*These topics are also required for articles of organization.

The articles of incorporation and operating agreements outline similar information; however, operating agreements delve into much greater detail. Their purpose is also different. Articles of incorporation are necessary to establish the corporation legally. This document identifies business information and covers the issuance of company stock. It also serves the explicit purpose of distinguishing the business as a separate entity from the business's owners.

Articles of organization provide the same purpose as articles of incorporation but are used for the other types of business structures. Additionally, no mandate exists for them to be filed with the state, although it is often a good idea.

Bylaws and Operating Agreements

There is often considerable confusion pertaining to the difference between bylaws and operating agreements. The difference is akin to that between articles of incorporation and articles of organization. Bylaws apply to corporations, and operating agreements apply to the other business structures.

> All members must sign the document; the document is only enforceable to signatories of the document.

The operating agreement or bylaw is a critical document for your business. This is an internal document that establishes the agreement between members on business operation and dispute resolution. Specifically, this enables your business to operate in a tailored manner agreed upon by the founding members. It also identifies all business and economic arrangements associated with your business. This document includes the following:

- Business Name and Official Location of Your Business
- Business Owner Names
- The Purpose of the Business
- Contributions (Capital and Property)
- Business Management
- Dispute Resolution Processes
- Distribution
- Meeting Conduct and Voting
- Duties, Rights, and Liabilities
- Business Amendments, Dissolution, Duration, and Termination
- Governing Law and Arbitration
- Indemnifications
- *Right of First Refusal* [67]
- Record Keeping

Step 4: Receive Your Federal and State Tax ID

When you register with the state, you will receive your state tax ID number. If your state requires businesses to pay taxes, you must obtain a tax ID number. Always verify the requirement for income taxes and employment taxes, as they vary by state.

Registering with the federal government will provide you with your Employer Identification Number (EIN), which represents your federal tax ID. Banks will require an EIN to open an account, and agencies that issue licenses or permits may as well. Your business entity will need an EIN if your business will perform any of the following functions:

- Pay Employees
- Be a Corporation or Partnership (File Tax Returns for Employment)

The application for an EIN should be accomplished immediately after registering your business.

67 Conditions established allowing for members to transfer owner interest to third parties.

DID YOU KNOW?

In February 2021, the U.S. Equal Employment Opportunity Commission (EEOC)[68] released litigation statistics detailing 67,448 charges of workplace discrimination received during Fiscal Year 2020. The breakdown of these charges is the following:

- Retaliation: 37,632 (55.8 percent)
- Disability: 24,324 (36.1 percent)
- Race: 22,064 (32.7 percent)
- Sex: 21,398 (31.7 percent)
- Age: 14,183 (21.0 percent)
- National Origin: 6,377 (9.5 percent)
- Color: 3,562 (5.3 percent)
- Religion: 2,404 (3.6 percent)
- Equal Pay Act: 980 (1.5 percent)
- Genetic Information: 440 (0.7 percent)

Objective: Utilizing Liability Protection

You may go about ensuring asset and liability protection in many ways. The difference between them pertains to the accepted level of risk. As I've stated previously, some investors will say these protections are unnecessary. If you're willing to operate with a high level of vulnerability when it comes to finances, taxes, protections, and potential litigations, then you may feel comfortable with the exposure. If you wish to mitigate some of these risks and pursue the aforementioned protections, you'll want to follow the tasks listed below.

68 U.S. Equal Employment Opportunity Commission (EEOC) (https://www.eeoc.gov/)

Tasks

- Determine personal and asset liability protection business structure.
    - Anonymity
    - Geography
    - Value threshold
    - Taxation

- Establish property insurance.

- Establish a business entity.
    - Select your structure
    - Identify your name
    - Register your business
    - Receive your tax IDs

- Trust current investment properties into business entities.

- Consider equity stripping (if appropriate).

- Investigate homestead exemptions for primary residence.

If while reading this chapter, there were concepts you wished to see that were either not covered or where you desired additional detail, please annotate and provide feedback via this QR code.

Visit our website (masterofleverage.info) by using this QR code to access key figures and references from this chapter.

Aloof Aaron, Cautious Carl, Sensible Sarah, and Risky Rick

There are those who are overly cautious, those that like to live life on the edge, and those who are somewhere in between. Carl is the former, Rick has built a home on the edge, and Sensible Sarah is somewhere in between. When it comes to leveraging protection, it's really an all-or-nothing proposition. When you (or your assets) are in danger, you're either protected or you're not.

Cautious Carl, generally speaking, likes to maximize his protection. He's the guy that has a lock-tight "prenup," insures his airline tickets, buys extended warranties on his electronic devices, and maxes out his term life insurance. Not surprisingly, he elects to maximize his real estate protection by creating one business entity per property.

Risky Rick doesn't believe in protection and chooses not to use it in hardly any aspect of his life. He believes leveraging business entities for protection are an unnecessary expense. Those horror stories about tenants going after landlords only happen to those people who deserve it. They would never happen to him; he would never become one of those statistics. He forgoes establishing any business entities as a form of liability or asset protection.

Sarah takes the sensible approach; she knows that protection is necessary; however, an abundance of protection can be costly. She is calculated in her risk taking; her approach to real estate is no different. For Sarah, she is comfortable partitioning her real estate portfolio by geography, cumulative value ($500,000), and investment/endeavor type. She wants to ensure she maintains both liability and asset protection for the real estate portfolio she has acquired.

Aloof Aaron is not one for using protection much, either.

Chapter 11: Retaining Your Leverage

A penny saved is worth two pennies earned … after taxes.
—Randy Thurman, *author*

In this chapter, we are going to cover the following:

Key Terms and Concepts

- Tax Preparer vs. Tax Advisor
- Active vs. Passive Business
- Capital vs. Passive Gains and Losses
- Real Estate Professional (Status)
- Property Use (Personal, Rental, Mixed-Use, and Arbitrage)

Business Entity Tax Considerations and Flow-Through Taxation

Decrease, Defer, Reclassify, Transform (DDRT)

- Decreasing Taxes through Business Deductions and Expenses
  - Deduction Categories
    - Current (Business) Expenses
      - Business Expense Qualifying Criteria
    - Depreciable Assets
    - Amortizable Costs
- Deferring Taxes through 1031 Exchange
- Reclassifying Taxable Income by Funding Retirement Accounts
- Transforming Income by Funding Investments through Retirement Accounts

Exit Strategies

- Cash-Out Refinancing – Part II
- Seller Financing – Part II
- Inheritance

> Always consult a taxation professional!
> —*Every successful real estate investor who has ever lived*

Congratulations! You've made it to the chapter that covers the single most complex and frustrating—yet potentially profitable—subject in this book. To build the suspense, let me give you a hint. The subject comes from a familiar adage about the two certainties for humans, and this chapter is not about death. You got it! Time to talk about taxes.

The U.S. government has established (federal) tax law within the *Internal Revenue Code (IRC)*. It is a never-ending aggregation of legal additions to govern the federal tax system. Notice I didn't write *adjustments,* which might imply additions and subtractions. That's because most of the adjustments are additions by Congress dating back to the inception of American taxation. To make matters even more complex, the aggregated case law, which elaborates upon the IRC, is substantially longer than the code itself. Most accountants rely upon this case law and on private rulings to interpret the IRC.

Now, the three-letter agency everyone only whispers in the comfort of their own home or among close friends, the *Internal Revenue Service (IRS),* is the agency chartered to enforce the laws and policies established within the IRC. In reality, the IRS isn't on patrol looking for citizens who are underpaying or not paying their taxes. They operate more like an audit agency, which relies on taxpayers to accurately report their earnings. The IRS audits a percentage annually. Much to our dismay, the IRS will be quick to identify and collect delinquent accounts, even if the error was an honest mistake. But they will not identify manners in which a taxpayer has overpaid because they missed legal deductions. Because of this, it is imperative that taxpayers understand their responsibility to correctly navigate this complex tax code and correctly account for all allowable deductions. In this chapter, I intend to assist you with navigating the IRC and provide potential tax strategies that may work for you. Please understand I am not a tax attorney or your CPA. Always consult a tax advisor to find what approach will ultimately be best for you.

Key Terms and Concepts

The tax code is complex, but it is possible to understand enough basics to lessen your tax burden. You need to be able to communicate with a qualified advisor so you and he or she can develop a strategy. Tax strategies are not one size fits all; they should be tailor-made for individuals and their respective businesses.

Before delving into these various tax strategies, you should first understand a few key terms and concepts specific to tax law and associated activities; these will be applicable regardless of the manner of tax strategy you choose to employ or whether you are leveraging a business entity. The five main concepts I wish to convey to you before going more in depth into other tax strategies are the following:

- Tax Preparer vs. Tax Advisor
- Active vs. Passive Business
- Capital vs. Passive Gains and Losses
- Real Estate Professional (Status)
- Property Use: Personal, Rental, Mixed-Use, and Arbitrage

Tax Preparer vs. Tax Advisor

You may be asking, "What is the difference between a *tax preparer* and a *tax advisor*? Aren't they both tax professionals?" They are, but the services they provide are very different and so is the outcome you will receive. Tax preparers can be very good at what they do. They assist those who are unfamiliar with how to complete their taxes. I had leveraged tax preparers prior to owning real estate to calculate and file my taxes; however, once I started investing in real estate, I quickly realized I needed a tax advisor, not just a tax preparer.

This is largely because tax preparers are reactionary—they take the information and records you provide and file them based on what they see. This is what you will find if you stroll into your local H&R Block. For many non-investors, this may suffice. Tax advisors, on the other hand, are more proactive. They are qualified to offer advice on how you may more effectively run your business and claim the appropriate expenses and deductions. The good ones are familiar with tax law specifically pertaining to real estate. Tax advisors are uniquely qualified to do what their title implies: give you advice about your taxes. I do not mean to appear disparaging toward tax preparers; they also provide a valuable service in line with their title. However, having your taxes prepared isn't the service a budding real estate investor requires.

Active vs. Passive Business

What is the difference between *active business* and *passive business*? In Chapter 1, I covered the differences between active and passive income. Active and passive business is the obvious corollary. Active business refers to a business that is providing a service through means of *material participation*.[69] Activities such as property management, construction, consulting, and being a real estate agent fall in the active category. Passive business occurs without the need for material participation. A business in which owning and leasing property is its primary purpose is passive business. The type of business you are operating, the associated provided services, and your level of material participation play a tremendous role in determining what you can claim as a deduction or expense, the amount you may deduct, and the amount of profit you may legally offset.

Capital vs. Passive Gains and Losses

The difference between how you categorize income and how the IRS taxes it is an important concept. Think of capital gains/losses as income earned/lost by conducting active business. All capital gains/losses are captured during the year in which they occurred (year sold when pertaining to a property). You can deem these gains/losses as either short-term or long-term. The tax code allows you to use *capital losses* to offset capital gains. The IRS factors short-term capital gains into income calculations and assesses taxes at the taxpayer's ordinary rate. They will calculate long-term capital gains[70] at a lower rate, also dependent upon the taxpayer's bracket.

69 Routinely being involved with the management and operations of your real estate investments.

70 Capital gains from assets with a holding period of more than one year.

> Excess capital losses may be used to offset up to $3,000 of ordinary income; you may carry additional excess losses to future years.

Passive income/losses are those accrued by means of passive business activity such as the collection of rental income or rents. The IRC limits the number of passive losses you can deduct during any given year to that of the taxpayer's total passive income. However, like capital losses, you may carry forward excess passive losses to future years.

I highlight these concepts so savvy investors such as yourself do not get blindsided by attempting to leverage capital losses (above $3,000) to offset passive gains or to leverage passive losses to offset capital gains (unless the property sold is the same for which passive losses have been carried over).

> Capital/passive losses are carried forward to future years until 1) capital/passive income offsets accrued capital/passive loss or 2) the property is sold, at which point the gains from sale offset the losses.

Real Estate Professional (Status)

What does it mean to be a real estate professional and what does this status gain you? You may think that you must be a real estate agent or broker who is in the business of buying and selling properties. That is not necessary. You may think you need to own your real estate license, even if you are not practicing. That is also incorrect. You also don't need to own your properties under a legal entity. In actuality, you could be all of these things and not be qualified as a real estate professional or have none of these things and still qualify.

To qualify as a real estate professional in the eyes of the IRS, you must meet three requirements:

1. Member spends 750 or more hours per year conducting real estate activities (including material participation)
2. More time is spent conducting real estate activities than other forms of employment combined
3. Accumulated time must be for one taxpayer, not a combined total of a team

Meeting these requirements is not insurmountable; however, it does require meticulous documentation. If working in real estate is your only job, this will be easy. If it isn't, and you have another job, you must document that you spent more time conducting real estate-related business than your other job.

Attaining status as a real estate professional removes the loss carryover limitation and permits passive losses to offset ordinary income. When combined with cost segregation and accelerated depreciation (concepts covered later in this chapter), this can be a powerful tool to reduce your tax liability.

Property Use (Personal, Rental, Mixed-Use, and Arbitrage)

The IRC classifies and taxes properties according to four classifications, depending on how you are using the property. Being aware of the classifications and using them effectively will reduce your tax liability. Here are the four main property use types:

- Personal
- Rental
- Mixed-Use
- Arbitrage

Personal Property

Typically, *personal property* is an individual's primary and/or secondary (vacation) home. Logic would dictate that if the primary purpose of a property is for you or your family to live in it, the IRC would classify it as your personal property. It's not that simple. A property must meet two criteria to be deemed personal use:

1. You live in the property for more than 14 days per year.
2. The property has been rented out for fewer than 15 days per year.

Meeting both of these requirements provides you with two tax advantages:

1. The (short-term) rental income is tax free.
2. You may claim 100 percent of the mortgage interest and property taxes for your home as a personal deduction.

Rental Property

The IRC classifies real estate as *rental property* when you breach one of the following thresholds (whichever is the larger threshold of the two):

1. When personal use days are fewer than 14 per month
2. When personal use days are less than 10 percent of the days rented

In this instance, the indirectly related expenses (including mortgage interest and property taxes) are prorated to the amount of time used for personal and rental purposes and taxed accordingly. You do not need to prorate expenses directly related to the rental portion of the property, but you can directly deduct them from the business as an expense.

Mixed-Use

The IRC defines the *mixed-use* classification to describe a property as a "dwelling unit used as a home." In this case, a property must meet the following criteria to qualify:

1. The property is lived in for more than 14 days or 10 percent of days rented (whichever is the larger threshold).
2. The property is rented out for more than 14 days.

A great example of a mixed-use property is a duplex in which you are living in one side. The indirectly related expenses would be prorated accordingly with one exception. The IRC does not permit indirectly related expenses to drive a passive loss of income; you may reduce the rental income to net zero. Directly related expenses would still be deducted as a business expense.

Arbitrage

Arbitrage, or *rental arbitrage* to be more specific, is the practice of renting a unit from an owner and subleasing the unit as a short-term rental or on a short-term basis. This is an approach commonly used by individuals who either cannot or do not wish to own property but want to earn money as a landlord. Taxation of arbitrage has a few nuances. For the most part, it is treated no differently than rental units, with the following exceptions:

1. There is no depreciation deduction on the property, but you can write off deductions on furniture.
2. You may deduct rent expenses.

The IRC property types are complex. Refer to Figure 11-1 for clarification.

> If you plan to perform a rental arbitrage, you may want to first check with your landlord. Some convenances have strict rules against subleasing to include arbitrage.

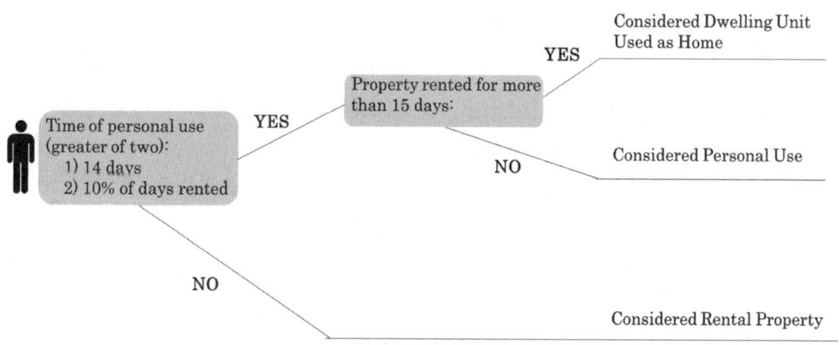

Figure 11-1: Property Use – Flow Chart

Business Entity Tax Considerations and Flow-Through Taxation

Flow-through or *pass-through taxation* is a tax distinction for business entities that are not legally dissociated from the owner. In these instances, you do not report and file the business income/losses as a separate entity. You report and file them on the owner's individual tax return. The business has no tax liability for the business income/losses since they have "flowed through" the business to the owner, where the income/losses are aggregated with the individual's other income and taxed at the owner's tax rate.

Take careful consideration when selecting your business entity structure due to the taxation implications. In the previous chapter, I outlined several benefits and differences between the business entities, specifically that of the C corporation and the S corporation. The following table outlines the differences in taxation:

	C-Type Corp	S-Type Corp
Taxation Type	Corporate	Personal
Taxation Method	Double	Pass Through
Tax Period	Fiscal Year	Calendar
Deductions	Increased	Standard

Table 11-1: C Corp and S Corp Comparison

Most other business entities have pass-through taxation and emulate the S corporation, as illustrated in the above table. LLC owners may elect how the IRS will tax their LLC based on the initiation of the entity. If you're establishing an LLC, you are likely starting as a disregarded entity or taxation as an S corp. If necessary, you can modify your classification at a later time; in fact, all businesses may change their entity type with the proper filing, but penalties may apply.

Decrease, Defer, Reclassify, Transform (DDRT)

Now that we've covered a few of the core concepts pertaining to real estate, we can address the act of retaining your leverage by managing your taxes efficiently. When looking for effective techniques to minimize your taxes, you have four actions you may take. Although several variations exist, the main techniques to minimize taxes fall into these four categories:

- Decrease taxes through business deductions and expenses
- Defer taxes through 1031 exchange
- Reclassify taxable income by funding retirement accounts
- Transform income by funding investments through retirement accounts

Remember, this doesn't mean you will always retain all of your hard earned money, but it may mean your money is spent in a manner that best benefits you and your business.

Decreasing Taxes through Business Deductions and Expenses

The most common technique for decreasing taxes is to offset the taxes according to IRS-approved business deductions and expenses. You don't need to be a business professional or leverage business entities to take advantage of this approach. Your only requirement is to have forethought and keep careful records. While daunting at first, it becomes second nature, especially when you understand the financial impact at tax time. First, you will need to understand the differences between the various deduction categories and how they are handled. Remember, all deductions are expenses, but not all expenses are deductions.

Deduction Categories

The IRC affords numerous deductions to real estate investors, but you must be responsible and savvy enough to track, record, and file them. A good tax advisor will prepare your tax returns and look into deductions you qualify for. Although numerous permissible deductions are available, they fall into one of three general categories:

- Current (Business) Expenses
- Depreciable Assets
- Amortizable Costs

In order to claim a deduction, you must have first incurred an expense, meaning you will need to spend capital. It is important to spend capital on things that enhance your business and, at the same time, qualify as a deductible expense.

Current (Business) Expenses

Business expenses are just that—expenses incurred in the act of running or maintaining a business. For the most part, the rules associated with expenses (as opposed to other deductions) are straightforward. You simply subtract the expenses from the profits; these are usually called *current expenses* because they are subtracted from the profit in the year in which the expense occurred. Refer to Figure 11-2 for a sample listing of current business expenses.

Some expenses have special governances dictating the extent to which they are deductible.

Legal entity constructs may either impose additional limitations or allow for greater deductions, depending on the type of entity and the situation.

- Advertising
- Appraisals
- Associations
- Assessments
- Bad Debts
- Bookkeeping
- Charitable Contributions
- Cleaning Services
- Conventions
- Dependent Care
- Education & Seminars
- Employee Wages
- Entertainment*
- Fees
    - Cleaning Services
    - HOA
    - Office Services
- Home Office
- Insurance
- Internet
- Leases & Rent
- Licenses
- Meals*
- Property Improvements
- Repairs
- Shipping
- Supplies
- Taxes
- Travel
- Utilities
- Vehicle Expenses*

Figure 11-2: Sample Listing of Current (Business) Expenses

*Expenses and deductions are only permitted under specific circumstances.

Business Expense Qualifying Criteria

The aforementioned list is not all-inclusive; you may add more expenses to this list as long as you (and your CPA) can justify them. It is important to ask, "What is justified in the eyes of the IRS?" The IRS determines a qualified business expense based on four primary questions or criteria. Generally, you must be able to answer *yes* to all four questions to classify an expense as a viable business-related expense rather than a personal expense:

1. Is the expense necessary for your business to produce income?
2. Is the expense an ordinary requirement for your type of business?
3. Is the expense reasonable for the size of your business and income?
4. Is the expense legally permitted under current statutes and limitations?

> A home office deduction requires two criteria: 1) The space must be your primary place of work for your business, and 2) the area must be used exclusively for business purposes—a space dedicated solely for work.

The first three questions are subjective. They require you to apply logic when exercising this approach to reduce your tax liability. Consult your CPA well in advance of tax filing season. If incurring any kind of expense, it is best to do so deliberately and in accordance with a plan. If you are traveling and plan to write off expenses during the trip, be sure to bookend your trip with business-related activities. You will need to be able to prove that the primary purpose of your trip was business-related if you want to write off 100 percent of your expenses.

Avoid generating unnecessary expenses so you can write them off on taxes. Simply capture and record the legitimate expenses you incur. Work from this perspective: give Uncle Sam his fair share, but not a penny more!

Depreciable Assets

The second category of deductions is *depreciable assets*. A depreciable asset is a means for legal entities to capture and recover (by deducting from taxes) some of the cost of age, deterioration, and other wear and tear on an asset, which, in a real estate context, is a property. This is calculated by prorating the purchase price of an asset over its *recovery period*[71] as determined by the IRS property class. You may deduct the annual prorate from your taxes. You can capture depreciation on a property, even when it is appreciating in value. It's not intuitive, but the IRC dictates that your real estate is both appreciating and depreciating at the same time. IRS Publication 946 covers the numerous ways in which you may depreciate a property. I have simplified the principles in Figure 11-3, which provides a small sampling of assets that may be depreciated. Also, see Table 11-2 for the depreciation table categories.

71 Time period over which an asset's basis may be deducted.

- Appliances
- Carpet & Flooring
- Computers & Devices
- Computer Software
- Cabinets & Countertops
- Fixtures
- Furniture
- Office Equipment
- Property Improvements
- Product Development
- Real Estate (Not Land)
- Tools
- HVAC
- Water Heaters
- Vehicles

Figure 11-3: Sample of Depreciable Assets.

Property Class	Recovery Period
3-Year Property	3 Years
5-Year Property	5 Years
7-Year Property	7 Years
Residential Property	27.5 Years
Nonresidential Property (Not Land)	39 Years

*General Depreciation System (GDS) method

Table 11-2: Property Class and Recovery Periods

Cost Segregation

There are other property classes in addition to those shown in Table 11-2; however, most aspects of real estate will fall into one of the aforementioned categories. When assessing depreciable assets, it is important to know: 1) that they may be deducted, and 2) their property class and associated recovery period. If you've incurred any of these expenses, you may claim the deduction over its associated recovery period rather than over the recovery period of the real estate dwelling (27.5 years). This is an advantageous manner to capture deductions when performing rehabs of distressed properties.

Amortizable Costs

Amortization is the act of capturing the cost of an asset over a duration of time. It sounds similar to depreciation, but it has some differences. The primary difference is that you leverage amortization for intangible costs and major expenditures. *Intangible* in this context is synonymous with *immaterial.* Some intangible expenditures related to real estate might include business setup expenses, any intellectual property costs, and possible product research and development. There are others, but they are less commonly associated with owning and maintaining real estate.

DID YOU KNOW?

In 2018, the Tax Foundation determined that property taxes comprised 71.7 percent of all U.S. locality tax collections across the nation and 31.1 percent of all U.S. state collections (a larger proportion than any other singular source of tax revenue).

States with the highest proportion of property tax revenue include:
1. New Hampshire – 63.8 percent
2. Alaska – 45.6 percent
3. New Jersey – 45.5 percent
4. Texas – 44 percent
5. Vermont – 43.1 percent

Note: most of these states have little to no state income tax as an offset to the higher proportion of property taxes.

Deferring Taxes through 1031 Exchange

The IRC Section 1031, commonly referred to as the *1031 exchange,* is a procedure that allows real estate investors to defer paying capital gains taxes when selling a property if the proceeds of that sale are used to purchase a like-kind property of equal or greater value within an approved time limit.

A like-kind investment is real estate—whether it be residential, commercial, or land—as long as the owner uses it for investment, not for resale or personal use. Investors should seek a replacement property (or properties) of equal or greater value to receive the full benefit of the 1031 exchange. Equal or greater value means that the property or properties purchased meet the following two requirements:

1. Purchase Price Target
2. EquityTarget

> The same legal entity that holds the original property must purchase the replacement property. If the first property is in your name, you must make the purchase; if it is in the name of an LLC, the LLC must make the purchase.

The *purchase price target* means the total purchase price of all the properties in the exchange must be equal to or greater than the sale price of the identified property. If Investor Bob sold a property for $200,000, the property's or properties' total purchase price must be $200,000 or more. The *equity target* means that the total amount of money you fund into the replacement property must be greater than or equal to the equity you received from selling the property. I refrain from referring to the amount of money as capital because it never actually touches your hands in the exchange. It's a transference of equity from one asset to one or multiple new assets. If, for whatever reason, you fall short of one of these two requirements, the total sum is not taxable. Only the deficit will be taxable.

While this is a useful tool to defer paying taxes, several restrictions as to what is eligible for the 1031 exchange are in place: the biggest being primary use (primary residences/secondary or vacation) properties and fix-and-flip properties.

Additionally, you have strict timelines to which you must adhere when pursuing a 1031 exchange; you must specify your intent at closing and identify a replacement property for the property sold within 45 days. You must also complete the exchange within 180 days.

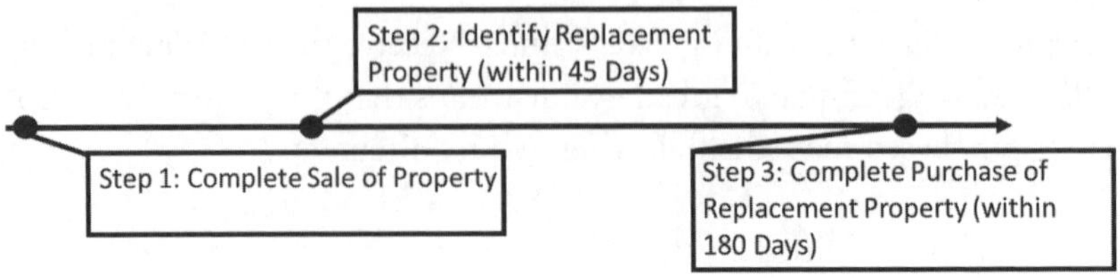

Figure 11-4: 1031 Exchange Timeline

Furthermore, you must also adhere to the following three rules:

- 3 Property Rule: Identify 3 properties for purchase (regardless of value)
- 200 Percent Rule: Identify unlimited properties (cumulative value < 200%)
- 95 Percent Rule: Identify unlimited properties (if acquired for > 95% of value)

If, for whatever reason, you cannot meet these timelines, the sum of the profit from the sale will become taxable. Because of this, many investors elect to execute a reverse 1031 exchange. It's not as complicated as it sounds; in fact, most details are the same with one caveat. It allows for the buyer to select, identify, and purchase a replacement property before the initial property is sold; this can be useful if you are in a competitive market and have the funds to do so. With either method of the 1031 exchange, you are playing a high-stakes game of keep-away with the IRS, but it might be worth it.

In order for a 1031 exchange to be valid, you must hire an independent third party to act as your intermediary. You must identify them before selling your asset.

Reclassifying Taxable Income by Funding Retirement Accounts

The third tax-saving technique is to offset what you are paying for taxes by funding your retirement account. The IRC has limits as to how much they permit you to invest each year. Leveraging business entities increases the limit of how much you can fund your retirement account.

Any growth your life investment experiences while in the retirement account will be tax free. You can retain your investments in a traditional retirement account, which is invested in various stocks, bonds, and certificates of deposit (CD), or you may elect to leverage a self-directed retirement account. Self-directed accounts provide you, as the taxpayer and investor, more flexibility in determining how your advisor invests your money and ultimately impacts your potential growth. The next section outlines how you may leverage these types of retirement accounts to aid you in expanding your real estate portfolio.

The question isn't at what age I want to retire, it's at what income.
—George Foreman, *professional boxer and entrepreneur*

Transforming Income by Funding Investments through Retirement Accounts

Funding real estate investments through your retirement accounts is a useful strategy if done correctly. Most retirement accounts are managed by a broker who invests your funds in a combination of stocks, bonds, certificates of deposit (CD), and so forth. Many people are unaware that some retirement accounts may be self-managed and, in fact, self-directed. These accounts permit the member to select and direct where their account's funds are invested—and real estate is an available option.

They are also unaware of the benefits and limitations associated with self-directed IRAs and other retirement vehicles, such as the *Solo 401(k)*.[72] One of the main perks of these plans is not only that they may be leveraged but also that any profits made from the entity will grow tax free—as long as all profits return to the investment vehicle.

Let's say Investor Bob stashed $200,000 into his retirement account largely because he wanted to live comfortably in the future, and because it allowed him to offset taxes. Now that Investor Bob is retired, he can transfer his retirement from a managed 401(k) to a self-directed retirement program. Figure 11-5 provides a non-all-inclusive list of self-directed retirement accounts.

72 Self-directed retirement account for individuals who are self-employed or own their own business with no employees.

- Traditional IRA
- Roth IRA
- SEP-IRA
- Spouse IRA
- Inherited IRA
- Solo(k)

Figure 11-5: Self-Directed Retirement Accounts

Investor Bob could self-direct the funds in his account toward another real estate acquisition. Let's say he found another property for $200,000; if he chooses to purchase the asset, any rental income he garners will automatically be tax free as long as all profits return to his retirement account. If Investor Bob decides to sell the property 10 years down the line and garners capital gains of $100,000, those gains are also tax free!

Solo 401(k) self-directed accounts have many other perks, including larger allowances for contributions than other retirement accounts. Be sure to do your research to fully explore this option.

Investor Bob could also choose to leverage funding from financial institutions by means of his retirement accounts. That's right. Lending institutions will provide loans to self-directed retirement accounts. Let's say Investor Bob found three properties worth $200,000. He could take out three loans, provide a total of $150,000 for down payments, and leverage the lender's $450,000 to acquire the assets. Not a bad approach, but you have to exercise caution. The IRS retains a provision called "Unrelated Debt-Financed Income" (UDFI). In short, this means that the percentage leveraged may be subject to taxes, which in this case is 75 percent. Assess the ROI and ROE to determine if leveraging lending within your retirement account provides a greater benefit or not. Transforming your income in this manner is another way of taking advantage of IRS incentives meant to promote good social behavior.

> Planning to retire? Before you do, find your hidden passion. Do the thing that you have always wanted to do.
> —Catherine Pulsifer, *author*

Isn't it great to also use your hidden passion to fuel your retirement?

Exit Strategies

Have you ever watched a TV show that built up to a disappointing climax? That's the disappointment I had with *Lost, Game of Thrones,* and *Star Wars Episodes VII, VIII,* and *IX.* I was in disbelief and despair because of all the time I had invested for a culmination that disappointed my expectations.

The same despair can occur in your investments if your strategy doesn't include a good exit plan. We call the exit plan of investing *estate planning.* It allows you to reap the benefits of your labors and secure your legacy for your beneficiaries.

Typically, people invest in real estate with one of two intentions: 1) to generate income to support a certain quality lifestyle, or 2) to provide a legacy for future generations. There are techniques you can leverage to accomplish both of these goals; however, they require active planning and a little forethought. Many tactics are available to you, but I want to emphasize three that are musts for your toolbox:

- Cash-Out Refinancing
- Seller Financing
- Inheritance

Cash-Out Refinancing – Part II

Pretend that Investor Bob is now a little older and wants to kick back and enjoy retirement in his senior years. If you recall, he purchased five investment properties 30 years ago for $200,000 each, a combined value of $1,000,000. Now Investor Bob wants to spend time with his wife and travel the world—and he wants his investment properties to fund their adventures. If he sells the properties, which have appreciated to a value of $450,000 each for a combined value of $2,250,000, the IRS will hand him a hefty tax bill for long-term capital gains. At 21 percent, the taxes due would be $472,500. Bob and his wife would have a significant amount of money they earned through real estate investing, but Uncle Sam would take about half a million dollars of it. Investor Bob knows there must be a better way, and he's smart enough to find legal strategies to keep his hard-earned money.

His first option is to cash-out refinance. This way, he could recoup his hard-earned capital and still maintain a profit-generating asset. If this is sounding familiar, it's because we have already discussed how to use cash-out refinancing to leverage your equity, reinvest, and increase your portfolio growth. This is using the same tactic Bob used when he was putting his foot on the accelerator and expanding his portfolio. At retirement, however, he eases off the petal and sustains his portfolio, allowing his tenants' rents to fund his retirement lifestyle.

Take a look at Figure 11-6 to compare Bob's options:

Sell		Cash-Out Refinance	
Total Sales Price:	$2,250,000	Total Value:	$2,250,000
Realtor Fees (6%):	$135,000	75% LTV:	$1,687,500
Total (Taxable) Gain:	$2,250,000	Total (Taxable) Gain:	$0
Taxes Due (@ 21%):	$472,500	Taxes Due (@ 21%):	$0
Funds in Pocket:	$1,642,500	Funds in Pocket:	$1,687,500
			& 4 income generating properties

Figure 11-6: Cash-Out Refinance – Part II

As you can clearly see, cash-out refinancing is the better approach for Investor Bob, as he possesses more cash in hand and retains the properties, which will continue to appreciate and fund his future endeavors.

Let's consider another scenario that isn't quite as rosy for Investor Bob. Imagine one of his properties hasn't fared too well and requires significant repairs soon; it is farther away from his centers of gravity and is in an area with a shifting market. Investor Bob should be hesitant to cash-out refinance that asset. At the same time, he is uncomfortable with giving Uncle Sam a large portion of his hard-earned income, so he looks for another option.

Seller Financing – Part II

I know we've covered seller financing in a previous chapter, but we'll discuss its advantages again, this time from the seller's perspective. The structure of seller financing is essentially two loans: one loan on the remaining mortgage debt and the other on the difference between the mortgage and the sale price.

Suppose Investor Bob wants to divest himself of his underperforming property. He has found an investor who is willing to purchase using seller financing. This is now an ideal solution for Investor Bob. With the mortgage paid off, Bob can negotiate the down payment quantity and associated interest rate directly with the buyer. Investor Bob will need to pay taxes on the negotiated amount of the down payment but may defer the remaining taxes over the life of the loan. The buyer is now responsible for maintaining the property as if it were his own, yet Investor Bob is secured against unfortunate downturns by maintaining possession of the note. To see the advantages, let's assume Investor Bob negotiates for a 5 percent down payment for the property in exchange for a 7 percent interest rate. Figure 11-7 identifies the differences in taxation between these two approaches.

Conventional Sale		Seller Financed	
Total Sale Price:	$450,000	Total Sale Price:	$450,000
Carryover Basis:	-	Carryover Basis:	-
Realtor Fees (6%):	$27,000	Realtor Fees (6%):	-
Total (Taxable) Gain:	$450,000	Total (Taxable) Gain:	$22,500
Taxes Due (@21%):	$94,500	Taxes Due (@21%):	$4,725
Funds in Hand:	$328,500	Funds in Hand:	$17,775

Figure 11-7: Seller Financing – Part II

At first glance, you may be tempted to say, "Not worth it. I rather take the $328,500!" That may be better for you, and it likely would be if you were still planning on growing your portfolio. Investor Bob isn't looking to continue expanding but rather to enjoy his retirement. And he will when he receives monthly payments of roughly $2,800 for the next 30 years. I think Investor Bob can manage to live comfortably off of that monthly stipend, especially since he already cash-out refinanced $1,670,000.

Inheritance

To give a *gift* or an *inheritance*—that is the question. In neither case does the recipient have to pay taxes, right? Wrong! It's true that the IRS will not collect taxes at the time of transfer; however, the *basis*[73] can be of monumental difference. When an asset is transferred as a gift, the basis of the gift is also transferred. Conversely, an asset transferred as an inheritance is granted a "basis step-up" to the FMV of the asset.

> Inheritance can be combined with the 1031 exchange program. If taxes have been deferred by means of the 1031 up to the point of your passing, your beneficiaries still gain the basis step-up despite years or decades of deferment. This is often referred to as "swap till you drop."

Investor Bob can help us understand why this matters. Let's now say it's 30 years later, and Investor Bob is nearing the end of his life. Naturally, he wants to pass along a financial legacy to his heirs. This legacy will be the four investment properties he purchased to generate wealth. He bought five of them 60 years ago for $200,000 each, a combined value of $1,000,000. He sold one via seller financing and retained the four remaining. Due to appreciation, they are now each worth $900,000, a combined value of $3,600,000. For one child, Investor Bob foolishly decides to gift two of the properties; the other child will receive two properties as an inheritance.

73 The purchase price plus any upgrades minus non-recouped capital expenditures or other debt obligations.

Here's how Investor Bob's legacy plays out. Since the 30-year note is paid off, there is no carryover basis (adjustment of basis to zero upon the death of the initial buyer); the IRS would consider the entirety of the sale profit, and it would be taxed accordingly.

Gift | Inheritance

Gift

Total Sale Price:	$1,800,000
Carryover Basis:	-
Total (Taxable) Gain:	$1,800,000
Taxes Due (@35%):	$630,000

Inheritance

Total Sale Price:	$1,800,000
Carryover Basis:	$1,800,000
Total (Taxable) Gain:	$0
Taxes Due (@35%):	$0

Figure 11-8: Gift vs. Inheritance

As you can see, one child fared considerably better with $1,800,000 in hand as opposed to $1,170,000. Although both fared well, Uncle Sam "inherited" $630,000 from Investor Bob's poor planning. Unless there is a pressing reason for your beneficiaries to possess an asset before your passing, it is better to transfer the asset via an inheritance rather than as a gift.

> If you are concerned about transfer of assets or who will receive which assets at the time of your passing, consider establishing an irrevocable trust assigning assets to specific individuals.

DID YOU KNOW?

The federal government and various states impose an estate tax if you reside in one of these states at the time of your decease. Your estate may be subject to the aforementioned tax. As of 2021, the following states impose an estate tax:

Connecticut, Hawaii, Illinois, Maine, Maryland, Massachusetts, Minnesota, New York, Oregon, Rhode Island, Washington, Vermont, and Washington, DC.

These various states' estate tax thresholds range from $1 million (Oregon and Massachusetts) to $5.74 million (New York). As of 2021, the federal threshold is $11.7 million.

Furthermore, some states also impose an inheritance tax, not to be confused with the estate tax. These states are Iowa, Kentucky, Maryland, Nebraska, New Jersey, and Pennsylvania. The estate is responsible for estate taxes; conversely, the beneficiary is responsible for inheritance taxes.

Always consult your financial and tax advisor to ensure your hard work is transferred in the manner in which you intended.

Objective: Retaining Your Leverage

I have presented several tax strategies in this chapter, and only some may apply to you. Familiarize yourself with the techniques that will likely apply to you and develop a strategy that works for your situation. If you are conducting business that is largely active business and garners capital gains, you'll likely need to plan for capital losses to offset them. If conducting business that is passive and garners passive income, passive losses may be used to offset gains.

Regardless of which techniques you employ, the most important aspect is that you are proactive in your tax planning. The most effective tax strategies are deliberate and require cognizance. An effective strategy is proactive, not retroactive or by happenstance. Remember, a good tax advisor will assist you in developing your strategy. The following tasks are a recap of the considerations previously covered within this chapter:

Tasks

- Acquire a good tax advisor.
- Assess proper business entity structures.
- Assess real estate portfolio property type uses.
  - Personal/Arbitrage property
    - Reclassify taxable income by funding retirement accounts
  - Rental/Mixed-use property
    - Decreasing taxes through business deductions and expenses
    - Deferring taxes through 1031 exchange
    - Transforming income by funding investments through retirement accounts
- Develop an exit strategy.
  - Cash-out refinance
  - Seller finance
  - Transfer via inheritance

If while reading this chapter, there were concepts you wished to see that were either not covered or where you desired additional detail, please annotate and provide feedback via this QR code.

Visit our website (masterofleverage.info) by using this QR code to access key figures and references from this chapter.

Aloof Aaron, Cautious Carl, Sensible Sarah, and Risky Rick

Retaining your leverage, or at least your hard-earned wealth, is something most people can get behind. Cautious Carl, Sensible Sarah, and Risky Rick have each garnered a reputable tax advisor to assist with planning and managing their portfolio. They are all adept at appropriately categorizing their income and annotating their deductions and expenses. Additionally, they each are knowledgeable on utilizing the 1031 exchange for those instances when they elect to sell a property. Furthermore, they have all been advised on how to reclassify their taxable income by funding their retirement accounts. Finally, each investor has learned how to transform their income by funding their investments through their retirement accounts.

Aloof Aaron is not familiar with these methods of retaining leverage (garnered income and wealth). Fortunately for him, his parents are familiar with these techniques.

Chapter 12: Maximizing Your Leverage with Networking

> **Networking is not about just connecting people. It's about connecting people with people, people with ideas, and people with opportunities.**
> —Michele Jennae, *author*

In this chapter, we are going to cover the following:

Types of Networking

- Relationships Are about Give and Take, Authenticity, and Consistency
- Professional Networking
- Personal Networking

Pre-Established Relationships

- High-Producing Agents and Team Members
- Family, Friends, and Word of Mouth
- Fellow Real Estate Investors

> Your network is your net worth.
> —Porter Gale, *author and international speaker*

Successful people perceive the role of networking differently. Some argue that networking is the most critical action you could take toward being successful. Others argue that it may be helpful, but they elevate a strong work ethic over networking. I would argue that both are correct. But the argument for work ethic may be reserved for the privileged or for those who have individuals networking for them—with or without their knowledge.

In the introduction of this book, I referred to a metaphor about a flower and what makes one grow more than another. Networking provides the ability for a flower to acquire nutrients it would not otherwise be able to organically obtain. Think about a flower isolated in the desert. A good gardener may bring resources to the flower or relocate it to a more nourishing environment. What a gardener does for a flower, a network does for you.

Networking enables the investor to identify opportunities, locate deals, and engage with team members they may not otherwise have access to or be able to engage with. If you already have easy access to all the properties, all the people, and all the resources, networking will not be as beneficial to you. But if you are still building your portfolio, networking may be the key to finding the right conditions for cultivating a successful career.

There is no one way to network; in fact, there are many. The three common threads among all of them are give and take, authenticity, and consistency. This chapter covers several methods to network effectively. Choose the ones you authentically enjoy and would be willing to leverage. As you lean in, you can help others, even when they may not be able to return the favor. You will begin to see connections grow; and with a growing network, your success will grow exponentially.

Types of Networking

We categorize networking as either professional or personal, but most networking is interrelated. Figure 12-1 reflects the connected relationship by highlighting places and instances where you naturally network. Keep in mind that this is not an all-inclusive list, but it may help you find inspiration within the constraints of your available time and interests.

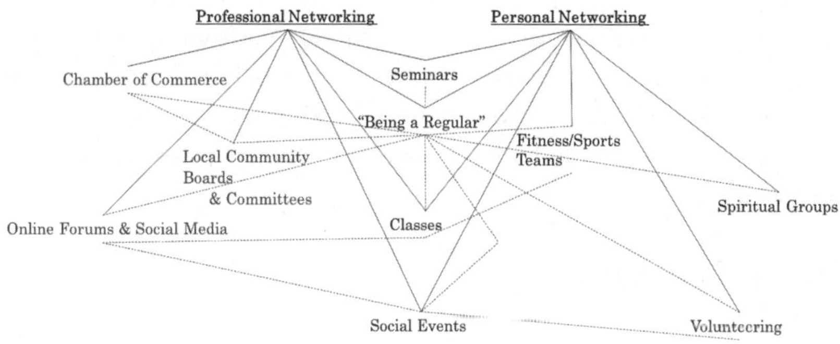

Figure 12-1: Networking

- Professional Networking
  - Chamber of Commerce
  - Local Community Boards and Committees
  - Online Forums and Social
  - Media
  - Seminars
- Personal Networking
  - Classes
  - Fitness/Sports Teams
  - Social Events
  - Religious/Spiritual
  - Groups
  - Volunteering

Relationships Are about Give and Take, Authenticity, and Consistency

Regardless of your choice to engage in professional or personal networking, there is one thing you must do: be consistent. You need to "become a regular." Consistency breeds familiarity, and familiarity wrapped in authenticity is the key to *trust.* Trust is the foundation upon which beneficial relationships are built, and establishing and maintaining beneficial relationships is the purpose of networking. You want to be the go-to guy in whatever venture you are establishing. This applies to networking as well.

You want to be the person people go to and refer others to for information or resources. That makes you, your skills, and your team the hot commodity, which is both powerful and valuable. An effective networker doesn't abuse his or her power. Networking is mutually beneficial, so seek to help others as much as possible. If you perceive that someone in your network is always taking but never giving, you may sever the bond and look for another relationship that is mutually beneficial.

Professional Networking

The difference between professional and personal networking is merely how they are perceived. One isn't necessarily more effective than the other; it comes down to what you are the most comfortable with and interested in. Professional networking tends to be more formal. If you are interested in more structured types of networking, you should take the time to look within your community for various associations that meet your interest. The following are merely a few examples of some activities I consider to be professional networking.

Chamber of Commerce

A great place to begin networking within your community professionally is your local chamber of commerce. Many cities' chambers of commerce are open forum, meaning that they are open to local business owners. Try attending meetings and events regularly to establish your reputation as a local. Once you've established a steady reputation, you'll be exposed to networking opportunities as well as other opportunities that rise within the chamber.

Local Community Boards and Committees

If the local chamber of commerce is too daunting or simply more than you are comfortable with, scale down to the local community boards and committees you may already be a part of. If you are a parent, consider your school's Parent Teacher Organization (PTO), a home or business owner association, or the zoning or transportation commission. These may not look as if they directly relate to real estate, but don't underestimate their value. You may be surprised by the networking opportunities they hold. While attending the PTO, conversations may arise pertaining to various issues ongoing within the community—issues that may impact the future value of real estate or, better yet, issues that may be turned into synergistic opportunities. Joining or attending the zoning and/or transportation commission may allow access to information you could use to determine the direction of growth for the populace. At the very least, professionals and residents of the neighborhood will look to your knowledge and advice; they may be willing to share theirs in return.

Online Forums and Social Media

Admittedly, joining or attending your chamber of commerce or local community committees is kind of old school. They are effective but often require you to be physically present. Social media and online forums, on the other hand, are the new-school approach. These media provide a phenomenal way to network. They're an efficient and relatively easy way to virtually meet people and establish yourself within the community as a trustworthy expert.

Keep in mind that online interactions are an aid, not a total replacement for in-person interaction. This is a both/and proposition. Eventually, you need face-to-face engagements with those whose relationships you are truly trying to codify. Be persistent in your online presence to build the bridge; then walk across the network bridge into face-to-face relationship building.

Seminars

Finally, do not forget about local seminars; they represent a sea of local real estate agents, potential buyers, various types of contractors, and fellow investors. All of these members are potential networking opportunities because they have the intent to be involved in real estate. Many people (novice and veteran alike) attend these forums and view them as transactional. Many such forums may be transactional, but they could also be uniquely lead- and opportunity-generating.

DID YOU KNOW?

In 2021, Smart Insights conducted a global social media statistics research summary to determine trends in consumer adoption and usage of social networking platforms. This study determined that 53.6 percent of the world's population currently uses social media and that the average daily usage of social media is just under 2.5 hours.

The study also determined the most popular networking and social media applications by accounting for the number of active users across the globe. The research provided the following number of active users for the following top five sites:

Facebook	2,740,000,000
YouTube	2,291,000,000
WhatsApp	2,000,000,000
Facebook Messenger	1,300,000,000
Instagram	1,221,000,000

The study also showed correlated high rates of consumer adoption growth for these top five social media platforms, with Gen Z (followed by Millennials) driving the surge.

Personal Networking

Not all networking needs to appear to be professional. Sometimes the best is seemingly coincidental. Most personal networking is accomplished this way because it tends to revolve around various hobbies or interests. There seems to be some natural cross pollination between a group of individuals you met professionally and a group of friends with which you associate.

Classes

As a fan of knowledge, taking a class is a significant way I build my network. It allows me to meet and engage with people of various interests and disciplines. When you are learning together, the environment is less intimidating; many students engage about life, hobbies, and careers. This allows for relaxed conversation about an unrelated topic like real estate in comparison to the more formal professional networking venues. Taking a class provides a great opportunity for you to learn something of interest, but it also allows you to contribute to others who will reciprocate by being part of your network.

Fitness/Sports Teams

Involvement with local athletics or fitness clubs is another effective way to build your network. You can pick a recreation league or fitness class to get involved with. Your body isn't the only thing that will be more fit; your network will grow stronger too. You entered real estate to accrue wealth; I consider good health and longevity to also be good personal wealth. You really can't go wrong in this area; find a physical activity you enjoy and do it with other people, and the networking will take care of itself.

Social Events

Thinking about hosting a dinner party? Going to a sporting event? Happy hour with friends? Technology expo? Charity ball? Costume party? Comic Con? The venue doesn't matter. Just say yes! These are all great ways to network with people. They also help melt the formality so people in your network can get to know each other for who they really are rather than the professional image we all project. No matter what social event you are attending, being yourself is the successful way to go.

Religious/Spiritual Gatherings

Networking is great for instances when there is a group of people with common interests that meets frequently. For those who are religious or spiritually minded, the common interest runs deep. But you should exercise caution in this arena: avoid going to a religious/spiritual event with the primary intent to conduct real estate networking.

Volunteering

Volunteering in the community is right up your alley if you are into developing a real estate portfolio. Improving properties not only improves our surroundings; it benefits those in need and makes everyone involved feel better. Working shoulder to shoulder with stable, trusted members of the community also affords a great networking opportunity. But volunteering does so much more than that.

Depending upon the venture, volunteering may also provide you with an education on how to accomplish projects more effectively or cost-efficiently. Habitat for Humanity, for example, is an international non-profit (volunteer) organization that constructs affordable housing for families in need. Many laborers and contractors volunteer their time to Habitat for Humanity as well as other organizations that seek to improve housing for the less fortunate. Being a volunteer on their work sites will make the world a little better, further your rehab skill set, and broaden your network.

DID YOU KNOW?

Although, networking tends to be transitioning to social media platforms, traditional networking still produces the most quality results. For example, LinkedIn conducted research that confirmed that 70 percent of jobs are found through personal connections.

GreatBusinessSchools.org posted a similar study indicating the following statistics of members from various professions:

- 84 percent prefer to meet in person
- 75 percent enjoy social interaction and the ability to bond
- 46 percent of people got their current position through traditional networking
- 26 percent identified and acquired a job from internet boards
- 14 percent were aided by agencies and recruiters
- 14 percent acquired the job directly or by other means
- 1 percent found a job in print media

Upwork also conducted a similar study and identified the following results:

- 46 percent – friends and family
- 40 percent – social media
- 38 percent – previous clients
- 36 percent – professional contacts

Pre-Established Relationships

Most of the methods detailed thus far have focused on finding new acquaintances through networking. While these methods are all useful, they may overlook valuable relationships you've already established but may have not considered: people who know you and know your hobbies, your tastes, and your interests. It is natural to share about your passion for real estate, too. Sharing information and ideas with people in your pre-established relationship network can assist both parties in expanding their network. Intentionally focus on these pre-established relationships to expand and leverage your network:

- High-Producing Agents and Team Members
- Family, Friends, and Word of Mouth
- Fellow Real Estate Investors

You may recall covering the concept of syndications in Chapter 4. Your pre-established relationships will be key to establishing a 506(b) syndication. This will work the best when you let people know what you're about and what you hope to accomplish. If they are interested, or better yet, like-minded, they may ask to be part of the process. Be careful in the process of building a syndication. According to IRS guidelines, you cannot solicit members to be part of your syndication; however, the regulations do not prohibit others from asking to join.

High-Producing Agents and Team Members

Of all the pre-existing relationships you have garnered, high-producing agents and trusted team members may be the most natural connection for active networking. One key to effective networking is viewing interaction as relationship-based rather than transactional. Ask them how you can help them with their endeavors. I've established great bonds with members of my team because I took the time to invest in their interests rather than being solely focused on my own.

If your team members are solid—and they shouldn't be on your team otherwise—they are in high demand. Their lack of free time and distaste for unnecessary complications afford you an opportunity to learn how they do business efficiently and remove hurdles in their interactions with you. Furthermore, sharing information is the essence of effective networking.

Several members of my team have asked me to be the second set of eyes on their projects and acquisitions. I offer my advice to them free of charge, and they find ways to return the favor. Other members have been part of my team so frequently that I have garnered loyalty status with them. They know that if I'm working on a project, I will contract with them. In return, if they see a project that might interest me, they bring it to me. In this way, we are helping with each other's job security. I have received better quotes, rates, deals, leads, heads-ups on pitfalls, invitations to collaborations, and preferences on competitive bids, all due to the pre-existing relationships and the willingness to help my teammates as much as they help me. Do the same, and you may garner the same loyalty and associated perks.

Family, Friends, and Word of Mouth

Your family and friends already provide moral support and encouragement. They also represent a critical part of your real estate network. If you are looking to expand your portfolio or hire a craftsman, they may have a friend of a friend who is looking to sell a home or possesses the skills your rehab requires. As with any referral, you should verify their findings, but if they bring you leads, look into them!

As odd as it may sound, my mother's hairstylist once gave me a lead on a property that I ended up buying. Another time, I was renovating a townhome I acquired via auction, and I struck up a conversation with the neighboring unit's owner—only to find out she was looking to sell in order to move into a larger place. I informed her that I was an investor willing to make a fair offer, and now both units are cash-flowing assets in my portfolio. Those are just two stories to highlight that you never know who will provide the information you need to progress along your journey.

I've provided real estate advice to numerous friends, family, and coworkers over the years. Most of the time, it's because they are inquisitive, but sometimes it is because they are actively looking to acquire real estate for their primary residence or for investments. Some of them became leads and shared details with me on a property I might be interested in. I've had other family and friends who shared their real estate successes and failures to benefit me in my pursuits. I've appreciated lessons on their various pitfalls as much as their successes.

> Find a way to filter friends and family who are self-proclaimed experts as opposed to those who are truly interested in real estate. Be kind, but don't feel bad when you don't take their advice. Others may deplete your time and effort asking for investment advice without intent to pursue or follow through with investing in real estate. Remember, networking is about give and take. They're friends and family, so don't blow them off, but recommend a few resources (like this book). If they read it, you'll have a basis for discussion.

Fellow Real Estate Investors

A rising tide lifts all boats.
—John F. Kennedy, *35th president of the United States*

It may seem counterintuitive to think of other real estate investors as a good source for networking. Aren't they the competition, or possibly, the enemy? Not really. A better way to think of it is the way the American military does. We have the Army to stomp through it, the Navy to sail around it, the Air Force to fly over it, and the Marines to kick the door down. The military branches are not in competition as much as in relationship. In the war against a declining neighborhood, a rehab done well by another investor makes your property value go up too.

Think of the bigger picture: it's incredibly unlikely all real estate investors in an area are in the same phase, eyeing the same property at the same time. Sometimes it feels like that—or that some investors have endless sources of funding. In reality, they will have cycles when they purchase and others when they reconstitute funds. Some will be looking to sell assets that no longer meet their profitability ratios but may meet yours. They may want to sell a property to purchase another one outside of your center of gravity. To say it clearly: opportunity is right around the corner, and you just need to find it. Sometimes your fellow real estate investors will be the ones to point it out.

I mentioned previously that purchasing real estate is much more like playing blackjack than poker. It's not every real estate investor against each other. Sure, you may or may not have a better hand than the other investors, but only two things matter: 1) you don't bust, and 2) you beat the dealer (the banks/lender). Everyone can win if everyone plays his or her hand correctly. It's not a zero-sum game.

I enjoy engaging with fellow investors because real estate is not just a passing interest; it's a passion, a profession, a lifestyle, almost a creed. You're almost certain to gain as much knowledge as you give. I've purchased properties at discount from investors who were motivated sellers. I've had investor friends who showed me properties that were just listed, but the timing wasn't right for them. I've honed my real estate strategy by engaging with trusted friends who were also real estate investors. In fact, the inception of this book came about at a real estate investor-friend's 30th birthday party as we were talking about life accomplishments and her desire to write a book. I say all of this only to affirm the notion that other investors are more friends than enemies. Sometimes they will be your competition, but they are making the tide rise for you too. That's capitalism at work!

Objective: Maximizing Your Leverage with Networking

Hopefully, I've convinced you of the benefits of networking. If I haven't, move on to the next chapter in hopes of reading information you'll find more useful. If I have, don't leave the networking knowledge on the pages of this book. Consider the activities you are currently involved in and assess which ones can be opportunities to network. You may surprise yourself when you take advantage of the opportunities that are readily available.

If you are not currently expanding your network, or if you want to continue expanding it, take a look at the following activities and prioritize your next steps:

Tasks:

- Assess professional networking opportunities.
    - Chamber of Commerce
    - Local community boards and committees
    - Online forums and social media
    - Seminars

- Assess personal networking opportunities.
    - Classes
    - Fitness/Sports teams
    - Social events
    - Religious/Spiritual groups
    - Volunteering

- Assess pre-established relationships.
    - High-producing agents and team members
    - Family and friends
    - Fellow real estate investors

- Conduct networking within available opportunities.

If while reading this chapter, there were concepts you wished to see that were either not covered or where you desired additional detail, please annotate and provide feedback via this QR code.

Visit our website (masterofleverage.info) by using this QR code to access key figures and references from this chapter.

Aloof Aaron, Cautious Carl, Sensible Sarah, and Risky Rick

Cautious Carl is not one who cares much for networking. Sensible Sarah and her husband are well-known members of the community, are involved in many social clubs, and network professionally/formally. Risky Rick seldom has time for networking socially; he does, however, spend a considerable portion of his time networking professionally. Fortunately for all three, their property management companies are excellent at networking, both professionally and personally.

Aloof Aaron is a natural at personal networking. He has no clue what professional networking is or what it entails.

SECTION IV:

MASTERY

Chapter 13: Strategizing Your Leverage

Everybody has a plan until they get punched in the mouth.
—Mike Tyson, *professional boxer*

In this chapter, we are going to cover the following:

Strategy Components

Operational Art and Operational Design

- Determine End State and Conditions
- Objectives and Effects (Operational Design)
- Determine the Centers of Gravity
  - Basing
  - Operational Reach
- Lines of Operation (LOO) and Lines of Effort (LOE)
  - Phasing
  - Timing and Tempo
  - Culmination
- Strategy-to-Task Framework
  - Decisive Points
  - Branches and Sequels

> Hope is not a strategy.
> —*Unattributed quote*

Lombardi got this one right: hope is not a strategy and will not by itself result in success. Diligent and deliberate planning followed by fervent execution will garner success.

Forgive me if I take on a tone of authority in this chapter on planning. I am going to leverage military terminology and methodologies—and I will bark out orders like a drill sergeant and dispense strategy like a field commander as though your life depends on it. In reality, your success as an investor does depend on having and executing a solid strategy.

As a person in business, you might be thinking that the military is not the most efficient organization compared to corporate entities. That's true, but the military has developed effective approaches to planning for complex operations. They have also developed efficient techniques to identify and mitigate risks. That's what you need to do. Once you have developed your plan, you are ready to execute your strategy and continue generating wealth.

Planning provides decision makers like you with awareness and affords an opportunity to assess potential outcomes among a myriad of alternatives within a controlled environment. Deliberate planning enables the analysis and evaluation of complex systems and problem sets by breaking them down into smaller, more manageable components. This increases the probability of success by enabling decision makers to create contingencies intended to counteract or mitigate identified risks associated with the proposed course of action (COA).

Strategy Components

> Dreams without goals are just dreams, and
> they ultimately fuel disappointment.
> —Denzel Washington, *American actor*

There are some aspects to developing a strategy that are so ingrained into the methodology that they have become part of its language. These aspects are the language of operational planning, and I call them the *strategic components*. We can distill the entirety of this book into one of these five components:

Environment (Where and When?): Describes the current environment as well as the future environment, which provides context to the strategy

Ends (Why?): Describes the desired goal or objective to be achieved

Ways (How?): Describes the manner in which you will apply resources to achieve the desired goal or objective

Means (Who and What?): Describes the resources required to accomplish the desired goal or objective

Risks: **(Danger, Peril, or Hazard?)**: Describes the inherent risks associated with achieving the desired goal or objective

The remainder of the chapter revolves around these components and your ability to plan effectively.

Operational Art and Operational Design

The Army defines operational art as the creative approach to integrating the ends, ways, and means through various echelons of a major operation or campaign. Leaders use this to conceptualize and determine the culmination of the endeavor. The decision maker may use operational art to assess the environment and mitigate the risks. *Operational design* is a similar creative approach used by the *joint community*[74] to achieve the same culmination of efforts and objectives. There are several elements of both operational art and operational design. Rather than cover them all, I've included the elements with the strongest correlation toward acquiring real estate.

74 Multiple military services (i.e., Air Force, Navy, Army, Marine Corp, etc.) working together.

Elements of Operational Art

- End State and Conditions
- Center of Gravity
- Decisive Points
- Lines of Operations (LOO) and Lines of Effort (LOE)
- Operational Reach
- Basing
- Tempo
- Phasing and Transitions
- Culmination
- Risk

Additional Elements of Operational Design

- Objective
- Effects

Determine End State and Conditions

Have you ever started a project without an end state in mind? Without a plan, what tends to happen? The project probably took longer and cost more. Dumpsters spontaneously caught fire, and the sun rose in the west and set in the east. Sound about right? You prevent this kind of chaos by establishing an end state based on *termination criteria*, which you use to establish *operational objectives* and *desired effects*.

The *end state* is the summation of conditions that constitutes the end. The termination criteria should be event-based determinations of objective achievement. The planner should consider how the determined operation's end state contributes to the overarching goals of your strategic real estate strategy. Remember, the end state satisfies the *why*. Why is your team performing the tasks you have assigned them?

Objectives and Effects (Operational Design)

Alternatively, an objective is a goal that directs action toward the defined end state. Furthermore, objectives (as well as effects) are the origin for defining subordinate tasks. Objectives should be specific and describe a singular end. They should not suggest any ways or means. You should express objectives in a concise and prescriptive statement.

One tool to express objectives clearly is the concept of SMART: Specific, Measurable, Actionable, Realistic, and Time-Bound. Leveraging this tool allows leaders to ensure they have developed effective objectives. I want to expand SMART to include additional components, making it SMART and what I call "SAFE." Go with me on this one.

Specific: An objective should be descriptive and detailed so that the goal of the endeavor is clearly understood by all.

Measurable: Progress toward and inevitably subsequent success of the endeavor should be quantitatively assessed. Qualitative assessments are possible but not preferred.

Actionable: The goal should be achievable with the resources and team members available.

Realistic: The proposed endeavor should be achievable. It cannot be an impossible goal.

Time-Bound: A specified duration of time must be included with every task and objective. Neglecting to do so is asking for failure.

Scalable: A good objective is one that can be tailored to various sizes and conditions. The objective indicates the "what," and the task defines the "how." Creating scalable objectives allows for repeatable processes.

Ambitious: Don't settle! Your objective should strive to achieve something significant—realistic, but significant. It's okay to strive for what you want as long as it does not unnecessarily deprive or impede another goal. Many leaders settle on their objectives or do not strive for their desires because of external perceptions and the fear of being viewed unfavorably. Sometimes, people hold back because they feel they are impeding someone else when, in reality, someone else is taking advantage of their kindness. Use market analysis to objectively assess equilibrium and have the courage to enforce a standard. And don't be apologetic about pursuing your goals when your aspirations do not impede upon others. Your knowledge, confidence, and wealth will be better for it.

Flexible: Your execution will not go according to plan! It's alright. Detours and delays happen. But having objectives that do not dictate the "how" allow for flexibility.

Enlightened: You are smart, but you don't have the answer to everything. Defer to individuals who are knowledgeable and develop objectives that make sense for the situation. Don't be a "bot" as they say; be an individual capable of individual thought with the humility to approach a professional when in doubt.

Alternatively, an *effect* is an outcome that is created by an action or set of actions. An effect is related to its objectives the way termination conditions define the end state. An effect should be directly associated with—but distinguishable from—an objective. It should be measurable but should not specify the ways or means of accomplishment.

Determine the Centers of Gravity

We've covered the concept of centers of gravity when discussing your team members. If you recall, the center of gravity is the entity or entities from which you project force. Carl von Clausewitz, Prussian general and military theorist, describes the center of gravity as "the hub of all power and movement, on which everything depends." Remember the people who make up your center of gravity: the deal finder, lender, property manager, and contractor. Other members of your team may be part of your center of gravity for any given endeavor, determined by the critical factors associated with each member of the team.

Basing

Basing is your place of operations, your home station if you will. It is the conceptual location where your centers of gravity reside and from which you project force. As I said, it is conceptual; it doesn't need to be so specific as to have an address but should be aligned regionally or around a city.

Operational Reach

When planning, you must consider your operational reach. This is an assessment of the team and resources (ways and means) available to accomplish the operation and the extent to which they may conduct an operation. Assess your team's *capability*, *availability*, and *geographic limitations*. Capability and availability limitations are self-explanatory; if a project is beyond your team's ability due to cost or skill, or if your team members are unavailable, you experience limitations. The most skilled team member is of little use if they are unavailable. A geographical limitation is one in which your team does not extend. This can be countered by establishing another base with its respective centers of gravity; however, this comes at a cost of time, effort, and/or money. Ignoring operational reach is one of the primary causes leading to the failure of an endeavor.

Lines of Operations (LOO)

You should also consider the various tasks linked together to accomplish an objective, achieve an effect, or establish a condition. We call these *lines of operations (LOO)* or *lines of effort (LOE)*. Similar activities should be aligned to accomplish an objective of the corresponding LOOs and achieve the desired end state. A plan may have one or multiple LOOs. Plans with a single LOO are often more simplistic, while those with multiple LOOs allow for greater flexibility in execution.

Lines of Effort (LOE)

An LOE is a sequence of tasks seeking to achieve a condition rather than a singular objective. LOEs align disparate team members working on separate tasks independent of one another yet toward the achievement of the same goal. Like LOOs*)*, a plan with a single LOE offers simplicity, while a plan with multiple LOEs offers flexibility. The most flexible plans combine LOOs and LOEs.

Phasing

A *phase* is a stage of an operation when a portion of team members, resources, and capabilities work toward a unifying or common purpose. The breaking up of tasks into these sequential stages is referred to as *phasing*. You may use phasing to integrate and synchronize efforts for any operation or campaign, regardless of size or complexity, by the implementation of sequencing and accounting of time and resources.

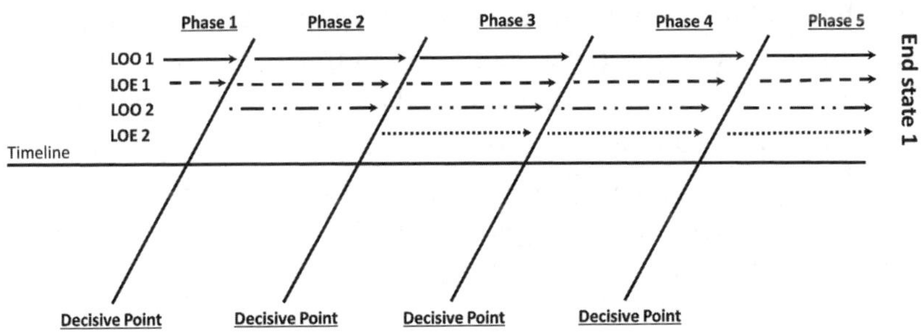

Figure 13-1: Sequencing and Phasing

You should infer from Figure 13-1 that the four LOOs*)* and LOEs cannot be initiated concurrently. LOO 1 and LOE 1 may both be initiated concurrently at the onset of the endeavor (referred to as *Phase 1*). LOO 2 may be initiated once Phase 1 is completed, assuming the required tasks are also completed. LOE 2 must wait until Phase 3 has been initiated.

Timing and Tempo

A good plan should define and elaborate upon the sequencing of the subordinate level's timing and tempo of the operation. You must accomplish some tasks in a specific (sequential) order; you may accomplish other tasks simultaneously or at any time. Determine which efforts and objectives are essential (main efforts). Tasks associated with main efforts should take priority of resources and scheduling over tasks associated with supporting efforts. The dissociation of main and supporting efforts (and subordinate tasks) is critical to avoid conflation of priority when task conflicts arise. For example, it takes longer to tape (in prep for painting) than to paint. If you start taping and someone else subsequently starts painting shortly thereafter, you run the risk of offsetting timing and tempo for task accomplishment.

Culmination

Culmination is why sequencing, timing and tempo, and phasing are important. Culmination is the apex of the operation—the point at which the LOOs*)* and LOEs converge and accomplish the desired end state. If an LOO or LOE does not occur on time, the mission may fail. Imagine a military operation in which the main ground force invading an area arrives before reconnaissance is complete or air support is provided. That's how you lose a battle. It would be akin to finishing drywall prior to running electrical and plumbing. Make sure you keep culmination in mind when developing your plan.

Strategy-to-Task Framework

The *strategy-to-task framework* (known as *strat-to-task*) is a process intended to parse the larger-level, strategic objectives into smaller, more granular objectives and tasks for the subordinate operations, efforts, and actions required to achieve the overarching goal. Within the military, the strat-to-task framework is depicted in Figure 13-2.

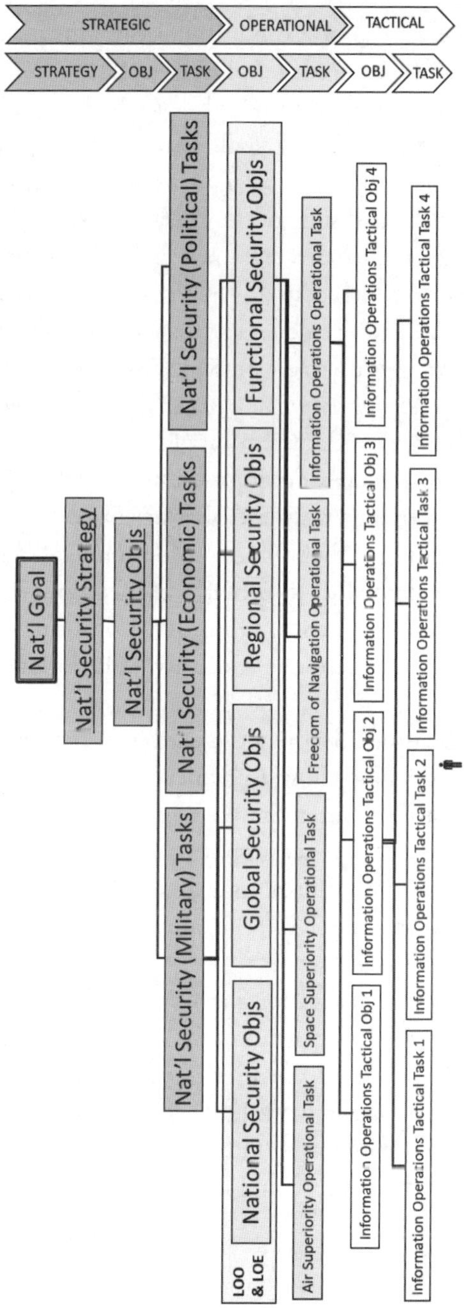

Figure 13-2: Strat-to-Task Framework

As you can see, it is complex, but it illustrates the necessity to delineate manpower and resources employed tactically and identify how they are leveraged to support the high-level operational and strategic objectives under the overarching goal. Tasks and objectives (or effects) directly support one another. A *strategic objective* (national security) is defined by parsing the end state of the goal. Each strategic objective has various *strategic tasks*. Each strategic task will have various lower level *operational objectives*, which contain their own sets of tasks and so forth. Your LOEs and LOOs*)* are generally associated with the operational objectives supporting the larger strategic initiatives. Your *operational tasks* become your *decisive points* in a plan. These tasks have smaller *tactical tasks* and *objectives* under them intended to be performed by team members seeking to achieve or complete the LOO*)* or LOE. Think of a tactical task as an activity a team member performs.

When I was serving in the military, some of my tasks as a cyber operations officer were aligned to Information Operations Tactical Task 2, Information Operations Tactical Objective 2, Information Operations Operational Task, Functional Security Operational Objectives, National Security (Military) Strategic Tasks, and National Security Objectives. The National Security Objectives were under the National Security Strategy detailing how to achieve the National Goals issued by the President of the United States. You can clearly see the different levels of operations. Other tasks supported entirely different operational objectives (and their subordinate tasks and objectives not shown in the depiction); all tasks, however, were in support of the National Security (Military) Strategic Tasks.

This same model is useful for aligning all of the tactical tasks that you and your team must perform in pursuit of the larger wealth acquisition goal we discussed in Chapter 2. The strat-to-task framework does not need to look the same; it just needs to logically and effectively organize and employ manpower and resources to achieve the objective. Figure 13-3 depicts what this could look like.

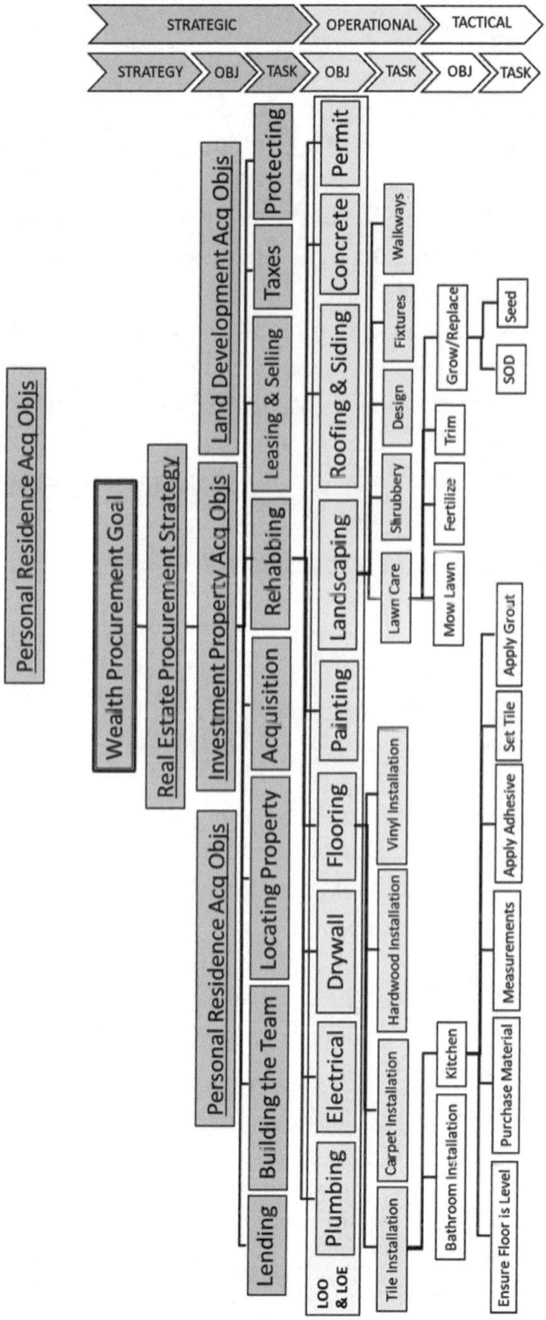

Figure 13-3: Strat-to-Task Framework (Real Estate)

Decisive Points

Decisive points pertaining to real estate differ from the traditional concept within the military's Joint Operation Planning Process. Usually, decisive points are key tasks or objectives that you must accomplish in order to diminish the adversary's ability to project power against an enemy. The real estate corollary is the developed essential tasks, both specified and implied. Decisive points also represent the gateways to the various phases of your operation or endeavor. The accomplishment of an objective or condition permits progression from one phase to another. Failure to accomplish an objective or condition may result in a delay or could prohibit flexible planning, which would force you to deviate from your original plan or even change your end state.

Development of Branches and Sequels

> Victory smiles upon those who anticipate the change in the character of war, not upon those who wait to adapt themselves after the changes occur.
> —Air Marshal Giulio Douhet, *Italian military strategist, WWI*

You will need to be flexible in your planning to adapt to unanticipated changes in the strategic components that occur during execution. It's often difficult and sometimes costly to react on the fly to an unforeseen problem without awareness of the impact it will have. You may have to explore your options for circumventing the problem without altering the overall project. Flexible planning offers more agile decision-making during changing conditions; this is afforded by the inclusion of *branches* and *sequels.*

Branches, simply put, are options built into a plan as counters to probable risks, or as alternatives to achieve the initial end state. Branches can also drive an alternative end state. On the other hand, sequels are continuations of a plan, or subsequent operations, from one phase to another. You may think of these as if/then decisions based upon decisive points or essential tasks. If the decisive point or essential task is successful, then continue with the sequel; if not, then initiate the branch.

LOEs and LOOs) that support multiple outcomes or end states often have associated decision criteria to assist you in how to progress from one phase into another.

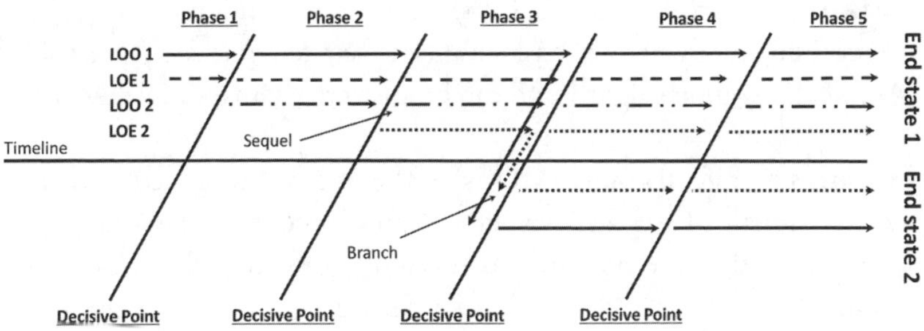

Figure 13-4: Branches and Sequels

In a plan schematic, branches and sequels are often portrayed in the manner indicated in Figure 13-4. Note, the branch occurs at the decisive point between Phase 3 and 4; that is the point upon which the decision maker must decide (based upon the progress assessment) whether to alter the plan from end state 1 toward end state 2. If you have not established a branch or have not established the conditions that permit the execution of the branch, you must assess termination criteria. For example, if while rehabbing a distressed property, you determine you've exceeded your budget and can no longer target 75 percent LTV, your sequel is to hold the property and refinance at a later time (after you have successfully lowered the LTV to less than 75 percent). Your branch is to sell the property for a small profit while also freeing up capital for another venture.

Risk (Task Assessment)

Task assessment describes the standards for determining task completion and, therefore, objective accomplishment. These determination measures are related to the termination criteria that dictate the end state for the overarching objective. This assessment is ultimately performed by the development and subsequent use of various indicators that portray progress (or lack thereof) in achieving stated objectives. The two primary means of assessing objectives and tasks are *measures of performance (MOPs)* and *measures of effectiveness (MOEs)* .

Measures of Performance (MOPs) : This is a quantitative or qualitative assessment of whether a task has been executed. It asks the question, "Are we doing things right?" and can be answered with a simple *yes* or *no*.

Measures of Effectiveness (MOEs) : This is a quantitative or qualitative assessment of the achievement of an objective or the attainment of an effect; they are intended to show progress toward a measurable threshold such as an end state. It asks the question, "Are we doing the right things?"

To be effective, MOPs and MOEs should be relevant, measurable, and responsive. Each should be relevant to a task, effect, or objective that furthers the end state. This assessment should be measurable, and quantitative assessments are inherently more measurable than qualitative. Finally, the assessment should be responsive; assessments that fail to detect changes quickly enough will not allow the investor to make decisions and/or enact change with enough expedience to be effective.

Objective: Strategizing Your Leverage

Develop a plan that contains the level of detail and/or simplicity that works for you and your team. If it doesn't work for both you and your team, don't do it. Find another system that will.

> A good plan, violently executed now, is better than
> a perfect plan executed next week.
> —General George S. "Old Blood and Guts" Patton,
> *U.S. Army General, WWII*

Do not let perfection be the enemy of success. Follow these steps to your comfort level and see a plan develop that you may then execute to achieve success:

Tasks:

- Determine end state and associated conditions.
- Determine various strategic objectives (or effects) required for the end state.
  - Determine subordinate (operational and tactical) objectives and tasks
- Assess adequacy of centers of gravity and basing.
  - Presence of basing
  - Limitations of operational reach
- Establish Lines of Operation (LOO) and Lines of Effort (LOE).
- Establish sequencing of tasks and objectives.
  - Phasing
  - Timing and tempo
  - Culmination
  - Decisive points
- Develop contingencies (branches and sequels).

Visit our website (masterofleverage.info) by using this QR code to access key figures and references from this chapter.

Aloof Aaron, Cautious Carl, Sensible Sarah, and Risky Rick

Cautious Carl, Sensible Sarah, and Risky Rick are all planners. Each of them has studied, understood, and enacted the operational art and design of planning as it pertains to real estate. They have each settled upon the following as their desired end state:

Generate enough wealth (capital and equity) to live comfortably while raising a family, to retire prosperously, and to provide my children (beneficiaries) with a legacy.

Additionally, our investor trio has elected to execute a combination of the following Lines of Operations and Lines of Effort in support of their desired end state:

Strategic Objective 1:	Acquire Cash-Flowing and Appreciating Assets
Strategic Objective 2:	Accelerate Leverage of Real Estate Assets
Strategic Effect 1:	Leverage the *Velocity of Money*
Strategic Effect 2:	Leverage the Inertia of (Real Estate) Equity

Cautious Carl has selected Strategic Objective and Strategic Effect 1. He refrains from the other effects and objectives, deeming them to be too risky for his liking. Sensible Sarah and Risky Rick elect to include all objectives and effects into their plan. Not so coincidentally, these objectives and tasks also become the lines of operations and lines of effort they will pursue to achieve their desired end state.

Aloof Aaron is just Aaron.

Chapter 14: Mastering Your Leverage

A pessimist sees the difficulty in every opportunity; an optimist sees the opportunity in every difficulty.
—Winston Churchill, *former Prime Minister of the United Kingdom*

In this chapter, we are going to cover the following:

Niceties, Necessities, and the Desired End State
Unlocking the *Momentum of Wealth*
- Determine End State and Associated Conditions
- Determine Various Strategic Objectives (or Effects) Required for the End State
    - Determine Subordinate (Operational and Tactical) Objectives and Tasks
- Assess Adequacy of Centers of Gravity and Basing
    - Presence of Basing
    - Limitations of Operational Reach
- Establish Lines of Operation (LOO) and Lines of Effort (LOE)
- Establish Sequencing of Tasks and Objectives
    - Phasing
    - Timing and Tempo
    - Culmination
    - Decisive Points
- Develop Contingencies (Branches and Sequels)

Perils of Overleveraging – Part II
Investor Journeys

Congratulations! You've made it to the final chapter in this book. This is where all secrets are revealed, and the path to unlocking the *Momentum of Wealth* is laid out before you. Actually, the first 13 chapters have revealed the secrets. Now we pull them all together and see the big picture.

In Chapter 2, we covered "Leveraging Key Real Estate Concepts." You could summarize that chapter like this: "Purchase real estate that is both cash-flowing and appreciating and reinvest passive income and equity capital through cash-out refinancing." That's simple enough. This chapter will help you navigate these activities by defining and elaborating upon these two actions: purchasing and reinvesting.

This chapter will point you in the direction of building a successful real estate portfolio. You must decide the extent of your ultimate destination and set upon the path. Ensure your goal is objective so you can assess your progress. If your goal is the subjective goal, "I want to be happy, wealthy, and in control of my destiny," you may have difficulty measuring your progress and lack the resolve to try. Being happy, wealthy, or in control are effects, or byproducts, not the goal to be achieved. Establishing a desired end state is imperative, as it guides your actions, enables necessary adjustments, and is the beacon that signals the culmination of your achievements. Having the improper end state may misguide your steps and undermine your efforts, preventing your success.

Niceties, Necessities, and the Desired End State

After you have decided upon your desired end state, you must consider your present activities and how they either support or detract from your goals. Early on in this book, we discussed the types of costs, specifically opportunity cost. Recall this diagram from Chapter 1.

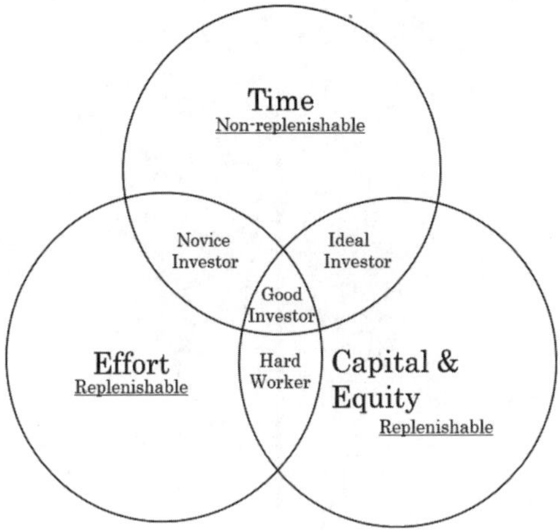

Figure 14-1 (1-13): Convergence of Effort, Money, and Time

Misappropriating these resources (time, effort, and money) may result in the opportunity cost of delaying the achievement of your end state. Similar to how to categorize your rehab, all of your present-day activities and the resources required to conduct them fall into one of three categories: niceties, necessities, and the end state. Niceties describe those activities in which you partake for your enjoyment but have little to nothing to do with achieving your goals. I'm not saying you shouldn't treat or reward yourself. You should, but you should do so deliberately, intelligently, and moderately. Necessities are those activities you must do to survive. The end state categorizes the achievement of the goal.

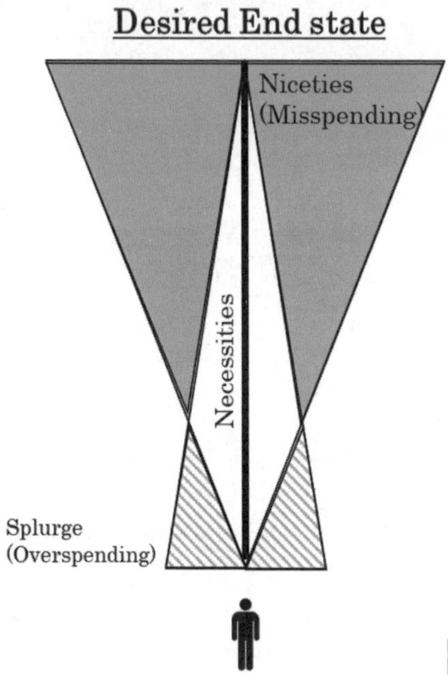

Figure 14-2: Niceties, Necessities, and the Desired End State

Spending resources you do not have may derail you from the path to achieving success. Conversely, if you perform nothing but the necessities, you will more than likely achieve the end state—but at what cost? As we've previously discussed, sometimes, when you can afford to reward yourself, do so! Just be wary of doing so excessively. Every reward detracts from the ultimate goal of building wealth. A reward now and then may be recuperated, but excessive rewards may delay you from achieving your goals.

The best way to define the necessities is to detail their conditions (constraints and restraints). Additionally, make an objective plan for how you will reward yourself and your family. This could be dining out every Saturday, taking one big family vacation per year, or taking every 10th cash-out refinance as a reward instead of reinvesting it. Whatever plan you develop, stick to it, and do not deviate from it unless absolutely necessary.

Unlocking the *Momentum of Wealth*

There are many ways to build your real estate empire and benefit from the subsequent wealth; even so, the principles remain the same. In the previous chapter, we outlined the process of strategizing your leverage. For your benefit, this objective and its subordinate tasks have been provided below.

Objective: Strategizing Your Leverage

Tasks:

- Determine end state and associated conditions.
- Determine various strategic objectives (or effects) required for the end state.
  - Determine subordinate (operational and tactical) objectives and tasks
- Assess adequacy of centers of gravity and basing.
  - Presence of basing
  - Limitations of operational reach
- Establish Lines of Operation (LOO) and Lines of Effort (LOE).
- Establish sequencing of tasks and objectives.
  - Phasing
  - Timing and tempo
  - Culmination
  - Decisive points
- Develop contingencies (branches and sequels).

Think of it this way: when you ask GPS for directions, it will ask for two points of reference: where are you going and where are you starting. Then the app provides you with several paths to arrive at your destination.

Let's follow Investor Bob as he advances from strategizing to planning to developing his real estate portfolio as he unlocks the *Momentum of Wealth*. First, Investor Bob must determine what the end destination looks like for him. He must determine where he is going—what his desired end state is.

1. Determine End State and Associated Conditions

Investor Bob, like most individuals, wants to be compensated for his efforts, live a prosperous life, and provide a legacy to his heirs. Here's what Bob's end state looks like:

Bob's Desired End State:

Generate enough wealth (capital and equity) for him and his wife to live comfortably while raising his family, to retire prosperously, and to provide his beneficiaries with a notable legacy.

Bob's Conditions (Constraints and Restraints):

1. *Be a present member and be part of the family (wife and two children) along the journey*
2. *Acquire 300 (cash-flowing and appreciating) units within 30 years*
3. *Ensure the collective real estate portfolio provides $4 million per year in passive income (capital) by year 30*
4. *Ensure the collective value of the real estate portfolio is $30 million (equity) by year 30*
5. *Take one major family vacation each year*

How do your desired end state and conditions compare with Bob's?

Clearly establishing your end state and associated conditions precedes effectively strategizing and planning when unlocking the *Momentum of Wealth* through real estate. Investor Bob clearly identified his end state as well as five constraints (must-do conditions). He will leverage these to determine the strategic components (Objectives, Effects, and Tasks) required to attain success.

2. Determine Various Strategic Objectives (or Effects) Required for the End State

The strategic objectives (or effects) are the major activities you must achieve to reach your end state. All other objectives, tasks, and effects are subordinate to these overarching initiatives; therefore, you need to define the objectives and effects in order to encompass the required activities and tasks. Investor Bob decided upon two strategic objectives and two strategic effects for his campaign:

Strategic Objective 1:	Acquire Cash-Flowing and Appreciating Assets
Strategic Objective 2:	Accelerate Leverage of Real Estate Assets
Strategic Effect 1:	Leverage the *Velocity of Money*
Strategic Effect 2:	Leverage the Inertia of (Real Estate) Equity

Note: each strategic objective or effect will have corresponding and subordinate tasks required to complete the component. Investor Bob identified the following five strategic tasks:

Strategic Task 1:	Strategizing and Planning (Preparation)
Strategic Task 2:	Acquiring Real Estate Assets
Strategic Task 3:	Rehabilitating and Force Appreciating Real Estate Assets
Strategic Task 4:	Operating and Maintaining Acquired Real Estate Assets
Strategic Task 5:	Securing and Retaining Acquired Real Estate Assets and Wealth

A subordinate task may support any one or a multitude of objectives or effects. The following tasks have been assigned as subordinate components to the aforementioned strategic objectives in the following manner:

Strategic Objective 1:

Acquire Cash-Flowing and Appreciating Assets

Strategic Tasks:

1. Strategizing and Planning (Preparation)
2. Acquiring Real Estate Assets
5. Securing and Retaining Acquired Real Estate Assets and Wealth

Strategic Objective 2:

Accelerate Leverage of Real Estate Assets

Strategic Tasks:

1. Strategizing and Planning (Preparation)
3. Rehabilitating and Force Appreciating Real Estate Assets

Strategic Effect 1:

Leverage the Velocity of Money

Strategic Tasks:

1. Strategizing and Planning (Preparation)
4. Operating and Maintaining Acquired Real Estate Assets

Strategic Effect 2:

Leverage the Inertia of (Real Estate) Equity

Strategic Tasks:

1. Strategizing and Planning (Preparation)
5. Securing and Retaining Acquired Real Estate Assets and Wealth

You will see that "Strategic Task 1: Strategizing and Planning (Preparation)" is a task that supports each strategic objective. Subjectively, Investor Bob could have also made "Strategizing and Planning" its own strategic objective rather than a strategic task that supports each objective. One could also make a convincing argument to split the strategic task "Securing and Retaining Acquired Real Estate Assets and Wealth" into two: "Securing and Retaining Acquired Real Estate Assets" and "Securing and Retaining Acquired Wealth." The former would remain a strategic task, and the latter could be its own strategic objective. It's a dealer's choice. What matters most is that Investor Bob does what makes the most sense for him.

Determine Subordinate (Operational and Tactical) Objectives and Tasks

Each strategic objective (and task) will also have subordinate operational and tactical objectives and tasks. A subordinate objective will directly correspond to the higher task. For example, the operational objective should directly pertain to the higher-level strategic task; similarly, the tactical objective should correspond to the operational task. After Bob determines the strategic objectives and tasks, he will need to determine the subordinate operational and tactical tasks. His plan looked like this:

Strategic Task/Operational Objective 1:

Strategizing and Planning (Preparation)

Operational Tasks:

1. *Leveraging the Basics*
2. *Leveraging Key Real Estate Concepts*
3. *Leveraging Your Team*
4. *Leveraging Location*
5. *Maximizing Your Leverage with Networking*
6. *Strategizing Your Leverage*

Strategic Task/Operational Objective 2:

Acquiring Real Estate Assets

Operational Tasks:

1. *Leveraging Other People's Money (Funding)*
2. *Leveraging Creative Financing*
3. *Leveraging the Acquisition*

Strategic Task/Operational Objective 3:

Rehabilitating and Force Appreciating Real Estate Assets

Operational Tasks:

1. *Leveraging the Rehab*

Strategic Task/Operational Objective 4:

Operating and Maintaining Acquired Real Estate Assets

Operational Tasks:

1. *Leasing the Real Estate Asset (Leveraging Your Equity)*
2. *Selling the Real Estate Asset (Leveraging Your Equity)*

Strategic Task/Operational Objective 5:

Securing and Retaining Acquired Real Estate Assets and Wealth

Operational Tasks:

1. *Utilizing Liability Protection*
2. *Leveraging Tax-Planning (Retaining Your Leverage)*
3. *Execute Cash-Out Refinancing (Retaining Your Leverage)*

Operational Tasks/Tactical Objectives and Tactical Tasks

Finally, Bob will need to establish the tactical objectives and tasks. You may have noticed the headers on the summaries located at the conclusion of each chapter. These summaries highlight an objective and specific, corresponding tasks. You may have surmised that these objectives are, in fact, the operational tasks/tactical objectives and their subordinate tactical tasks. For your convenience, I have included them here:

Tactical Objective:

Leveraging the Basics

Tactical Tasks:

- *Calculate your DTI.*
- *Assess your current realized and unrealized wealth efficiency.*

Tactical Objective:

Leveraging Key Real Estate Concepts

Tactical Tasks:

- *Assess your current investments' (real estate or otherwise) ROI and ROE.*

Tactical Objective:

Leveraging Other People's Money

Tactical Tasks:

- *Improve and maintain creditworthiness.*
- *Research and assess available lending options.*
    - *Lending institutions*
    - *Loan types*
    - *DPA programs*

Tactical Objective:

Leveraging Creative Financing

Tactical Tasks:

- *Determine if you are eligible for low- to no-money-down financing.*
- *Determine if you are eligible for DPA programs.*
- *Determine if you have the capital for "live and upgrade" ventures.*
- *After having conducted a property assessment*
- *Consider seller financing.*
- *After having assessed the property's pertinent details*
- *Consider syndication to acquire larger, more profitable investments.*

Tactical Objective:

Leveraging Your Team

Tactical Tasks:

- *Honestly assess your personality type, personal skills, and aptitude for managing and operating real estate, as well as your ability and willingness to invest your personal time and effort.*
- *Identify and research team members for your centers of gravity.*
    - *Deal finder*
    - *Lender*
    - *Property manager*
    - *Applicable contractors*
    - *Determine which additional core and ancillary team members you may acquire for any property in which you are interested.*

Tactical Objective:

Leveraging Location

Tactical Tasks:

- *Determine the region of interest.*
    - *Assess climate, economy of force, laws, and natural hazards*
- *Determine the city (or cities) of interest.*
    - *Assess employment opportunities*
    - *Assess other enticements*
- *Determine the neighborhood(s) of interest.*
    - *Assess desirability and demand*
    - *Assess availability and supply*
- *Assess if you're in a buyer's or seller's market.*
- *Assess the property.*
    - *Assess property value trends*
    - *Assess Price-to-Rent ratios*

Tactical Objective:

Leveraging the Acquisition

Tactical Tasks:

- *Decide if you're pursuing a turnkey and/or distressed property.*
    - *If distressed property, determine cause of distress*
- *Assess property pertinent details (Amount owed, condition, FMV, homeowner's situation, property situation, etc.).*
- *Conduct a property assessment.*
    - *Income and expenses*
    - *Expenditures*
    - *Costs*
    - *ROI and ROE*
    - *Target price range*
- *Submit an offer.*

Tactical Objective:

Leveraging the Rehab

Tactical Tasks:

- *Research and understand the norm for the area.*
- *Understand your constraints.*
- *Conduct your walk-through (virtual or in-person).*
- *Determine necessities and niceties within your budget.*
- *Work exterior to interior (depending on season).*
    - *Develop a practical order of work*
- *Don't exclude miscellaneous components.*
- *Target forced appreciation (if practical).*
- *Garner contractor bids.*

Tactical Objective:

Leveraging Your Equity

Tactical Tasks:

- *Decide upon selling or leasing and assess profitability.*
- *If leasing (and not using a property manager) …*
    - *Advertise.*
    - *Conduct a preliminary screening.*
    - *Disseminate applications.*
    - *Conduct an in-depth screening.*
    - *Accept or reject tenants and solidify lease agreement.*
    - *Turn over the keys.*
- *Furnish property for short-term rentals.*
- *If selling (and not using a real estate agent) …*
    - *Determine listing price by assessing FMV.*
    - *Prepare property for sale (cleaning and staging).*
    - *Conduct marketing.*
    - *Negotiate potential sales.*
    - *Navigate closing.*

Tactical Objective:

Utilizing Liability Protection

Tactical Tasks

- *Determine personal and asset liability protection business structure.*
    - *Anonymity*
    - *Geography*
    - *Value threshold*
    - *Taxation*
- *Establish property insurance.*
- *Establish a business entity.*
    - *Select your structure*
    - *Identify your name*
    - *Register your business*
    - *Receive your tax IDs*
- *Trust current investment properties into business entities.*
- *Consider equity stripping (if appropriate).*
- *Investigate homestead exemptions for primary residence.*

Tactical Objective:

Retaining Your Leverage

Tactical Tasks:

- *Acquire a good tax advisor.*
- *Assess proper business entity structures.*
- *Assess real estate portfolio property type uses.*
    - *Personal/Arbitrage property*
        - *Reclassifying taxable income by funding retirement accounts*
- *Rental/Mixed-use property*
    - *Decreasing taxes through business deductions and expenses*
    - *Deferring taxes through 1031 exchange*
    - *Transforming income by funding investments through retirement accounts*
- *Develop an exit strategy.*
    - *Cash-out refinance*
    - *Seller finance*
    - *Transfer via inheritance*

Tactical Objective:

Maximizing Your Leverage with Networking

Tactical Tasks:

- *Assess professional networking opportunities.*
    - *Chamber of Commerce*
    - *Local community boards and committees*
    - *Online forums and social media*
    - *Seminars*
- *Assess personal networking opportunities.*
    - *Classes*
    - *Fitness/Sports teams*
    - *Social events*
    - *Religious/Spiritual groups*
    - *Volunteering*
- *Assess pre-established relationships.*
    - *High-producing agents and team members*
    - *Family and friends*
    - *Fellow real estate investors*
- *Conduct networking within available opportunities.*

Tactical Objective:

Strategizing Your Leverage

Tactical Tasks:

- *Determine end state and associated conditions.*
- *Determine various objectives (or effects) required for the end state.*
    - *Determine subordinate (operational and tactical) objectives and tasks*
- *Assess adequacy of centers of gravity and basing.*
    - *Presence of basing*
    - *Limitations of operational reach*
- *Establish Lines of Operation (LOO) and Lines of Effort (LOE).*
- *Establish sequencing of tasks and objectives.*
    - *Phasing*
    - *Timing and tempo*
    - *Culmination*
    - *Decisive points*
- *Develop contingencies (branches and sequels).*

Once the required tactical tasks have been established, Investor Bob will have completed the strat-to-task framework. The final product should resemble the following (using Strategic Objective 1 as an example).

Strategic Objective 1:

Acquire Cash-Flowing and Appreciating Assets

Strategic Tasks/Operational Objectives:

1. Strategizing and Planning (Preparation)

Operational Tasks/Tactical Objectives:

- *Leveraging the Basics*

  Tactical Tasks:

  - *Calculate your DTI.*
  - *Assess your current realized and unrealized wealth efficiency.*
- *Leveraging Key Real Estate Concepts*

  Tactical Tasks:

  - *Assess your current investments' (real estate or otherwise) ROI and ROE.*
- *Leveraging Your Team*

  Tactical Tasks:

  - *Honestly assess your personality type, personal skills, and aptitude for managing and operating real estate, as well as your ability and willingness to invest your personal time and effort.*
  - *Identify and research team members for your centers of gravity.*
    - *Deal finder*
    - *Lender*
    - *Property manager*
    - *Applicable contractors*
  - *Determine which additional core and ancillary team members you may acquire for any property in which you are interested.*
- *Leveraging Location*

Tactical Tasks:

- *Determine the region of interest.*
    - *Assess climate, economy of force, laws, and natural hazards*
- *Determine the city (or cities) of interest.*
    - *Assess employment opportunities*
    - *Assess other enticements*
- *Determine the Neighborhood(s) of interest.*
    - *Assess desirability and demand*
    - *Assess availability and supply*
- *Assess if you're in a buyer's or seller's market.*
- *Assess the property.*
    - *Assess property value trends*
    - *Assess Price-to-Rent ratios*

- *Maximizing Leverage with Networking*

  ...... and so forth
- *Strategizing Your Leverage*

  ...... and so forth

Investor Bob would then move on to Strategic Task 2 (Acquiring Real Estate Assets), but at this point, I'm hoping you're able to deduce how the rest of the process will continue.

3. Assess Adequacy of Centers of Gravity and Basing

If you're a novice in real estate investing, you may be wondering if this step is necessary. Remember, when seeking directions from a GPS, you must define your current location—what we call your *base of operations.* If you plan to grow your real estate portfolio and expand into areas where you are not physically present (investing remotely/long-distance real estate investing), this step is critical. While you can forgo this step and still be successful, you will likely do so inefficiently in terms of time, effort, and money. You may sacrifice or delay a long-term advantage for the sake of a short-term gain. I'm not saying you can't or that you won't encounter opportunities that arise outside of your centers of gravity or areas of basing. But the opportunity presented must simply be worth more than the generated inefficiencies. Alternatively, if you elect to pursue an opportunity in an area in which you are sure you do not wish to expand, you may not need to establish a new center of gravity or a new basing area. It would not be efficient to develop lasting relationships with more than one or two essential team members (probably a property manager), nor would it be worth the effort to do so.

Presence of Basing

When assessing adequacy, the first component to assess is basing. If you've established a center of gravity, it becomes your base of operations. If you haven't, your present location is your base of operations. Some investors consider their family members or friends to be another base of operations. You may need to utilize this approach when getting started; however, if possible, don't be *that* person. Relying on family and friends can muddle relationships, and the employer/employee dynamics can inflict undue stress in an area where it is unwelcome.

Limitations of Operational Reach

Hopefully, thinking through this section is little more than a formality since this concept has been covered in both Chapter 5 and Chapter 13. You need to determine the reach to which your center of gravity can extend your operations. This is your operational reach. Opportunities occurring outside of this area (and in an area in which you want to continue expanding) may require an additional center of gravity to combat inefficiencies of resource utilization.

4. Establish Lines of Operation (LOO) and Lines of Effort (LOE)

Establishing LOOs*)* and LOEs*)* (and subsequently establishing sequencing of tasks and objectives) is when the fun begins. Prior to this, you have a vague sense of where you are, where you are going, and a cloudy notion of the actions you need to take. But you have no plan of action to put it all together. Establishing the LOOs and LOEs is when you establish the plan. It's when you bring it all together and plan the path from your base of operations toward accomplishing your end state.

Conveniently, Investor Bob has already established his LOOs and LOEs; they are the strategic objectives and strategic effects, respectively. For the sake of this example, let's imagine you've chosen the same LOOs and LOEs as Investor Bob.

Line of Operation/Strategic Objective 1: *)*
Acquire Cash-Flowing and Appreciating Assets

Line of Operation/Strategic Objective 2: *)*
Accelerate Leverage of Real Estate Assets

Line of Effort/Strategic Effect 1: *)*
Leverage the Velocity of Money

Line of Effort/Strategic Effect 2:
Leverage the Inertia of (Real Estate) Equity

5. Establish Sequencing of Tasks and Objectives

In order to effectively sequence the respective objectives and tasks, you'll need to account for the order of operations and efforts. As you are well aware, this is where you determine the sequence of tasks.

Figure 14-3 is a representation of LOOs and LOEs in pursuit of attaining your end state. Remember, you cannot pursue all endeavors at once. The only LOO*)* which you may initially pursue is to "Acquire Cash-Flowing and Appreciating Assets." There is an order in which you must execute these LOOs and LOEs because of their interdependencies. But in this graph, it isn't clear which LOOs and LOEs*)* are required for the initiation (or continuation) of others.

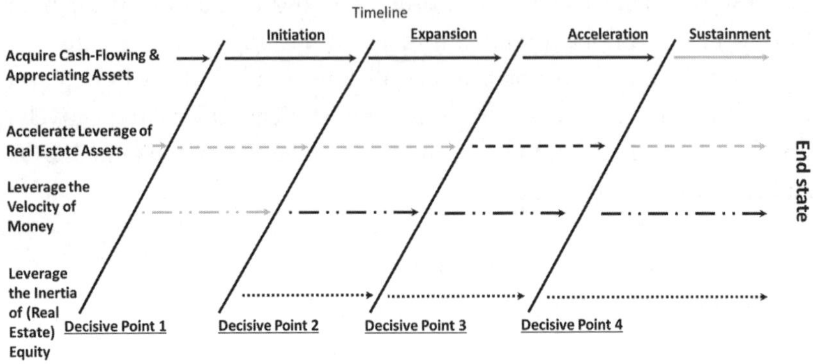

Figure 14-3: LOO and LOE Sequencing

If you are to understand these interdependencies, you would need to construct a modified input-output model, as demonstrated by Figure 14-4.

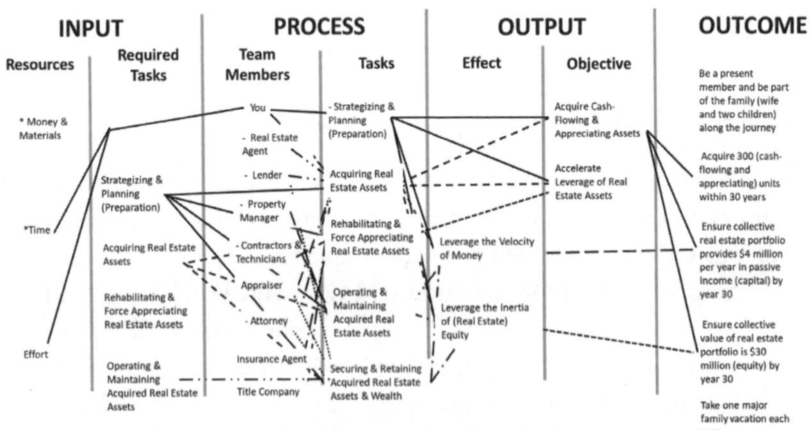

Figure 14-4: LOO and LOE Input-Output Model

Simple, right? It isn't as complex as it may appear once you assess each column individually. Doing this better enables you to determine effective resource allocation in addition to true sequencing of subordinate objectives and tasks to better ascertain the interdependencies of the various LOOs and LOEs. The pertinent details for each column are the following:

Resources

1. Money and/or materials will be required to hire/utilize team members other than yourself (or your significant other/partner).
2. Time (yours or your team members') will be required for any endeavor.
3. Your effort will be required for strategizing and planning.

Required Tasks

This column becomes interesting because you are meant to deduce the following order of tasks:

1. Strategizing and Planning (Preparation)
2. Acquiring Real Estate Assets
3. Rehabilitating and Force Appreciating Real Estate Assets
4. Operating and Maintaining Acquired Real Estate Assets

Note that strategic tasks three, four, and five have dependencies upon strategic tasks one and two, not with one another. Even so, in the sequencing diagram, the forced appreciation LOO)doesn't initiate until later. You will find this to be a result of either limited resources or constrained conditions.

Team Members

With certainty, you are going to need team members to aid you in your endeavor. Even if you could accomplish all of the tasks on your own, you shouldn't. You won't be as efficient performing many of the tasks, and it will not be an efficient utilization of your resources. Match the appropriate team member to each of the following tasks to achieve optimum efficiency:

Real Estate Agent
Acquiring Real Estate Assets

Lender
Acquiring Real Estate Assets
Securing and Retaining Acquired Real Estate Assets and Wealth

Property Manager
Operating and Maintaining Acquired Real Estate Assets

Contractor and Technicians
Rehabilitating and Force Appreciating Real Estate Assets
Operating and Maintaining Acquired Real Estate Assets

Appraiser
Acquiring Real Estate Assets
Securing and Retaining Acquired Real Estate Assets and Wealth

Attorney
Securing and Retaining Acquired Real Estate Assets and Wealth

Title Company
Acquiring Real Estate Assets
Securing and Retaining Acquired Real Estate Assets and Wealth

Note: these are the tasks with which the team members are going to assist you. These members will often learn how to complete tasks outside of their trade out of convenience or efficiency. They may even offer these services to you. The above simply indicates their primary focus or areas of expertise.

Tasks

You should deduce that the strategic tasks in the chart support the respective strategic objectives and effects:

Strategizing and Planning
(Objective) Acquire Cash-Flowing and Appreciating Assets
(Objective) Accelerate Leverage of Real Estate Assets
(Effect) Leverage the *Velocity of Money*
(Effect) Leverage the Inertia of (Real Estate) Equity

Acquiring Real Estate Assets
(Objective) Acquire Cash-Flowing and Appreciating Assets
(Objective) Accelerate Leverage of Real Estate Assets
(Effect) Leverage the *Velocity of Money*
(Effect) Leverage the Inertia of (Real Estate) Equity

Rehabilitating and Force Appreciating Assets
(Objective) Accelerate Leverage of Real Estate Assets

Operating and Maintaining Acquired Real Estate Assets
(Effect) Leverage the *Velocity of Money*
(Effect) Leverage the Inertia of (Real Estate) Equity

Securing and Retaining Acquired Real Estate Assets and Wealth
(Effect) Leverage the *Velocity of Money*
(Effect) Leverage the Inertia of (Real Estate) Equity

Effects and Objectives
Finally, we will assess how the strategic effects and objectives in the chart correspond to the predefined conditions to constitute Investor Bob's desired end state.

(Objective) Acquire Cash-Flowing and Appreciating Assets
Acquire 300 (cash-flowing and appreciating) units within 30 years.

(Objective) Accelerate Leverage of Real Estate Assets
N/A

(Effect) Leverage the *Velocity of Money*
Ensure the collective real estate portfolio provides $4 million per year in passive income (capital) by year 30.

(Effect) Leverage the Inertia of (Real Estate) Equity
Ensure the collective value of the real estate portfolio is $30 million (equity) by year 30.

Once these components have been assessed, you should be able to establish which resources are required for completion of the various LOOs*)* and LOEs. The LOOs, in this case, pertain to the objectives, whereas the LOEs pertain to the effects.

Outcome

The outcome column is simply Investor Bob's five desired end state conditions. You are meant to determine the relationships between the LOOs and LOEs to the second, third, and fourth conditions. You may infer that other LOOs or LOEs to support the first and fifth conditions are required to achieve the desired end state.

In Investor Bob's example, the latter conditions don't actually pertain to investing in real estate but more so pertain to maintaining and supporting his family while striving to invest in real estate. Take note: in this example, LOO "Accelerate Leverage of Real Estate Assets" is not a required LOO for completion of the desired end state. Resources assigned to this LOO*)* should be utilized when opportune, never in instances where utilization is detrimental to other LOOs and LOEs.

Phasing

Phasing, as you are now aware, is the segmentation of the identified sequencing into distinct parts often dissociated by changes in conditions; this distinction is an imperative part of planning. From a military planning perspective, the rules of engagement are often different and dependent upon the phase of a campaign in which you are currently engaged. Phasing for this real estate investment strategy is no different. I've found that segmenting this strategy into the following four phases offers the most straightforward approach to understanding the rules of engagement you'll want to adhere to throughout your journey.

Phases:

1. Initiation
2. Expansion
3. Acceleration
4. Sustainment

> Dependent upon your means and goals, the "Expansion" and "Acceleration" phases may be executed in inverse order, parallel, or with only one and not the other.

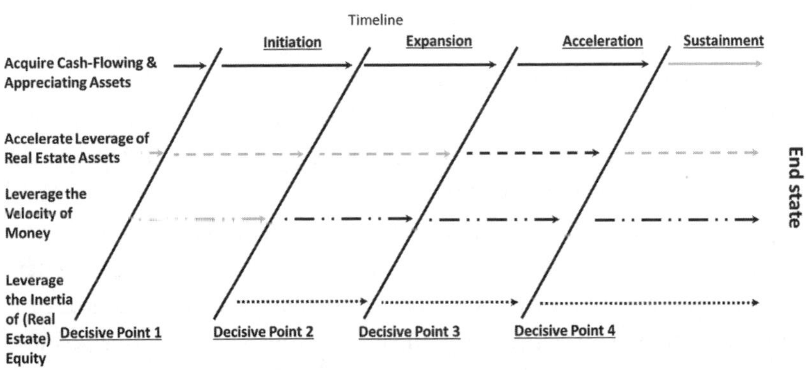

Figure 14-5: LOE and LOO)Phasing

Consider the following focus or emphasis for each phase:

Initiation
Establish and accrue cash-flowing and appreciating units leveraging low interest rates and low- to no-money-down conventional loans, as well as DPA programs. *Minimize capital expenditures to the greatest extent practical; leverage capital to generate and grow equity.*

Expansion
Continue accruing cash-flowing and appreciating units by leveraging portfolio and commercial loans. *Trade generated equity for additional growth of capital and equity to be reinvested for real estate portfolio expansion.*

Acceleration
Leverage capital to acquire distressed properties, with the intent to force appreciate value (equity). *Accelerate growth by trading force appreciated equity into additional growth of capital and equity to be reinvested for real estate portfolio expansion.*

Sustainment
Maintain operations, upkeep, and security of the acquired real estate portfolio. *Trade accrued equity for capital intended for additional growth while retaining passive income (capital) for other use,* or *leverage passive income (capital) for additional growth while retaining accrued equity for other use,* or *retain accrued equity and capital for other use.*

Each phase places emphasis on certain actions to achieve certain conditions. This does not mean that actions (tasks or objectives) associated with other LOO/s and LOEs cannot be conducted within a certain phase. You may have the means to skip phases of this plan altogether. If you do not have those means, conducting activities intended for later phases may not be advisable, even if currently achievable. Doing so may be detrimental to your overall strategy and cause you to plateau in progression rather than experience consistent growth. Alternatively, some phases, such as acceleration and sustainment, may not be pertinent to your desired end state.

Timing and Tempo

Where the process of sequencing and phasing is more of a design, the process of timing and tempo is more of an art. Timing and tempo pertain to the coordination and scheduling of subordinate objectives and tasks. Typically, the driving factors of timing and tempo include team member and resource availability, space limitations (team members working on top of one another), additional incurred costs, requirements, or limitations, etc. If actions are not completed in a certain order, you will see a disruption or delay. While timing and tempo is relevant for all subordinate objectives and tasks, it is most pertinent for Leveraging the Rehab and Retaining Your Leverage (taxes). Review Chapters 8 and 11 for examples specific to those topics.

Culmination

Culmination is the point when you've made it. You have completed at least the main (if not all) LOOs*)* and LOEs required to satisfy the desired end state conditions.

At this point, your efforts are purely focused on sustaining—but not expanding—your assets and wealth and reaping the rewards of your endeavor. This does not preclude you from continuing to expand. It merely signifies that it is no longer necessary for achievement of your desired end state.

Decisive Points

Decisive points are integral to an investment strategy and achievement of your desired end state in that they determine if and/or when you may advance from one phase to another. If conducting activities out of phase may be detrimental, advancing phases prior to the proper time increases the likelihood of dire effects, or at best, introduces costly inefficiencies.

That being said, you may find opportunities that are so enticing you can't help but pursue them. This may violate the conditions of your current phase, so if you choose to go after them, make sure the opportunity is enticing enough to offset any penalty incurred from deviating from your strategy. The numbers may work in your favor. When these moments arise, if pursued, identify this as a branch in your plan.

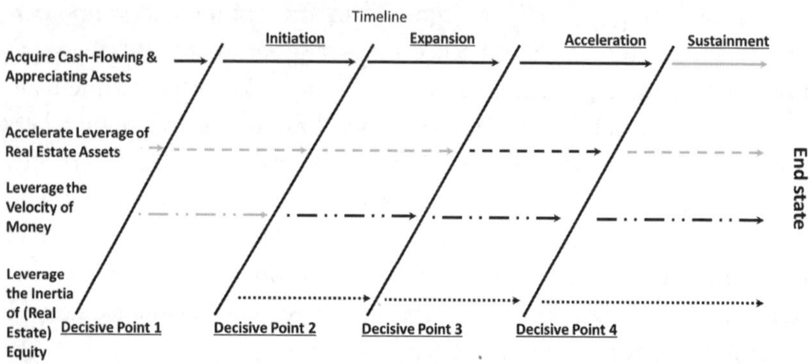

Figure 14-6: Decisive Points

A decisive point should be a criterion, which when met, allows progression from one phase to another (sequel). If failed or altered, it results in a change of the plan, or a branch. It is important to note that these criteria are more effective when they are quantitative rather than qualitative. This is so they may be more objectively assessed.

Investor Bob's decisive points, listed below, seem simple enough. For many individuals, advancing through the first few phases and satisfying the decisive points criteria will take time. I recommend you maintain similar criteria for your plan. You should assume most of your journey will be spent in the expansion and/or acceleration phase of this strategy.

Decisive Point 1

- Preparation, strategy, and planning is complete (as much as possible).
- Enough capital has been accrued to initiate first acquisition (varies per location and endeavor).
- DTI is under 43 percent.

Decisive Point 2

- Nine cash-flowing properties (plus primary residence) have been acquired using conventional loans (20 total if married … 10 per person).

Decisive Point 3

- (Subjective Criteria) Enough capital has been accrued (or equity transferred) for required capital expenditures (varies per location and endeavor).

Decisive Point 4

- Culmination has been attained.

6. *Develop Contingencies (Branches and Sequels)*

Finally, you will need to establish contingencies for the most probable and most detrimental impediments to the plan. As we've discussed, sequels are the continuation of a plan from one phase to another. Branches are when a deviation from the initial plan is required, typically for either a catastrophic failure to achieve a decisive point's criteria or from an intentional choice not to follow the original plan. There are far too many contingency possibilities to enumerate. Devise branches and sequels that fit your design and plan.

Perils of Overleveraging – Part II

Despite the immense benefit and generational wealth you may acquire using this strategy, you must maintain situational awareness if the plan starts to go awry. This can happen if you overleverage. Overleveraging occurs when a real estate investor borrows too much money without the ability to pay the property's operating expenses and/or their debt from the mortgage payments. In a world where there is good and bad debt, overleveraging can be a catastrophic debt. The housing crisis of 2008 was due to real estate investors' overleveraging combined with predatory and poor lending practices. Fortunately, many of the predatory lending practices have been mitigated by various legislation. Unfortunately, lending practices have become increasingly stringent, resulting in a higher barrier to entry for many novice investors. While additional safeguards against overleveraging exist today, investors must be wary of the pitfalls.

Even in today's world, many investors pursue opportunities that are above their reach or choose investment opportunities unwisely. If we are going back to gambling analogies, this equates to hitting on Blackjack when the dealer holds a bust hand; it can cause you to bust and be detrimental to the entire table. A player should be savvy in choosing when to hit and when to stay, just as an investor should be savvy in knowing when to pursue an opportunity and when to forgo. To put it simply, just because an opportunity exists doesn't mean it's the right opportunity for you.

Let's identify the most common ways investors subject themselves to overleveraging. This will help you to steer clear of making these mistakes. Most of the actions I recommend are within your control; the few that are not can be counteracted with deliberate planning. In real estate, economic downturn is a cyclical certainty. Hoping it doesn't occur is not a strategy—planning is. Sometimes the best mitigation to a peril is to steer clear. The following are the most common manners in which investors overleverage:

Overleveraging:

- Overextending
- Overborrowing
- Overassessing
- Excessive Ambition

Overextending

Overextending refers to an investor who leverages his/her capital to the extent that insufficient reserves remain to resolve unanticipated capital expenditures or lapses in passive income. This results in the investor needing to take on more debt to overcome the impediment. This, in turn, requires resolution for the continuation of generating income. Overextension is commonly caused by not maintaining sufficient reserves, not projecting/budgeting for repairs, and/or not accounting for vacancies or late/unpaid rents.

Think of it this way: you invested all of your supplemental income into cash-flowing and appreciating real estate. Then you need to replace a roof unexpectedly. While this may be deducted or depreciated, you still must expend several thousand dollars—capital you no longer have. You could take out a bridge loan, but you may become overextended (negative cash flow).

Using the *10 percent rule* will help you avoid this crisis. Apply the 10 percent rule like this:

- Plan for a 10 percent vacancy rate.
- Project for 10 percent of rental income to be used for repairs.
- Retain 10 percent (capital) of investment portfolio value for capital expenditures.

Another strategy to prevent this crisis is projecting capital expenditures and/or assessing if a tenant is tenuous. Awareness of these issues in advance may increase your preparedness against being overextended.

Overborrowing

Overborrowing occurs when an individual or investor borrows more money for an investment than he or she should, resulting in expenses amounting to more than the FMV of monthly rents. The culmination is a negative or non-existent cash flow. While some investors employ this approach with assets that are appreciating in value, it is not recommended for novice investors (those in Phase 1).

Many investors find themselves in this situation when they inappropriately leverage low- to no-money-down loan options or when they ignore the 1 percent and 2 percent rule for rents. Overborrowing can also occur when investors take out adjustable-rate mortgages. Imagine this: you purchase a property with an adjustable-rate mortgage with a marginal positive income ratio and an inconsistent increase in rental demand. You need to be wary of the interest rate adjustments and their impact on the assets-income ratio. If you do not address these adjustments properly, they may result in overleveraging. The best methods to avoid overborrowing in manners that result in overleveraging are the following:

- Adhere to the 1-percent (or 2-percent) rule for rental income to property value.
- Buy down or sell adjustable-rate mortgages if interest rates cause a negative income ratio.

Overassessing

Overassessing means improperly assessing market or environment conditions when you investigate a property to acquire. Even if you accomplish everything else correctly, overassessing sets you on a path toward overleveraging because you chose a property that can become a sinkhole. This can result in draining resources from other properties in your portfolio. Overassessing occurs when an investor fails to perform trend analysis to determine the direction of the conditions. If you focus too much on the snapshot of the present but ignore the trendanalysis, you may set yourself up for failure.

Trends to look for include decreasing property values, decreasing school performance or failed school levies, increasing crime rates, and major industry departing the area—without tourism or niche factors to compensate. Weaker investors ignore what trends tell them. They incorrectly assess the indicators of future performance by focusing too much on the present situation. Negative indicators of future performance will result in decreasing equity and declining rental demand, resulting in decreased earnings or capital. This is a death spiral to your real estate investments. Accurately assessing indicators of future performance doesn't guarantee you will never make mistakes or overassess a property. It will, however, minimize the chance that any acquisition mistake will torpedo your broader strategy. The best method to counter overassessing a potential acquisition is to adhere to these activities:

- Establish a trend.
- Adhere to the process of narrowing your search for a profitable investment property.

Excessive Ambition

Being overambitious means you are trying to take on more than you can handle. Where overextending pertains to misallocation, misuse, or underestimation of required capital reserves for your venture, excessive ambition means misallocation, misuse, or underestimation of required resources (capital, equity, time, or effort).

This occurs most often when you pursue an endeavor that is beyond your ability to execute but you believe is within your ability if resources are traded and managed effectively. For example, let's assume Investor Bob located and identified a property he could force appreciate that had the following figures:

ARV:	$125,000
Total Sales Price:	$50,000
Renovations:	$40,000
Refinance Fees (2%):	$2,500
75% ARV (Cash-out Refinance):	$93,750
Total Expenses:	$92,500

Figure 14-7: Excessive Ambition

This is a great opportunity! Investor Bob could essentially force appreciate, cash-out refinance, then walk away with an appreciating and cash-flowing property with essentially the same amount of capital as when he started. The only problem with this is that Investor Bob only has $70,000 of capital available and doesn't have the ability to finance. He figures he can offset the $22,500 deficit by putting in his own time and effort to the renovations and pursues this endeavor. If it works out, his gamble will pay off. But if additional capital is required or if his time and/or effort is insufficient, he is sunk. He would own an asset incapable of generating any revenue to offset or recoup his expenditures. If any additional liability arises with this asset or others within his portfolio, his excessive ambition would have then led to his being overleveraged.

DID YOU KNOW?

WalletHub conducted an assessment in 2021 to determine the most overleveraged cities in the United States. It assesses the average mortgage compared to the average home value to determine the cities' debt-to-value ratios. The top results of this study are provided below:

City:	Median Mortgage Debt:	Median House Value:	Mortgage Debt Ratio:
McKees Rocks, PA	$114,874	$56,500	203%
Willis, TX	$141,804	$84,500	168%
Blacklick Estates, OH	$147,661	$93,700	158%
York, PA	$126,807	$80,700	157%
Trenton, NJ	$141,312	$100,400	141%
Dumfries, VA	$280,392	$213,300	131%
Canton, MS	$147,745	$124,200	119%
Richmond, TX	$186,870	$167,900	111%

Economic Downturn

Now that we've discussed the things that you can control (to avoid overleveraging), you may be asking about the things that you cannot. While you cannot control economic downturns, you may become adept at predicting when downturns may occur—and prepare for them by following the same mitigations to avoid overleveraging. If you're savvy, you may even posture yourself to take advantage of economic valleys.

Preparing for the lows efficiently begins by predicting when a downturn will occur. You know the old adage, "Buy low, sell high." Let me add a layer: "Buy low, sell high if appropriate, and avoid selling low unless you must." Seems simple (and it is), but too many individuals do not adhere to this principle.

Let's apply the principle to an economic downturn. You buy low so that you have immediate equity available. If you purchased a property for 70 percent of its FMV and the bubble bursts, you maintain a 30 percent margin against the decrease in value to offset an upside-down mortgage.

If you must sell a property, sell high. Remember, the objective of this strategy is to acquire assets that are appreciating in value and generating cash flow. If a property is not appreciating in value, is marginally cash-flowing, and/or the market indicators suggest a downturn and/or decreasing rents, sell when it is worth more (sell high) rather than waiting until the value decreases and you have to sell low. Investors who were overleveraged during the last housing crisis were the ones who lost out because they were forced to sell low. Even when the value of properties plummeted, the rental demand did not. Although the downturn diminished their accrued equity, investors who held on to their assets were still generating passive income because their units were still cash-flowing. In other words, the investment strategy still worked; it merely slowed down. You will also find that investors who did not sell their assets during the burst have recouped their equity and then some. Figure 14-8 highlights the average value of homes in the U.S. from 2000 through 2020. On average, home values achieved and exceeded the pre-bubble high of 2005 by 2019.

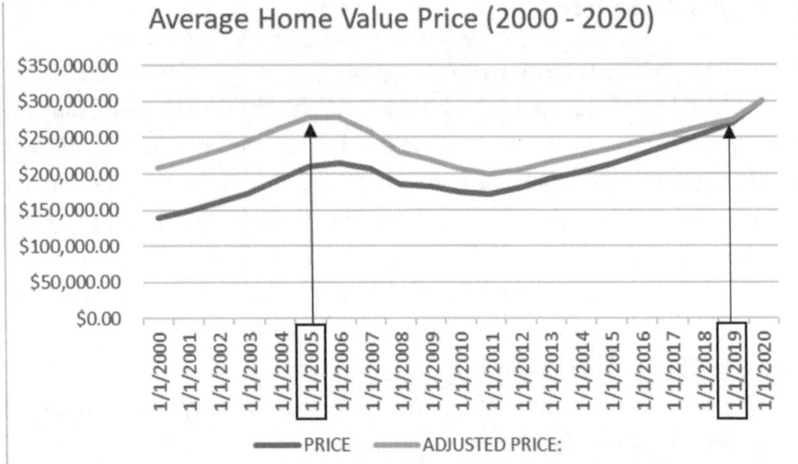

Figure 14-8: Home Values Over Time

Don't get me wrong. A housing crisis can be a tragic event for many investors. However, it can be a glorious, life-altering event for those who are prepared. By this, I mean investors who have capital available to purchase appreciating assets will leverage the crisis to buy properties for pennies on the dollar. To accomplish this, you must have enough capital readily available to pay in cash or leverage finance to purchase from those who are overleveraged. This is a win-win.

We circle back to an earlier principle: apply common sense. The multimillion-dollar question is how to predict the economic upturns and downturns so that you don't have copious amounts of underleveraged capital for extended periods of time. Predicting economic downturns is an art that advisors get paid millions to determine. It is a complicated calculation. However, consistent indicators or triggers for an economic downturn, recession, or housing crisis typically include the following:

- Widespread property prices increasing faster than salaries
- Abundance of overleveraging by investors and homeowners
- Increasing interest rates after periods of low rates (adjustable-rate mortgages)

If you notice several of these indicators occurring simultaneously or within a small window of time, a downturn may be imminent.

Prepare yourself to take advantage of the imminent crisis and see your portfolio's growth accelerate far more expediently than you would have otherwise.

> As sure as the spring follows the winter, prosperity and economic growth will follow recession.
> —Robert Foster Bennett, *American politician and businessman*

Sensible Sarah's Journey

Here we are, at the end of this journey for our investors. It is time for us to see just how well the pursuit of this investment strategy met Sensible Sarah's desired end state. We will recap the impacts of the various choices executed by Sarah throughout her journey to demonstrate her effectiveness in leveraging this strategy.

Prior to initiating this strategy, Sensible Sarah had planned and prepared. In doing so, she researched and studied the principles identified within this book and started saving for her first real estate acquisition. Up until then, she and her family had been renting a two-bedroom, two-bathroom apartment for $900/month. It worked because her children were young and could share a room with twin beds. Fortunately, Sensible Sarah had been saving for the past two years and had been able to set aside $10,000 for purchasing a home. She identified a duplex property, discussed it with her husband, and decided to purchase it as their new primary residence/investment property. Sarah leveraged an FHA loan to acquire this asset due to the low down payment required for the purchase. The property details are the following:

Price: $150,000 **Taxes:** $200/month
Size: 2 Bed, 2 Bath (Each) **Insurance:** $40/month
Avg Rental Demand: $850 (Each)/month

Down Payment: $3,500
Closing Costs: ~$4,000 (Funding fee ~3%, MIP fee ~1%)
P&I: $380/month
MIP: $60/month

Sensible Sarah will need only $7,500 to cover the out-of-pocket expenditures, leaving $2,500 in reserve. While Sensible Sarah is coordinating the few minor alterations and managing the logistics of the move, her husband is advertising and conducting background checks on potential tenants for the neighboring unit. They find a tenant to rent the unit for $850, resulting in a monthly profit of $170 ($2,040/year). Sarah, being sensible, decides to continue saving the $850/month she could otherwise garner in rents from the side of the unit her family is occupying. Between savings and passive income, she is able to set aside $1,020 per month ($12,240/year).

Meanwhile, there are other properties Sensible Sarah believes would be ideal to acquire as an investment property. For simplicity, they have similar specifications to the duplex she has already purchased. Purchasing a duplex as an investment property will require a down payment of 25 percent ($37,500). Purchasing an investment property that is a single-family home requires a down payment of 20 percent ($30,000). It will take four years to save enough capital to purchase another (duplex) investment property.

Price: $150,000 **Taxes:** $200/month
Size: 2 Bed, 2 Bath (Each) **Insurance:** $40/month
Avg Rental Demand: $850 (Each)/month

Down Payment: $37,500
Closing Costs: ~$4,000
P&I: $280/month

During this time, Sensible Sarah also decided to establish an LLC to shelter her real estate investments. Rather than wait another four years for her next acquisition, she elected to acquire a single-family home to be her primary residence using the USDA program (after one year of residing in the duplex). Examine this unit's financing specifications.

Sarah must pay only for closing costs since the USDA loan can be 100 percent. Additionally, there is no monthly MIP for this loan, lowering her monthly out-of-pocket expenses to $540/month. Now, she may lease the other half of the original duplex for FMV. She also trusts the duplex into her LLC.

At the three-year mark, Sensible Sarah has conducted yet

another sensible act. She has acquired her third property (duplex) through her LLC. Once acquired, both sides of this property are leased, and $1,180/month ($14,160/year) becomes the garnered income for that unit. The total passive income from the two acquisitions grows to $2,180/month ($26,160/year). It will take Sarah another two years to accrue enough capital to purchase a fourth property. Sarah has also established a second LLC in which to purchase her fourth property, and a fifth property is on the horizon. Sarah places the first single-family unit (purchased with USDA) into the first LLC.

Sarah has also been carefully assessing her first duplex's value and the available equity. She has now accrued enough equity that when cash-out refinanced will enable her to purchase a fifth unit. Furthermore, refinancing her first unit makes the FHA loan another available option, an option that will enable her to acquire her sixth unit in only her seventh year of investing in real estate. This acquisition will be another single-family home.

At this point, her monthly income is $6,220/month ($74,640/year). Not bad at all! Sarah has positioned herself to purchase an additional three properties every two years. She can also cash-out refinance her second property to leverage a 10th mortgage. At the end of her eighth year, she will have 10 properties in her portfolio. They generate $11,000/month ($132,000/year) in passive income. Sensible Sarah has the leverage to purchase five properties every two years.

In year 12, rather than purchasing two properties, Sensible Sarah and her family decide they are ready to take on their first major rehab. They establish a fifth LLC, which they use specifically for purchasing and rehabilitating properties. Once they've completed the rehab, the property is trusted into another LLC under their portfolio. She identifies a property with the following characteristics:

Price: $60,000
ARV: $150,000
Renovation Costs: $40,000
Size: 3 Bed, 3 Bath
(Refi) Closing Costs: ~$4,000
P&I: $300/month
Taxes: $200/month
Insurance: $40/month
Avg Rental Demand: $1500/month

This represents an immense opportunity for the Sensible family. They know they could purchase and renovate the distressed property with cash, rent the unit for a profit, and cash-out refinance the unit after the seasoning period. Furthermore, they are generating more equity than the amount of capital invested, so much so that they may conclude this endeavor with more capital in hand than when they started—all while maintaining a cash-flowing property. For example:

ARV: $150,000
(75% ARV): $112,500
Price: $60,000
Renovation Costs: $40,000
(Refi) Closing Costs: ~$4,000
Holding Costs: $1,000 (Utilities, etc.)
Profit: $7,500

While working on this rehab, one of the neighbor kids trespasses onto the property and injures himself. The parents consider suing but realize the Sensibles purchased under an LLC that has no other assets. Since the only repayment they could possibly obtain is an unfinished house, they decide to forgo suing.

For the next few years, Sensible Sarah and her family perform one rehab per year as a family activity to involve their kids in the business. Sarah continues to expand her portfolio in the manners previously detailed with a few minor exceptions: 1) She no longer has the need (nor is she eligible) for FHA or USDA loans. 2) After year 11, when she and her husband have attained 20 properties using conventional lending, she will need to leverage portfolio loans from her lenders.

You get it, right? You see how "sensible" Sarah's journey was. Rather than expound in narrative form, let me sum it up and provide a graphic overview.

Sarah achieved her desired end state by year 20. She may continue expanding her portfolio or rest on her laurels.

This example assumes she continued to purchase small single-family and multifamily units to achieve this goal. She could have progressed to commercial properties, large multifamily complexes, etc., to continue her expansion. When you get to that point in your journey, your network will guide you to those more efficient methods reserved for investors with the capital to pursue them.

(Objective) Acquire Cash-Flowing and Appreciating Assets:
(Goal) - Acquire 300 (cash-flowing and appreciating) units within 30 years
(Actual) - Acquired 243 (cash-flowing and appreciating) units within 20 years

(Objective) Accelerate Leverage of Real Estate Assets:
(Goal) - Rehab properties to accelerate other objectives and effects
(Actual) - Rehabilitated eight properties to accelerate other objectives and effects

(Effect) Leverage the Velocity of Money:
(Goal) - Ensure the collective real estate portfolio provides $4 million per year in passive income (capital) by year 30
(Actual) - Real estate portfolio provides $4.85 million per year in passive income (capital) by year 20

(Effect) Leverage the Inertia of (Real Estate) Equity:
(Goal) - Ensure the collective value of the real estate portfolio is $30 million (equity) by year 30
(Actual) - Real estate portfolio value would be worth $36.3 million (equity in today's dollars) by year 20

Having reached her desired end state in year 20, Sarah can conclude her journey or continue her plan for the full 30 years. Continuing would garner $257.4 million per year and would be valued at $2.6 million—figures that far exceed anything Sarah could have ever imagined. She has achieved a legacy and leaves an inheritance of generational wealth. It all came about through knowledge, favorable happenstance, deliberate effort, and discipline.

Sensible Sarah's Journey

Year	Income/Yr	Property Acquired	Property Refinanced	Business Entity Established	Total Value	Events	Phase
1	Preparation						Initiation
2						Decisive Point 1	
3	$ 2,040.00	1			$ 150,000.00	FHA Loan	
4	$ 12,240.00	2		1	$ 300,000.00	USDA Loan	
5	$ 12,240.00				$ 300,000.00		
6	$ 12,240.00				$ 300,000.00		
7	$ 26,160.00	3			$ 450,000.00		
8	$ 26,160.00				$ 450,000.00		
9	$ 74,640.00	4,5,6	1	2	$ 900,000.00	FHA Loan	
10	$ 79,040.00	7	2	3	$ 1,500,000.00		
11	$ 132,000.00	8,9,10		4	$ 1,950,000.00		
12	$ 146,400.00	11		5	$ 2,100,000.00	Sued	
13	$ 218,400.00	12-15,16	3	6	$ 2,850,000.00		
14	$ 304,800.00	17-21,22		7,8	$ 3,750,000.00	Decisive Point 2,3	
15	$ 488,880.00	23-33,34	4,5,6	9,10,11,12	$ 5,550,000.00		Expansion / Acceleration
16	$ 701,280.00	35-48, 49	7	13-16	$ 7,800,000.00		
17	$ 1,012,800.00	50-70,71	8, 9, 10	17-22	$ 10,950,000.00		
18	$ 1,423,440.00	72-99,100	11	23-30	$ 15,000,000.00		
19	$ 3,462,480.00	101-143,144	12,13,14,15,16	31-42	$ 21,600,000.00		
20	**$ 4,850,160.00**	145-242,243	17-22	43-72	**$ 36,300,000.00**	**Goal Achieved**	
21	$ 10,301,760.00	244-384,385	23-34	73-114	$ 57,750,000.00		Sustainment
22	$ 19,845,600.00	386-674	35-49	115-202	$ 101,100,000.00	Economic Downturn	
23	$ 27,336,240.00	675-1,203		203-360	$ 180,450,000.00		
24	$ 37,658,880.00	1,204-1,932		361-578	$ 289,800,000.00		
25	$ 51,878,873.00	1,933-2,937		579-880	$ 440,550,000.00		
26	$ 71,462,153.00	2,938-4,320		881-1,296	$ 648,000,000.00		
27	$ 98,436,953.00	4,321-6,225		1,297-1,866	$ 933,750,000.00		
20	$135,606,746.00	6,226-8,850		1,867-2,654	$ 1,327,500,000.00		
29	$186,811,853.00	8,851-12,466		2,655-3,738	$ 1,869,900,000.00		
30	$257,352,008.00	12,467-17,477		3,739-5,242	$ 2,621,550,000.00		

Cautious Carl's Journey

Let's assess Cautious Carl's journey through this strategy. Carl is less comfortable taking the risks associated with leveraging (cash-out refinancing) than Sarah. He elected to refrain from force appreciating properties by executing various rehab projects, due to the risks associated with the endeavor and his lack of knowledge. Let's recap the impacts of Carl's choices and assess how his pursuit of this investment strategy worked in achieving his desired end state.

Cautious Carl planned and prepared before initiating his strategy. He researched and studied the principles within this book while saving for his first real estate acquisition. Like Sarah, his children were young and could share a room in the rented, two-bedroom, two-bathroom apartment for $900/month. Fortunately, Cautious Carl had been saving for the past two years and had been able to set aside $10,000 for purchasing a home. His cautious nature prompted him not to leverage low-money-down payment options. This strategy will require another three years to attain enough capital for the 15 percent down payment, networked with lenders for the ideal rate. Carl identified a target property, discussed it with his wife, and decided to purchase a duplex as their primary residence/investment property. The property details are the following:

Price: $150,000 **Taxes:** $200/month
Size: 2 Bed, 2 Bath (Each) **Insurance:** $40/month
Avg Rental Demand: $850 (Each)/month

Down Payment: $22,500
Closing Costs: ~$3,000
P&I: $300/month

Together the Cautious family located a tenant to rent the adjacent unit for $850, resulting in a monthly profit of $360

($4,320/year). Carl, being cautious, decides to continue saving the $850/month he could otherwise garner in rents should his family not occupy the residence. Between savings and passive income, he is able to set aside $1,210 per month ($14,520/year).

Meanwhile, there are additional properties Carl would like to purchase as additional investments. They have similar specifications to the duplex he has already purchased. It will take two years to save enough capital to purchase a second property.

Price: $150,000 **Taxes:** $200/month
Size: 2 Bed, 2 Bath (Each) **Insurance:** $40/month
Avg Rental Demand: $850 (Each)/month

Down Payment: $37,500
Closing Costs: ~$4,000
P&I: $280/month

Carl established an LLC to shelter his real estate investments and maximize asset and personal liability protection. Two years later, Carl may afford a third duplex.

Carl maintains this approach and continues to leverage the *Velocity of Money* to fund his expansion (as depicted on the following page).

He also was able to achieve his desired end state; it just took longer … seven years longer.

When a tenant attempted to sue Carl, he had both insurance and asset and liability protection. When the housing market dipped, Carl experienced minimal impacts due to his highly selective approach to acquiring assets. He did, however, have an absurd number of LLCs (890) at the end of his journey. He accrued a notable legacy that he and his wife may enjoy during their lifetime and pass along as an inheritance.

The Cautious family achieved the objectives and effects required to attain their desired end state. For Cautious Carl, preparation and advancement to Decisive Point 1 required five years. In year 18, he advanced from Phase 1 to Phase 2. Nine years later, Carl progressed to Phase 3 (Sustainment), representing the culmination or attainment of the end state.

(Objective) Acquire Cash-Flowing and Appreciating Assets:
(Goal) – Acquire 300 (cash-flowing and appreciating) units within 30 years
(Actual) – Acquired 333 (cash-flowing and appreciating) units within 27 years

(Objective) Accelerate Leverage of Real Estate Assets:
Not Leveraged

(Effect) Leverage the Velocity of Money:
(Goal) – Ensure the collective real estate portfolio provides $4 million per year in passive income (capital) by year 30
(Actual) – Real estate portfolio provides $4.88 million per year in passive income (capital) by year 27

(Effect) Leverage the Inertia of (Real Estate) Equity:
Not Leveraged

Like Sensible Sarah's example, this model assumes he continued to purchase duplexes to achieve this goal. In actuality, he could have progressed to larger ventures to generate greater returns. It's important to note the difference in the rate of growth for both Carl and Sarah. Should they continue to expand their portfolios, Sarah's growth will grow at a notably higher rate due to the compounding effects of the *Inertia of Real Estate* that amount to the *Momentum of Wealth.*

Cautious Carl's Journey							
Year	**Income/Yr**	**Properties Acquired**	**Properties Refinanced**	**Business Entity Established**	**Total Value**	**Events**	**Phase**
1	**Preparation**						
2							
3							
4							
5						**Decisive Point 1**	
6	$ 4,320.00	1		1	$ 150,000.00		
7	$ 4,320.00						
8	$ 18,480.00	2		2	$ 300,000.00		
9	$ 18,480.00						**Initiation**
10	$ 32,640.00	3		3	$ 450,000.00		
11	$ 32,640.00						
12	$ 46,800.00	4		4	$ 600,000.00	Sued	
13	$ 60,960.00	5		5	$ 750,000.00		
14	$ 75,120.00	6		6	$ 900,000.00		
15	$ 103,440.00	7,8		7,8	$ 1,200,000.00		
16	$ 145,920.00	9,10,11		9,10,11	$ 1,650,000.00		
17	$ 202,560.00	12,13,14,15		12,13,14,15	$ 2,250,000.00		
18	$ 273,360.00	16-20		16-20	$ 3,000,000.00	**Decisive Point 2**	
19	$ 376,580.00	21-27		21-27	$ 4,050,000.00		
20	$ 518,776.00	28-37		28-37	$ 5,550,000.00		
21	$ 714,665.00	38-50		38-50	$ 7,500,000.00		
22	$ 984,522.00	51-69		51-69	$ 10,350,000.00	Economic Downturn	**Expansion**
23	$ 1,356,277.00	70-95		70-95	$ 14,250,000.00		
24	$ 1,868,407.00	96 131		96-131	$ 19,650,000.00		
25	$ 2,573,917.00	132-170		132-170	$ 25,500,000.00		
26	$ 3,545,828.00	171-238		171-238	**$ 35,700,000.00**		
27	**$ 4,884,732.00**	239-333		239-333	$ 49,950,000.00	**Goal Achieved**	
28	$ 6,729,206.00	334-463		334-463	$ 69,600,000.00		
29	$ 9,270,154.00	464-643		464-643	$ 96,450,000.00		Sustainment
30	$12,770,564.00	643-890		643-890	$133,500,000.00		

Risky Rick's Journey

Carl did well in his real estate venture, but Sarah did better. Risky Rick, in all his competitiveness, desired far more than both of them. He has always wanted to be the best, to have the most, or be the fastest. Rick is willing to take risks to be the frontrunner, and his investment strategy is no different. Let's see how effective Rick's boldness was toward achieving his goals.

Like Sarah and Carl, Rick diligently assessed the principles in this book, developed his strategy, and set about developing his portfolio. Rick saved the necessary $10,000 to acquire his first property. Prior to this time, Rick and the Risky family rented a three-bedroom, two-bathroom house for $1,200/month. His children were young enough to share a room, but Rick wanted more for them if possible. He identified the perfect property without consulting his wife and decided to purchase a duplex as their new primary residence/investment property. He also decided to leverage the FHA loan to acquire this asset due to the low down payment required for the purchase. The property details are the following:

Price: $150,000 **Taxes:** $200/month
Size: 2 Bed, 2 Bath (Each) **Insurance:** $40/month
Avg Rental Demand: $850 (Each)/month

Down Payment: $3,500
Closing Costs: ~$4,000 (Funding fee ~3%, MIP fee ~1%)
P&I: $380/month
MIP: $60/month

Rick's wife was not pleased with the selection. She had her heart set on a single-family home with more room. Instead, their kids needed to share a room, and they had less of a yard. The tension between Rick and his wife resulted in her refusal to assist with finding a property manager or locating tenants to reside on the other side. Risky Rick had to do it all himself. He found a tenant to rent the unit for $850, resulting in a monthly profit of $170 ($2,040/year). He promised to find another single-family home as a residence for his family.

Rick, like Sarah, sets aside $1,020 per month ($170 profit plus $850 savings), equating to $12,240 per year. Rick identifies the following single-family home for his family to live in and elects to use the USDA loan to purchase. He also leases the now vacant half of the duplex for FMV. Unlike Sarah and Carl, Risky Rick believes that establishing a business is a costly waste of time. He maintains the properties in his name.

Price: $150,000 **Taxes:** $200/month
Size: 4 Bed, 3 Bath **Insurance:** $40/month
Avg Rental Demand: $1500/month

Down Payment: $0 (USDA)
Closing Costs: ~$4,000
P&I: $300/month

Rick's wife does not like the single-family property Rick found. She appreciates the size and the amenities but doesn't like living so far away from the city. Rick promises that he will find a single-family home closer to the city for their family. Meanwhile, Rick continually researches other properties that have similar specifications to the duplex he already purchased. Purchasing a duplex as an investment property will require a down payment of 25 percent ($37,500).

Normally, it would take another three years to save enough capital to purchase another duplex. But at the expense of time with his family, Rick earns his real estate license and spends numerous hours working real estate as a side hustle to acquire the required capital within one year.

Price: $150,000 **Taxes:** $200/month
Size: 2 Bed, 2 Bath (Each) **Insurance:** $40/month
Avg Rental Demand: $850 (Each)/month

Down Payment: $37,500
Closing Costs: ~$4,000
P&I: $280/month

Rick uses this garnered capital to purchase his third property, bringing his annual income (from his real estate) to $26,400. Rick knows it will take another two years to generate enough capital to purchase his fourth property. If he continues to earn commissions from selling properties, he can purchase another unit in one year. His real estate agent job also lets him get away from hearing how much his wife doesn't enjoy living further from the city. Risky Rick earns the required capital and purchases the fourth property in the sixth year. Rick's properties now garner enough passive income for him to purchase another property each year. Rick purchases his fifth property in the seventh year.

Rick still isn't satisfied with his progress. He knows that if he continues to garner additional income through being a real estate agent, he can procure one additional property per year. Furthermore, he elects to cash-out refinance the first unit to leverage the accrued equity toward the purchase of another unit. By the end of year eight, Rick has purchased properties six, seven, and eight. Together these units garner $97,200 per year, enough to purchase two properties per year, and with a little more active income, three per year.

Rick begins to listen to his wife's complaints about him working so much and not spending enough time with the family. So Risky Rick takes a year to enjoy increased family time, but he still longs to build a real estate empire. He decides to work even harder the next year to make up for the year when he was investing in family but not in real estate. Risky Rick hires an assistant to help locate viable properties to procure. The assistant doesn't quite master finding viable turnkey properties with the proper ROI or ROE potential; she does, however, have a great knack for identifying distressed properties. She encourages him to leverage the funds garnered during his off year to rehabilitate and force appreciate distressed properties in addition to acquiring turnkey properties. The assistant identifies a property with the following characteristics:

Price: $60,000
ARV: $150,000
Renovation Costs: $40,000
Size: 3 Bed, 3 Bath
(Refi) Closing Costs: ~$4,000
P&I: $300/month
Taxes: $200/month
Insurance: $40/month
Avg Rental Demand: $1500/month

This represents an immense opportunity for Risky Rick. He and his assistant know they can purchase and renovate the distressed property with cash, rent the unit for a profit, and cash-out refinance after the seasoning period has concluded. Furthermore, they are generating more equity than the amount of capital invested, so much so that they may conclude this endeavor with more capital in hand than when they started, all while maintaining a cash-flowing property. For example:

ARV: $150,000
(75% ARV): $112,500
Price: $60,000
Renovation Costs: $40,000
(Refi) Closing Costs: ~$4,000
Holding Costs: $1,000 (Utilities, etc.)
Profit: $7,500

So far, Rick's endeavor has proven successful. He renovated the property, rented it, and earned a profit on the endeavor that he gave to the assistant. Needless to say, Rick's wife is not happy that he spends most of his time away from home. Rick's behavior causes stress in his marriage.

Rick doesn't sleep well on the couch and figures if he can't sleep, he may as well be working. Together, Rick and his assistant work hard. In year 10, they rehab two properties, acquire three properties with passive income, acquire one property with active income, and acquire another from the cash-out refinance of Rick's third property. Rick realizes he needs to leverage portfolio loan options to acquire many of these units. He has surpassed his allotment of Fannie May-backed conventional loans. This was worth the effort since he was now making $196,000 per year, enough to purchase five properties per year—or at least so he thought.

Meanwhile, Rick's wife suspects that her husband and his assistant are romantically involved. A private investigator confirms her suspicions, and she serves him divorce papers. True to his nature, Risky Rick has all of his assets in his name and unprotected. His wife sues for divorce, and the judge gives her seven pieces of Rick's real estate—the ones with the most equity. She also receives a sizeable percentage of his capital. She promptly sells those properties and purchases a single-family home in the city.

Rick has to take another off year to put parts of his life back together and to garner additional passive income. With eight properties, he must still leverage portfolio loan options; alimony and child support elevate his DTI. In year 11, he and his assistant rehab two properties and earn enough active income to buy a third for a total of 11.

Risky Rick continues with his investment strategy, and he and his assistant move in together. They rehab properties and work as real estate agents. They execute two rehabs annually, using the same approach. This continues to work well until, in year 14, a tenant's child shocks himself on faulty wiring. Risky Rick has neither insurance nor business entities to provide asset liability protection. The tenant sues, and the court awards $500,000 for medical bills and pain and suffering. This slows down Rick's ability to acquire additional assets. He has been working hard and finally realizes the strain managing 33 properties was causing him. He grudgingly hires a property manager to oversee the day-to-day activities.

He continues to do well until the economy takes a turn at year 20. He experiences a 20 percent vacancy rate during this time, which plateaus his *Velocity of Money*. Furthermore, the value of his real estate assets drops 20 percent, eliminating his ability to leverage the *Inertia of Real Estate*. Even so, he is able to attain his goal by year 22. He could choose to enjoy the fruits of his labor or continue to expand his portfolio. If he chooses the latter, by year 30, he will have accrued a portfolio worth $346 million and garnered an annual (passive) income of $17.5 million.

The following example illustrates the remainder of Risky Rick's journey toward achieving his objectives.

* Properties acquired listed in parenthesis indicate properties renovated then leased by Risky Rick.

In the end, Risky Rick did not accomplish his goal of being the fastest to reach the monetary objectives. He surpassed his monetary goals but did so at an intolerable cost. He achieved his goal two years later than Sensible Sarah, exerted considerably more effort doing so, and lost his family along the way.

(Objective) Acquire Cash-Flowing and Appreciating Assets:
(Goal) - Acquire 300 (cash-flowing and appreciating) units within 30 years
(Actual) - Acquired 513 (cash-flowing and appreciating) units within 22 years

(Objective) Accelerate Leverage of Real Estate Assets:
(Goal) - Rehab properties to accelerate other objectives and effects
(Actual) - Rehabilitated 24 properties to accelerate other objectives and effects

(Effect) Leverage the Velocity of Money:
(Goal) - Ensure the collective real estate portfolio provides $4 million per year in passive income (capital) by year 30
(Actual) - Real estate portfolio provides $4.1 million per year in passive income (capital) by year 22

(Effect) Leverage the Inertia of (Real Estate) Equity:
(Goal) - Ensure the collective value of the real estate portfolio is $30 million (equity) by year 30
(Actual) - Real estate portfolio value would be worth $76.9 million (equity in today's dollars) by year 22

Risky Rick did better than Carl financially but not nearly as well as Sarah. This illustration also assumes Rick learned from his lessons and conducted himself appropriately for the remainder of his journey. It also does not account for the ex-wife continuing to draw a significant portion of his income after the divorce for child support until the children are 18, all of which would impact his ability to achieve these goals and objectives.

Risky Rick's Journey

Year	Income/Yr	Properties Acquired	Properties Refinanced	Business Entity Established	Total Value	Events	Phase
1	Preparation						Initiation
2						**Decisive Point 1**	
3	$ 2,040.00	1			$ 150,000.00	FHA Loan	
4	$ 12,240.00	2			$ 300,000.00	USDA Loan	
5	$ 26,400.00	3			$ 450,000.00		
6	$ 40,560.00	4			$ 600,000.00		
7	$ 54,720.00	5			$ 750,000.00		
8	$ 97,200.00	6,7,8	1		$ 1,200,000.00		
9	$ 97,200.00		2		$ 1,200,000.00	Year with Family	
10	$ 196,320.00	9-13,(14,15) ~~3-9;~~			$ 2,250,000.00	Sued/divorced (Ex took 7 properties (properties 3 - 9) & $100K plus alimony & child support)	
11	$ 139,680.00	9,(10,11)			$ 1,650,000.00	**Decisive Point 2,3**	
12	$ 220,743.00	12-14,(15,16)			$ 2,400,000.00		Expansion / Acceleration
13	$ 332,415.00	17-21,(22,23)			$ 3,450,000.00		
14	$ 486,254.00	24-31, (32,33)			$ 4,950,000.00	Tenant Sues for medical bills, takes $500K; Rick hires Property Manager & Insurance	
15	$ 514,574.00	(34,35)	3,4,5,6		$ 5,250,000.00		
16	$ 779,677.00	36-51,(52,53)	7,8,9		$ 7,950,000.00		
17	$ 1,144,883.00	54-88,(89,90)	10,11,12,14		$ 13,500,000.00		
18	$ 1,676,308.00	91-142,(143,144)	15-22		$ 21,600,000.00		
19	$ 2,450,881.00	145-219,(220,221)	23-32		$ 33,150,000.00		
20	$ 3,546,253.00	222-317,(318,319)	33,34		**$ 47,850,000.00**	Economic Downtum	
21	$ 3,953,566.40	320-402,(403,404)			$ 60,600,000.00	Vacancies (20%)	
22	**$ 4,118,287.20**	405-513			$ 76,950,000.00	****Goal Achieved****	
23	$ 4,538,681.96	514-634			$ 95,100,000.00	Vacancies (20%)	Sustainment
24	$ 5,001,990.61	635-767			$115,050,000.00	Vacancies (20%)	
25	$ 5,512,593.81	768-914			$137,100,000.00	Vacancies (20%)	
26	$ 6,075,319.39	915-1,076			$161,400,000.00	Vacancies (20%)	
27	$ 6,695,488.00	1,077-1,254			$188,100,000.00		
28	$ 9,223,704.00	1,255-1,500			$225,000,000.00		
29	$12,706,574.00	1,501-1,838			$275,700,000.00		
30	$17,504,576.00	1,839-2,305			$345,750,000.00		

Aloof Aaron's Journey

Aloof Aaron is quite a bit different from our other investors. Unlike the other investors, he is a free-spirited single guy who drifted his way through life rather than adhering to any sort of plan. His investment strategy is in line with his life philosophy: a little cavalier and rather opportunistic. Aaron, unlike our other investors, had not done any research or prepared to initiate real estate investing.

Aaron was living rent free in his parent's guest house. One day, while lounging at the local Starbucks, he overheard Risky Rick and his wife arguing. One was trying to explain the benefits of low- to no-money-down loan options, and the other wasn't listening. Aaron, however, was. Unfortunately, he hadn't been saving any capital for investing in real estate. He did what any free spirit would have done: he asked his mom and dad for money. His parents were so excited that he expressed interest in anything pertaining to his future that they gave him $10,000. In their minds, this was a small price to pay to get him out of their guest house and into adulthood.

Aaron located a property to his liking. It was in a decent neighborhood, but most importantly, it was within walking distance from several bars and had a sorority house on the same block. Aloof Aaron walked into his parent's bank and inquired about various loans. He proceeded to purchase a residence with the following characteristics using the FHA loan:

Price: $150,000 **Taxes:** $200/month
Size: 4 Bed, 3 Bath **Insurance:** $40/month
Avg Rental Demand: $1500/month

Down Payment: $3,500
Closing Costs: ~$4,000 (Funding fee ~3%, MIP fee ~1%)
P&I: $380/month
MIP: $60/month

To his parent's surprise, Aaron finally owned a piece of property. Aaron was living the dream—except he wasn't making the money he overheard Risky Rick describe at Starbucks. He realized his error in purchasing a single-family home and found a duplex he would like to purchase. He reapproached the bank to acquire another loan. The bank informed him that he was authorized only one FHA loan at a time. He could leverage a USDA loan, but his DTI was too high since he was not generating any passive income on the single-family property.

Aaron consoled himself by throwing a party and inviting the sorority to his place. While immersed in activities, he realized that four women lived in the sorority house, and each one rented a room individually. He had a stroke of genius: he could rent rooms in his house! The next day Aaron reached out through his bro-network of friends to assess their interest. He found three friends who were each willing to rent a room for $500 per month. Aaron was now generating $820/month ($9,840/year), which, combined with his day job, brought his DTI under 43 percent. He threw another party to celebrate. During this party, one of the sorority sisters mentioned a party the night before at a beautiful house in the countryside. Oh, how she wished her sorority house had a place further out of town where they could maximize their fun.

Aaron, motivated like most young men are, had another stroke of genius: he could use the USDA loan his lender informed him about to purchase a place in the countryside for no money down, and he could invite all of his closest sorority friends every weekend. A year later, Aaron purchased another property with similar characteristics:

Price: $150,000
Size: 4 Bed, 3 Bath
Avg Rental Demand: $1500/month
Taxes: $200/month
Insurance: $40/month

Down Payment: $0 (USDA)
Closing Costs: ~$4,000
P&I: $300/month

This time he learned from his previous mistake and made sure to rent out rooms—one to a close friend and the others to two of the sorority sisters that were at his party and looking for a more remote spot. Aloof Aaron could not be more pleased. Little did his friend know, Aaron was charging him $700 per month in rent while charging each of the ladies only $400 per month. His new income was $27,360 per year. His parties become legendary, and he set his sights on purchasing other investment properties.

Another year elapsed, and Aaron began to pursue a secret relationship with one of the sorority roommates, Adrift Alice. She enjoyed a free entrepreneurial spirit just like Aaron. But Aaron's friend had always been enamored with Adrift Alice, too. One day his jealousy erupted in an argument that uncovered Aaron and Alice's covert relationship. At the climax of the battle, Alice let slip that she paid $400 per month in rent and can do what she wants, where she wants, with whom she wants! In a fit of rage, Aaron's friend stormed out of the house to plot his revenge.

A week later, Aaron was served with court papers alleging that he had violated the fair housing laws associated with leasing a property: he had unfairly charged his former friend/roommate with higher rent than the other tenants based solely on gender—one of the seven discrimination categories. Aaron lost the case, and the court required him to relinquish $27,360 in damages—an amount equivalent to his profits from the past year.

Aaron found another roommate and charged him only $400 per month, bringing his total annual income to $17,760. Aaron decided he needed to step up his game and purchased another property. He found a duplex with the following characteristics:

Price: $150,000 **Taxes:** $200/month
Size: 2 Bed, 2 Bath (Each) **Insurance:** $40/month
Avg Rental Demand: $850 (Each)/month

Down Payment: $37,500
Closing Costs: ~$4,000
P&I: $280/month

It would take him another year to acquire the capital necessary to purchase this property. He did so and told Alice they could live on one side and rent out the other. She was not ready for that kind of commitment and promptly left him. He decided to stay in the party house and rent both sides of the duplex. After a few parties, he got over his loss, consoled by garnering $27,480 per year in passive income. Aaron went on to purchase one property every two years with this income. In his seventh year, he purchased his fourth property, increasing his income to $41,640 per year, enough to purchase an additional property each year. The following year, he purchased his fifth and the year after, his sixth property, bringing his total passive income to $69,960.

Alice drifted back into his life and said she was ready for more of a commitment as long as Aaron shared some of his hard-earned passive income. He made his way to the local florist to celebrate their newfound love. While at the florist, he heard a couple (Sensible Sarah's family) discussing how well their latest cash-out refinance went. True to form, Aaron inquired about leveraging the equity from his first unit to expand his portfolio. Unfortunately, his property had not increased in value over the last six years because he had chosen a neighborhood that was stagnating (probably due to frequent house parties). To make matters worse, Aaron had not maintained the property's condition (also due to frequent house parties). He dismissed the notion of cash-out refinancing, thinking that the other couple didn't know what they were doing or that it was just a fluke.

Even so, Aaron had enough passive income to purchase

two properties per year. In year 12, he purchased properties 9 and 10, increasing his passive income to $126,600. In the 13th year, Adrift Alice wanted to become Aloof Alice. She pleaded with Aaron to marry her and instantly morphed into a bridezilla, demanding a gargantuan wedding. They spent the entire year's passive income on the ultimate party-style wedding. The following year (year 14), Aaron looked for another property. He discovered that he was unable to procure a conventional loan. Furthermore, the lender was unwilling to provide Aaron with their portfolio loan options due to his erratic spending habits, comingling of business and personal funds, and numerous late payments. As he was exiting the bank, Aaron stopped by Starbucks to pick up a peppermint mocha for his bride. While waiting in line, he overheard Risky Rick with his younger mistress/assistant. They were discussing rehabbing a property. Aaron figured if they could do it, he could too.

He found a property with the following specifications:

ARV: $150,000
Price: $60,000
Renovation Costs: $40,000
Holding Costs: $1,000 (Utilities, etc.)

Aaron had enough capital to purchase the distressed property and renovate it. Aloof Alice wanted to assist and see how Aaron worked. Together they stumbled their way through the project; however, it took eight months of hard labor to renovate, and the repair costs were double what they had budgeted. In the end, they spent $140,000 to procure a property that was worth $150,000. They were able to lease the unit, bringing their total passive income to $140,720 per year. Aaron and Alice decided they had had enough manual labor. They set aside half of their passive income to live on and invested the rest in rentals. Aaron calculated he could purchase one property every two years with cash.

This process of acquiring a new property with cash continued each year until year 22, when the economy took a downturn. Aaron was still able to acquire additional properties. However, due to his tenant selections, he experienced vacancies in 20 percent of his units. Additionally, his property value was impacted across his portfolio. Aaron concluded his journey, having attained 19 properties valued at $2.85 million and garnering $253,680 per year. It's difficult to measure Aaron's effectiveness or performance in attaining his goal because he didn't really have an end state when he set out on this journey. His endeavors are depicted in the following graphic:

Aaron concluded his venture by failing to meet the same goals and objectives as our other investors. Even the depiction above is overly ambitious for what Aaron could hope to achieve should he learn from his many lessons appropriately. In reality, the best moniker Aaron could hope for would be a slumlord due to buying poorly and continuing to neglect his properties. More than likely, he'll never reach the potential profits above due to his cavalier nature and potential foreclosures due to back taxes or other consequences of negligent acts.

(Objective) Acquire Cash-Flowing and Appreciating Assets:
(Goal) - Acquire 300 (cash-flowing and appreciating) units within 30 years
(Actual) - Acquired 19 (cash-flowing and appreciating) units within 30 years

(Objective) Accelerate Leverage of Real Estate Assets:
(Goal) - Rehab properties to accelerate other objectives and effects
(Actual) - Rehabilitated 1 property to accelerate other objectives and effects

(Effect) Leverage the Velocity of Money:
(Goal) – Ensure the collective real estate portfolio provides $4 million per year in passive income (capital) by year 30
(Actual) - Real estate portfolio provides $253,680 per year in passive income (capital) by year 30

(Effect) Leverage the Inertia of (Real Estate) Equity:
Not Leveraged

Aloof Aaron's Journey							
Year	Income/Yr	Properties Acquired	Properties Refinanced	Business Entity Established	Total Value	Events	Phase
1	$ (680.00)	1			$ 150,000.00	FHA	Initiation
2	$ 9,840.00				$ 150,000.00		
3	$ 27,360.00	2			$ 300,000.00	USDA	
4	$ 17,760.00				$ 300,000.00	Sued	
5	$ 27,480.00	3			$ 450,000.00		
6	$ 27,480.00				$ 450,000.00		
7	$ 41,640.00	4			$ 600,000.00		
8	$ 55,800.00	5			$ 750,000.00		
9	$ 69,960.00	6			$ 900,000.00		
10	$ 84,120.00	7			$ 1,050,000.00		
11	$ 98,280.00	8			$ 1,200,000.00		
12	$ 126,600.00	9,10			$ 1,500,000.00		
13	$ 126,600.00				$ 1,500,000.00	Wedding	Expansion
14	$ 140,720.00	11			$ 1,650,000.00		
15	$ 140,720.00				$ 1,650,000.00		
16	$ 154,840.00	12			$ 1,800,000.00		
17	$ 154,840.00				$ 1,800,000.00		
18	$ 168,960.00	13			$ 1,950,000.00		
19	$ 168,960.00				$ 1,950,000.00		
20	$ 183,080.00	14			$ 2,100,000.00		
21	$ 183,080.00				$ 2,100,000.00		
22	$ 197,200.00	15			$ 2,250,000.00	Economic Downturn	
23	$ 157,760.00				$ 1,800,000.00	Vacancies (20%)	
24	$ 169,056.00	16			$ 1,920,000.00	Vacancies (20%)	
25	$ 169,056.00				$ 1,920,000.00	Vacancies (20%)	
26	$ 180,352.00	17			$ 2,040,000.00	Vacancies (20%)	
27	$ 180,352.00				$ 2,040,000.00	Vacancies (20%)	
28	$ 191,648.00	18			$ 2,160,000.00	Vacancies (20%)	
29	$ 239,560.00				$ 2,700,000.00		
30	$ 253,680.00	19			$ 2,850,000.00		

Visit our website (masterofleverage.info) by using this QR code to access key figures and references from this chapter.

Final Thoughts

Here's the most important thing you can take away from this book: the best strategy is one that fits your lifestyle and your risk tolerance. Even a bad investment is better than not investing if you learn from it, treat it as part of your education, and move forward with knowledge. Controlling your future instead of allowing others to control it is a critical component to independence. Whatever choices you make to chart your future, commit to them.

Happenstance will change over time, hopefully for the better. Do not haphazardly approach life's endeavors, or you will limit your potential. Disparity aside, effort remains and should persist as the discriminating determinant of success. Learn to be humble and ask for assistance when appropriate. Investing in real estate is a team sport, but it requires individual effort. Whatever you do, make sure you invest in assets that provide value and always assess the ROI and ROE.

Finally, after sharing my knowledge of real estate with you, I leave you with this thought:

Dare greatly, act with purpose, live your best life, and pay it forward!
—Ryan Henderson, *wealth strategist and real estate investor*

Appendix A: Key Topics

Good Idea

1 – 1: Most costs of business are tax deductible.

3 – 1: When rate shopping, try to target a 30-day window in which to narrow and select a loan; the bureau will group the inquiries and treat them as one.

3 – 2: You may be able to deduct your premium from your taxes; it is likely you will need to itemize your deductions.

3 – 3: Gifts from family members, grants, and contributions from sellers are also permitted to be used toward closing costs of VA loans.

3 – 4: Gifts from family members, grants, and contributions from sellers are also permitted to be used toward closing costs of USDA loans.

3 – 5: Always, always, always ask if you are eligible for DPA programs.

4 – 1: You may refinance any of these deals to a conventional/portfolio loan to enable their re-use!

4 – 2: You can actually use the VA, then FHA, then USDA consecutively in back-to-back (to-back) years!

5 – 1: Leverage the handyperson to the greatest practical extent, then follow up with the licensed specialist where needed.

5 – 2: Bring both the home inspector and general contractor on site together and early. The GC can develop estimates for issues identified by the home inspector.

5 – 3: If major plumbing work is not required, consult your handyperson first.

6 – 1: Look for areas that have military installations; they have stable employment and move every few years, resulting in many choosing to rent instead of purchase their residence.

6 – 2: As a general rule of thumb, the ideal property for an investor is the worst house in the best area. This property will offer the best opportunity for appreciation while also maintaining demand.

7 – 1: If possible, try to be "all in" for 75 percent ARV or less. This includes purchase price, renovations, transaction costs, and holding costs. This will ensure you have immediate equity in the property and provide you a buffer if something goes wrong. It also adds the possibility of procuring an income-generating asset after having an immediate 100 percent ROE.

7 – 2: Closing costs, home warranty, contingencies, earnest money, appliances, move-out date, rent collection, utility transfer, and necessary repairs are all excellent terms that can be used during negotiations to sweeten the deal for both parties until settling on agreed-upon terms.

7 – 3: If you have the capital, provide cash offers to increase your competitiveness; cash-refinance after the seasoning period to recoup your capital.

8 – 1: You don't need to hire a master craftsman when a handyperson is more than capable.

8 – 2: If possible, have your project manager and property inspector conduct the walk-through alongside you. They will start to develop efficiencies that will benefit you.

8 – 3: If possible, take a video of the walk-through for you to reference and to send to contractors when disclosing the work you wish for them to perform.

8 – 4: Ask if your contractor has an account with the vendor you intend to use; if so, purchase on their account. You ensure that you are not paying markup and they get the loyalty points and can arrange logistics. It's a win-win!

8 – 5: Installing gutter covers eases maintenance and extends the life of gutters. It's a good idea for wooded lots.

8 – 6: Note that if you're going from dark to light paint color schemes, you may need additional coats.

8 – 7: Always bring an expert (engineer or qualified contractor) to verify work.

8 – 8: Do not buy expensive plants.

8 – 9: Talk with local investors to find a good and affordable concrete layer.

8 – 10: If acquiring a functioning washing machine, draft a general clause for the washer excluding it from the repair agreement; otherwise, do not provide a washer/dryer.

8 – 11: Consider installing floors after painting has been completed (unless solid hardwood).

8 – 12: Residents and other individuals living near your property will take advantage of your dumpster. Try to do all the demo at one time near the beginning of the project.

8 – 13: It's not a bad idea to have a portable toilet on site if there is no running water.

8 – 14: Add a ceiling fan if there are lights already in the ceiling.

9 – 1: Offer a small reward payment to current tenants for referrals, but be sure to pay them only after the new lease has been signed.

10 – 1: Establishing a website to show "flip" remodels is a great way to advertise and potentially solicit distressed properties.

11 – 1: Inheritance can be combined with the 1031 exchange program. If taxes have been deferred by means of the 1031 up to the point of your passing, your beneficiaries still gain the basis step-up despite years or decades of deferment. This is often referred to as "swap till you drop."

Remember

3 – 1: Always ask your lender if they are willing to offer a letter of pre-approval.

3 – 2: Always ask if the institution allows mortgage loans on investment properties and infer their limit.

3 – 3: Financial gifts from family members or grants for down payment assistance are acceptable for down payment and closing costs of FHA loans.

3 – 4: DPA programs are offered to first-time and repeat home buyers alike.

3 – 5: If intending to refinance a property owned for less than a year, always ask if the lending institution has a seasoning period and if the lender uses LTV or LTC for their cash-out refinance ratio.

4 – 1: The FHA 203(k) loan program is capped at 110 percent of the value of the home. Additionally, licensed contractors must perform the work.

4 – 2: Seller financing is unlikely to show up on a member's credit report (unless the seller registers and reports the debt).

5 – 1: Accountant services are tax deductible.

5 – 2: When hiring an electrician, ensure you find one who is licensed, bonded, and insured. Inspect the final work.

6 – 1: Property management companies and attorneys are great assets to help navigate the complexities of the landlord-tenant statutes. You, however, are ultimately responsible.

6 – 2: Research crime before you buy.

7 – 1: Make sure your spouse (or significant other) is supportive of ventures in distressed properties. It is not an easy path and requires a lot of commitment.

7 – 2: Ensure you conduct a title search and check for all liens on the property.

7 – 3: When performing your valuation, conduct all three and use the most conservative approach. When making an offer, you can leverage this figure, and when refinancing, you will minimize most surprises (appraisers love to take the most conservative estimate).

8 – 1: The contractors should provide a bid that itemizes materials and labor. Do not accept a vague offer that does not itemize the work being performed. They should also indicate the time the project will take.

8 – 2: Whatever you do, make sure you make your selection above reproach; your decision criteria cannot be discriminatory in any nature.

8 – 3: If you see water damage or suspect a leak, check the gutters and flashing first before jumping to replace the roof.

8 – 4: Always consult with qualified professionals/engineers on the final product.

8 – 5: New or dark walls will need a primer!

8 – 6: For most investment properties, a framed semi-stock MDF and wooden veneer will suffice. Refer to Figure 8-2.

8 – 7: A good handyperson can do most flooring and small tile jobs.

8 – 8: Always check your county website or local building department for codes and regulations on permits; these vary by state/area.

9 – 1: Do not post the address of the property; make the prospective tenant call for the address.

9 – 2: Always check special provisions in your state governing landlord-tenant relationships and lease agreements.

10 – 1: Always verify with an attorney to ensure your business entity is structured correctly to accomplish this imperative.

10 – 2: If the homestead exemption in your state is greater than the value of your home, there is little risk in paying off your mortgage; if the exemption is less, take actions to strip equity from the asset.

10 – 3: All members must sign the document; the document is only enforceable to signatories of the document.

11 – 1: Excess capital losses may be used to offset up to $3,000 of ordinary income; additional excess losses are carried forward to future years.

11 – 2: Capital/passive losses are carried forward to future years until 1) capital/passive income offsets accrued capital/passive loss or 2) the property is sold, at which point the gains from sale offset the losses.

11 – 3: The same legal entity that holds the original property must purchase the replacement property. If the first property is in your name, you must make the purchase; if it is in the name of an LLC, the LLC must make the purchase.

11 – 4: In order for a 1031 exchange to be valid, you must hire an independent third party to act as your intermediary. You must identify them before selling your asset.

Note

1 – 1: There is only so much work (active income) any one person can accomplish due to physical limitations or time. When work stops, income stops.

1 – 2: Unrealized wealth/equity value is speculated on demand, meaning that it can increase or decrease in value while possessed.

1 – 3: You may also own industrial real estate; however, that is not covered in this book.

1 – 4: Although lesser routine expenses are not included in hard debt, lending institutions do review credit card balances. Make sure to keep your balance beneath 43 percent.

3 – 1: Banks typically only offer HELOCs on primary residences. Always inquire.

3 – 2: Not all banks offer the most competitive loans on investment properties.

3 – 3: Lenders from credit unions may not be able to assist or offer the same rates for properties outside of their lending jurisdiction.

3 – 4: Conventional loans have loan limits for standard areas and higher limits for high-cost areas. Be sure to check the loan limits when buying a home.

4 – 1: Since a real estate syndication is a business, the regulations and policies establishing governance are dictated by the Securities & Exchange Commission (SEC).

5 – 1: Many investors refer to these members that I call the centers of gravity as the Core-4.

5 – 2: Be sure to find an agent who specializes in the property type in which you are interested.

5 – 3: In an ideal world, partnering with a wholesaler is a win for everyone. In the real world, people are greedy, and one person's greed is usually at the expense of someone else.

5 – 4: Look into Loss-of-Rents (business interruption) coverage for bigger assets and/or if it works for your level of risk.

5 – 5: Property managers can also be your deal finder. They often know other investors who are looking to sell their property before it goes on the market, allowing you to engage prior to other investors.

5 – 6: I recommend contacting your lender to see which appraisers they frequently work with. Look to develop a relationship with one of them.

5 – 7: Don't micromanage. Don't ask them to work for free. Don't pester them with small stuff. This will ruin your relationship with a valuable member of the team.

5 – 8: Do not undervalue landscaping when developing your real estate portfolio. It is essential in developing curb appeal and ensuring your house is the hottest prospect on the block.

6 – 1: Technology is your friend. Use it advantageously to automate the process of searching through these criteria.

6 – 2: This is an ideal situation for owning Section 8 housing, but that is not advised for novice investors.

6 – 3: If the economy takes a turn, high-growth jobs are hit the hardest.

6 – 4: Typically, highly educated tenants take better care of your property and tend to generate higher wages, which enable them to afford higher rents.

6 – 5: Look for nice restaurants and nice car dealerships; they are usually on the "path to progress."

6 – 6: Look for new interstates, highways, and metros. Cities will not invest in infrastructure unless there are demand signals showing growth. Also, look for major retailers such as Walmart or Target.

6 – 7: The neighborhood level of research is where your deal finder will come in handy.

6 – 8: Establish a trend to determine school rankings.

6 – 9: The quality of roads and streets is a simple and telling assessment. Cities invest and maintain areas they value.

6 – 10: Properties adjacent to roads with high traffic volume will appraise for less than comparable properties.

6 – 11: Consult with your property manager or research online to determine trends in rent prices.

6 – 12: A shifting market does not always denote positive growth. It simply identifies ideal conditions preceding a high demand market environment.

6 – 13: It's better to have lower rents to ensure a lower vacancy rate.

6 – 14: Some properties that are low demand may be ideal for Section 8 housing. While inherently riskier, this can be a lucrative endeavor for the more experienced investor.

7 – 1: Some states have statutes limiting a property from being sold for less than a certain percentage of its listed value. For example, Ohio's limit is 66 percent.

7 – 2: For homeowners, the rule of thumb for monthly expenses is no more than 28 percent. For investors, assess ROI and ROE.

7 – 3: P&I combined with Taxes and Property Insurance is typically referred to as PITI.

7 – 4: The rule of thumb for investors is to set aside 10 percent of monthly rental income for repairs and anticipated vacancies.

7 – 5: The buyer may include additional contingencies; however, this decreases the competitiveness of the offer.

8 – 1: Good property management will offer services ranging from minor repairs to extensive rehabs and renovations.

8 – 2: Upgrading the service meter to 200 amp will ensure the property can handle the demand of modern technology.

8 – 3: R22 (Freon) is used in older cooling units and is no longer available. If acquiring an older unit that has an R22 cooling system, keep in mind it will eventually need to be replaced.

8 – 4: Some states mandate disclosures to buyers.

9 – 1: A positive rate of ROE denotes appreciation of value; a negative rate of ROE denotes depreciation.

10 – 1: Grantor trusts are not impenetrable; a judge can order you (or your business) to disclose the owner grantor of an asset. Proper adherence to business practices may prevent a judge from making such a mandate.

10 – 2: Grantor trusts on their own do not offer any tax advantages.

10 – 3: A HELOC cannot be used as an equity-stripping method on investment properties.

10 – 4: There are specific differences between a joint venture and a syndication. Consult your attorney for advice.

10 – 5: The general manager will need to pay self-employment taxes.

10 – 6: Using the same name for each registration is not required; doing so is good for advertising, but refraining is more discreet.

11 – 1: Some expenses have special governances dictating the extent to which they are deductible.

11 – 2: Legal entity constructs may either impose additional limitations or allow for greater deductions, depending on the type of entity and the situation.

11 – 3: A home office deduction requires two criteria: 1) The space must be your primary place of work for your business, and 2) the area must be used exclusively for business purposes—a space dedicated solely for work.

11 – 4: Solo 401(k) self-directed accounts have many other perks, including larger allowances for contributions than other retirement accounts. Be sure to do your research to fully explore this option.

11 – 5: If you are concerned about transfer of assets or who will receive which assets at the time of your passing, consider establishing an irrevocable trust assigning assets to specific individuals.

Caution

1 – 1: Failing to analyze trends is a mistake of a novice investor that could have ruinous repercussions.

2 – 1: Be careful not to refinance too often. There are transaction costs associated, which will eat away at the profitability of this strategy or cause you to invest additional capital of your own if you're not careful.

3 – 1: While applying for your loan, try to avoid co-signing on another loan and making any large deposits. **DO NOT UNDER ANY CIRCUMSTANCE** 1) quit your job or 2) spend money set aside for closing.

3 – 2: Avoid falling behind on your other accounts and mortgages.

3 – 3: Inquiries may have a more detrimental impact if you are early on in your credit journey (few accounts or short credit history). Avoid making large purchases (vehicles, etc.).

3 – 4: A Chapter 7 bankruptcy will remain and impact your credit report for 10 years. A Chapter 13 bankruptcy will do the same to a lesser extent for 7 years.

3 – 5: The biggest risk associated with collateral loans (and lines of credit) is the possibility of losing the asset should the debtor fail to repay in accordance with the terms. Take caution when leveraging this option on your primary residence.

3 – 6: Not all lending institutions allow cash-out refinancing on investment properties. Always verify when first engaging with a lender.

4 – 1: If the seller still has a mortgage when attempting to seller finance a deal, the lending institution may elect to invoke the "due-on-sale" clause. This allows the bank to demand that the remainder of the loan be paid in full, effective immediately. If the owner is not able to pay, the lender may repossess/foreclose upon the home.

5 – 1: You may consider using TurboTax or H&R Block for your taxes to save on expenses. Don't do it! Leveraging a CPA who specializes in real estate will often cost roughly the same amount but result in far more deductions and savings.

5 – 2: Try to avoid the conflict of interest with dual agencies. Develop rapport with an agent who is loyal to you.

5 – 3: When dealing with a wholesaler, the transaction is treated as if it is for sale by owner (FSBO); they have no duty to care about any of your interests. This offers a phenomenal opportunity but also has inherent risks—risks that may be perilous for novice and more junior investors.

5 – 4: Make sure you have a good appraiser. Appraisers that lowball your property value will diminish your real estate inertia. Appraisers with a reputation for inflating asset values are unlikely to be accepted by financial institutions and are, therefore, equally problematic. Leverage your network!

5 – 5: Be careful not to get a home inspector who is persnickety and nitpicks unnecessarily.

6 – 1: Junior investors should be cautious using this method to increase wealth. Identifying these opportunities may not be difficult but timing often is. Poor timing can easily result in you acquiring a property that takes too long to mature and undermines your overall investment strategy.

6 – 2: Be wary about rents increasing 15 percent or more per year. These are signs of a potentially overinflated market.

7 – 1: Interacting with properties involving personal distress is often a time-consuming, emotionally draining, and frustrating task. You need to be thick-skinned and resilient. Understand that people who are drowning will do anything not to drown, and that may include trying to take you with them.

7 – 2: Some auctions will inflate the valuation of a property in efforts to drive up the bids for the property. A higher valuation mandates a higher minimum accepted bid, which also diminishes profits for any investor pursuing the property.

8 – 1: Be wary if a contractor requests all funds (material and/or labor) up front. Many horror stories from investors start by accepting these terms.

8 – 2: Do not put a new coat of latex over an old coat of oil-based paint; it will cause the paint to peel.

8 – 3: Dealing with septic tanks is not something investors do on their own. Hire a professional and save yourself a headache, time, and potentially a large mess.

8 – 4: If there are major structural issues to the foundation and you discover them before you've acquired the property, my advice is to let this deal pass so a better deal does not become your opportunity cost.

8 – 5: Be wary of adding square footage when the residence is already the largest in the neighborhood. The ARV will not increase commensurately, but rental demand may increase.

8 – 6: Stay away from installing bathtubs with jets. This is a maintenance nightmare waiting to happen. Remember, "no one cares about your property …"

9 – 1: Do not cash-out refinance a property that is depreciating in value; doing so may result in a situation where the amount owed is more than the value of the home.

9 – 2: Be wary of posting "For Rent" signs in certain areas. These signs highlight that the unit is available but also broadcast the unit's vacancy (or impending vacancy), which makes it an easy target for vandalism.

9 – 3: Be sure to check state laws to avoid discrimination. Protected statuses include disability, familial status, national origin, race, religion, sex, and skin color. DO NOT inquire about any of the protected statuses or traits of your prospective tenants, because it may appear to be discriminatory.

9 – 4: DO NOT allow the tenant to move in prior to completing the move-in report, signing the lease, or paying the security deposit and first month's rent. If you allow them to move in and they decline to do any of the above items, they are technically considered a resident and must therefore be evicted. This is a slow and expensive process, especially for a tenant from whom you have not collected any rent.
10 – 1: I am not an attorney. I am not offering legal advice. I am offering information for educational purposes. You should consult an attorney to determine which business structure is most appropriate for you.

10 – 2: Do not trust the residence into a business entity; homestead exemption is for natural persons only.

10 – 3: Not all states recognize the grantor trust; always consult your attorney or business advisor.

11 – 1: If you plan to perform a rental arbitrage, you may want to first check with your landlord. Some convenances have strict rules against subleasing to include arbitrage.

12 – 1: Find a way to filter friends and family who are self-proclaimed experts as opposed to those who are truly interested in real estate. Be kind, but don't feel bad when you don't take their advice. Others may deplete your time and effort asking for investment advice without intent to pursue or follow through with investing in real estate. Remember, networking is about give and take. They're friends and family, so don't blow them off, but recommend a few resources (like this book). If they read it, you'll have a basis for discussion.

Appendix B: Index

1031 exchange, 284, 293, 298-300, 306, 309-310, 358
Active business, 287, 308
Active income. See Wealth (Types): Realized: Active
Actual Value, 175, 231
Advertising, 26, 234, 239-240, 249, 252, 278, 382
  Networking, 239-240
  Online, 239-240, 241
  Signage, 239
American Apartment Owners Association (AAOA), 139
Amortization, 33, 35, 38, 55, 69, 71, 81, 297
Anonymity, 258, 260-262, 266, 282, 358
Appreciation, 22, 33-37, 40, 93, 100, 103, 118, 140, 147, 159, 161, 164, 172, 178-179, 194, 201, 229, 232, 235, 238, 306, 357, 365
Archimedes, 33-34,51
Asset liability protection, 258-260, 282, 358, 396
Assets, 16, 39, 41, 65, 69, 77, 89, 119, 122, 138, 176, 255, 259-263, 265-266, 268-270, 273-274, 277, 283-284, 287, 294, 296-297, 299, 302, 307, 321-322, 344, 351-354, 360-361, 363, 365-368, 371, 376, 379-380, 385-386, 389-390, 396-397, 405, 407
  Depreciable, 284, 294, 296-297
    Recovery period, 296-297
  Unrelated Debt-Financed Income (UDFI), 302
Auctions and Sheriff Sales, 244
Bach, Richard, 118
Basing, 328, 331, 334, 343, 345, 349, 359, 361-362
Bennett, Robert Foster, 381
Buckle, Henry Thomas, 151
Buffet, Warren, 41
Business, 4, 10, 22, 24-26, 41, 74, 80-81, 83, 105-106, 113, 116, 118, 122, 124, 128, 134, 145, 169-170, 247, 258-262, 265-269, 272-280, 282-284, 286-296, 298, 300-301, 308-309, 314-315, 321, 329, 358, 385, 393, 396, 404
Business entity, 24, 80-81, 105, 116, 169-170, 258, 260-262, 265-269, 272-273, 278, 280, 282-284, 286, 292, 309, 358
  Bylaws, 258, 278-279
  Registered agent, 278-279
  Structure, 258-259, 272-276, 279, 282, 358
    Cooperative (Co-op), 24, 273, 275
    Corporation, 258, 273, 275-276, 278-280, 292
    Joint venture, 258, 273-274
    Limited partnerships, 274
    LLC, 258, 273, 276
    Partnership, 113, 115, 273-274, 276, 280
    Umbrella company, 258, 273, 277
  Tax ID, 258, 272, 280, 282, 284, 292
Buyer's Market, 135, 149-150, 159
Capital. See Wealth (Types): Realized
Capitalization rate, 182
Carnegie, Andrew, 112
Cash-out refinance, 48-49, 86-87, 89, 236, 270, 304,
348, 358, 378, 384-385, 394-396, 403
Chamber of commerce, 313-315, 324, 359
Churchill, Winston, 345
Closing date, 184-185
Commercial Real Estate (CRE), 55, 80-81, 182
Condo Owners Association (COA), 173, 177
Consumer surplus, 13-14, 149
Contingencies, 164, 184-186, 193, 329, 343, 345,
349, 359, 373
  Appraisal, 55-56, 58, 66, 125, 186-187
  Inspection, 186
  Loan, 186-187
Corcoran, Barbara, 234
Cost (Types), 10, 25
  Cost of Business, 10, 25-26
  Opportunity cost, 10, 25, 27-28, 31, 40, 78, 119, 216, 235-239, 346-347
  Transaction cost, 10, 25-26, 40, 84, 87, 184, 234,
  248-249, 252
Cost Approach, 181-182
Credit Score, 2, 55, 59-63, 65, 73, 75-77, 79, 123, 239, 241, 243
  Bankruptcy, 55, 59, 65, 77, 118-119
    Chapter 13, 65, 362
    Chapter 7, 65, 78, 118, 249-250, 252, 265
  History, 61-63
  Outstanding Debt, 62
  Payment history, 61
  Properties owned, 59, 63, 118

Recent inquiries, 62
Type of Credit, 63
Debt-to-Income (DTI), 10, 29-30, 59
Decisive Points, 328, 331, 338, 340, 343, 345, 349, 359, 371-372
Decrease, Defer, Reclassify, Transform (DDRT), 284, 293
Demand barrier, 18
Desirability and Demand, 135, 150, 156, 162-163,
356, 361
Crime Statistics, 151
Days on Market (DOM), 151, 154, 159
Increasing rents, 151, 155
New construction, 77, 135, 156, 247
School Rankings, 151-152
Transit Score, 151-152
Vacancy period, 151,155
Walkability Score, 151-154
Desired End State, 334, 336, 344-346, 348-350, 367-368, 370-371, 382, 386-389
Distressed property, 118, 165, 169, 183, 192, 341, 356, 385, 395, 404
Personal Distress, 118, 164, 166-167, 170
Four Ds, 166
Dodd-Frank Act, 69-70
Douhet, Giulio, 340
Dumas, Alexandre, 55
Earnest money, 164, 185-186, 188, 190
Equilibrium price, 13-16, 18, 29-30, 166
Equilibrium quantity, 17
Equity, 6, 22, 33-37, 39-41, 45-47, 52, 62, 66-67, 72,
77-78, 86-87, 89, 93-94, 100-101, 104, 111, 119, 147, 166-167, 171, 173, 179, 184, 195, 231, 234, 236-237, 247, 253, 255, 258, 264, 266-267, 270-271, 282, 299, 304, 344, 346, 350-352, 354, 357-358, 363, 367-368, 370, 373, 377, 379, 384-386, 390, 394-396, 398, 403, 406
Available, 35, 39-40, 46-47, 52, 86-87, 94, 101, 195, 239-237, 270, 379, 384
Generated, 33, 35, 37, 40, 72, 100, 370
Rapid generation, 184
Strip, 258, 264, 270-271, 282, 358
Equity stripping, 40, 258, 264, 270-271, 282, 358
Equity target, 299
Exit Strategies, 284, 303
Expenses, 22, 24, 26, 30-31, 33, 41-44, 69, 85, 96, 98, 116-117, 137, 164, 170,172-180, 187, 192, 234, 238, 247-249, 263, 273, 275, 284, 286, 290-291 ,293-298, 309-310, 356, 358, 373, 376, 383
Additional Living, 174-175
Advertising costs, 26
Capital (CAPEX), 173,176
Cash Flow, 164,179-180,247,255,375-376,379
Closing Costs, 26,41,46,50,55,66,68,75-77,80,
82,95-99,102,177-178,185,195,382-383,385,
388-389,392-395,400,402-403
Current, 31,294
Down Payment, 38,46,49-50,55,60,72-73,75-76,
78-79,82,87,92,94-99,102-104,177-178,187,
305,382-383,388-389,392-394,400,402-403
Holding Costs, 256, 257, 341
Interim, 156,175,238
Offset, 238
Operating (OPEX), 176
Out-of-pocket, 256
Preparation, 234, 248-249
Property Management, 26, 42-43, 96,122-123, 125, 135, 137-138, 160, 173, 176-177, 195, 239, 287, 325
Replacement Cost, 175
Utilities, 173, 176, 178, 244, 385, 395, 404
Vacancies, 173, 177
Expenses Extended Replacement Cost, 175
Fair Market Value (FMV), 10, 13, 29-30
Federal Deposit Insurance Corporation (FDIC), 67
Federal Home Loan Mortgage Association, 69
Federal National Mortgage Association (Fannie Mae), 69
Fellow Real Estate Investor, 117, 119
For Sale By Owner (FSBO), 121, 183
Forced Appreciation, 100, 194, 201, 229, 232, 357, 365
Foreman, George, 301
Gale, Porter, 312
Garages, 79, 174, 212
Gentrification, 145
Governance, 22, 105
Grantor trusts, 268-269
Home Equity Lines of Credit (HELOCs), 67 See also Lending
Home Owners Association (HOA), 236, 251, 255

Income Capitalization, 158, 181-182
Increased demand, 10, 15, 147, 150
Increased supply, 10, 14-15, 149
Inertia of Real Estate, 27, 33-35, 40, 47, 54, 89, 390, 397
Inflation, 33, 35-37, 42
Inheritance, 284, 303, 306-309, 358, 387, 389
Insurance, 26, 42-43, 57, 60, 66-67, 73-74, 86, 94-98, 102, 112, 121-122, 124, 127, 131, 137, 139, 160, 173-175, 178, 186, 214, 245, 258,260,265-266, 272, 282-283, 358, 382-383, 385, 388-389, 392-396, 400, 402-403
Internal Revenue Service (IRS), 285
Jennae, Michele, 311
Joint community, 330
Kennedy, John F., 322
Key Values
- **After Restoral Value (ARV),** 10, 29
- **As-Is Value (AIV),** 10, 29
- **Loan-to-Value (LTV),** 10, 29, 31

Key Values and Ratios, 10, 29
Landlord and tenant laws, 138
Lease, 24, 98, 103, 138, 199, 234-235, 238-239, 241, 243-246, 252-254, 357, 383, 404
- **Agreement, 334**

Lending, 10, 22, 25-28, 30-31, 40, 55-56, 58-60, 63,
65-70, 73-74, 77-78, 81, 83-85, 87-89, 102-104, 111, 122, 133, 168, 170, 173, 178, 185, 187, 191, 205, 272, 302, 355, 373-374, 385
- **Adjustable-Rate,** 55, 71-72, 86, 166, 376, 380
- **Adjustable-Rate Mortgage. See Amortization**
- **Collateral loans,** 55, 77-78, 80
  - **HELOC,** 62, 67, 78, 264, 270-271
  - **Home Equity**, 62, 67, 77, 78
- **Commercial Real Estate (CRE),** 55, 80
- **Debt-Service Coverage Ratio (DSCR),** 80, 81, 173
- **Down Payment Assistance (DPA),** 55, 82, 92, 95, 99
- **Expedience,** 85, 342
- **FHA 203(k) Improvement,** 79
- **Fixed Rate**
  - **Conventional**, 55, 64-65, 73, 75-76, 181, 370, 373, 396, 404
  - **Federal Housing Administration (FHA),** 55, 71, 74-75, 95
  - **Jumbo**, 120, 134
  - **Renovation**, 98, 120, 132
  - **USDA**, 55, 65, 71, 76-77, 82, 95, 97-99, 383-385, 393, 401-402
  - **Veterans Affairs loans**, 55, 75
- **Flexible Approval,** 85
- **Flexible Terms,** 85
- **Hard money,** 56, 83-85, 178, 293, 304
- **Loan-to-cost (LTC),** 87
- **Nonqualified loan,** 69-72
- **Notices of Default (NODs),** 168
- **Portfolio Loans,** 55, 67-68, 72, 74, 83, 89, 386
- **Prepayment Penalties,** 80-81
- **Principal and Interest (P&I),** 173
- **Process,** 57, 58, 67, 86
  - **Application**, 239, 242
  - **Appraisal**, 55-56, 58, 66, 125
  - **Pre-Approval**, 55, 57-58, 188, 190
  - **Underwriting**, 55-56, 58-59, 65-66, 69, 73, 85
- **Qualified loans,** 69, 70
- **Refinancing,** 49, 51, 56, 66, 86, 89, 125, 284, 303-304, 346, 354, 384, 388, 403
- **Repayment Schedules,** 80-81
- **Risk Factors,** 55, 58-59, 69
- **Second mortgage,** 77-78, 82, 104, 264, 270

Leverage, 34, 41, 56, 60, 72, 77-78, 83, 87, 93-94, 96, 101, 115, 121, 126, 128, 132, 146, 165, 167, 178, 181, 191, 229, 231, 238, 246, 253, 260, 270, 284, 288, 293, 297, 301-304, 308, 310-312, 320, 323, 328-329, 342, 344-345, 349-354, 358-359, 361, 363, 367-368, 370-371, 376, 380, 384-386, 388-390, 392, 394-398, 401, 405-406
- **Accelerate,** 487

Loan-to-Value (LTV), 10, 29, 31
Local regulations and statutes, 230
Location
- **City,** 146, 148, 378
  - **Direction of Growth**, 134, 147-148, 156, 315
  - **Economic barriers**, 147
  - **Education**, 127, 142-143, 226, 318, 407
  - **Employment Opportunities**, 134, 139-140, 142, 162-163, 356, 361
  - **Enticements**, 134, 145, 148, 162-163, 356, 361
  - **Geographic barrier**, 147
  - **Income and Wages**, 203, 211
  - **Industry**, 134, 141-142, 197, 377
  - **Unemployment**, 134, 141, 144-145
- **Grow out or grow up,** 156

Neighborhood, 100, 135-136, 144-145, 148, 152-154, 156-157, 162, 169, 177, 184, 198-199, 213, 230, 240, 251, 315, 322, 356, 361, 400, 403
Buyer's market, 135, 149-150, 159
Price-to-Rent ratio, 135, 157, 160, 162, 356, 361
Region, 134, 136-138, 162, 356, 361
Climate, 134, 137, 141, 162, 356, 361
Economy of Force, 134, 137, 162, 356, 361
Natural Hazards, 134, 137, 139, 162, 356, 361
Marine Expeditionary Unit (MEU), 113
Market Data Approach, 181-182
Market Distress, 164, 166, 236
Momentum of Wealth, 1, 33-34, 39, 47, 49-51, 53-54, 345-346, 349-350, 390
Mortgage Insurance Premium (MIP), 60, 73-74
Myers-Briggs, 115
National Association of Realtors, 72, 80, 157, 172
Necessities and Niceties, 194, 197-198, 232, 357
New Price (P_2), 17
Offer strategies
Best Offer Up Front, 190
Cash offer, 187-188
Early bird, 188
Earnest money, 164, 185-186, 188, 190
Escalation clause, 188, 190
Pre-approval letter, 188, 190
Offer Strategies, 164, 187
Open house, 252
Operational Reach, 328, 331, 334, 343, 345, 349, 359, 362
Limitations, 343, 345, 349, 359, 362
Original Price (P_1), 17
Other People's Money, 55, 87, 89, 353, 355
Overassessing, 374, 376-377
Overborrowing, 374, 376
Overextending, 181, 374, 377
Overleveraging, 92, 99, 345, 373-374, 376, 379-380
Passive business, 284, 286-288
Passive Income. See Wealth (Types): Realized: Passive
Path of growth, 17
Patton, George S., 342
Personal liability protection, 258-260, 265-266, 275-276, 389
Portfolio expansion, 370
Price and quantity, 11, 15
Price ceiling, 18
Price floors, 17
Price to Rent Ratio, 157, 160
Primary Assumptions (Four), 4
Primary residence homestead exemption, 258, 260, 263
Private Mortgage Insurance (PMI), 73, 86
Producer surplus, 10, 13-14, 149
Profit potential, 18
Profit return. See Return on Investment, Return on Equity
Profitability Ratios, 33, 45, 179
Properties (Types), 10, 22, 77
Properties in Disrepair, 169
Property (Types), 10, 22, 77
Apartments, 10, 23, 240
Attached housing, 10, 23-24
Commercial Property, 23, 25, 80
Condominiums (Condos), 24
Co-Operative, 24
Mixed-Use Property, 23, 25, 290, 309, 358
Single-family home, 24, 94, 96-98, 383-384, 392-393, 396, 401
Townhomes, 10, 23-24
Undeveloped Land, 10, 23, 25
Property Assessment, 110, 164, 171, 192, 355-356
Property Condition, 169, 171
Property Insurance, 95, 173-174, 282, 358
Liability, 174-175
Property use, 284, 286, 289, 291
Arbitrage, 284, 286, 289, 291, 309, 358
Mixed-use, 10, 23, 25, 284, 286, 289-290, 309, 358
Rental, 42, 290, 309, 358
Property valuation, 125, 158, 223
Property Value Trend, 135, 158
Pulsifer, Catherine, 302
Purchase price target, 299
Real estate professional, 284, 286, 288-289
Rehabbing, 135, 194-196, 198, 207, 341, 404
Accepting the bid, 194, 206
Bedrooms, 120, 182, 225, 229-230, 240
Contractor bids, 194, 200, 203, 232, 357
Decks/porches, 194, 207, 211
Demolition, 131, 194, 225-226
Landscaping, 79, 129, 194, 207, 213, 249, 251
Paint, 79, 169, 194, 201, 207, 210, 213, 217, 222-223, 336

Roofing, 79, 130, 137, 194, 207, 212
Forced appreciation, 100, 194, 201, 229, 232, 357, 365
Inspections, 125, 129-130, 194, 225-226, 228
Interior, 165, 177, 194-195, 198, 201, 207, 209, 211, 216, 221-222, 225, 232, 357
Bedrooms, 120, 182, 225, 229-230, 240
Cabinets & countertops, 112, 130, 194, 216, 223, 230, 231
Carpentry, 194, 197, 216, 221-222
Drywall, 194, 207, 216, 221, 223, 336
Electrical, 79, 127-129, 194, 197, 216, 218, 227, 229, 336
Flooring, 79, 182, 194, 202, 204, 216, 224-225
Framing, 130, 194, 207, 211, 216, 220-221
Hardwood, 112, 131, 197, 206, 224-225
HVAC, 112, 128, 176, 194, 196, 216, 219, 227
Insulation, 194, 216, 220-221
Kitchen, 79, 198, 223, 225, 229, 231, 251
Linoleum, 224-225
Painting, 135, 211, 216, 221-224, 251, 336
Plumbing, 79, 129-130, 194, 197, 216-218, 227, 336
Location, 196
Permits, 156, 194, 225-227, 280, 289, 340
Season, 196
Septic system, 207, 214-215, 218
Walk-through, 194, 200-202, 232, 246, 357
Rental income (rent), 28, 33, 41-42, 44, 47, 93, 96-98, 103, 177, 237-238, 288, 290-291, 302, 375-376
Renting
Keys, 234, 239, 246, 254, 357
Screening, 234, 238-239, 241-243, 254, 357
Application, 234, 239, 242
Application fee, 242
Background check, 243, 382
Short-term, 246, 248, 254, 290, 291, 357
REO, 68, 78, 120, 168, 170
Repayment schedule, 81, 85
Replacement Cost, 175
Residential properties, 23
Return on Equity (ROE), 63, 81, 82, 84-87, 90-93, 96
Low, 236
Negative, 236, 255
Return on Investment (ROI), 33, 45-46, 179
High, 236
Low, 236-237, 255
Negative, 237-238, 255
Rommel, Erwin, 113
Roosevelt, Theodore, 10
SAFE, 332
Sales Comparison, 158, 181-182
Sales volume, 135, 150, 159
Seller's market, 135, 149-150, 159, 162-163, 180, 356, 361
Selling, 21, 26, 78, 120, 125, 149, 160, 166, 185, 197-198, 226, 228, 234, 237-238, 248-250, 254-255, 263, 275, 288, 298-300, 354, 357, 379, 394
Closing, 65-66
Financing, 92-93, 102-104, 110, 284, 303, 305-306, 355
List price, 234, 249
Negotiate, 102
Staging, 238, 249-252, 254-255, 357
Steps, 235, 250
Sensibles, 385
Shortage, 10, 16-17, 157, 180
SMART, 332
Stanford marshmallow experiment, 6-7
Strategizing
Components, 328-330, 340, 350
Constraints and Restraints, 348, 350
Culmination, 328, 331, 336, 343, 345-346, 349, 359, 371, 373, 379, 390
Desired End State, 334, 336, 344-346, 348-350,
367-368, 370-371, 382, 386-389
Lines of Effort (LOE), 328, 331, 334-335, 344-345,
349, 359, 362
Lines of Operations (LOO), 331, 334, 344
Operational Art, 328, 330-331
Operational Design, 328, 330-331
Phasing, 328, 331, 335-336, 343, 345, 349, 359, 369, 371
Sequencing tasks and objectives, 343, 345, 349, 359, 362-363
Strategy-to-task framework, 328, 336
Task assessment, 341
Termination criteria, 331, 341
Measures of Performance (MOPs), 342
Measures of Effectiveness (MOEs), 342
Timing and tempo, 328, 336, 343, 345, 349, 359, 371
Supply and demand, 10-13, 15, 196

Curve, 12-13
Demand Curve, 12-16
Supply Curve, 13-15
Supply barrier, 17, 147
Surplus, 10, 13-14, 16, 149, 157
Sustainment, 369-370, 390
Target Price Range, 164, 179-180, 192, 356
Tax advisor, 284-286, 293, 308-310, 358
Tax preparer, 284, 286
Taxation, 22, 275-277, 282, 284-285, 291-292, 305, 358
Taxes, 2, 26, 42-43, 74, 94-98, 102, 116-117, 125, 145-146, 160, 173-174, 178, 234, 248, 250, 274,
280-281, 284-287, 289-290, 293, 296, 298-303,
305-306, 308-309, 358, 371, 382-383, 385, 388-389, 392-395, 400, 402-403, 405
Capital gains, 26, 298
Deductions, 284, 293, 309, 358
Team Dynamic, 112-113
Team members, 112-113, 115-116, 132-133, 233,
311-312, 320, 324, 332-335, 338, 355, 359-360, 362, 365-366, 371
Ancillary, 112, 115, 125, 132, 185, 355, 360
Appraiser, 58, 112, 125-126, 158, 181, 187, 222, 366
Contractors, 101, 112, 114, 118, 126, 131-132, 196-197, 199-201, 203-204, 207, 315, 318, 355, 360
Dumpster Companies, 112, 127
Electrician, 112, 127-128
Handyperson, 128, 130, 197, 204, 215, 222, 224
Home inspector, 112, 129
HVAC technician, 128, 196
Other Specialists, 130-131
Plumbing Technicians, 130
Roofing Technician, 130
Centers of Gravity, 112, 116, 118, 132, 138, 162-163, 304, 328, 333-334, 343, 345, 349, 355, 359-361
Core, 11, 112, 115-116, 132-133, 198, 293, 355, 360
Certified Public Accountant (CPA), 116
Deal Finder, 112, 117-122, 124, 133, 137, 333, 355, 360
Insurance Agent, 112, 121, 265
Property Manager, 112, 116, 122-123, 132-133, 155, 160, 200, 214, 238-240, 254-255, 334, 355, 357, 360, 362, 366, 392, 396
Real Estate Attorney, 116
Real Estate Lender, 112, 123
Title Company, 112, 124, 253, 366
Thurman, Randy, 284
Title commitment, 124
Title insurance, 66,124
Trend, 10, 18, 20, 42, 50-51, 135, 151-152, 157-158, 179, 376-377
Trend analysis, 10, 18, 376
Trend of value, 158
Turnkey property, 165, 169, 255
Amount owed, 169-170, 192-193, 237, 271, 356
Twain, Mark, 25, 92, 258
Tyson, Mike, 328
Underperforming property, 305
Underwriters, 58-60
Valuation, 22, 125, 158, 168, 181-182, 222-223
Vector, 10, 18-20
Velocity of Money, 33-34, 41-42, 44-47, 54, 255, 344, 351-352, 363, 367-368, 386, 389-390, 397-398, 406
WalletHub, 378
Washington, Denzel, 329
Wealth (Types), 10,21
Realized, 10, 21-22
Active, 10
Passive, 21-22
Unrealized, 10, 21-22, 32, 36-37, 354, 360
Wholesale agent, 121, 167
Winfrey, Oprah, 164
Xerxes, 194